KT-446-492

Lesbian, Gay, Bisexual, Trans and Queer Psychology

This exciting and engaging textbook introduces students to the psychology of lesbian, gay, bisexual, trans and queer lives and experiences. It covers a broad range of topics including diversity, prejudice, health, relationships, parenting and lifespan experiences from youth to old age. The book includes 'key researcher' boxes, which outline the contributions of significant individuals and their motivations for conducting their research in their own words. Key issues and debates are discussed throughout the book, and questions for discussion and classroom exercises help students reflect critically and apply their learning. There are extensive links to further resources and information, as well as 'gaps and absences' sections, indicating major limitations of research in a particular area. This is the essential textbook for anyone studying LGBTQ Psychology, Psychology of Sexuality or related courses. It is also a useful supplement to courses on Gender and Developmental Psychology.

VICTORIA CLARKE is a Reader in Sexuality Studies at the University of the West of England, Bristol.

SONJA J. ELLIS is a Principal Lecturer in Psychology at Sheffield Hallam University.

ELIZABETH PEEL is a Senior Lecturer in Psychology at Aston University, Birmingham.

DAMIEN W. RIGGS is a Visiting Research Fellow in the School of Psychology at the University of Adelaide and Lecturer in the School of Social Work at Flinders University.

Lesbian, Gay, Bisexual, Trans and Queer Psychology

An Introduction

Victoria Clarke
Sonja J. Ellis
Elizabeth Peel
and
Damien W. Riggs

CAMBRIDGE
UNIVERSITY PRESS

CAMBRIDGE UNIVERSITY PRESS
Cambridge, New York, Melbourne, Madrid, Cape Town, Singapore,
São Paulo, Delhi, Dubai, Tokyo

Cambridge University Press
The Edinburgh Building, Cambridge CB2 8RU, UK

Published in the United States of America by Cambridge University Press, New York

www.cambridge.org
Information on this title: www.cambridge.org/9780521700184

© Victoria Clarke, Sonja J. Ellis, Elizabeth Peel and Damien W. Riggs 2010

This publication is in copyright. Subject to statutory exception
and to the provisions of relevant collective licensing agreements,
no reproduction of any part may take place without the written
permission of Cambridge University Press.

First published 2010

Printed in the United Kingdom at the University Press, Cambridge

A catalogue record for this publication is available from the British Library

ISBN 978-0-521-87666-7 Hardback
ISBN 978-0-521-70018-4 Paperback

Cambridge University Press has no responsibility for the persistence or
accuracy of URLs for external or third-party Internet websites referred to
in this publication, and does not guarantee that any content on such
websites is, or will remain, accurate or appropriate.

Contents

Boxes

Introduction: how to read and use this book

The book is intended as a specialist textbook that will support a course or lecture block on LGBTQ psychology (or the psychology of sexualities and genders). At the same time, each chapter is intended to stand alone, and provide an introduction to a particular aspect of LGBTQ psychology, so LGBTQ perspectives and experiences can be incorporated into a wide range of psychology topics such as, for example, lifespan development, prejudice, health, research methods, family and relationships. Readers 'dipping in' to some of the later chapters can consult the glossary for definitions of key concepts.

What's in this book?

The book is divided into three sections plus a concluding chapter.

Section I (History, contexts and debates in LGBTQ psychology) provides an overview of the theoretical, methodological, political and practical issues and debates that inform LGBTQ psychological research. Chapter 1 explores the history and development of the field of LGBTQ psychology. It discusses the work of early sexologists, the 'founding fathers' of sexuality and gender research, the emergence of 'gay affirmative' psychology in the 1970s and the subsequent development of LGBTQ psychology as a recognised sub-field of psychology. Chapter 2 summarises some of the key theoretical and political perspectives that inform research in the area, and examines the relationship between LGBTQ psychology and related areas of research such as queer theory and feminist psychology. It also examines the relationship between LGBTQ psychology and positive social change for LGBTQ communities and individuals. Chapter 3 provides insight into doing LGBTQ psychological research. It explores some of the issues that psychologists encounter when researching LGBTQ populations and the main methods used in LGBTQ psychological research. It also provides practical guidance for readers undertaking research projects in LGBTQ psychology and outlines the core principles of non-heterosexist and non-genderist research. Chapters 2 and 3 will also equip you with tools for critically evaluating research in LGBTQ psychology and mainstream psychology.

Section II (Understanding social marginalisation in LGBTQ lives) overviews one of the core concerns of LGBTQ psychology: understanding and challenging the social marginalisation of LGBTQ individuals and communities. Chapter 4 examines aspects of diversity within LGBTQ communities, and the different and intersecting forms of social marginalisation that members of these communities encounter. Some LGBTQ psychologists might disagree with our decision to have a separate chapter on diversity on the grounds that this serves to make diversity a 'special issue'. However, we think it is important both to integrate discussion of diversity throughout the book and to allocate some separate space within the book to focus specifically on issues around diversity. Chapter 5 overviews the most well investigated topic in LGBTQ psychology: prejudice and discrimination against members of LGBTQ communities. Research has focused both on the implications of prejudice and discrimination for members of LGBTQ communities and on understanding and challenging the negative attitudes and behaviours of hetero-sexual and non-trans people, as well as on broader institutional heterosexism. Chapter 6 explores social marginalisation in relation to the sexual, mental and physical health of LGBTQ people. This chapter highlights the distinctive experi-ences and needs of LGBTQ communities in relation to health and health care.

Section III (LGBTQ experiences across the lifespan) outlines research on significant events in the LGBTQ lifespan: from youth to old age and death. Chapter 7 centres on the experiences of LGBTQ young people and the significant ways in which these differ from those of heterosexual and non-trans youth. This chapter also summarises the literature on coming out and the development of non-heterosexual and trans identities. Chapters 8 and 9 consider significant events in the lives of LGBTQ adults, namely, forming and maintaining relationships and creating families and parenting children. Chapter 10 examines ageing in LGBTQ communities and the lives of older LGBTQ people, as well as issues around dying and bereavement. Finally, Chapter 11 concludes the book by considering future directions for LGBTQ psychology, highlighting some of the issues that have been neglected to date and outlining key concerns for future research. For readers contemplating undertaking a research project in this area, this chapter might give you some ideas for your research!

There are some topics that we simply did not have the space to discuss, including growing bodies of work on LGBTQ concerns in relation to sport and leisure, and the workplace (see Clarke and Peel, 2007a). We hope that work in these areas continues to develop and that a future edition of this book or other books on LGBTQ psychology will include a discussion of LGBTQ issues in sport and leisure, and the workplace.

Pedagogical features of the book

A number of pedagogical features support the main text:

- **Chapter overviews and summaries.** Each chapter starts with an overview, which signposts the major topics dealt with in the chapter, and each chapter ends with a summary of the main points covered.

> **Overview**
> - What is LGBTQ psychology and why study it?
> - The scientific study of sexuality and 'gender ambiguity'
> - The historical emergence of 'gay affirmative' psychology
> - Struggling for professional recognition and challenging heteronormativity in psychology

> **Main chapter points**
>
> This chapter:
>
> - Defined LGBTQ psychology as a branch of psychology that seeks to challenge the privileging of heterosexuality within society and provides a range of psychological perspectives on the lives and experiences of LGBTQ people.

- **'Key researcher' boxes.** Each chapter (except for Chapter 8) contains a box (or boxes) written by a key researcher in the field, which outlines their contribution to, or vision of, LGBTQ psychology.

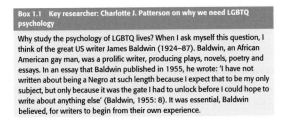

> **Box 1.1   Key researcher: Charlotte J. Patterson on why we need LGBTQ psychology**
>
> Why study the psychology of LGBTQ lives? When I ask myself this question, I think of the great US writer James Baldwin (1924–87). Baldwin, an African American gay man, was a prolific writer, producing plays, novels, poetry and essays. In an essay that Baldwin published in 1955, he wrote: 'I have not written about being a Negro at such length because I expect that to be my only subject, but only because it was the gate I had to unlock before I could hope to write about anything else' (Baldwin, 1955: 8). It was essential, Baldwin believed, for writers to begin from their own experience.

- **'Key study' boxes.** Chapters 1, 2 and 4–10 contain boxes that summarise the findings of an important study in the area.

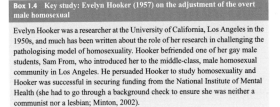

> **Box 1.4   Key study: Evelyn Hooker (1957) on the adjustment of the overt male homosexual**
>
> Evelyn Hooker was a researcher at the University of California, Los Angeles in the 1950s, and much has been written about the role of her research in challenging the pathologising model of homosexuality. Hooker befriended one of her gay male students, Sam From, who introduced her to the middle-class, male homosexual community in Los Angeles. He persuaded Hooker to study homosexuality and Hooker was successful in securing funding from the National Institute of Mental Health (she had to go through a background check to ensure she was neither a communist nor a lesbian; Minton, 2002).

- **'Highlights' boxes.** Each chapter contains boxes that foreground key issues and debates, provide examples of research instruments or summarise the pros and cons of particular approaches.

> **Box 1.2** *Highlights: the Kinsey scale*
>
> 0 Exclusively heterosexual behaviour
> 1 Primarily heterosexual, but incidents of homosexual behaviour
> 2 Primarily heterosexual, but more than incidental homosexual behaviour
> 3 Equal amounts of heterosexual and homosexual behaviour
> 4 Primarily homosexual, but more than incidental heterosexual behaviour
> 5 Primarily homosexual, but incidents of heterosexual behaviour
> 6 Exclusively homosexual behaviour

- **'Gaps and absences' sections.** At the end of each chapter (except Chapter 4) we identify a number of gaps and absences in the relevant research area. These suggestions for future research signal some of the major limitations of work in a particular area and will help readers critically to assess the strengths and weaknesses of the existing literature. They might also provide inspiration for research projects on LGBTQ issues.

> **Gaps and absences**
>
> Every chapter will highlight gaps and absences in a particular area of research. In this chapter, we note some of the major gaps and absences across the field of LGBTQ psychology as a whole:
>
> - *The lives of LGBTQ people outside of the USA*: As will quickly become apparent, a lot of the research we draw on in this book was conducted in the USA. This is partly because the field was first established in the USA and because there are lots of LGBTQ psychologists there. We hope that as the field continues to develop, we will learn more about LGBTQ people living in other countries.
> - *Diversity within LGBTQ communities*: Research has tended to focus on the experiences of gay men and lesbians who live in urban areas (often major gay

- **Questions for discussion and classroom exercises.** Each chapter includes questions and exercises that are designed to help readers to reflect critically on the issues covered in the chapter and to guide you in further exploring some of the issues. Many of the questions and exercises can be used as a focus for seminar discussions, assignments or research projects.

> **Questions for discussion and classroom exercises**
>
> 1. List all the terms and associations you can think of for the categories 'lesbian', 'gay man', 'bisexual' and 'heterosexual'. These can be slang terms, stereotypes, famous people, behaviours or practices. It doesn't matter if some people would consider the words offensive or whether you would use them; the point of this exercise is to identify all the positive and negative cultural associations for these categories. Once you've listed all the associations you can think of, can you spot any themes or patterns?

- **Further reading.** Each chapter includes suggestions for further reading to guide readers' independent study. LGBTQ psychological research tends to be scattered over a wide range of books and journals and some of these may not be very accessible. We have been careful to include only sources in the suggestions for further reading and throughout the book that are (hopefully) relatively easy to access. In addition, although we encourage greater dialogue between psychologists and academics in other disciplines, this book is intended as a celebration of the work of LGBTQ psychologists and we only draw on work outside of psychology when psychological research is minimal or absent.

> ### ■ Further reading
>
> Barker, M. (2007) Heteronormativity and the exclusion of bisexuality in psychology. In V. Clarke and E. Peel (eds.), *Out in psychology: lesbian, gay, bisexual, trans and queer perspectives* (pp. 95–117). Chichester: Wiley.
> British psychologist Meg Barker analyses the representation of homosexuality and bisexuality in introductory psychology textbooks. She highlights the heteronormative assumptions that are widespread in psychology and the invisibility of bisexuality in discussions of non-heterosexuality.

- **Glossary.** A comprehensive glossary at the end of the book includes definitions of all the key terms and concepts used in the book and should be the reader's first port of call if you are not clear about the meaning of any words. If you start by reading some of the later chapters first, you will come across some words or concepts that have been explained in earlier chapters, and we encourage you to check the glossary for definitions. When a term that is defined in the glossary first appears in the main text it is printed in **bold** type.

> **additive models of identity** Models based on the assumption that it is possible and appropriate to examine a single aspect of someone's identity in isolation from the other aspects of their identity (e.g., it is possible to examine and understand a person's experience as a gay man in isolation from his status as a white, middle-class, middle-aged, able-bodied man). An alternative approach to identity is the intersectional approach, which understands all the different aspects of our identity as interconnected and impossible to separate and examine in isolation (see Chapters 4 and 11).
>
> **androgyny** The phenomenon of not clearly fitting into either of the binary categories of 'male' or 'female', typically on the basis of physical appearance, dress or mannerisms.

- **Additional resources.** We also include lists of websites, documentaries and feature films that are important, alternative sources of information on LGBTQ lives and experiences. These suggestions are intended to help readers further their understanding of particular issues, and can be used as a basis for group discussions in lectures and seminars.

> ### Documentaries and feature films
>
> **History of LGBTQ psychology**
>
> *Kinsey* (Bill Condon Dir., 2004). The story of the life and work of Alfred Kinsey, the 'founding father' of modern sexology. The film provides an insight into Kinsey's research and methods, especially the less widely publicised aspects of his work.

Our approach

Although this book is recognisable as a textbook, and we map the terrain of LGBTQ psychology as we perceive it, we are critical of the notion that textbooks are simply dispassionate, 'objective' overviews of a body of research and theory. We therefore aim both to outline the themes and perspectives of the existing field of LGBTQ psychology, and to present a vision of how LGBTQ psychology should develop in the future. (We suspect that our vision of the field may be too radical for some and not radical enough for others!) This means that our mapping of the field is far from dispassionate and the book invites the reader to engage critically with LGBTQ research. We particularly emphasise 'criticality' in areas where we feel the field has been dominated by mainstream perspectives and assumptions, and there is a lack of *accessible* critique of mainstream perspectives. For example our discussion of the essentialism versus social constructionism debate in Chapter 2 focuses on critiques of mainstream approaches to understanding the aetiology of homosexuality.

In Chapter 1, we discuss our decision to name the field 'LGBTQ psychology' rather than the more conventional title of lesbian and gay psychology, or, more recently, LGB or LGBT psychology. The name LGBTQ psychology signals, among other things, our commitment to an inclusive approach to this area of psychology, one that acknowledges and explores the diversity of LGBTQ communities and engages with a wide range of theories and methodologies, as well as with research and theory on LGBTQ issues in other academic disciplines. Some authors choose to change the ordering of 'LGBTQ' (to 'TBQLG' for example, and some authors vary the order each time they use the acronym) to signal an inclusive approach and to recognise that the experiences and agendas of gay men and (to a lesser extent) lesbians have (problematically) dominated the field. We applaud this strategy, but feel it is impractical for a textbook, so we have chosen to use consistently one of the most orthodox and recognisable orderings of the acronym (the other being 'GLBTQ').

We have thought carefully about the language and concepts we use in the book and how we present research. Readers may be unfamiliar with the use of inverted commas around certain words and concepts (e.g., 'gender ambiguity' and 'gay affirmative' psychology in Chapter 1). Although not common in mainstream psychology, in fields such as LGBTQ psychology and feminist psychology inverted commas are used (often rather liberally!) to signal that a particular word or concept is problematic in some way or that the author does not fully subscribe to the use of particular terminology (and alternative terminology may be equally problematic or simply unavailable). We have also been careful to indicate briefly the geographic origins of particular studies and/or researchers (and which academic field researchers work in). This is because LGBTQ psychology has been dominated by the work of North American researchers and it is important to locate research within its cultural context and acknowledge the contributions of researchers outside of North America.

When writing this book we have been aware of the limitations of our experience both as researchers and as members of LGBTQ communities. As we discuss in Chapter 3, writing about groups to which one does not belong is a precarious task. We are particularly aware of speaking from positions of relative privilege (we are all, like most academics, white and middle-class) and of our lack of personal experience of living as trans. We have attempted to incorporate a range of perspectives on living out particular identity categories and have consulted guidance produced by members of the trans community on non-trans people writing about and representing trans lives and perspectives.

Who we are

To give readers an idea of who we are, we now provide brief outlines of our research interests and approaches. Victoria Clarke is a Reader in Sexuality Studies at the University of the West of England, Bristol, UK. She has published on the history of LGBTQ psychology, lesbian and gay parenting, same-sex relationships and civil partnership, LGB sexualities and appearance, LGBT issues and education, and qualitative methodology. In collaboration with Elizabeth Peel, she has edited a number of books and Special Issues of journals on LGBTQ psychology. She uses mainly qualitative approaches to research, particularly critical qualitative approaches such as discourse analysis, and she has commitments to feminism, social constructionism, post-structuralism and queer theory. She used to identify and write as a radical lesbian feminist, but now identifies and writes as a non-heterosexual.

Sonja J. Ellis is a Principal Lecturer in Psychology at Sheffield Hallam University, UK. She has published on attitudes and moral reasoning around lesbian and gay rights issues, and on homophobia at university, and is currently completing a small project on the sexual health education needs of LBQ young women. Sonja's research to date has mainly employed a mixed-method approach (i.e., studies using both quantitative and qualitative methods) and has focused on facilitating positive social change for lesbians and gay men. Sonja identifies as both a lesbian and a feminist and some of her work is informed by these perspectives.

Elizabeth Peel is a Senior Lecturer in Psychology at Aston University, Birmingham, UK. She has published on heterosexism, diversity training about sexualities and same-sex relationships. She predominantly uses qualitative methods and aims for criticality in her research. She is the editor (with Victoria Clarke) of the books *Out in psychology* and (with Victoria Clarke and Jack Drescher) *British lesbian, gay, and bisexual psychologies*. Elizabeth also conducts critical health psychology research about chronic illness (e.g., diabetes) and is interested in the intersections between health, illness, gender and sexuality.

Damien Riggs is a Visiting Research Fellow in the School of Psychology, University of Adelaide, and Lecturer in the School of Social Work at Flinders

University, Australia. He has published on psychoanalysis and queer theory, race privilege and lesbians and gay men (and LGBTQ psychology more broadly), gay men's health and sexual practices, lesbian and gay parents, embodiment and non-gender normativity, lesbian and gay rights, and heteronormativity in psychological practice. He is the editor (with Gordon Walker) of the first Australasian book on lesbian and gay psychology (*Out in the Antipodes*) and the editor of the Australian Psychological Society's *Gay and Lesbian Issues and Psychology Review*. He is the author of a book about queer rights and race privilege (*Priscilla (white) queen of the desert*) and a book about lesbian and gay parenting (*Becoming parent*). Damien mainly uses qualitative approaches to research (and in particular thematic analysis and discourse analysis), though he has recently used content analysis to quantify research findings.

Although we speak and write in one authorial voice throughout the book, it is inevitable that we don't agree on everything! The choices we have made in writing this book have involved compromises of our individual perspectives and politics. However, we feel that bringing together a group of people with different interests and areas of expertise, and varied perspectives and approaches to research, has substantially enriched the book. We have certainly learnt a great deal from each other in the process of writing it. As you might imagine, four authors writing together is a challenging process but we hope you'll agree that the whole is greater than the sum of its parts! We decided to nominate a lead author for each chapter who wrote the first draft of the chapter (some sections of the chapter may have been written by one of the other authors), incorporated the others' feedback and produced the final draft, taking responsibility for any final decisions about language and content. Victoria wrote the Introduction and Chapters 1, 2, 3, 9 and 10, Sonja Chapters 5 and 7, Elizabeth Chapters 6 and 8, and Damien Chapters 4 and 11.

We hope you enjoy reading this book and that it provides an informative and engaging introduction to LGBTQ psychology. We have certainly enjoyed writing it and welcome readers' feedback.

Acknowledgements

We would like to thank our commissioning editor Andrew Peart (who left Cambridge University Press for another position during the writing of the book), particularly for his enthusiasm about the project, and Hetty Reid and Carrie Cheek at Cambridge University Press. A number of reviewers commented on the book proposal and the book itself – and we would like to thank them all for their considered and insightful feedback, which helped us greatly in developing the book. Thanks to all of the key researchers who met our many demands (!) with good humour, and for making an important contribution. In terms of individual 'thank yous', Victoria would like to thank Celia Kitzinger for inspiring her critical engagement with lesbian and gay psychology, the many students who have participated in her lectures and seminars on LGBTQ psychology for allowing her to 'test out' a lot of the material that she presents in this book, and her colleagues at UWE. Sonja would like to thank the Psychology Subject Group at Sheffield Hallam and Michelle Boughton for supporting her endeavours in the field of LGBTQ psychology; and also the students on her Psychology of Sexuality module, whose interest in our work has made it worthwhile. Elizabeth would like to thank Rosie Harding, Adam Jowett, Celia Kitzinger (for the same reason as Victoria), colleagues at Aston, and the students who take her Human Sexualities module for their enthusiastic engagement with the field. Damien would like to thank the students in his qualitative lecture series who have provided him with feedback on this teaching and his extensive inclusion of LGBTQ topics in the lectures.

SECTION I

History, contexts and debates in LGBTQ psychology

1 Introducing LGBTQ psychology

> **Overview**
> - What is LGBTQ psychology and why study it?
> - The scientific study of sexuality and 'gender ambiguity'
> - The historical emergence of 'gay affirmative' psychology
> - Struggling for professional recognition and challenging heteronormativity in psychology

What is LGBTQ psychology and why study it?

For many people it is not immediately obvious what **lesbian**, **gay**, **bisexual**, **trans** and **queer** (LGBTQ) psychology is (see the glossary for definitions of words in bold type). Is it a grouping for LGBTQ people working in psychology? Is it a branch of psychology about LGBTQ people? Although LGBTQ psychology is often assumed to be a support group for LGBTQ people working in psychology, it is in fact the latter: a branch of psychology concerned with the lives and experiences of LGBTQ people. Sometimes it is suggested that this area of psychology would be more accurately named the 'psychology of sexuality'. Although LGBTQ psychology is concerned with sexuality, it has a much broader focus, examining many different aspects of the lives of LGBTQ people including prejudice and discrimination, parenting and families, and **coming out** and identity development.

One question we're often asked is 'why do we need a separate branch of psychology for LGBTQ people?' There are two main reasons for this: first, as we discuss in more detail below, until relatively recently most psychologists (and professionals in related disciplines such as psychiatry) supported the view that **homosexuality** was a mental illness. 'Gay affirmative' psychology, as this area was first known in the 1970s, developed to challenge this perspective and show that homosexuals are psychologically healthy, 'normal' individuals. Second, and related to the **pathologisation** of homosexuality, most psychological research has focused on the lives and experiences of **heterosexual** and **non-trans** people. LGBTQ people are given little or no consideration within **mainstream psychology**. For example, most research on mothers is based on heterosexual mothers, and prejudice against LGBTQ people is given scant attention in social psychological research on prejudice. LGBTQ psychologists believe that if psychology is to be a true 'psychology of people', then it must examine the experiences of all people and be open to the ways in which people's lives differ (see Box 1.1).

Box 1.1   Key researcher: Charlotte J. Patterson on why we need LGBTQ psychology

Why study the psychology of LGBTQ lives? When I ask myself this question, I think of the great US writer James Baldwin (1924–87). Baldwin, an African American gay man, was a prolific writer, producing plays, novels, poetry and essays. In an essay that Baldwin published in 1955, he wrote: 'I have not written about being a Negro at such length because I expect that to be my only subject, but only because it was the gate I had to unlock before I could hope to write about anything else' (Baldwin, 1955: 8). It was essential, Baldwin believed, for writers to begin from their own experience.

For those of us in psychology who identify as LGBTQ, it can also be important that our work is based in lived experience. Studying the psychology of sexual orientation and gender identity may or may not be the only work we do, but it can often be a door that we must unlock. Publishing LGBTQ scholarship does indeed almost literally open closet doors for some of us; doing this work can sometimes be one way of declaring our sexual and gender identities. More than that, however, studying LGBTQ lives can help us to understand our own lives.

As Baldwin also noted, however, 'it must be remembered that the oppressed and the oppressor are bound together within the same society' (Baldwin, 1955: 21). In saying this, Baldwin was claiming that the experiences of all US citizens are inextricably linked, regardless of race. In the same way, it is important to recognise that LGBTQ lives are bound together with those of people around us. Without comprehending the lives of both LGBTQ and non-LGBTQ people, no psychology can claim to be comprehensive.

Why, then, must we insist on the importance of LGBTQ psychology? First, we need to do this because it is essential for those of us who identify as LGBTQ to care about our own lives. If we fail to do this, how could we achieve any kind of integrity, or call ourselves psychologists? Second, we must insist on this because any psychology that fails to include us will never be complete. Without understanding the experiences of LGBTQ people, how could any psychology possibly apply to all?

Woven together, psychologies of LGBTQ and non-LGBTQ lives will create a stronger and more durable fabric than either one could make alone. 'Negroes are Americans and their destiny is the country's destiny', wrote Baldwin in the 1950s (1955: 42). Could Baldwin possibly have imagined that the US would some day elect an African American to be President? I am not sure. I am, however, certain that Baldwin's writings contain a message for us as psychologists. Any psychology of human experience that is worthy of the name must include the psychology of LGBTQ experiences.

It is important to note that there are no universally agreed definitions of the terms 'lesbian', 'gay', 'bisexual', 'trans' and 'queer' and as you will discover when you read this book there are lots of other words and phrases that are used to categorise sexuality and gender identity. These terms are most often associated with **western** cultures; non-western cultures use different language and concepts to describe variation in sexual and gender identities and practices (see Chapters 2 and 4).

The term 'gay affirmative' psychology is no longer used; it was replaced by the term 'lesbian and gay psychology' in the 1980s to signal that the research area examined the lives of both gay men and lesbian women. More recently, the terms 'LGB', 'LGBT' and occasionally 'LGBTQ' or 'LGBTQI' have been used. Not only can these increasingly lengthy acronyms be confusing, but there is also considerable debate about the scope of the field. Should it just focus on same-sex sexuality and the experiences of lesbian, gay and bisexual people? Or should it also include the experiences of trans and **intersex** people, who, in societies that assume a direct correspondence between gender identity and **natal sex**, are positioned outside of social norms around **sex/gender**? Should queer perspectives be incorporated? Our view is that this area of psychology should be inclusive (Clarke and Peel, 2007b). Although there are important differences between LGBTQ people (see Chapter 4), the shared experience of living outside dominant sexuality and sex/gender norms, and the close links between sexuality and sex/gender, merit an inclusive approach. In addition, as we discuss further in Chapter 2, there has been considerable debate about the usefulness of identity categories such as 'bisexual' and 'lesbian'. Whereas some LGBT theorists and activists argue for the importance of such categories, for example, to claim rights and give people a voice, others – particularly **queer theorists** – have argued that identity categories are **instruments of regulation** and **normalisation**. We use the term 'LGBTQ' to signal our inclusion of both of these perspectives in our discussion of the field.

Because the field of LGBTQ psychology has primarily concentrated on the experiences of younger, white, middle-class, able-bodied, urban-dwelling gay men and lesbians, there has been little examination of the breadth and diversity of experiences within LGBTQ communities. This means that our adoption of an inclusive approach will often be limited by this emphasis on the experiences of particular groups of gay men and lesbians in existing research. We highlight the breadth and diversity of experience within LGBTQ communities where possible and draw your attention to the gaps and absences in current knowledge. Another reason for using the term 'LGBTQ psychology' is to signal our concern for diversity and to emphasise that LGBTQ psychologists are not in agreement about the remit of the field, the types of research questions we should ask, or the methodologies we should use to answer these questions. This is of course similar to the wider discipline of psychology, where multiple paradigms and theories all rub shoulders together. As such, LGBTQ psychology is a microcosm of psychology and it embraces a plurality of perspectives about on whom or what we research and the theories and methods we use in conducting research. Debates among LGBTQ psychologists are often as lively as (or livelier than) those between LGBTQ psychologists and mainstream psychologists!

With all of that in mind, our definition of LGBTQ psychology is as follows: LGBTQ psychology is a branch of psychology that is affirmative of LGBTQ people. It seeks to challenge prejudice and discrimination against LGBTQ people and the privileging of heterosexuality in psychology and in the broader society. It seeks to promote LGBTQ concerns as legitimate foci for psychological research and promote **non-heterosexist**, **non-genderist** and inclusive approaches to psychological research and practice. It provides a range of psychological perspectives on the lives and experiences of LGBTQ people and on LGBTQ sexualities and genders.

Another question we're often asked is 'can heterosexuals (and non-trans people) be LGBTQ psychologists?' Like all other areas of psychology, LGBTQ psychology is open to any psychologist with a scholarly interest in the area (see Peel and Coyle, 2004). The phrase 'LGBTQ psychologist' means a psychologist involved in this type of psychology. As Kitzinger *et al.* (1998: 532) noted: 'No implications are intended as to the characteristics of the psychologists themselves: a "lesbian and gay psychologist" can be heterosexual, just as a "social psychologist" can be anti-social or a "sport psychologist" a couch potato.' However, as will become apparent, many of the psychologists who work in this area are LGBTQ-identified (see Box 1.1). We now explore the historical development of LGBTQ psychology, starting with the work of early sexologists who founded the scientific study of sexuality and 'gender ambiguity'.

The scientific study of sexuality and 'gender ambiguity'

Sexology is the systematic study of sexuality and gender identity. Although sexuality and gender ambiguity have been written about for centuries (for example, we know of numerous ancient texts on sexuality including the Indian text the *Kama Sutra*), it was only in the nineteenth century that these issues were treated as formal subjects of scientific and medical investigation. Whereas contemporary researchers would tend to classify trans as an example of gender diversity and LGB sexualities as sexual diversity, early sexologists classified both '**cross-gender identification**' and same-sex sexuality under the broad rubric of '**inversion**', which was associated with homosexuality (Meyerowitz, 2002).

Magnus Hirschfeld and Karl-Heinrich Ulrichs

The first social movement to advance the rights of homosexual and trans people was established in Germany in 1897. The Scientific Humanitarian Committee was founded by a medical doctor, Magnus Hirschfeld (1868–1935), and an openly homosexual lawyer, Karl-Heinrich Ulrichs (1825–95), among others, and adopted the motto 'justice through science' (Kitzinger and Coyle, 2002). The Committee sponsored research, published a journal, the *Yearbook for Intermediate Sexual Types*, produced information for the public, including leaflets and a film, *Different from the others* (1919), and conducted one of the earliest sex surveys (which found that 2.2 per cent of the population was homosexual). Hirschfeld also headed the Institut für Sexualwissenschaft (the Institute for Sexual Science), an early private research institute in Berlin, that was founded in 1919 and destroyed by the Nazis in 1933. Much early experimentation with **sex change surgery** was undertaken here in the 1920s and 1930s, supervised by Hirschfeld (Meyerowitz, 2002).

Ulrichs and Hirschfeld developed the theory of a third, intermediate, sex between women and men (which included people who would now be called trans, intersex, lesbian, gay and bisexual). Ulrichs introduced terminology in 1864 and 1865 to describe a natural 'migration of the soul', a woman's soul in a man's body and vice versa (Oosterhuis, 2000). An Urning was a male-bodied person with a female psyche who desired men and an Urningin was a female-bodied person with a male psyche who desired women. Ulrichs also introduced terms for 'normal' (heterosexual and feminine) women (Dioningin), and 'normal' (heterosexual and masculine) men (Dioning), female and male bisexuals (Uranodioningin and Uranodioning respectively) and intersexuals (Zwitter). This terminology reflects a theory popular among early sexologists, that of universal human bisexuality, which held that each individual contained elements of both sexes. Masculine men and feminine women were thought to be ideal types, the opposing poles of a continuum of human sexual and gender expression.

Although Ulrichs refined his typology to acknowledge that not all male-bodied people who desired men were feminine and that people varied in relation to who they desired, their preferred sexual behaviour (passive, active or no preference) and their gender (feminine, masculine or in between), the **gender inversion theory of homosexuality** was to be his lasting contribution to sexology. The theory was developed by Hirschfeld and was to influence the work of other leading sexologists (Bullough, 2003). Hirschfeld also wrote about **transsexualism** (and **transvestism**), describing it as a form of neurological intersex in his book *Die Transvestitien* (1910). Hirschfeld argued that **transsexuals**, intersexuals and homosexuals were all distinct types of 'sexual intermediaries', natural (if inferior) variations of the human condition.

Recent reappraisals of Hirschfeld's contributions to sexology suggest that, although his ideas were more or less ignored in the English-speaking world for the second half of the twentieth century, his conceptualisation of sexuality and gender was perhaps the most radical to emerge from early sexology (Brennan and Hegarty, 2007; Bullough, 2003).

Richard Freiherr von Krafft-Ebing and Henry Havelock Ellis

Richard Freiherr von Krafft-Ebing (1840–1902), an Austro-German psychiatrist, and one of the world's leading psychiatrists of his time, is generally regarded as the 'founding father' of sexology. His major work, *Psychopathia sexualis* (first published in Germany in 1886; it was translated into English and published in the USA in 1939), challenged the view that 'sexual perversion' was a sin or a crime, and instead presented it as a disease. The first edition of the book proffered forty-five case histories of sexual perversion (including what we would now call male homosexuality, lesbianism and transsexualism). The book was intended as a forensic reference for doctors and judges and some portions were written in Latin to discourage lay readers. However, the book was very popular with lay readers and went through many editions and translations (the twelfth edition published in 1903 contained over 300 case histories). A number of people wrote to Krafft-Ebing after reading the book to share with him their histories of sexual and gender 'deviance'. Krafft-Ebing included some of these autobiographical accounts in later editions of the book. His views on sexual perversions such as homosexuality were complex and changed throughout his lifetime. Dutch historian Harry Oosterhuis (2000), the author of an excellent book on Krafft-Ebing, argues that Krafft-Ebing died supporting the homosexual rights movement and viewing homosexuality as compatible with mental health. However, for the most part, his work reflected rather than challenged the prevailing orthodoxy that homosexuality was pathological, and did much to link **non-reproductive sexuality** with disease. *Psychopathia sexualis* is still widely available and provides a fascinating insight into the lives of Victorian people whose sexual and gender identities and practices departed from **normative** heterosexuality.

Henry Havelock Ellis (1859–1939), a British doctor whose wife, Edith, was openly lesbian, is a central figure in the modern study of sexuality. Ellis's major work was the six-volume *Studies in the psychology of sex*, published between 1897 and 1910 (a seventh volume was published in 1928). Ellis, along with his contemporary Sigmund Freud (see below), opened up sexuality to serious research and challenged the moral values that blocked public and scientific discussion of sexuality. His volume on homosexuality, *Sexual inversion* (first published in Germany in 1896 and published in England the following year; see Ellis and Symonds, 2007), presented homosexuality as a biological anomaly, akin to colour blindness. This was a radical argument that challenged the dominant view that homosexuality was the result of choice and therefore sinful or criminal behaviour. Gay scholars generally view Ellis's work as sympathetic and helpful, whereas some lesbian scholars have been critical of Ellis for presenting stereotypes of lesbian identities and sexual practices as scientific fact (Jeffreys, 1985).

Ellis's work further contributed to the construction of homosexuality and trans as distinct categories. Ellis defined 'eonism' as a separate category from homosexuality that included cross-gender identification as well as **cross-dressing** (the contemporary distinction between transsexualism and transvestism was first promoted by a US-based doctor, Harry Benjamin (1885–1986) who challenged the prevailing orthodoxy about the treatment of transsexualism in his book *The transsexual phenomenon* (1966) and developed the contemporary **Standards of Care** for the treatment of transsexualism and **Gender Identity Disorder**). Ellis, along with Edward Carpenter (1844–1929), an open homosexual and socialist reformer, founded the British Society for the Scientific Study of Sex Psychology in 1914, a scholarly scientific organisation that was also committed to social change. The Society focused on public education, and sponsored public lectures and produced a variety of pamphlets on sexuality.

Sigmund Freud

Sigmund Freud (1856–1939) was an Austrian neurologist and psychiatrist and the founding father of psychoanalysis. Although psychoanalysis is not considered part of mainstream psychology, most readers have probably heard of Freud and have some understanding of concepts associated with Freud's work such as 'the unconscious', 'penis envy' and the 'Oedipus complex'. Freud published numerous books and papers on sexuality including *Three essays on the theory of sexuality* (1905). He is famous for redefining sexuality as a primary force in human life and for his rich and complex writing about sexuality. For instance, Freud argued that humans are born 'polymorphously perverse', meaning that any number of objects (including people) could be a source of sexual pleasure, and that we become heterosexual after negotiating various stages of psychosexual development. This means that Freud rejected the notion, popular among other sexologists, that homosexuality and heterosexuality are inborn and instead viewed all forms of sexuality as the product of the family environment.

Homosexuality and bisexuality are often viewed as forms of 'arrested psychosexual development' in psychoanalytic theory and there has been a lot of debate about what Freud really thought about homosexuality. Sympathetic commentators have pointed out that Freud was a supporter of homosexual law reform, which suggests that he viewed homosexuality as compatible with mental health (Abelove, 1993). However, many of his followers used and developed his ideas in support of a pathologising model of homosexuality, including advocates of **conversion therapy** (see Box 1.3 below).

Freud was critical of the notion that homosexuals constitute a third sex on the grounds that: 'A very considerable measure of latent or unconscious homosexuality can be detected in all normal people. If these findings are taken into account, then, clearly, the supposition that nature in a freakish mood created a "third sex" falls to the ground' (1953: 171). More radically perhaps, Freud's focus was on pleasure rather than on reproduction and although he viewed **penis-in-vagina**

intercourse as the ultimate expression of mature, healthy adult sexuality, he did not uphold the 'reproductive sexuality = healthy/non-reproductive sexuality = pathological' distinction to the same degree that many of his sexological colleagues did. Freud's original theories have been extended and reworked by a wide range of scholars including the feminist theorist Juliet Mitchell (1974), the **post-structuralist** thinker Jacques Lacan (1968) and, more recently, the queer theorist Judith Butler (1997).

Early sexologists are hugely important in the historical development of LGBTQ psychology for a number of reasons:

- They established sexuality and gender identity as legitimate foci of scientific investigation.
- They developed many of the concepts and language that we use today.
- They challenged the prevailing orthodoxy regarding sexual and gender diversity.
- They established sexuality and gender identity as central to individuals and to human existence.
- They enabled the voices of sexual and gender 'deviants' to be heard.
- They viewed scientific research and social activism as compatible endeavours.

It has been widely argued that the most significant impact of the work of first-wave sexologists was the popularisation within western culture of the idea that we all possess an innate **sexual orientation** that organises our sexual behaviours. In the words of the French post-structuralist theorist Michel Foucault (1978: 43): 'Homosexuality appeared as one of the forms of sexuality when it was transposed from the practice of **sodomy** onto a kind of interior **androgyny**, a hermaphroditism of the soul. The sodomite had been a temporary aberration; the homosexual was now a species.' In other words, early sexologists were influential in the development of the concept of sexual identities: there was a shift from viewing sexuality in terms of behaviour (practising sodomy or non-reproductive sexual acts) to viewing it as central to our sense of self (being a 'sodomite'). Foucault was also commenting on the popularisation of a gender inversion model of homosexuality alongside the linking of sexuality and identity.

Alfred Kinsey and colleagues

As we can see, LGBTQ psychologists inherit a long European tradition of emancipatory scholarship and social activism (Kitzinger and Coyle, 2002). Although doctors in the USA had studied and written about variant sexuality for as long as European sexologists had (see Terry, 1999), it wasn't until the 1950s and the work of Alfred Kinsey (1894–1956) and colleagues that the scientific study of sexuality was truly established in the USA.

Kinsey, a biologist and an expert on the gall wasp, founded the Institute for Research in Sex, Gender and Reproduction at Indiana University in 1947, now called the Kinsey Institute for Research in Sex, Gender and Reproduction. Kinsey and his colleagues published two books, *Sexual behavior in the human male* (1948) and *Sexual behavior in the human female* (1953), more widely known as the Kinsey Reports, which detailed the findings of comprehensive sexual histories collected from over 10,000 people. Kinsey's methods and findings have generated a huge amount of controversy (Ericksen and Steffen, 1999). In terms of his contributions to LGBTQ psychology, he challenged the notion that homosexual behaviour was relatively infrequent. Kinsey found that many people have had same-sex sexual experiences and people's sexual preferences could change over the course of their lifetime: 50 per cent of the men and 28 per cent of the women in his studies had had same-sex sexual experiences. Furthermore, 38 per cent of the men and 13 per cent of the women had had orgasms during these experiences.

Kinsey and his colleagues developed a seven-point scale for measuring sexual preference (see Box 1.2). Rather than using discrete categories, Kinsey and colleagues placed people along a continuum of sexual behaviour. A number of researchers, including the feminist sexologist Shere Hite, who published the ground-breaking book *The Hite report: A nationwide study of female sexuality* (1976), criticised the emphasis on sexual behaviour and the neglect of the meanings that people give to their experiences in Kinsey's work. However, classifying people in terms of behaviour and sexual practices, rather than discrete identity categories, allowed Kinsey to observe greater diversity and flexibility in human sexuality than in much previous (and subsequent) research. Researchers at the Kinsey Institute have undertaken wide-ranging research on sexuality since Kinsey's death in 1956, including a ground-breaking study of nearly a 1,000 gay men and lesbians in San Francisco, beginning in 1968, by the psychologist Alan Bell and the sociologist Martin Weinberg. The study resulted in two books – *Homosexualities* (Bell and Weinberg, 1978) and *Sexual preference* (Bell *et al.*, 1981).

Kinsey is widely regarded as the 'father' of modern sexology and his work is often associated with the 'sexual revolution' in the USA in the 1960s. Kinsey's research had a profound impact on social and cultural values in the USA and in other western countries and his findings challenged widely held beliefs about sexuality.

Box 1.2 *Highlights: the Kinsey scale*

0 Exclusively heterosexual behaviour
1 Primarily heterosexual, but incidents of homosexual behaviour
2 Primarily heterosexual, but more than incidental homosexual behaviour
3 Equal amounts of heterosexual and homosexual behaviour
4 Primarily homosexual, but more than incidental heterosexual behaviour
5 Primarily homosexual, but incidents of heterosexual behaviour
6 Exclusively homosexual behaviour

The historical emergence of 'gay affirmative' psychology

The pathologisation and de-pathologisation of homosexuality

Kinsey demonstrated that homosexuality was far more widely practised than previously assumed and for this reason could be regarded as 'normal' sexual behaviour. However, at the time the Kinsey Reports were published most psychiatrists and psychologists regarded homosexuality as 'abnormal'. In 1952, the American Psychiatric Association decided to include homosexuality in the second edition of its *Diagnostic and statistical manual of mental disorders* (DSM). As Kitzinger and Coyle note (2002: 1): 'lesbians and gay men were characterised as the sick products of disturbed upbringings … Psychology textbooks routinely presented material on lesbians and gay men under headings implying sickness (for example, "sexual deviation" or "sexual dysfunction").' Given that most research on homosexuality relied on samples drawn from prisons, treatment centres for the mentally ill and therapists' client lists it is not surprising that these individuals were found to be less well adjusted than the average person (Bohan, 1996). Morin (1977) found that as much as 70 per cent of pre-1974 psychological research on homosexuality was focused on three questions: 'Are homosexuals sick?', 'How can homosexuality be diagnosed?' and 'What causes homosexuality?' Many psychologists and psychiatrists attempted to treat homosexuality and to convert LGB people (especially gay men) into heterosexuals. Psychotherapy was one of the most common treatments (Bohan, 1996). Numerous forms of behaviour therapy were also used such as aversion therapy (associating electric shocks or nausea-inducing substances with homosexual stimuli) and orgasmic reconditioning (associating heterosexual stimuli with masturbation). Other, more extreme, treatments included the use of hormones such as oestrogens (to decrease 'abnormal' sex drive) or androgens (to increase 'normal' sex drive), castration and clitoridectomy, and even lobotomies. See Box 1.3 for a discussion of the controversy surrounding the contemporary use of aversion (or 'conversion') therapy.

Box 1.3 *Highlights: contemporary advocates of the treatment of homosexuality*

Shockingly, some psychologists and psychiatrists still adhere to the view that homosexuality is pathological and advocate the treatment of homosexuality and the use of 'reparative' or 'reorientation' therapy. We think such terms suggest that the therapist is benevolently helping the client to repair something that was broken or to return him or her to a 'natural' state, which is why we prefer the term 'conversion therapy'. Conversion therapy implies wilfully turning someone from one state to another (Riggs, 2004a).

The National Association for the Research and Therapy of Homosexuality (NARTH) is a US organisation that promotes the treatment of homosexuality.

NARTH, alongside religious organisations such as Exodus International (that offers people 'freedom from homosexuality through the power of Jesus Christ'), views homosexuality as chosen behaviour and therefore open to change. As recently as 2003, a paper was published in the *Archives of Sexual Behavior* by a prominent US psychiatrist, Robert Spitzer, reporting a study examining the effectiveness of conversion therapy. Spitzer's highly controversial and much debated findings were that most participants reported a change from a predominantly or exclusively homosexual orientation to a predominantly or exclusively heterosexual orientation as a result of undergoing conversion therapy.

US-based social scientist Theo Sandfort (2003) argued that Spitzer's methodology was flawed in a number of ways, including the use of a biased sample, drawn mainly from members of religious organisations like Exodus International. Other critics have raised questions about the ethics of Spitzer's study and whether it falls short of the principle of avoiding harm. A study by US psychologists Michael Schroeder and Ariel Shidlo (2001), based on interviews with 150 clients of conversion therapy, found evidence of poor and questionable clinical practice and ethical violations by providers of conversion therapy. In 2002, Shidlo and Schroeder reported the findings of a study of 202 consumers of conversion therapy: most participants indicated that their efforts to change their sexuality had failed and many felt that such interventions were harmful.

One of the first psychologists to challenge the view that homosexuals were mentally ill was Evelyn Hooker (1907–96). Box 1.4 provides a summary of Hooker's most important study. The publication of Hooker's research prompted other similar studies and gay activists used this research in their campaigns for the removal of homosexuality from the DSM. Gay activists began a series of protests and demonstrations in 1968 and the American Psychiatric Association voted to remove homosexuality five years later in 1973. However, homosexuality was replaced by a new diagnosis 'ego-dystonic homosexuality', to be applied to people who fail to accept their homosexuality, experience persistent distress and wish to become heterosexual. (Unsurprisingly a parallel category of 'ego-dystonic heterosexuality' was not incorporated into the DSM!) This condition remained in the DSM until 1987 (homosexuality also remained in the World Health Organisation's International Classification of Diseases, a diagnostic manual used widely outside of North America, until 1993). Two years after the removal of homosexuality from the DSM, the American Psychological Association (APA) adopted the official policy that 'homosexuality, per se, implies no impairment in judgement, stability, reliability, or general social or vocational capabilities'. The APA also urged 'all mental health professionals to take the lead in removing the stigma of mental illness that has long been associated with homosexual orientations' (Conger, 1975: 633). See Box 1.5 for a discussion of the inclusion of transsexualism in the DSM.

Box 1.4   Key study: Evelyn Hooker (1957) on the adjustment of the overt male homosexual

Evelyn Hooker was a researcher at the University of California, Los Angeles in the 1950s, and much has been written about the role of her research in challenging the pathologising model of homosexuality. Hooker befriended one of her gay male students, Sam From, who introduced her to the middle-class, male homosexual community in Los Angeles. He persuaded Hooker to study homosexuality and Hooker was successful in securing funding from the National Institute of Mental Health (she had to go through a background check to ensure she was neither a communist nor a lesbian; Minton, 2002).

Hooker noted that most research and clinical experience was with homosexual subjects who came to clinicians for psychological help, were patients in mental hospitals, were in prison or were in disciplinary barracks in the armed services. Hooker sought to obtain a sample of 'overt homosexuals who did not come from these sources; that is, who had a chance of being individuals who, on the surface at least, seemed to have an average adjustment' (p. 18). Hooker also wanted to obtain a sample of homosexuals who were 'pure for homosexuality; that is, without heterosexual experience' (p. 20) and she largely succeeded. Her heterosexual sample was also largely 'pure'.

Hooker administered three standard personality tests (the Thematic Apperception Test, the Rorschach Test and the Make a Picture Story Test (MAPS)) to samples of thirty homosexual men and thirty heterosexual men, matched for age, intelligence and education. Hooker asked three expert clinicians to examine the test results. The clinicians were unaware of the men's sexual identities and could not distinguish between the two groups on the basis of their test results (except for the results of the MAPS in which the men often explicitly identified their sexuality). There were also no significant differences between the homosexual and heterosexual men in terms of psychological adjustment.

Hooker concluded that homosexuality is not necessarily a symptom of pathology and that 'there is no single pattern of homosexual adjustment' (p. 29). She argued that some clinicians might find it difficult to accept that some homosexuals 'may be very ordinary individuals, indistinguishable, except in sexual pattern, from ordinary individuals who are heterosexual' (p. 29), and some 'may be quite superior individuals, not only devoid of pathology ... but also functioning at a superior level' (p. 29).

Box 1.5   *Highlights: transsexualism and the DSM*

Although there have always been people who have 'cross-dressed' and lived as the 'other' gender or between genders for a number of different reasons, the phenomenon of 'changing sex' was only brought to public attention in the 1950s. A media sensation was created when a New York newspaper announced in 1952 that Christine Jorgensen, a former soldier, was surgically reassigned from male to female. Since then, the definition, causes and treatment of transsexualism have been widely debated. The diagnosis 'transsexualism' was introduced into the DSM-III in 1980; this was replaced by 'Gender Identity Disorder (GID) in Adolescents and Adults' in the DSM-IV in 1994. GID is applied to people who exhibit persistent cross-gender identification and a persistent discomfort with their sex or a sense of inappropriateness in the gender role of that sex.

The inclusion of GID (and sub-categories such as GID of childhood; see Chapter 7) in the DSM is controversial. Some trans people welcome the diagnosis because it allows them to access treatment. Others are critical of the pathologisation of **transgender** practices. Transgender activist Riki Anne Wilchins (1996, quoted in Mackenzie, 1999: 200) argued that the American Psychiatric Association 'has their *own* disorder – GenderPathoPhilia – which we define as "an abnormal need or desire to pathologise any gender behaviour which makes you uncomfortable"'.

Proving the normality of homosexuals

At the time of the removal of homosexuality per se from the DSM, research on gay and lesbian issues was concentrated in clinical psychology. As Kitzinger and Coyle (2002: 2) noted:

> mainstream psychology – dealing with staple topics such as education, work and leisure, lifespan development, parenting, health and so on – simply ignored lesbians and gay men altogether, as though lesbians and gay men never attended school, didn't have jobs or leisure activities, didn't grow up or grow old, never had children, never got ill and so on.

By leaving lesbians and gay men (and BTQ people) out of the 'everyday' psychology of people and only including them as examples of sexual and gender deviance, mainstream psychology provided a highly distorted image of the lives and well-being of LGBTQ people.

It is perhaps unsurprising then that the earliest gay affirmative psychological research sought to emphasise the normality of gay men and lesbians and their similarities to heterosexuals. Siegelman (1972) compared the adjustment of non-clinical samples of lesbians and heterosexual women and found no differences between the samples. Similarly, Thompson *et al.* (1971) found no important differences in the personal adjustment and psychological well-being of matched samples of lesbians and gay men and heterosexuals. Both of these studies were unusual for including lesbians, as early affirmative research, like pathologising research, tended to focus on gay men. Early researchers were strong advocates of positivist-empiricism and were critical of what they viewed as the bad science underpinning the pathologising model. They sought to replace the biased assumptions, samples and measures of the pathologising model with a more objective approach to research (Kitzinger, 1987).

Early gay affirmative research also focused on measuring heterosexuals' attitudes to homosexuality (MacDonald and Games, 1974) (see Chapter 5) and understanding the coming out process and the formation of homosexual identities (Cass, 1979) (see Chapter 7). Some early studies also examined the **sexual identity** development of children in lesbian mother families (see Chapter 9). The psychiatrist Richard Green (1978) examined the sexual identity development of children raised by homosexual and transsexual parents. Green found that the children's gender role behaviour was consistent for their sex and the older children were all heterosexually oriented. Green concluded that children being raised by homosexual or transsexual parents 'do not differ appreciably from children raised in more conventional family settings' (pp. 696–7).

Even now, Green's study stands as one of only a small number of 'affirmative' investigations into transsexual people and their families. Most psychological research on trans has focused on the causes and treatment of trans and on the psychological adjustment of trans people. Some psychologists have also used trans as a lens through which to explore the **social construction** of gender (see Kessler and McKenna, 1978, for an early example of this). These researchers are interested in what we can learn about gender as a category by exploring the practices of trans people and the ways in which they 'do' gender in everyday life. Some trans identified researchers have been critical of this research when it ignores the lived experience of trans people, and the ways in which socially constructed categories are lived and embodied (Hale, 2006); this criticism is arguably not applicable to Kessler and McKenna's work (see Crawford, 2000).

Homosexuality and trans were widely regarded as distinct entities by the early 1970s; however, research on trans was often incorporated under the umbrella of research on homosexuality. Including both homosexuals and transsexuals in the same sample, as Green did, was unusual. More common were comparisons of the psychological adjustment and gender roles of samples of lesbians and **transwomen** (McCauley and Ehrhardt, 1978), and of gay men and **transmen** (Roback *et al.*, 1978). Such comparisons often presented transsexuals as conservative in attitude and less well adjusted than gay men and lesbians. For instance, Kando (1976: 45) remarked that, 'unlike liberated females and other sexual minorities, transsexuals lack all militancy and desire only middle-class acceptance'.

A dichotomous heterosexual/homosexual model of sexuality constrained the development of research on bisexuality. In early gay affirmative research, bisexuality was often stigmatised as 'a passing phase' and bisexuals were presented as confused about their sexuality or 'in denial' about their homosexuality and seeking to avoid the stigma associated with a fully realised lesbian or gay identity (see, for example, Cass, 1979). Although a **dichotomous model of sexuality** continues to dominate research on sexuality and negative assumptions about bisexuality linger on, from the late 1970s researchers began to challenge the dichotomous model. Early attempts to develop alternative, multidimensional models of sexuality include the groundbreaking book *The bisexual option: a concept of one hundred percent intimacy* (1978) by US psychiatrist and sex researcher Fritz Klein (see Chapter 7).

As Fox (1995) outlines, early affirmative research on bisexuality sought to validate bisexuality as a sexual identity and identify the factors involved in the development of positive bisexual identities, and, like early research on homosexuality and lesbianism, set out to prove the normality of bisexuals.

The emergence of a critical alternative to proving the normality of homosexuals

Early affirmative research has been criticised for reinforcing the normative status of heterosexuality by treating heterosexuals as the basis for comparison (Kitzinger, 1987). In short, early gay affirmative research promoted a 'just the same as' message, which, like the pathologising model before it, assumed that differences between people were problematic, rather than just differences.

Most early gay affirmative research was conducted in the USA, and there was very little European research offering positive images of gay men and lesbians until the 1960s, and then just a handful of instances (affirmative research on homosexuality began even later in Australasia). One of those early European studies was June Hopkins's pioneering study of the lesbian personality, which is summarised in Box 1.6. Research in Britain only began to flourish in the 1980s, when two important books were published, both of which signalled a departure from the **liberal-humanistic** 'just the same as' message and the positivist-empiricist model that pervaded research in the USA (Clarke and Peel, 2007c). In 1981, John Hart and Diane Richardson published *The theory and practice of homosexuality*. They were critical of the male bias in existing research and were careful to distinguish differences in the experiences of gay men and lesbians. They also emphasised the importance of acknowledging the **political** implications of theories of homosexuality. The publication of this text marked the early beginnings of a **critical psychology** approach to lesbian and gay issues.

> **Box 1.6   Key study: June H. Hopkins (1969) on the lesbian personality**
>
> June Hopkins conducted one of the first affirmative studies that focused specifically on lesbians. Hopkins was born in Texas and moved to England with her husband in the 1960s, where she secured a post as a clinical psychologist. Although Hopkins was married she knew she was a lesbian (Clarke and Hopkins, 2002). When Hopkins served in the airforce in the 1950s, a number of her friends were dishonourably discharged for being lesbian. She was also troubled by the use of 'lesbian' and 'gay' as diagnoses when she began working as a psychologist. She intended her study to 'fill the void in objective investigation into the personality factors of lesbians' (p. 1433) and to test whether the prevailing view that lesbians were neurotic had any objective, quantifiable base.
>
> Hopkins's hypothesis was that there would be no personality factors that would be statistically significantly different between lesbian and heterosexual women.

The main measure was the 16 Personality Factor (16 PF) Questionnaire. Hopkins compared samples of twenty-four lesbians and twenty-four heterosexual women matched for age, intelligence and professional or educational background. Most of the lesbians were recruited from a lesbian organisation set up to support research, the Minorities Research Group, and the heterosexual women were recruited from among Hopkins's own networks.

Hopkins's hypothesis was not confirmed: there were a number of differentiating factors on the 16 PF between the lesbian and the heterosexual groups, but 'the traditionally applied "neurotic" label [was] not necessarily applicable' (p. 1436) to lesbians. Some of the differences between the lesbians and the heterosexual women suggested that the lesbians had a resilient personality, which contradicted the vulnerable personality implied by the neurotic label. Furthermore, the differences suggested that 'a good, descriptive generic term for the average lesbian would be "independent"' (p. 1436).

Hopkins concluded her report by noting that 'the following terms are suggested as appropriately descriptive of the lesbian personality in comparison to her heterosexual female counterpart: 1. More independent. 2. More resilient. 3. More reserved. 4. More dominant. 5. More bohemian. 6. More self-sufficient. 7. More composed' (p. 1436).

This critical approach was further developed in Celia Kitzinger's *The social construction of lesbianism* (1987; see Clarke and Peel, 2004; Peel and Clarke, 2005, for a discussion of this landmark book). Like Hart and Richardson, Kitzinger was critical of the male bias of gay affirmative research and chose to focus her research on lesbians because of the neglect of lesbian experience within gay affirmative psychology and because of the differences between lesbians and gay men. Kitzinger also provided a searing critique of the positivist-empiricist and liberal-humanistic assumptions that guided much research in the USA (see Chapter 2).

In the 1980s, lesbian and gay psychology began to diversify and move away from a narrow focus on proving the psychological health of lesbians and gay men towards a focus on how lesbians and gay men live their lives. By the start of that decade, lesbian and gay psychologists in the USA were convinced that the time was right to seek professional recognition of this area of psychology and to begin to challenge the **heteronormativity** of psychology from the inside.

Struggling for professional recognition and challenging heteronormativity in psychology

Groupings within professional bodies such as the American Psychological Association (APA) and the British Psychological Society (BPS) provide a forum for research and other activities in particular areas of psychology. They typically organise specialist events and publish newsletters and journals that communicate the latest developments to researchers and practitioners. Most areas of mainstream psychology (such as social, clinical, health, developmental, education, forensic, and sport and exercise psychology) are represented within professional bodies, as are newer areas of psychology or areas affiliated with alternative approaches to psychology (such as the **psychology of women** and **qualitative psychology**; see Chapter 2). In 1984 the APA approved the establishment of Division 44, The Society for the Psychological Study of Lesbian and Gay Issues. Division 44 was the first professional body for lesbian and gay psychologists and represented a huge step forward in establishing lesbian and gay psychology as a legitimate area of psychological research and practice (see Box 1.7 for details of all the current major professional bodies).

Lesbian and gay psychologists in Britain endured a much longer struggle to achieve professional recognition. A Lesbian and Gay Psychology Section was finally established in the BPS in 1998 after nearly a decade of campaigning and

---

Box 1.7 *Highlights: major professional bodies for LGBTQ psychologists*

- *Division 44 (The Society for the Psychological Study of Lesbian, Gay, Bisexual and Transgender Issues)*, originally established within the APA in 1984. Membership is open to anyone with an interest in LGBT issues. Division 44 publishes a regular newsletter and various resolutions on LGB concerns, organises events, task forces (that raise awareness of particular topics such as ageing), and grants and awards to recognise and promote contributions to LGBT psychology. For further details see: www.apadivision44.org
- *Gay and Lesbian Issues and Psychology (GLIP) Interest Group*, established within the Australian Psychological Society (APS) in 1994. GLIP publishes a journal and a newsletter, organises events and has produced guidelines and position statements promoting non-heterosexist approaches to psychological practice with LGBT people. Membership is open to anyone with an interest in the area. For further details see: www.groups.psychology. org.au/glip/
- *Psychology of Sexualities Section* (formerly the Lesbian and Gay Psychology Section), established within the BPS in 1998. Membership is only open to BPS members, although non-members can subscribe to the Section journal, *Psychology of Sexuality Review* (formerly *Lesbian and Gay Psychology Review*), and join the Section email listserv. The Section organises various events and awards prizes for achievements in student research. For further details see: www/bps.org.uk/pss/pss_home.cfm.
- *Section on Sexual Orientation and Gender Issues (SOGII)*, founded within the Canadian Psychological Association in 2002. Membership is open to anyone. For further details see: www.sogii.ca/

four rejected Section proposals. BPS procedures require a membership ballot before new Sections are formed and shockingly 1,623 members voted against the formation of the Section (1,988 voted for it) – this was the biggest 'anti' vote in any comparable ballot in the history of the BPS. Even more shocking is the fact that members of the working group that proposed the Section received abusive hate mail from other Society members (Kitzinger and Coyle, 2002).

Why was the formation of the Lesbian and Gay Psychology Section within the BPS so controversial? Sadly, we think the answer to this question is that hetero-normativity remains deeply embedded in the discipline of psychology. Although few psychologists nowadays would describe homosexuality as pathological or promote the use of conversion therapy, psychological theories and research are riddled with **heterosexist** assumptions. Psychology continues subtly and not so subtly to present heterosexuality as the norm or the ideal. For instance, devel-opmental theories that assume that all children are raised in heterosexual house-holds continue to be taught widely in psychology without anyone querying the heterosexist assumptions on which such theories are based.

Sections, divisions and interest groups within professional bodies are vital components in challenging heteronormativity in (and beyond) psychology. LGBTQ psychologists have been very active in promoting non-heterosexist approaches to psychological research and practice. Psychologists in the USA have developed guidelines for avoiding heterosexist bias in research (see Chapter 3), for inclusive psychology curricula (APA, 1998), and for unbiased psychotherapeutic practice with gay men and lesbians (Garnets et al., 1991).

One of the biggest changes to the field in recent years has been the inclusion of bisexual, trans and queer concerns. Although, as Kitzinger and Coyle (2002) point out, this area of psychology has always included work on bisexuality and trans, until relatively recently most research has been based on the experiences and perspectives of gay men and lesbians. As we noted above, the inclusion of BTQ perspectives is controversial, but we very much welcome the expansion of the field in this way. Some of the more recently formed professional bodies reflect this wider remit in their title (for example, the Section on Sexual Orientation and Gender Issues in the Canadian Psychological Association), and expanded titles have been called for in the more established professional bodies (for example, the Lesbian and Gay Psychology Section of the BPS was in 2009 renamed the Psychology of Sexualities Section). BTQ psychologists have been critical of the marginalisation of BTQ experiences in lesbian and gay psychology. We write this book at a time when there is still little in the way of specifically bisexual, trans and queer psychology and most research and practice continues to focus on gay men and lesbians. As we have shown, the early decades of this area of psychology were very much focused on challenging the pathologisation of homo-sexuality and establishing gay and lesbian concerns as legitimate foci of psycho-logical research. We hope that the publication of this book signals a new era, in which LGBTQ psychologists document the lives of LG *and* BTQ people in all their richness and diversity.

Gaps and absences

Every chapter will highlight gaps and absences in a particular area of research. In this chapter, we note some of the major gaps and absences across the field of LGBTQ psychology as a whole:

- *The lives of LGBTQ people outside of the USA*: As will quickly become apparent, a lot of the research we draw on in this book was conducted in the USA. This is partly because the field was first established in the USA and because there are lots of LGBTQ psychologists there. We hope that as the field continues to develop, we will learn more about LGBTQ people living in other countries.
- *Diversity within LGBTQ communities*: Research has tended to focus on the experiences of gay men and lesbians who live in urban areas (often major gay centres such as New York, San Francisco, London and Sydney), and have access to the commercial 'gay scene' and gay and lesbian communities. Most research participants also tend to be younger, white, middle-class, highly educated, professional and able-bodied. This means that there are significant gaps in our knowledge about the lives of BTQ people, and LGBTQ people who experience both heterosexism and social marginalisation relating to race, culture, gender, old age, disability, rural isolation, social class and poverty.
- *Marginalised sexual and gender identities and practices outside the cultural West*: We also know little about the experiences of **non-heterosexual** and trans people living in non-western cultures (see Chapters 2, 4 and 11). It is important to note that 'western' is both a cultural and a geographic designation and some countries outside of the geographic west subscribe to western values (e.g., Australia, New Zealand), and countries in the geographic west also incorporate non-western cultures and communities (e.g., gay Muslim communities in Britain).
- *Lenses other than sexuality*: Research tends to emphasise sexuality and sexual prejudice as the defining features of gay and lesbian experience, and neglects the ways in which race, culture, age, gender, social class and ability shape the lives of gay men and lesbians and BTQ people. Although it is important to include, for example, black LGBTQ people in research, it is also necessary to explore the ways in which social norms around race shape the lives of *all* LGBTQ people.
- *Alternative models of sexuality*: Most research is based on a dichotomous heterosexual/homosexual model of sexuality and overlooks the challenges that bisexuality presents to this model. Furthermore, little is known about the sexuality of research participants other than their self-identification as lesbian or gay (and bisexual). We can only speculate about how a more nuanced conceptualisation of sexuality might alter research findings.
- *Theoretical diversity*: LGBTQ psychology has little engagement with related areas of research within and outside of psychology such as **feminist psychology** and **queer theory** (see Chapter 2). We think engaging with related areas of research and theory would invigorate LGBTQ psychology.

- *Methodological diversity*: Positivist-empiricism dominates LGBTQ psychological research, although qualitative and critical approaches are gaining momentum in the UK and Australasia. We encourage further engagement with a wide range of methods and approaches to research.
- *Intersex*: We chose not to include 'I' for intersex in our naming of the field, partly because most research focuses on intersex as a theoretical category (e.g., Kessler, 1998), rather than on the lives and experiences of individual intersex people and intersex communities (but see Kitzinger, 2000a; Liao, 2007), and partly because there is ongoing debate within intersex and LGBTQ communities about the inclusion of intersex people under the LGBTQ banner.

Main chapter points

This chapter:

- Defined LGBTQ psychology as a branch of psychology that seeks to challenge the privileging of heterosexuality within society and provides a range of psychological perspectives on the lives and experiences of LGBTQ people.
- Highlighted the contributions of early sexologists to the establishment of sexuality and gender identity as legitimate foci of scientific investigation and to the development of the modern concepts of sexuality and gender identities.
- Outlined the emergence of 'gay affirmative' psychology, following the declassification of homosexuality as a mental illness, and the emphasis on proving the psychological health of gay men and lesbians and their similarities to heterosexuals in early gay affirmative research.
- Noted the emergence of an alternative, critical, approach to lesbian and gay psychology in Britain in the 1980s, which challenged the 'just the same as' model that prevailed in gay affirmative research in the USA.
- Documented the struggles that LGBTQ psychologists have undergone to achieve professional recognition for their work and to challenge heterosexism in psychology.

Questions for discussion and classroom exercises

1.   List all the terms and associations you can think of for the categories 'lesbian', 'gay man', 'bisexual' and 'heterosexual'. These can be slang terms, stereotypes, famous people, behaviours or practices. It doesn't matter if some people would consider the words offensive or whether you would use them; the point of this exercise is to identify all the positive and negative cultural associations for these categories. Once you've listed all the associations you can think of, can you spot any themes or patterns?

Are most of the terms for each category positive or negative? Could you think of more terms for some categories than for others? Why do you think that is? What do the terms reveal about cultural attitudes towards lesbianism, homosexuality, bisexuality and heterosexuality? (For further information on this exercise, see Peel, 2005.)

2.   Without consulting anyone else or giving it too much thought, write down what you think makes a 'real man' and a 'real woman', and ask other people (preferably people of different ages, backgrounds and so on) to do the same. Compare your definitions of the two categories and the language you have used to describe them. Are there any similarities? Any differences? What do the answers tell us about gender? Are the categories 'real man' and 'real woman' enough to capture our experience of gender? (For further information on this exercise, see Bornstein, 1998.)

3.   Do you think it is more useful to conceptualise sexuality in terms of distinct categories (lesbian, gay and bisexual) or in terms of Kinsey's continuum of sexual behaviour and preferences? What do you think of the argument that we are all bisexual to a degree?

4.   Identify some of the strengths and weaknesses of early affirmative research on homosexuality.

5.   Reflect on the heteronormativity you have encountered within psychology. Have social psychology courses included discussion of **homophobia, transphobia** and **biphobia**? Have discussions of parenting and child development been based on theories that assume all children develop in heterosexual households and that our gender role is fixed at an early age? Are heterosexist and genderist assumptions reflected in your textbooks and other teaching materials? What can be done to challenge heteronormativity in psychology?

Further reading

Barker, M. (2007) Heteronormativity and the exclusion of bisexuality in psychology. In V. Clarke and E. Peel (eds.), *Out in psychology: lesbian, gay, bisexual, trans and queer perspectives* (pp. 95–117). Chichester: Wiley.
British psychologist Meg Barker analyses the representation of homosexuality and bisexuality in introductory psychology textbooks. She highlights the heteronormative assumptions that are widespread in psychology and the invisibility of bisexuality in discussions of non-heterosexuality.

Dreger, A. D. (1998) *Hermaphrodites and the medical invention of sex*. Cambridge, MA: Harvard University Press.

The prologue (pp. 1–14) to Alice Dreger's fascinating account of the treatment of hermaphrodites (intersex people) in Europe in the late nineteenth and early twentieth centuries explores how ideas of sex, gender and sexuality are formed and changed.

Greene, B. (2000) Beyond heterosexism and across the cultural divide: developing an inclusive lesbian, gay, and bisexual psychology: A look to the future. In B. Greene and G. L. Croom (eds.), *Education, research and practice in lesbian, gay, bisexual, and transgendered psychology: a resource manual* (pp. 1–45). Thousand Oaks, CA: Sage.
In this chapter US psychologist Beverley Greene develops arguments around inclusivity and diversity and the need to explore the 'different lenses and realities' of LGBTQ people.

Meyerowitz, J. (2002) *How sex changed: a history of transsexuality in the United States.* Cambridge, MA: Harvard University Press.
Chapter 1 of Joanna Meyerowitz's comprehensive history of transsexuality provides an engaging insight into the work of early sexologists and the development of the concept of 'sex change' and of sex change surgery.

Sullivan, N. (2003) *A critical introduction to queer theory.* Edinburgh: Edinburgh University Press.
Chapter 1 of Nikki Sullivan's accessible introduction to queer theory provides an overview of the work of early sexologists and explores how their work contributed to the contemporary organisation of sexuality into sexual identity categories such as 'gay' and 'lesbian'.

2 Key debates and perspectives

Overview

- Social constructionism versus essentialism
- Liberalism versus radicalism
- The relationship between LGBTQ psychology and feminism
- The relationship between LGBTQ psychology and queer theory
- The relationship between LGBTQ psychology and critical psychology
- The relationship between LGBTQ psychology and positive social change

In Chapter 1, we introduced you to the history and contemporary development of LGBTQ psychology as a recognised sub-field of psychology. In this chapter, we further equip you to be an LGBTQ psychologist by exploring some of the theoretical and political issues that inform the field. We start by exploring two key debates underpinning much work within LGBTQ psychology: confrontations between essentialist and constructionist theories and between liberal and radical ideologies. Don't panic about our mention of theory, **ideology** and politics (things that make a lot of psychologists panic!) – these concepts can all be defined simply as an organised collection of ideas, a way of looking at things, a way of explaining things. At the same time, we acknowledge that these debates are rather complex and we encourage you to return to them once you have read some of the topic-based chapters and you have an understanding of the empirical research on which these debates are brought to bear.

In discussing the essentialism versus social constructionism debate we touch on a controversial issue – the aetiology or origins of homosexuality. Our view is that research on the aetiology of homosexuality is deeply problematic, as we explain below. However, understanding how individuals and groups of people come to identify with particular labels and conceptions of sexuality and gender, and how particular understandings of sexuality and gender come into being in particular moments in history, *is* interesting and very different from the search for (say) a 'gay gene'. Our discussion of the essentialism versus social constructionism debate is designed to provide you with tools to engage critically with 'origins' research.

Our exploration of key debates is followed by a discussion of some of the broad theoretical and political movements both within and outside of psychology that have influenced the work of LGBTQ psychologists. We focus on three broad traditions: feminism, queer theory and critical psychology. These are not the only traditions to shape the work of LGBTQ psychologists, but they are the ones that are least likely to be familiar to readers. We end the chapter by exploring the relationship between LGBTQ psychology and positive social change for LGBTQ communities.

Social constructionism versus essentialism

Essentialist theories

As Kitzinger *et al.* (1998) noted, until the mid-1980s gay affirmative psychology (as it was known then) was for the most part rooted in essentialist theories. Sexuality was 'assumed to be an inner state or "essence", which the individual "represses" or "discovers", "denies" or "acknowledges"' (p. 531). Essentialist theories often conceptualise sexuality in terms of 'sexual orientation', which implies the existence of an inner psychological or biological structure that organises people's sexual feelings and desires and directs their sexual behaviours and practices (as typically either homosexual or heterosexual). Although it is acknowledged that people sometimes behave in ways that conflict with their essential sexual orientation (in homophobic social climates people may 'repress' their true desires and act in accordance with social convention), the 'truth' of their sexuality is thought to reside in their sexual orientation. Essentialist theories of sexuality assume that sexual orientations are either biologically determined (in some way) or acquired very early in life (as a result of early childhood social-isation or an interaction of nature and nurture), and are fixed and unchanging. Similar theories have been proposed for the origins of trans (see Box 2.1) and gender identity.

Many non-heterosexuals feel that their sexuality has a biological basis (Gottschalk, 2003), and many lesbian and gay political movements and campaigns have used essentialism to argue that homosexuality is not chosen and should not therefore be a basis for discrimination. The first people to harness essentialist arguments were early sexologists and reformers such as Magnus Hirschfeld and Havelock Ellis, who challenged the prevailing view of homosexuality as wilful and immoral (and therefore criminal) behaviour by instead presenting homosexuality as **congenital inversion** (see Chapter 1).

There have been numerous attempts to discover the 'cause' of homosexuality and numerous different theories have been proposed for the origins of homo-sexuality. Our brains (LeVay, 1991), our genes (Hamer *et al.*, 1993), the lengths of our fingers (Martin *et al.*, 2008), our map reading abilities (Rahman *et al.*, 2005) have all been thought to provide clues (or the answer) to the origins of homo-sexuality (see Box 2.1). The findings of such studies tend to be widely reported in

Box 2.1   *Highlights: essentialist theories of the aetiology of homosexuality, bisexuality and trans*

The 'gay gene' theory. Some researchers have argued that there is a genetic basis to homosexuality and point to evidence from family, twin and genetic studies (Bailey, 1995). Some family studies of homosexuality have found that gay men have more gay brothers than straight men (Pillard and Weinrich, 1986). An early twin study found a 100 per cent concordance rate for thirty-seven male monozygotic twin pairs, compared to 15 per cent for twenty-six dizygotic pairs (Kallman, 1952). However, the methodology of this study has been severely criticised. Although subsequent twin studies have produced varied and inconsistent results, Bailey (1995) concluded that the evidence from twin studies suggests that both male and female homosexuality are moderately heritable. In 1993, the geneticist Dean Hamer and colleagues reported evidence of a 'gay gene' associated with the Xq28 marker of the X chromosome.

The 'gay brain' (or neuroendocrine) theory. This theory posits that the brains of gay men have something in common with those of heterosexual women and that the same is true of the brains of lesbians and heterosexual men. The brain differences between men-preferring and women-preferring individuals are thought to be largely innate and result from pre-natal hormone exposure, although parental socialisation may also play a role (Bailey, 1995). Evidence for this theory includes an association between sexual orientation and (recalled) childhood gender nonconformity (Green, 1987). The UK-based psychobiologist Qazi Rahman and colleagues have conducted a number of studies testing the neuroendocrine theory. They have found that, for example, gay men use a blend of male and female map-reading strategies (Rahman *et al.*, 2005).

Nurture during the 'developmentally critical' early years. The psychoanalyst Irving Bieber (1965) notoriously proposed that male homosexuality was the product of a 'close-binding-intimate' mother and a 'detached and hostile' father. In Bieber's theory, homosexuality was viewed as a pathological reaction to poor parenting.

Bisexuality. Most biological studies exclude bisexuals or classify them as homosexuals (e.g., LeVay, 1991). There is very little evidence supporting the proposition that bisexuality has a biological basis; however, some researchers have attempted to discover whether bisexuals are more like homosexuals or heterosexuals in relation to variables such as childhood gender nonconformity. A common finding is that bisexuals occupy an intermediate position between homosexuals and heterosexuals (Bell *et al.*, 1981).

Trans. Various essentialist theories have been proposed to explain transsexualism: some theorists suggest early nurture is key (Stoller, 1968), whereas others argue that transsexualism is determined by biological factors (Zhou *et al.*, 1995); indeed, some researchers have recently claimed that transsexualism should be understood as a form of neurological intersex (see Jeffreys, 2008).

the media and instigate debates about whether homosexuals are 'born that way' or 'made that way'.

Let's consider a classic example of one of these types of studies: Simon LeVay's (1991) 'A difference in hypothalamic structure between heterosexual and homosexual men'. LeVay dissected and compared the INAH nuclei in the hypothalami of forty-one subjects: nineteen homosexual men (including one bisexual man), sixteen presumed heterosexual men, and six presumed heterosexual women. All of the homosexual men, six of the heterosexual men and one of the women had died from AIDS-related causes. LeVay categorised some of the men as homosexual on the basis of their disclosures to their doctors and he assumed the other men to be heterosexual on the basis of 'the numerical preponderance of heterosexual men in the population' (p. 1036).

There are four INAH nuclei in the anterior hypothalamus – INAH 1, 2, 3 and 4. LeVay replicated the previous finding that INAH 2 and 3 are sexually dimorphic (that is, systemically different in form between men and women), but failed to replicate the previous finding that INAH 1 was sexually dimorphic. LeVay's key finding was that the INAH 3 of the homosexual men were smaller than those of the heterosexual men and similar in size to those of the heterosexual women.

Numerous critiques have been made of this and other essentialist studies:

- *Some critics have asked why the origins of homosexuality matter.* They highlight the dearth of research on the origins of heterosexuality, which indicates that heterosexuality is widely regarded as normal and natural, and not in need of explanation, whereas homosexuality is seen as a developmental anomaly that demands explanation.
- *Some critics have argued that essentialist research relies on social formations of sexuality.* In a queer reading of LeVay's study, British-based LGBTQ psychologist and key researcher (see Box 2.2) Peter Hegarty (1997) argued that LeVay's claim to discovery relied on the social construction of sexuality as 'sexual orientation'. In other words, LeVay and other essentialist researchers present as fact (as universal, ahistorical and acultural) a model of sexuality that is one among many possible models of sexuality, and that is particular to contemporary western culture (Hegarty, 2003a).
- *Bisexuality is ignored or is treated as a variant of homosexuality.* LeVay classified his participants as either homosexual or heterosexual (something that is common in other studies), and included a bisexual-identified man in the homosexual group. In doing so, LeVay 'assumes and reinforces the norm that there are two types of person, homosexuals and heterosexuals, and that they can be considered biologically distinct' (Hegarty, 1997: 361). By including a bisexual man in the homosexual group, LeVay recycles the belief that 'one drop' of homosexuality makes someone totally homosexual. As we discussed in Chapter 1, bisexuality troubles the dichotomous heterosexual/homosexual

Box 2.2   Key researcher: Peter Hegarty on why I study the sexual politics of science

About fifteen years ago, I moved from Ireland to California, began my PhD research at Stanford University, and came out. At the time, the US media were enamoured of recent claims about the discovery of a gene that could predict who will come out, and my sense that such knowledge would have made the coming out process harder, not easier, for me got me thinking about what kinds of science lesbian, gay, bisexual, and transgender people do, and do not, need, want, and deserve. Since then my research has taken me down three interlocking paths. First, I became sceptical of the hypothesis that biological research brings about improvements in heterosexual people's attitudes to LGB people. The survey evidence supporting this claim was a robust correlation between tolerant attitudes and biological determinist beliefs among heterosexual people. I observed that the correlation between tolerance and biological beliefs was found only among students who also thought that biological determinist attitudes expressed tolerant views toward lesbian and gay people (Hegarty, 2002). More recently, I've found that essentialist views predict prejudice against trans people (Tee and Hegarty, 2006), and that teaching people biological beliefs doesn't affect their attitudes toward stigmatised groups (Hegarty and Golden, 2008).

In the last paragraph, I wrote 'students' where 'straight students' might have been more precise. Did you notice? My second line of research examines how privileged identities are taken as the norm. (Try and make 'LGB students' the norm for 'students'. It feels different, right?) In social science thinking these slips lead published psychologists' and psychology students' explanations of group differences to focus on lower-status groups such as lesbians and gay men (Hegarty and Pratto, 2001, 2004), and women (Hegarty and Buechel, 2006). As a result, these groups are more likely to be stereotyped in 'expert interpretations' of data.

My third way of working is historical. Some of my attempts to inform psychological science with LGBTQ studies have led me to research how psychological technologies like the Rorschach test (Hegarty, 2003b) and the IQ test (Hegarty, 2007a) intersect with LGBT history in the USA. Throughout, I've been inspired most by critical thinking in fields like queer theory, feminist studies and science and technology studies. But I also find psychological science to be too important, and too much fun, either to allow it to escape criticism, or to engage with it only by critique. This positions me betwixt-and-between opposing sides in debates about quantitative and qualitative methods and **realism** and social construction. Is my work 'mainstreaming' critical LGBT ideas or reclaiming the psychology lab as queer space? I want you to be the judge.

model of sexuality (Hegarty, 1997). As Hegarty outlines, the only alternative to including bisexuals in the homosexual group is to abandon a dichotomous model of homosexuality and (possibly) the concept of 'sexual orientation', and to acknowledge that sexuality is more fluid and messy than the dichotomous model suggests.

- *Homosexuals are assumed to be 'gender inverts' or to have an excess of gender.* Many biological theories draw on and reinforce the notion that gay men and lesbians are 'gender inverts', that gay men have an excess of femininity (they have feminised brains or bodies) and lesbians have an excess of masculinity (they have masculinised brains or bodies). In western thought, desire for a man is often understood as a feminine desire and desire for a woman as a masculine desire. In the words of the feminist philosopher Judith Butler (1990), sexual desire (even same-sex sexual desire) is conceived of within a 'heterosexual matrix'. Interestingly, some findings suggest that gay men are more masculine than heterosexual men; however, this is also presented as an excess, a developmental anomaly, and the bodies of heterosexuals are assumed to be 'normal' – appropriately masculine or appropriately feminine (Hegarty, 2003a).

- *Some critics have asked what manifestation of sexuality biological studies are seeking to explain.* Some men identify firmly as heterosexual but have regular sex with other men (e.g., men in prison or in the armed forces and other men who might be labelled 'situational homosexuals' or men who have sex with men (**MSM**)). Some people identify with a particular sexual identity because of political or ideological reasons (e.g., **political lesbians**). Some people identify as bisexual but are in a long-term monogamous relationship with someone of a different sex. Some people feel that their engagement in particular sexual communities or practices is a more important indicator of their sexuality than the sex/gender of the people they have sex with (e.g., some people who engage in **BDSM**). These are just a few examples of the complexities in how people identify their sexuality and experience and express their sexual desires. If these people were invited to participate in a biological study, how would they be classified? Which aspect of sexuality – how we label and identify our sexuality (now or in the past), how we behave (now or in the past), what we desire (now or in the past) – counts as 'the truth' of our sexuality? Typically, essentialist researchers ignore the meanings people give to their sexualities and attempt to classify them in terms of the dichotomous heterosexual/homosexual model (see Chapter 3 for a detailed discussion of defining populations in LGBTQ research).

Social constructionist theories

In the mid-1980s, social constructionists began to challenge essentialist conceptualisations of sexuality, arguing that the categories 'lesbian', 'gay', 'bisexual' and 'heterosexual' are the products of particular historical, cultural and political contexts (e.g., Kitzinger, 1987). Social constructionist research on sexuality and gender identity has explored how people actively construct their identities (e.g., Flowers and Buston, 2001; Kitzinger and Wilkinson, 1995; Mason-Schrock, 1996), how sexual and gender identity categories are made 'real' through social processes and interactions, and the variations in the conceptualisation of sexuality and gender identity across time, place and culture (see Box 2.3). Social constructionists have also sought to unravel the taken-for-granted status of 'heterosexuality' and the ways in which individual heterosexuals construct their identities (e.g., Demasi, 2003; Wilkinson and Kitzinger, 1993).

Box 2.3   Key study: Peter Jackson (2000) on the categorisation of sexual and gender diversity in Thai culture

The experience of sexuality and gender in non-western cultures is often very different from how they are experienced in western cultures. Australian-based Asian studies scholar Peter Jackson points to the limitations of western theories of sexuality for understanding same-sex cultures within Thailand. Thai culture categorises sexuality in terms of different forms of 'phet', eroticised genders, rather than in terms of sexual identities. A person's location on the gender scale of phet (from 100 per cent masculine to 100 per cent feminine) determines their erotic preference. It is more important to know how masculine or feminine someone is, than to know the types of sexual bodies and gender performances they find erotically appealing.

Jackson has identified at least seven contemporary forms of phet: (1) man (in western terms, 100 per cent butch masculine and heterosexual), (2) gay king and (3) gay queen (both categories for what western cultures would call gay men, kings taking a sexually insertive role and queens a receptive role), (4) kathoey (previously considered an intermediate or third sex/gender incorporating the western categories of homosexuality and transsexuality, now referring more specifically to trans and intersex people), (5) tom and (6) dee (both categories for what western cultures would call lesbian women, toms being masculine and dees feminine), and (7) woman (100 per cent feminine and heterosexual). There are four distinctive sexual communities in Thailand based on identification with one of four erotically paired categories: (1) man and woman, (2) gay king and gay queen, (3) kathoey and man, and (4) tom and dee.

It is important to note that gay and kathoey are not distinguished as a type of sexuality and type of gender respectively, they are both forms of phet. Many 'gay men' describe themselves as 60/40, 70/30 and so on – these refer to imagined percentage blendings of king (sexually insertive) and queen (sexually receptive), and reflect an increasing recognition that homosexually active men engage in a wide variety of sexual behaviours. But this versatility is understood as emerging from a masculine/feminine blending.

Jackson argues that it is impossible to sustain a difference between sexual identity and gender identity in Thai culture because personal identification as a man or as a gay king is simultaneously erotic and gendered. Whereas western cultures tend to privilege sexuality over gender, many non-western cultures privilege gender over sexuality. Jackson argues that it is important not to see the western history of sexuality as true and Thai culture as underdeveloped.

It is important not to confuse social constructionism with socialisation theory. Socialisation theory presents sexuality and gender as a product of early childhood experiences and conditioning by the media and other social institutions (and sex as the product of biology). The idea that social norms or 'gender stereotypes' determine the boundaries of acceptable gender role behaviour for women and men, and that these norms are historically and culturally specific, is relatively non-controversial (Kitzinger, 1995). Social constructionism goes much further than socialisation theory and explores the ways in which the most basic categories for organising our experience of ourselves and of the world in which we live (woman, man, homosexual, heterosexual) are themselves social constructions, products of social processes and interactions.

Social constructionists reject the 'sex = biology, gender = culture' formula, and argue that both sex and gender are socially derived. The 'natural fact' (Garfinkel, 1967) of two, and only two, sexes is thought to be an ideological (rather than a 'natural') system, a lens through which we view and interpret the world. The US historian Thomas Lacquer (1990) maintained that the **two-sex model** is a relatively new way of understanding sex, which was invented during the eighteenth century alongside the development of modern science. Prior to the emergence of the two-sex model, a one-sex model was dominant, in which women's bodies were understood as different (and inferior) versions of men's bodies. As the Norwegian sociologist Tor Folgerø (2008: 137) outlines: 'the new scientific disciplines prepared the way for an understanding of the sexes as essentially different, and the differences were manifested in everything from the reproductive cells to a person's character and personality'.

Some theorists have suggested that the existence of intersex people (people who are born with 'sex' chromosomes, external genitalia and/or an internal reproductive system that are not considered 'standard' for either male or female) and trans people troubles the two-sex model and the homosexual/heterosexual model of sexuality. For example, US social psychologist Suzanne Kessler (1998) argued that rather than treating the existence of intersex people as a sign that there are not two natural sexes, the bodies of intersex infants are altered in line with the two-sex model, in order to maintain that model as a natural fact (e.g., some infants born with ambiguous genitalia have had their phallus reduced in size, so that it looks like a 'normal' clitoris, and have had a 'vagina' constructed). The existence of the categories homosexual and heterosexual relies on the two-sex model: heterosexuals are attracted to the 'opposite' sex and homosexuals to the same sex. If the two-sex model is an ideological system, then it follows that the categories of 'homosexual' and 'heterosexual' are also the products of an ideological system rather than 'natural' expressions of sexuality.

Social constructionists maintain that in essentialist theories sexuality and gender are reified: for social constructionists, sexuality and gender are abstract concepts but essentialists treat them as real things. One question we are often asked about social constructionism is 'if something is socially constructed does that mean it is not real?' Social constructionists argue that our socially constructed realities are intensely powerful; as Victoria and her colleague New Zealand feminist psychologist Virginia Braun put it, the effects of language and **discourse** 'can feel as real as the sun on our skin or the wind in our hair' (Clarke and Braun, 2009: 241). We find the following quotation about AIDS from US professor of art history and AIDS activist Douglas Crimp a really useful way of explaining the relationship of social constructionism to things like 'reality', 'biology' and the 'material world'. Crimp (1988: 3) wrote that:

> AIDS does not exist apart from the practices that conceptualise it, represent it, and respond to it. We know AIDS only in and through these practices. This assertion does not contest the existence of viruses, antibodies, infections, or transmission routes. Least of all does it contest the reality of illness, suffering, and death. What it does contest is the notion that there is an underlying reality of AIDS, upon which are constructed the representations, or the culture, or the politics of AIDS. If we recognise that AIDS exists only in and through these constructions, then hopefully we can also recognise the imperative to know them, analyse them, and wrest control of them.

Crimp's argument is that social constructionism does not deny the existence of a material reality; we clearly have bodies and 'minds' that do and feel things, that, for example, experience sexual desire and pleasure and arouse desire and pleasure in others. At the risk of sounding like a cheesy romance novel (!), when we experience such feelings, we may also experience our pulses quicken, our hearts race – even though our experience of sexuality is mediated through socially constructed categories, it nonetheless has a material 'reality'. It is important, however, to distinguish between materiality and biological determinism. To say that sexuality has a material reality is very different from claiming that our genes or our brains determine (at least in part) our experience of sexuality.

Just as many people feel that their sexuality has a biological basis, some people feel that their sexuality is chosen or a product of social processes (Gottschalk, 2003). Some gay and (especially) lesbian movements have used choice or social constructionist theories as a basis for political action. In the 1970s, feminist challenges to essentialist theories of sexuality empowered women to feel that they could reject heterosexual relationships and choose lesbian relationships (Gottschalk, 2003). This is not to say that social constructionist theories of sexuality are commensurate with the notion that we can *choose* our sexual identities. Rather, social constructionism creates the possibility of choice and agency in relation to sexuality more readily than theories that present sexuality as biologically determined or fixed at an early age.

Weighing up essentialism and social constructionism

Although social constructionism is an important strand of contemporary LGBTQ psychology, essentialism continues to dominate the field. Debates about the aetiology of homosexuality reached their peak in the early 1990s. As Kitzinger *et al.* (1998: 531) noted, 'debates between social constructionists and essentialists … left neither side convinced, and research now proceeds in parallel within each framework'. This is partly because of the impossibility of resolving the essentialist/social constructionist debate (Kitzinger, 1995). It is possible to claim that sexuality has a basis in biology and that the expression of sexuality is influenced by cultural and social mores (indeed, some researchers argue for 'integrationist' understandings of sexuality that take account of biological, psychological and social influences). It is also possible to argue that sexuality is socially constructed and sexuality has a material 'reality'. However, essentialist and social constructionist explanations of sexuality are fundamentally incompatible: homosexuality cannot be both a social category and a genetically determined trait. Kitzinger (1995) argued that social constructionism does not provide alternative answers to questions posed by essentialists; rather it raises a whole different set of questions about the social and historical processes through which particular categorisation systems are produced, and the ways in which people live out particular categories (e.g., how the **heterosexual/ homosexual binary** came into being, and how and why individual people come to identify with particular sexual categories).

Both the essentialist commitment to science and the essentialist construct of 'the homosexual' have been useful to campaigns for LGBTQ rights. Essentialist arguments have also been used to undermine LGBTQ rights (some people have welcomed the 'gay gene' theory because it allows for the possibility of aborting gay foetuses). Some LGBTQ activists have been critical of the use of essentialist arguments because they are defensive and apologetic. As Kitzinger (1995) pointed out, essentialist theories call for tolerance and acceptance on the grounds that LGBT people 'cannot help it' and being LGBT 'is not contagious'. Essentialist arguments present non-heterosexuals as a minority, a group that has always existed and always will exist as a variation from the heterosexual majority. As such, essentialism supports the notion that heterosexuality is normal and natural, rather than a socially constructed social institution.

Just as essentialist conceptions of sexuality have been used in political campaigns, so have social constructionist arguments. For example, as noted above, **lesbian feminists** have maintained that if sexuality is socially constructed, it can be changed, and women can choose to be lesbians in opposition to **patriarchal oppression** (e.g., Rich, 1980). As we noted in Chapter 1, some therapists and some religious groups have argued that homosexuality is chosen behaviour that can be changed through therapy or religious practice. Like essentialism, social constructionism also has its critics. For example, British psychobiological researcher Qazi Rahman (1999) has argued that constructionist accounts are 'intellectually weak' (p. 8). The emphasis on fluidity and narrative in constructionist work draws attention away from the regularities of sexuality, and constructionist research fails to provide empirically robust accounts that allow us to differentiate between and evaluate competing models on the basis of the strength of evidence.

Kitzinger (1995) concluded that neither social constructionist nor essentialist arguments are inherently 'lesbian and gay positive'; both can be used to support and to undermine LGBTQ rights.

Liberalism versus radicalism

In certain social contexts, to be considered liberal is generally a good thing; liberal people are thought to be tolerant and accepting of diversity. This view is reinforced by much LGBTQ psychological research. As we discuss further in Chapter 5, research on homophobia has found that people who score low on homophobia tend to be more liberal in outlook and are less likely to be sexist and racist or to hold conservative religious beliefs. Anti-homophobia education often centres on encouraging people to adopt a more liberal perspective on homosexuality – to see LGBTQ people as the same as heterosexual people and not to 'judge' people in terms of their sexuality. Liberal-humanism is a dominant ideology in late modern western cultures and emphasises the uniqueness and rights of the individual. In relation to sexuality, this ideological framework stresses the essential humanness of LGBTQ people and the relatively trivial nature of their sexuality. As Celia Kitzinger (1989: 85) outlined, the liberal-humanist 'rejects classifications that pigeonhole people into labelled boxes and emphasises that the lesbian [or the gay man] should not be segregated as an alien species, but accepted as part of humanity in all its rich variety'. Many LGBT political movements are founded on liberal principles and seek equal rights for LGBT people. Such political organisations seek social reform rather than social revolution: they campaign for, for example, partnership, parenting and employment rights on a par with heterosexual and non-trans people.

Radical theorists and activists have criticised liberal political movements as **assimilationist** or normalising (see Clarke, 2002a, 2002b). They argue that the goal of such movements is achieving the acceptance and tolerance of the majority (tolerance literally means putting up with something you don't like), in other words, fitting in. The liberal message that 'we are all the same' has been criticised for ignoring the ways in which LGBTQ people are socially marginalised (Brickell, 2001), and therefore different from heterosexual and non-trans people.

Other political movements – like **gay liberation**, lesbian feminism and queer – have had more radical goals. Such movements have tended to argue that LGBTQ people should not seek to 'fit in' with the heterosexual majority, and that heterosexual norms should not be the baseline for equality and social justice. Radical movements have demanded social transformation rather than equality within the existing social system and sought respect for LGBTQ people's lives and perspectives.

In many contemporary cultural contexts, radicalism is often viewed with suspicion; self-proclaimed radicals (of any variety) are viewed as militants, as extremists. What radicalism literally means is 'going to the root', so LGBTQ radicals, such as gay liberationists, lesbian feminists and queer activists, have understood themselves as going to the root of LGBTQ social marginalisation, and seeking completely to transform that state of affairs. For example, lesbian feminists have argued that lesbians as a group are socially marginalised, and **hetero-patriarchy** (the organisation of society around male dominance and heteronormativity) lies at the root of this social marginalisation (Rich, 1980). Lesbian feminists have sought to resist and challenge heteropatriarchy, and to bring about a new social order based on principles of economic equality and anti-capitalism, peace and anti-militarism, and so on.

From a liberal standpoint, radical movements are often seen as (hopelessly) idealistic and as achieving very little, while liberal campaigns seek and achieve concrete goals (such as partnership recognition). Concern has also been expressed about the potential for radical campaigns to 'go too far' and alienate potential allies by using 'in your face' tactics and making 'unrealistic' demands.

Debates between liberals and radicals have also played out within LGBTQ psychology. The British psychologist Celia Kitzinger, in her groundbreaking text *The social construction of lesbianism* (1987), critiqued the liberal assumptions of gay affirmative psychology from her standpoint as a **radical lesbian feminist**. Kitzinger argued that liberal models of lesbianism present it 'as no more than a choice of lifestyle, a sexual preference, the outcome of "true love", or a route to "true happiness"' (p. vii). By contrast Kitzinger as a radical feminist rejected **individualised** interpretations of lesbianism and theorised lesbianism as a political institution and challenge to heteropatriarchy.

One example of Kitzinger's critique is her analysis of the (then) emerging body of research on homophobia and homophobia scales. As we discuss further in Chapter 5, homophobia scales typically consist of a number of items, with a response format ranging from strongly agree to strongly disagree: 'The diagnosis of homophobia thus depends upon the investigators' decision as to which items to count as "pro" and which as "anti" gay. The decision is made uniformly, throughout the homophobia literature, in accordance with the dictates of liberal ideology' (p. 59). For a summary of Kitzinger's critique of homophobia scales see Box 2.4. Kitzinger argued that if a radical lesbian feminist completed a homophobia scale, she might be given a 'high on homophobia' score. This is because radical lesbian feminists view lesbians as different from heterosexual women, they view lesbianism as a threat to the social order and to the nuclear family, and many advocate political lesbianism and invite and encourage heterosexual women to identify and live as lesbians.

The liberal solution to homophobia is to educate and change the attitudes of individual homophobic heterosexuals (by countering 'myths' and 'stereotypes' with

Box 2.4 *Highlights: Celia Kitzinger's (1987) radical feminist analysis of homophobia scales*

Kitzinger's critique	Examples of homophobia scale items
Homophobia scales equate a lack of prejudice with the notion that there are no differences between homosexuals and heterosexuals; homosexuality is merely a sexual preference or a choice of lifestyle. The non-homophobe must agree with items such as those listed opposite:	Homosexuals are just like everyone else, they simply chose an alternative lifestyle (Hansen, 1982). A person's sexual orientation is a totally neutral point upon which to judge his or her ability to function in any situation (Thompson and Fishburn, 1977).
Homophobia scales adhere to the liberal humanistic belief that homosexuality is natural, normal and healthy. Non-homophobes must disagree with the items listed opposite:	Homosexuality is unnatural (Price, 1982). Homosexual activities are abnormal (Hansen, 1982). Homosexuals are sick (Black and Stevenson, 1984).
Following on from this non-homophobes must agree with the items listed opposite:	Just as in other species, homosexuality is a natural expression of sexuality in humans (Millham *et al.*, 1976). If homosexuality is allowed to increase it will destroy our society (Price, 1982).
A lack of prejudice is equated with the belief that homosexuals can play a productive role in society; they are not a threat to the social order and the nuclear family. Non-homophobes must disagree with the items listed opposite:	Most homosexuals will attempt to seduce 'straights' if given the opportunity (Thompson and Fishburn, 1977). Homosexuals should not be allowed to vote (Aguero *et al.*, 1984).

sound empirical data – see, for example, Fiona Tasker's (2002) summary of the lesbian and gay parenting literature). For radicals, this is at best 'tinkering around the edges' of a problem that requires major social change (compare Tasker's approach to lesbian and gay parenting with that of Victoria's (Clarke, 2002b) lesbian feminist social constructionist analysis). Just as debates between social constructionists and essentialists are impossible to resolve, it seems likely that liberals and radicals will continue to disagree about the goals of the LGBTQ movement, the nature and causes of LGBTQ marginalisation and how best to challenge it.

The relationship between LGBTQ psychology and feminism

Feminism

Feminism is often referred to (jokingly) as the 'F word' because it is perceived as a 'dirty' word, something that should not be mentioned in 'polite company'! As university educators with a strong interest in feminism, we often perceive a great deal of hostility to feminism, as well as a great deal of misunderstanding of feminist goals and perspectives. The first thing to note is that feminism is not a homogeneous body of thought, and that there is as much (or probably more) debate among feminists as between feminists and others. Broadly speaking, feminism comprises a number of different movements and theories concerned with social relations between women and men, and women's rights and interests. Feminists are often negatively stereotyped as man-hating, angry lesbians who want to rule the world. While some feminists identify as lesbian and there are branches of feminist theory and practice specific to lesbian communities (such as lesbian feminism), lesbianism and feminism are not synonymous. Furthermore, although some (**separatist** and radical) feminists identify men as a social group as their 'political opponents', most feminists do not hate men as individuals (rather they are critical of the **power** and **privilege** invested in men) and have very little inclination to rule the world!

Over the years, many different subtypes of feminist theory and practice have developed, far too many to summarise here (for an overview see Beasley, 1999; Douglas, 1990). Feminism has been a hugely influential social force. Feminists in the nineteenth and early twentieth centuries, known as first-wave feminists, campaigned successfully for women's right to vote. Second-wave feminists (from the late 1960s onwards) have campaigned (often successfully) for, among many other things, women's abortion and reproductive rights, women's right to protection from rape, sexual assault, domestic violence and sexual harassment, and women's rights in the workplace (including maternity leave and equal pay).

Although it is often claimed that we now live in a 'post-feminist' era (McRobbie, 2004) and, more colloquially, that 'everything is equal now', feminists remain concerned about the infringement of women's rights. Contemporary feminism is also concerned with understanding how women's experience intersects with racism, classism, heterosexism and colonialism. For much of its history, the voices and concerns of white, middle-class, western women have dominated feminism. Since the 1980s, the alternative feminisms proposed and developed by women of other races and cultures have gained increasing prominence; alongside this, there is an increasing awareness of the rights of women in non-western countries. For some, this backlash against an over-emphasis on the concerns of white, middle-class, western women constitutes a 'third wave' of feminism (see Springer, 2002).

Feminist psychology

There has always been tension between the (heterosexual) women's movement and lesbian feminism to a greater or lesser extent: lesbian feminists have been highly critical of the neglect of lesbian issues within feminism, and lesbians have been singled out as the 'lavender menace', as dividing and discrediting the women's movement, by heterosexual feminists. These tensions are also evident in the relationship between feminist psychology (sometimes called the psychology of women) and LGBTQ psychology. Like LGBTQ psychology, feminist psychology is a recognised sub-field of psychology, with groupings in all of the major professional bodies (see Unger and Crawford, 2003, for an excellent introduction to feminist psychology). Feminist psychology has been defined as a 'psychological theory and practice which is explicitly informed by the political goals of the feminist movement' (Wilkinson, 1997a: 247) and is concerned with topics of relevance to women's lives and the operation of gender within society. The different topics studied by feminist psychologists are too numerous to list here, but include issues like: pregnancy and motherhood (Marshall and Woollett, 2000), the lives of women immigrants in western countries (Espin, 1995), gender and language (Crawford, 1995), masculinity (Archer, 2001) and violence against women (Gavey, 1996).

Lesbian psychologists such as Celia Kitzinger (1996a: 120) have criticised feminist psychology for relegating lesbian concerns to 'the token lesbian chapter' (feminist psychology has also largely ignored bisexual and trans women, whose interests rarely warrant even token coverage). Kitzinger's argument is that lesbian issues are given only token attention within feminist psychology (usually under headings like 'difference' or 'diversity' or in relation to sexuality), while feminist psychology as a whole remains resolutely heterosexual. Kitzinger highlights the 10 per cent rule: 'While a token lesbian presence is considered very important, anything more than tokenism is construed as a "takeover"' (1996a: 132). The exclusion of lesbian and bisexual women's experience from discussions of, for example, childhood and adolescence, pregnancy, motherhood, work and violence against women suggests that lesbian and bisexual women do not grow up, do not get pregnant, do not mother, do not work and do not experience violence (as women). Lesbianism and bisexuality are reduced to sexualities, things to be discussed in relation to sex, but not in relation to any other aspect of women's lives. The tokenistic treatment of lesbianism within feminist psychology parallels other forms of tokenism (for example, in relation to black women and disabled women), and signals a failure on the part of many feminist psychologists to give thorough-going consideration to differences between women.

At the same time, as we briefly noted in Chapter 1, some lesbian psychologists have been critical of the male bias of much LGBTQ psychology. Some have felt so frustrated by the ignorance of feminist and gay psychologists that they have attempted to establish a separate psychology of lesbianism (Boston Lesbian Psychologies Collective, 1987). A number of lesbian psychologists have called for separate organisations to promote lesbian research under the banner both of feminist and of lesbian and gay organisations (e.g., Rothblum, 1992) and some continue to call for a separate psychology of lesbianism (e.g., Rothblum, 2004). Several lesbian psychologists have chosen to align with feminist psychology and others with LGBTQ psychology (and some have a foot in both camps), and many feel frustrated with the marginalisation of lesbian concerns in both camps (Clarke and Peel, 2005).

There have also been tensions between some feminist and trans and queer scholars and communities. The radical feminist theorist Janice Raymond is famous (or notorious) for writing a book, *The Transsexual Empire: The Making of the She-male* (1979), that is widely perceived as transphobic within trans communities. In this book, Raymond argued, among other things, that **male-to-female (MTF) transsexuals** and the doctors who treat them promote sexist notions of gender and that MTF transsexuals are part of a plot by men to infiltrate the women's movement. There has been a great deal of discussion of Raymond's arguments (see trans feminist Sandy Stone's (1991) much cited response to Raymond). A number of radical feminists remain highly critical of trans people and trans politics (e.g., Jeffreys, 2003, 2008), and some feminist community events have sought to exclude trans women (by requiring women who attend to be 'women born women'). At the same time, some feminist scholars (including trans feminists) have sought to develop a feminist analysis of trans that is sympathetic to the needs and goals of trans people (see Elliot, 2009). For more information about historical and contemporary political tensions between members of LGBTQ communities see Clarke and Peel (2007b). It is important to acknowledge that an inclusive LGBTQ psychology has a complex history, and that LGBTQ communities are heterogeneous (and often non-harmonious) in constitution (Elliot, 2009).

To conclude this section, feminism and feminist psychology are important to LGBTQ psychology because many LGBTQ psychologists identify as feminist or are strongly influenced by feminist ideas (including all of us), even if they don't locate their work within feminist psychology. Furthermore, feminist ideas and feminist activism have shaped the perspectives of many LGBTQ people. There is some debate about whether men can call themselves feminist. Some men do, whereas others identify as 'pro-feminist' in response to the argument that feminism as a theory and a practice is grounded in the experience of being, and living as, a woman, so only women can authentically identify as feminist.

The relationship between LGBTQ psychology and queer theory

Queer theory

Queer theory is a body of work concerned with the critique of heteronormativity. US psychologist Henry Minton (1997) argued that the key to understanding queer theory is its reclamation of the word 'queer'. Queer used to be a term of abuse for non-heterosexuals, and connoted strangeness and peculiarity. In reclaiming this word, queer activists and theorists invested queer with positive, and often defiant and confrontational, meanings. Queer is 'in your face'; queers do not want to fit in, they want to rebel against and resist heteronormativity.

Queer theory developed in the 1990s out of the fields of **lesbian and gay studies** and **women's studies**. Key queer theorists include Judith Butler (1990), Eve Kosofsky Sedgwick (1990) and David Halperin (1990). Queer theory is strongly influenced by the work of the French post-structuralist theorist Michel Foucault (1926–84), famous for his critiques of social institutions such as psychiatry and the prison system and his work on the history of sexuality. Foucault's (1978) *History of sexuality*, vol. I is regarded by many as the most influential book within queer theory (Hegarty and Massey, 2006). In this book, Foucault theorised power as operating through the production of sexuality and sexual categories as much as by their repression. This was a radically different model of power from that offered by gay liberationists and lesbian feminists: these groups understood power as a possession (something that men or heterosexuals have) and as repressive (power is used to marginalise individuals and groups). By contrast, Foucault understood power as relational (power operates between people and institutions, rather than through a top-down model where some people have power and some people don't) and productive (power produces knowledge rather than simply repressing it). This means that power is everywhere: we cannot liberate ourselves from power and **oppression**, and freedom cannot operate outside of power (Minton, 1997). The goal of queer is working against power not seeking freedom *from* power.

Queer theory built on feminist critiques of essentialist constructions of gender and sexuality. Judith Butler (1990, 1993, 2004), in particular, is famous for her theorisation of the performativity of gender. To simplify her rather complex and subtle argument, Butler theorised gender as performative, as something that people do, or more accurately that is done, rather than as something that people have or are (see Clarke and Braun, 2009). The things that we typically treat as outward expressions of our inner gender identity – the type of jewellery we wear, how we style our hair, what clothes we wear, what type of bag we carry, how we walk and hold our bodies – are actually how gender is done. This is not to suggest that gender is simply voluntary and we can take off gender just as we would take off a coat. Butler uses the concept of 'performativity' rather than 'performance' to signal that gender is not something within our conscious control; that the whole of society is organised around the belief that there are two and only two genders, and that our gendered practices are shaped by and read through that lens. So any attempt on our part to 'queer' gender risks being undone by the two sex/gender system.

Queer defines itself against conventional lesbian and gay and feminist politics. One of the hallmarks of queer is its rejection of the sexual identity categories on which the conventional **lesbian and gay movement** was built. Following Foucault, queer theorists view sexual identity categories such as 'gay' and 'lesbian' as regulating and limiting the expression of sexual desire (see Box 2.5). Butler (1990: 13–14) argued that: 'identity categories tend to be instruments of regulatory regimes, whether as the normalising categories of oppressive structures, or as rallying points for a liberatory contestation of that

---

Box 2.5   Key study: Daniel Warner (2004) on the normalisation and regulation of homosexual identities in Evelyn Hooker's research

In Chapter 1, we summarised Evelyn Hooker's (1957) comparative study of the adjustment of homosexual and heterosexual men, and noted that it is generally assessed very positively as making a groundbreaking contribution to the development of gay affirmative psychology and the declassification of homosexuality as a mental illness. US psychologist Daniel Warner offers a slightly different view of Hooker's research, drawing on queer theory. He argues that it both selectively normalised homosexuality and represented a new development in the regulation and control of homosexual subjectivities. Hooker's research did not eliminate the notion that there are differences between homosexuals and heterosexuals; rather it created a distinction between 'normal' homosexuals and deviant queers.

Hooker chose explicitly to avoid people who had been the subject of research on homosexuality up until that point – prisoners, patients and sex workers. If Hooker's intention was simply to show that there is no psychological difference between homosexuals and heterosexuals (and to challenge prejudice based on an assumption of difference) she could have easily used a prison or a clinical population. She could have shown that despite both groups' 'deviancy' from social norms, there was nothing that distinguished them as heterosexual and homosexual. Such a strategy would have avoided making any statement about norms and avoided dehumanising prison or clinical populations.

Hooker's task was in fact twofold: to show that homosexuals are no different from heterosexuals and to show that homosexuals are 'normal'. Hooker secured funding for her research partly because she had access to a hidden population of 'normal' homosexuals, many of whom were members of the Mattachine Society (part of a wider gay and lesbian political movement prominent in the 1950s and 1960s known as the homophile movement). In the 1950s, locating 'homosexuals' meant not finding men with a certain desire but finding men who were willing to name their desire in a way that could be recognised and measured by researchers. The men Hooker considered 'normal' were not normal if normal means the way most homosexual men of the time lived their lives and made sense of their sexuality and their identity. The men Hooker knew were mostly white, middle-class men in monogamous relationships, who understood themselves as part of a gay community and were committed to advancing gay rights. The Mattachine Society encouraged members to participate in research, and as such Mattachine homosexuality 'got its name and face out there first, and thus established a new grid in the matrix of intelligibility, perfectly suited for their kind of sexual deviance' (Warner, 2004: 331).

In Hooker's study, models of 'normal' homosexuality are mapped onto class and race, and, in extending the boundaries of 'the normal' to include white, middle-class gay men, working-class, non-white 'queers' remain on the outside, the deviant sexual other. It is this model of white, middle-class, monogamous homosexuality that represents the 'normal homosexual' in contemporary discourse. Hooker's research did not discover the normal homosexual; rather it constructed it, and provided a baseline against which other non-heterosexuals' 'normality' would be judged.

very oppression'. From a queer standpoint, because power operates through sexual identity categories, **deconstructing** and refusing sexual identity catego-ries is the key to meaningful **resistance**. This means that there are no clear membership criteria for queer, unlike the lesbian and gay movement, in which self-identification as lesbian or gay is key. Queers are defined not by their sexual identities but by their opposition to heteronormativity (which raises the con-troversial possibility of **queer heterosexuals** (see Thomas, 2000, on queer heterosexuals, and Walter's, 1996, critique of this notion). Queer draws its boundaries more inclusively than the lesbian and gay movement, including potentially anyone, especially non-heterosexual and trans people, who reject heteronormative concepts of sex/gender and sexuality.

Queer psychology

Insights from queer theory have been applied to a wide range of topics in psychology, including the aetiology of homosexuality (Hegarty, 1997), the con-cept of 'locus of control' (Riggs, 2005) and anti-homosexual prejudice (Hegarty and Massey, 2006). In spite of the growing application of queer theory within psychology, it remains highly controversial and has been the subject of heated debates within academia (see Clarke and Peel, 2007b, for a summary of the numerous criticisms that have been made of queer theory). Some lesbian and gay psychologists have argued that queer theory has little to offer this area of psychology (Wilkinson and Kitzinger, 1996a), whereas others vigorously dis-agree. For instance, Warner (2004: 335) suggests that a queer-informed LGBTQ psychology would stop demonstrating that queers are normal and abandon the search for the origins of homosexuality. Instead, queer psychology would focus on how particular sexual categories come to be, how individuals and groups of people come to identify with particular sexual categories, and how these categories are lived on a daily basis. In Warner's (2004: 335) words:

> This would be a methodology of the margins that does not seek to make things intelligible in terms of the heteropatriarchy, but tries to find the words of the margins itself. Ultimately, it would be a methodology that understands the performative nature of identity and does not seek to found the social in the biological.

The relationship between LGBTQ psychology and critical psychology

Critical psychology is not a unified approach to psychology, but an umbrella term for a range of radical approaches to the discipline that share some key assumptions (see Fox, Prilleltensky and Austin, 2009, for an accessible introduction to critical psychology). Critical psychology developed out of a critique and rejection of the core principles of mainstream psychology (see Gergen, 1973). Critical psychologists have developed alternative approaches to psychology drawing on a variety of theoretical traditions that are usually overlooked by mainstream psychology. These traditions include feminism, **Marxism**, **post-modernism**, **post-structuralism** and social constructionism. As the editors of an early collection on critical psychology noted, critical psychologists 'believe that psychology's traditional practices and norms hinder social justice, to the detriment of individuals and communities in general and of oppressed groups in particular' (Prilleltensky and Fox, 1997: 3). Critical psychologists argue that psychology is not a neutral and value-free discipline detached from the larger social and political context; rather the theories and practices of mainstream psychology are value-laden and support an unjust society. Gough and McFadden (2001: 14) discuss this argument in relation to the pathologising model of homosexuality. For psychologists and psychiatrists to 'proclaim heterosexuality as normal and homosexuality as alien, for example, is not to state the nature of things … but to produce one powerful version of reality within contemporary society'.

Although not all critical psychologists would accept the label 'social constructionist', many of the assumptions of social constructionism form the foundations of critical psychology (see Box 2.6). Let's consider one of the central propositions of critical psychology and social constructionism – that knowledge is partial and subjective and it is not possible to accumulate objective facts and complete knowledge about the world – in more detail. Mainstream psychologists attempt to minimise the impact of the researcher as much as possible (reduce 'bias', minimise 'extraneous variables') and knowledge is viewed as something the researcher 'discovers' or 'finds' through the correct application of scientific procedures. By contrast, critical psychologists view knowledge as something that is generated by the researcher in interaction with the participants. In other words, knowledge isn't out there waiting passively to be uncovered; knowledge is something that we actively create.

Take an interview study, for example: a mainstream psychologist would attempt to ask the participants the same questions in exactly the same way, and to minimise the impact of the researcher on the interview. The interview is viewed as a tool for discovering what participants think and feel (the participant is viewed as a container of feelings and cognitions that is emptied out by the researcher), but like all self-report instruments, interviews are hampered by 'selective recall' and 'interviewer bias'.

Box 2.6 *Highlights: key differences between mainstream psychology and critical psychology*

Key issues	Mainstream psychology	Critical psychology
What is psychology?	The science of mind and behaviour	A set of discourses and practices that produce particular versions of reality and that regulate and normalise particular versions of subjectivity
What is the goal of psychological research?	To measure, understand and predict human behaviour and cognitions, to produce reliable and valid knowledge about the world	To challenge oppression and promote social change; research should be useful
Guiding epistemic frameworks	Positivist-empiricism, realism, essentialism	Social constructionism, post-structuralism, **critical realism**
Core methods	Quantitative and experimental: surveys and structured interviews, questionnaires, experiments, statistical analysis	Qualitative and critical: **discourse analysis**, **Q-methodology** (Kitzinger, 1987), interviews, focus groups, **naturalistic data** (see Chapter 3)
Position on truth and objectivity	The goal of research is hypothesis testing and discovering facts about the world; objective knowledge (truth) is possible, through the appropriate application of scientific procedures	It is not possible to discover objective facts about the world; all knowledge is partial and subjective; there is no one truth; the goal of research is to construct and deconstruct meaning; good research is rigorous and **reflexive**
View of language	Language reflects reality, it is a window on the world; we look through language (e.g., responses to questionnaire items) to discover what is going on inside people's heads or in the world	Language constructs reality; language is a form of social action, and has a performative role in constructing our social and psychological worlds; language (or discourse) per se is the focus of research

| View of the person | The 'lab' is the most appropriate place to study human behaviour, because relevant variables can be controlled and measured, it is possible to discover generalisable rules and patterns about human behaviour | People are always located in social contexts and always occupy positions of marginality and privilege in relation to social norms; these contexts must not be stripped away by the research process; human experience is varied and complex; research should capture the contradictions and complexity of people's lives |
| Relationship between the researcher and the researched | The researcher has control over the research process and the subjects' engagement in the research | Researchers should acknowledge the power they hold in the research process; measures can be taken to attempt to minimise the power and control of the researcher and empower participants |

For the critical psychologist, the interview is a flexible tool for generating accounts of experience, and interviewing is an organic process; new questions might occur to the researcher throughout the interview and the interviewee might raise unanticipated issues. Researchers inevitably shape the interview process and the knowledge generated from it: their standpoint shapes the questions they ask, what they perceive to be relevant, what they sideline as unimportant, how they interact with the participant, and the choices they make in analysing and presenting the data. The social location of the researcher is viewed as a positive resource rather than something that can be engineered away through the appropriate application of scientific methodology. The researcher's influence on the research process is openly acknowledged (there is no such thing as 'researcher bias' in critical psychology!), and it is usual for researchers to give some consideration to how their social positioning may have shaped their research.

Hopefully this brief discussion gives you some indication of major differences between mainstream and critical psychology. Our discussion of qualitative methodologies in Chapter 3 will provide further insight into the theoretical assumptions and methodological practices of critical psychologists. Critical psychologists work in many of the major sub-fields of psychology, including social psychology (e.g., Ibáñez and Íñiguez, 1997), health psychology (e.g., Murray, 2004b; see also Chapter 6), clinical and counselling psychology (e.g., McNamee and Gergen, 1992) and developmental psychology (e.g., Burman, 1994). Many LGBTQ psychologists are increasingly drawn to critical psychology because of its explicit concern for social change and the generation of liberatory knowledge, and because of their desire to understand the lives of LGBTQ people in all their complexity. LGBTQ psychologists are also drawn to critical psychology's concern for power (something that it rarely acknowledged within mainstream psychology) and its analysis of the role of psychological knowledge in supporting the status quo (see Chapter 9).

The relationship between LGBTQ psychology and positive social change

Over the decades, LGBTQ psychologists have sought to contribute to social change in myriad ways:

- Some LGBTQ psychologists argue that simply doing (affirmative) research on LGBTQ issues is a political act, especially when there is huge pressure not to do such research. Some of the early pioneers of LGBTQ psychology risked their reputations and their careers in conducting their research.
- At the most basic level, LGBTQ psychological research can give members of LGBTQ communities 'a voice'. One of the ways in which people and communities are socially marginalised is by silencing them, denying them an opportunity to 'have their say'. On an individual level, the opportunity to have one's experiences listened to and documented can be extremely empowering.
- Research can be a tool to raise awareness of issues, especially if the findings of a study are well publicised in the media and/or brought to the attention of key stakeholders such as policy makers.
- Research can challenge faulty and prejudiced assumptions. The history of LGBTQ psychology provides numerous examples of this. For instance, Evelyn Hooker's research challenged the assumption of homosexual pathology and was used by gay and lesbian activists to support their case against the inclusion of homosexuality as a mental illness in the DSM.
- Through research we can gain a better understanding of the unique perspectives and experiences of LGBTQ people. This knowledge can be used productively to improve services for LGBTQ individuals and communities.
- The work of LGBTQ psychologists can lead to positive social change for LGBTQ people *and* heterosexual and non-trans people: by examining the experiences of people who live outside of social norms, we can understand something about how social norms operate in the lives of all people.

- Some research has an applied focus in that it tests out the efficacy of inter- ventions (for example, the best way to reduce prejudice) and helps practitioners to engage effectively in social change.
- Research can also feed into social change in a more indirect way. Some research invites us to pause and consider the implications, costs and benefits of our interventions and proposes alternative strategies for facilitating social change.

Many LGBTQ psychologists seem to assume that the steady accumulation of scientific knowledge about LGBTQ lives is the best way to influence policy and practice in relation to LGBTQ communities. Celia Kitzinger (1997: 214) argued that:

> As long as the legal and political apparatus that governs us is (or affects to be) responsive to scientific 'evidence' in making decisions about who is allowed to teach what in state-run schools, who is permitted to adopt or foster children or to use medically provided artificial insemination services, who is imprisoned, and what acts of violence count as crimes, one can argue that it is important for gay and lesbian psychologists not to vacate the field [of mainstream psychology].

Kitzinger illustrates that LGBTQ psychologists are frequently torn between the (often opposing) goals of helping individuals and transforming society. Let's consider an example: As we discuss in Chapter 9, since the 1970s psychological studies have shown that children of lesbian mothers are remarkably similar to the children of heterosexual mothers (i.e., most are heterosexual and 'appropriately' gendered). These studies helped to change the attitudes of the courts in many western countries towards lesbian mothers, and a mother's lesbianism is now extremely unlikely to be grounds for denying her custody of her children (as it was in the 1970s). However, critics have argued that these studies reinforce many traditional norms and values (that it is better to be heterosexual, that it is better to conform to gender norms), and some LGBTQ psychologists want to challenge such assumptions and conduct research that contributes to longer-term social transformation. There are no easy or obvious answers to the dilemma of how best to contribute to positive social change, and we encourage readers to develop their own standpoints on this issue.

Gaps and absences

- Although there were debates about social constructionism and essentialism in the 1980s, on the whole, positivist-empiricism and essentialism continue to dominate LGBTQ psychological research and there has been little examination of the theoretical and political foundations of LGBTQ psychology.
- Following on from this, non-mainstream theories and approaches such as critical psychology and queer theory occupy a more or less marginal status within LGBTQ psychology. We think LGBTQ psychology would be enriched by a more active engagement with these and other non-mainstream approaches.

This is not to say that LGBTQ psychologists should abandon mainstream psychology, but that, for example, insights from queer theory might advance the use of experimental methodologies in important ways (Hegarty and Massey, 2006).

- There has been little consideration of how LGBTQ psychologists can best contribute to social change for LGBTQ people. Although some scholars have highlighted the limitations of liberal and essentialist approaches to LGBTQ psychology, they have been less forthcoming about demonstrating the effectiveness of alternative approaches.

- As we highlighted in Chapter 1, and as we will continue to highlight throughout the book, LGBTQ psychological research is often based on the experiences of relatively privileged – white, middle-class, educated, professional, urban-dwelling – gay men and lesbians. This means that LGBTQ psychologists often develop theories that are based on the lives of a particular sector of the LGBTQ population and are problematically generalised to include all LGBTQ people. One such theory (see Chapter 8) is that **same-sex relationships** are based on principles of equality and are not organised around hierarchical power imbalances. Given that a lot of relationship research is based on samples of white, middle-class, educated, professional couples, where both partners have similar backgrounds, this may well be true for these couples. It may also be the case that if researchers look for equality, they find it! Some researchers, such as the sociologists Christopher Carrington (1999) and Jacqui Gabb (2004), have found evidence to challenge the 'equality norm' for same-sex partners. Interestingly, their research was based on more socio-economically diverse samples and, in the case of Carrington, on the use of intensive qualitative data collection (he actually lived with some of the families he studied), rather than one-off interviews. We suspect that these researchers were more open to the possibility of generating evidence that challenged the 'equality norm' for same-sex relationships; and their samples and methodologies may have pointed the way to this evidence. What this brief example hopefully demonstrates is the need for more **intersectional** theorising within LGBTQ psychology and more consideration of how participants' positioning in relation to race, culture, gender, social class, ability and age both shapes how they live and shapes our theories of their lives.

Main chapter points

This chapter:

- Outlined debates between essentialists and social constructionists about the origins of homosexuality, bisexuality and trans.

- Outlined debates between liberals and radicals about the goals of LGBTQ politics and LGBTQ psychology.
- Summarised some of the key features of feminism and feminist psychology and the links between feminist psychology and LGBTQ psychology.
- Summarised some of the key features of queer theory and the relationship between queer theory and LGBTQ psychology.
- Overviewed some of the core aspects of critical psychology and the relationship between critical psychology and LGBTQ psychology.
- Discussed the relationship between LGBTQ psychology and positive social change for LGBTQ communities.

Questions for discussion and classroom exercises

1. In 1989, US psychologist and feminist therapist Laura Brown proposed an alternative model for psychological inquiry based on the experiences of lesbians and gay men in a groundbreaking article entitled '*New voices, new visions: toward a lesbian/gay paradigm for psychology*'. She argued that lesbian/gay reality is defined by biculturalism (membership of mainstream and lesbian/gay culture), normative creativity (there are no rules or role models for lesbians and gay men to follow in living their lives *as* lesbians and gay men, so they have to create their own) and marginality. In what ways would psychology be different if it was based on a lesbian/gay (and BTQ) standpoint rather than a heterosexual one? Can you 're-imagine' one of your psychology textbooks or courses from a lesbian/gay (BTQ) standpoint?

2. Why are people heterosexual? Do people choose to be heterosexual? Is it a product of socialisation and early childhood experiences? Are people born heterosexual?

3. Reflect on some of the questions from the 'heterosexuality questionnaire' (Rochlin, 2003); e.g., What do you think caused your heterosexuality? When and how did you first decide you were a heterosexual? Is it possible your heterosexuality is just a phase that you may grow out of? Is it possible your heterosexuality stems from a neurotic fear of others of the same sex? What assumptions do these questions, and the heterosexuality questionnaire as a whole, draw our attention to?

4. What are the desired and expected qualities of girls/women and boys/men in your culture? Why do you think gender conformity is so strictly enforced? Imagine you are a 'gender terrorist' for a day: what would you do to transgress gender norms?

5.   Compare and contrast Fiona Tasker's (2002) mainstream and liberal
        approach to lesbian and gay parenting with Victoria's (Clarke, 2002b)
        critical and radical approach. What are some of the strengths and
        weaknesses of each approach (see Kitzinger and Coyle, 2002)? Which
        approach do you prefer and why?

Further reading

Clarke, V. and Braun, V. (2009) Gender. In D. Fox, I. Prilleltensky and S. Austin (eds.),
Critical psychology: an introduction, 2nd edition (pp. 232–49). London: Sage.
In this chapter, Victoria and Virginia Braun explore different models of gender and
sexuality within mainstream and critical psychology, and critically examine the concepts
of gender and sexuality from a queer-informed, feminist social constructionist standpoint.

Clarke, V. and Peel, E. (2007b) From lesbian and gay psychology to LGBTQ psychologies: a journey into the unknown (or the unknowable)? In V. Clarke and E. Peel (eds.), *Out
in psychology: lesbian, gay, bisexual, trans and queer perspectives* (pp. 11–35).
Chichester: Wiley.
This chapter explores the shift from lesbian and gay psychology to LGBTQ psychology
and examines some of the debates that have taken place between members of LGBTQ
communities.

Kitzinger, C. (1987) *The social construction of lesbianism*. London: Sage.
In Chapter 2 of her classic text Kitzinger outlines her critique of the liberal assumptions of
gay affirmative psychology from her standpoint as a radical lesbian feminist.

Myerson, M., Crawley, S. L., Anstey, E., Kessler, J. and Okopny, C. (2007) Who's zoomin'
who? A feminist, queer content analysis of 'interdisciplinary' human sexuality textbooks.
Hypatia, 22(1), 92–113.
An incisive analysis of the heteronormative assumptions underpinning most human
sexuality textbooks that provides a great introduction to queer theory, and in particular a
queer-informed feminism.

Wilkinson, S. (1997a) Feminist psychology. In D. Fox and I. Prilleltensky (eds.), *Critical
psychology: an introduction* (pp. 247–64). London: Sage.
In this chapter, British feminist psychologist Sue Wilkinson provides an accessible introduction to feminist psychology.

3 Doing LGBTQ psychological research

> **Overview**
>
> - Research methods and approaches
> - Issues in doing LGBTQ psychological research

Imagine you are undertaking a research project in LGBTQ psychology (some readers may not have to imagine). Your first step is to identify your theoretical assumptions (see Chapter 2). Do you subscribe to the assumptions of social constructionism, positivist-empiricism or something else? Your theoretical assumptions will (generally) determine your methodology (quantitative, qualitative or a combination of the two), and your methodology, in turn, determines which methods of data collection and analysis you may use. The earliest research on LGBTQ people – the work of sexologists such as Krafft-Ebing and Havelock Ellis – relied on case studies, that is the sexual and gender histories of individual homosexuals, transsexuals and others living outside of social norms around sex/gender and sexuality. Today LGBTQ psychologists use a wide range of methods to collect and analyse data about the lives of LGBTQ people and LGBTQ sexualities and genders. This chapter outlines the main methods used by LGBTQ psychologists and considers the strengths and weaknesses of different approaches to research. The chapter also has a broader focus on the issues and dilemmas that psychologists encounter when researching LGBTQ populations. It provides guidance to researchers undertaking their first project on LGBTQ issues and highlights good practice in researching LGBTQ populations.

Research methods and approaches

We have organised our discussion of the different methods and approaches used by LGBTQ psychologists around the conventional, if problematic, quantitative/qualitative divide. Box 3.1 summarises some of the advantages of quantitative and qualitative approaches for researching LGBTQ populations.

Box 3.1   *Highlights: summary of the advantages of qualitative and quantitative approaches for studying LGBTQ populations*

Why qualitative approaches are useful for studying LGBTQ populations	Why quantitative approaches are useful for studying LGBTQ populations
They prioritise participants' meanings, concepts and language.	They provide concrete information about incidences of particular behaviours and practices, and of patterns of behaviour and practices within and across communities (e.g., patterns of anti-trans prejudice on college campuses).
They are ideally suited to 'giving voice' to marginalised and invisible groups.	
They are useful for exploratory research and for studying topics about which little is known.	
	They are useful for exploring relationships between different phenomena.
They can be used to explore the meanings that people attach to experiences, and provide vivid and detailed narrative accounts of the impact of particular experiences (e.g., being subjected to anti-trans prejudice) on an individual.	They more readily allow for comparison across participants because the researcher constructs the categories that inform the research.
They can be used to provide compelling case studies to support statistical findings.	Given the weight placed on 'hard' data in the wider society, quantitative approaches can be useful in supporting claims for equality.

Quantitative approaches and experimental methods

Quantitative approaches to the study of LGBTQ psychology are typically associated with mainstream psychology and the positivist-empiricist paradigm (although see Box 3.2 for a discussion of the use of these approaches in critical psychology). Positivist-empiricist psychology is primarily concerned with formulating laws to account for happenings in the social world, with a view to being able to predict and control these happenings. This type of research aims to explore patterns of similarity between people and therefore is carried out on fairly large samples from which the research findings can be generalised to a wider population. Almost always, mainstream psychology is hypothetico-deductive, which means that the research question is derived from a theory (a hypothesis) and tested in the research context. Therefore, research that employs this approach centres largely on measurement of phenomena, and the systematic testing of hypotheses. This research design facilitates the process of determining causality. For example, a psychologist might be interested in what situations give rise to an LGBTQ person 'coming out'. Similarly, she might be interested in what conditions cause a

Box 3.2 *Highlights: is critical psychology necessarily qualitative?*

Critical psychology developed out of a critique and rejection of the main tenets of mainstream, positivist-empiricist psychology and is strongly associated with critical qualitative approaches to research such as different versions of discourse analysis. This means that it is unusual for critical psychologists to use quantitative and experimental methods. However, some psychologists have questioned the neat division of research into quantitative/mainstream (and often also liberal, essentialist) and qualitative/critical (and often also constructionist, radical). Peter Hegarty (2002: 163) notes that lesbian and gay psychology in the USA 'remains invested in liberal humanist morality and positivist-empiricist methods... In contrast, European lesbian and gay psychology is developing through more explicit conversations with critical psychological frameworks.'

While Hegarty welcomes the latter development, he argues that there are still convincing political and empirical reasons to employ quantitative methods such as engaging with critiques of essentialism. He demonstrates the latter point in a complex analysis of symbolic beliefs about sexual orientation. He notes that there is widely assumed to be a correlation between tolerant attitudes to lesbians and gay men and the belief that sexuality is immutable. In two studies, Hegarty found that tolerant attitudes towards lesbians and gay men and belief in the immutability of sexuality were correlated – but only among participants who consistently judged that people who are more tolerant of homosexuality would express immutability beliefs. He argues that the link between immutability and tolerance depends more on the social construction of immutability beliefs as signalling tolerance and less on the content of such beliefs. So, Hegarty used conventional measures such as homophobia scales and questionnaires to explore the meaning and social construction of particular beliefs about sexuality.

In a groundbreaking edited collection on critical psychology (Fox and Prilleltensky, 1997), Celia Kitzinger (1997) examined whether liberal and positivist-empiricist lesbian and gay psychology could be regarded as critical psychology. Kitzinger's provocative argument was that scientific and quantitative methods were effective in producing positive social change (and so in some ways should be regarded as critical psychology), whereas there was very little evidence of concrete changes produced by discourse analysis and other critical methods.

Arguments about the strategic use of quantitative methods are more well developed in feminist psychology, where many have advocated the importance of using 'the master's tools to dismantle the master's house' (Unger, 1996); that is, using empirical science to provide support for feminist arguments about women's rights (see, for example, Wilkinson, 1997b).

person to engage in homophobic hate crime. This type of research makes use of categories (e.g., 'lesbian', 'gay') and constructs (e.g., 'homophobia') created and defined by the researcher with the assumption that (if well constructed) they hold the same meaning for different people. In terms of its theoretical grounding, mainstream psychology is underpinned by the notion that there is a single underlying truth about the social world, which can be identified and understood through objective investigation.

Experimental research

Despite a long history of experimental research within the broader subdiscipline of social psychology, this approach is uncommon within LGBTQ psychology, and is represented by only a few isolated studies. These include studies exploring: men's reactions to lesbians and gay men (Kite, 1992), the effects of sexual orientation on hireability ratings (van Hoye and Lievens, 2003), and the effectiveness of getting heterosexuals and non-heterosexuals working together on collaborative tasks as a method for reducing homophobia (Grack and Richman, 1996).

Although experimental research potentially provides valuable insights into the issues and concerns of LGBTQ people, there is a range of reasons why this framework has seldom been employed. First, mainstream social psychologists have shown little interest in LGBTQ issues. This is to suggest not that mainstream social psychologists are dispassionate homophobes (although there may be some of these!), but rather that experimentation relies on being able to control factors in the environment in order to measure the effects of a given stimulus. Although there are some aspects of individuals (e.g., brain function and reaction time) that can be studied under controlled laboratory conditions, issues such as homophobia and coming out are a function of many external, interacting factors, which it is simply not possible to control for. One of the key aspects of LGBTQ psychology is its commitment to making positive social change at the applied level. Since the whole purpose of experimental methodology is to control the context of behaviour, it inevitably creates an artificial setting. The setting may therefore refine the behaviour to such an extent that its relevance to real life and its generalisability become lost. So, although we can employ experimental methodologies to study some aspects of LGBTQ psychology, their utility here is perhaps more limited than is true of other areas of psychology.

The lack of experimental work within LGBTQ psychology can also be attributed to the discipline of psychology itself: in particular, the history of LGBTQ research within psychology and the methodological trajectory of the discipline. As we outlined in Chapter 1, early experimental studies on sexuality tended to stigmatise and pathologise LGBTQ people. Although some early pioneers (e.g., Hooker, 1957) used experimental approaches to challenge this pathological work, those working within gay affirmative psychology tended to steer clear of this approach. This was, in part, a rejection of a methodological tradition that had been responsible for injustice towards LGBTQ people. However, it was also facilitated by the fact that by the end of the 1970s psychology was moving away from a purely experimental research base to employing a wider range of methods, including surveys and questionnaires.

Surveys and questionnaire-based research

In contrast with experimental research, surveys and questionnaires are widely used in LGBTQ psychology, particularly in the USA. Although the terms 'survey' and 'questionnaire' are often used interchangeably, in psychology they represent two distinct forms of data collection (although the research instruments themselves may look very similar).

A survey is essentially a structured paper version of an interview, designed to elicit self-reported information. Its purpose is primarily to generate descriptive statistics. Therefore, this method is often too limited for psychologists who are more interested in testing hypotheses about, rather than describing, social phenomena. However, because there are lots of topics and issues within LGBTQ psychology about which little is known, surveys are often used to provide baseline data. They are also useful for establishing how common a particular occurrence is (e.g., homophobic bullying) or identifying general perceptions of how 'gay-friendly' a particular setting is (e.g., a workplace, a university campus).

Although surveys are usually quantitative, they can be used to collect qualitative data also (see the qualitative and quantitative UK National Lesbians and Health Care Survey, Fish and Wilkinson, 2000; Fish and Anthony, 2005; see also Chapter 6). Qualitative surveys can be useful for facilitating the collection of detailed information from large numbers of people, although as British social scientist Julie Fish (1999) can testify, the investment of time and effort required for open-response formats make it much more difficult both to recruit participants and to elicit detailed written responses. However, *online* qualitative surveys can generate a large amount of data quickly, especially if the participant group is highly motivated (Harding and Peel, 2007a).

In contrast with surveys, questionnaires are sophisticated test instruments designed to elicit information about cognitive constructs (e.g., attitudes, self-esteem, body image). They comprise discrete measures of a particular psychological phenomenon (e.g., self-esteem, homophobia, stress), and are usually structured in a uniform format, requiring responses to each item to be evaluated on a comparable scale (e.g., a Likert-type 'strongly agree' to 'strongly disagree' five-point scale). Questionnaires are much more rigorous than surveys, and through multiple piloting on large samples are refined to ensure that they have a high level of validity and reliability. Questionnaires are fairly easy to distinguish from surveys as they are often called scales or indexes (e.g., Attitude Towards Women Scale; Index of Homophobia), are usually described as having been 'validated' and/or 'standardised', and are scored (i.e., responses are added up to give an overall score or set of scores). Within LGBTQ psychology the most common example of a questionnaire is the homophobia scale, of which there are several (see Davis *et al.*, 2004; see also Chapter 5).

When homophobia scales are combined with other established instruments (e.g., personality measures; measures of self-esteem, stress or health) psychologists can use questionnaires not only to describe phenomena and document rates and frequencies of particular activities and behaviours, but also to find relationships between phenomena (e.g., between fear of rejection and coming out). In addition, questionnaires can be used to explain and predict phenomena (e.g., people who fear rejection are less likely to come out). This characteristic enables psychologists to identify, for example, the types of people who tend to be homophobic, or the types of LGBTQ people who are more likely to cope well with coming out. For this reason, and many others, questionnaire research (and survey research) are popular in applied settings such as education, law, health care and social policy.

Qualitative and critical methods

Broadly speaking, qualitative research centres on generating meaning and under-standing about the world and people's experience of it. Although qualitative methods are occasionally used within mainstream psychology, most qualitative researchers subscribe to one or more of a wide range of philosophies (e.g., **phenomenology**, **contextualism**, **standpoint theory**, social constructionism, post-structuralism) that view meaning as in some way contextual or subjective. In other words, qualitative researchers tend to reject the view that it is possible to generate objective, universal truths, and instead focus on understanding the mean-ings produced in a particular context by a particular group of people. Although qualitative approaches (such as case studies and interviews) have a long history in LGBTQ research, they have only become popular within LGBTQ psychology, particularly in Europe and Australasia, relatively recently. The growing popularity of qualitative methods within LGBTQ psychology reflects the growing popularity of these methods within psychology more broadly (for a good overview of qualitative approaches, see Madill and Gough, 2008). At the same time, qualita-tive methods hold a particular attraction for some LGBTQ psychologists because of the emphasis on participants' meanings and the potential for critiquing domi-nant norms.

In simple terms, there are two main qualitative approaches: experiential and critical. Experiential approaches aim to map out and interpret the meanings people attach to their experiences and how those meanings are influenced by prevailing cultural ideas. Critical approaches are concerned with interrogating dominant meanings and exploring the effects of particular patterns of meaning. There is a huge variety of techniques for collecting and analysing qualitative data: from collecting data that already exist in the world (such as media reports on lesbian and gay adoption, parliamentary debates about trans rights, or telephone conversations between a bisexual man and his friends and family) to generating data (through interviews or focus groups) for the purposes of research. We now outline some of the main qualitative methods of data collection and analysis used by LGBTQ psychologists.

Interviews and focus groups

Interviews are one of the most widely used methods of data collection in psychology and interviews have been used extensively in LGBTQ psychology. For instance, the sexologist Alfred Kinsey and his team of researchers used highly structured interviews to collect data about people's sexual behaviour (see Chapter 1). Although interviews are used to collect data for quantitative, statistical analysis, we are going to concentrate on the use of interviews in qualitative research. Interviews are used to collect in-depth data from individual participants and occasionally from couples or families in relationship and family research. Researchers typically devise a schedule of questions or topics to guide the discussion. Researchers may use the telephone, email or the Internet to conduct interviews with geographically dispersed or 'hard to engage' (see below) participants (van Eden-Moorefield *et al.*, 2008), although face-to-face interviews are generally regarded as generating richer data. This is because the researcher has access to a range of social and interactional cues (such as facial expressions, gaze, gestures and posture) that augment the spoken or written word.

Another increasingly popular method is focus groups (sometimes referred to as group interviews or group discussions), where a group of people is invited to discuss a number of questions or topics or some kind of stimulus material (such as a film clip, vignette or information leaflet) and the discussion is facilitated and moderated by a researcher. Some qualitative researchers value focus groups because they are characterised by collective discussion of topics and interaction between participants (Frith, 2000). Agreement between group members can build a fuller picture of the views of participants and disagreement may also lead participants to provide further explanation of their views. Awareness of shared experience may encourage discussion of difficult and sensitive issues and more confident group members may 'break the ice' for shyer participants. Focus groups also provide an efficient way of obtaining a wide variety of information quickly.

Interviews and focus groups have been used by LGBTQ psychologists to study a wide range of topics, including older gay men's lives (Lee, 2008), gay men's use of sexual language (Mays *et al.*, 1992), and money management practices in same-sex relationships (Burns *et al.*, 2008).

Interviews and focus groups are usually tape-recorded (sometimes video-recorded) and transcribed. Data collected through interviews and focus groups can be analysed in a number of different ways. You may be familiar with common methods of qualitative analysis such as thematic analysis, grounded theory and interpretative phenomenological analysis, which often centre on searching for common themes and patterns in data (see Box 3.3 for examples of studies using particular qualitative methods).

Interviews and focus groups are useful for exploratory research into under-researched topics (many topics in LGBTQ psychology would fall into this category!) and for generating testable hypotheses for quantitative research. Because focus groups tend to have a more unstructured format than interviews,

Box 3.3 *Highlights: qualitative methods of data analysis in action*

Thematic analysis (TA) is one of the most widely used qualitative methods (see Braun and Clarke, 2006, for a clear and accessible introduction to TA) and is often regarded as a foundational qualitative method. TA centres on the systematic generation of themes or patterns within data. Unlike other qualitative approaches, TA is not embedded within a particular theoretical tradition, so can be flexibly deployed within different theoretical frameworks. Examples of studies using TA include Victoria and colleagues' (Clarke *et al.*, 2007) constructionist-informed TA of same-sex couples' views on civil partnership and marriage, and Elizabeth's (Peel, 2002) discursively informed TA of the problems and dilemmas gay and lesbian identified trainers encounter in conducting lesbian and gay awareness training.

Grounded theory (GT) originally developed in sociology and is now used extensively in psychology. GT aims to generate theory from the ground (the data, the participants' experiences) up (Willig, 2001). However, many applications of GT fall short of theory generation and instead produce something akin to thematic analysis – a mapping of themes and categories within data. Over the years different varieties of GT have developed. Brendan Gough (2002) uses GT in combination with discourse analysis to explore the ways in which young heterosexual men talk about homosexuality. Matthews *et al.* (2005) use GT to understand lesbians' recovery from addiction.

Interpretative Phenomenological Analysis (IPA) is associated with the work of psychologist Jonathan Smith and colleagues (Smith and Osborn, 2003) and is particularly popular in health, clinical and counselling psychology (see Willig, 2001, for an accessible introduction to IPA). IPA aims to understand lived experiences and the meanings people attach to their experiences (this is the phenomenological aspect). It also acknowledges that researchers cannot access a participant's world directly, but have to make sense of that world using their own interpretative resources (this is the interpretative part). Examples include Bennett and Coyle's (2007) exploration of the experiences of gay men with intellectual disabilities (see Chapter 4), and Paul Flowers and colleagues' (2003) research on Scottish gay men and HIV testing (see Chapter 6).

Narrative analysis (NA), unlike most other qualitative methods, focuses on individual narratives rather than on themes and patterns across a data-set (although some forms of NA identify patterns of similarity and difference across narratives). As with other qualitative methods, there are lots of different forms of NA. Examples include Reid's (2008) research on the meanings of family and ways of 'living' family for non-heterosexuals, and Langdridge's (2007a) critical NA of young gay men's expectations for parenthood.

they are particularly useful for identifying unanticipated issues. Focus groups and interviews are also useful for exploring the language and social worlds of participants (Wilkinson, 1998a). It is important to note that the use of interviews and other qualitative approaches does not guarantee that participants' meanings will be respected. Interviews and other self-report techniques have been widely used in pathologising research, as key researcher (see Box 3.4) Celia Kitzinger (1987: 66) pointed out: 'some of the most virulently anti-gay and anti-woman investigators have never sullied their work with a de-humanizing statistic, or contaminated their intuitions with a controlled experiment'.

Box 3.4   Key researcher: Celia Kitzinger on why I study the social construction of reality

In the early 1970s, aged just seventeen, I was expelled from school for suspected lesbianism. I wasn't even sure what 'lesbianism' was: there was no acknowledgement back then – at least not in my small Oxfordshire village – of people like me. Searching for information about my 'perversion', I consulted psychology books in the local library: they told me I was sick and perverted. A suicide attempt, and four months in a mental hospital enduring clumsy attempts at diagnosis and cure, contributed to my developing sense of psychology as dangerous and oppressive to lesbians. Outraged at the way I was being treated, I knew from very early on that I wanted to challenge the way in which lesbians were socially constructed – in psychology and beyond it.

By the time I started my doctoral research (in 1980) things had moved on. The new field of lesbian and gay psychology was challenging negative stereotypes with studies showing that we were just as mentally healthy as straight people, that we didn't pose any threat to the family or to society, and that our children turned out just as sex-stereotyped as everyone else's. While this was obviously an improvement on the psychology I had read as a teenager, it seemed equally problematic. My involvement in the radical feminist movement of the late 1970s and early 1980s gave me a strong and coherent basis from which to challenge both sides' depoliticised claims about lesbian and gay lives and their use of positivist **rhetoric** to disguise their value commitments. My first book, *The social construction of lesbianism*, used Q-methodology and interviews to explore how the new 'gay-affirmative' psychology constructed 'the lesbian' as a particular kind of human being and to challenge the objectivity (and political value) of that construction.

Today I am still interested in the social construction of reality but my interest has shifted from how psychology constructs lesbianism (or other sexualities and genders) to how we all contribute to the social construction of reality in our everyday interactions. I explore the mundane reproduction of sexism, heterosexism and other forms of power and oppression (and resistance to them) at the level of everyday life (Kitzinger, 2000b, 2005a, 2005b). Detailed analysis of actual interactions (rather than interviews or focus groups) reveals the warp and weft of everyday conversations – as when a dentist receptionist, hearing a woman ask for an appointment for her partner, asks for 'his' name, or when a doctor designs his questions very differently for a 'wife' phoning about her 'husband' compared with a 'friend' calling about a (same-sex) 'friend' (Kitzinger, 2005a; Land and Kitzinger, 2005). The routine and insidious construction of heteronormative reality marginalises LGBTQ people as 'Other' and contributes to our oppression. It is worth documenting it, and challenging it, in order to create a world that better respects the diversity of the people in it.

Naturalistic data

The term 'naturalistic data' has a range of meanings, but we use it to refer to 'data-in-the-world'; that is, data generated for purposes other than research. As we noted above, this might include newspaper reports, records of parliamentary debates (Ellis and Kitzinger, 2002), teaching and training sessions (Peel, 2002), psychology textbooks (Barker, 2007), children's books (Riggs and Augoustinos, 2007), talk shows (Clarke and Kitzinger, 2004), self-help literature (Clarke and Rúdólfsdóttir, 2007), telephone calls (Land and Kitzinger, 2007), interactions between doctors and patients (Speer and Green, 2007) – the list goes on! One clear benefit of naturalistic data is that some forms such as newspaper reports and talk shows are very easy and economical to access. Other forms of naturalistic data may be relatively easy to access for some LGBTQ psychologists because of their professional activities. For example, Elizabeth's work as a lesbian and gay awareness trainer (see Peel, 2002; see also Chapter 5) permitted her easy access to lesbian and gay awareness training sessions for her research on this topic. Other forms of naturalistic data can be harder to capture. For example, audio and/or video-recording doctor–patient interactions requires the use of expensive recording and data management equipment, and it can be complex and time consuming to find a group of doctors and patients who are willing to have their consultations recorded. For LGBTQ psychologists concerned with the social world, naturalistic data give direct access to that world. For instance, if a researcher wants to explore dominant social perceptions of homosexual rights, collecting media coverage of these issues might be more contextually appropriate than collecting psychology students' responses to a homophobia scale.

Discourse analysis

Discourse analysis (DA) emerged in the 1980s and is an increasingly popular approach to qualitative research among LGBTQ psychologists. Within psychology, DA is strongly associated with critical psychology and with the work of a diverse group of British social psychologists such as Derek Edwards (Edwards and Potter, 1992), Wendy Hollway (1989), Ian Parker (1992), Jonathan Potter (Potter and Wetherell, 1987) and Margaret Wetherell (Wetherell and Potter, 1992). DA centres on the detailed analysis of textual data (such as interview and focus group transcripts, media reports and counselling sessions) and challenges many of

Box 3.5 *Highlights: core assumptions of realist/essentialist versus discursive approaches to language*

Realist/essentialist approaches	*Discursive approaches*
Language reflects reality. Language is generally viewed as a window on the world (whether that is the inner world of our minds or the 'world out there'). We look through language in order to uncover the meaning that lies beneath.	Language is active, does things, has discursive (and, some would say, material) effects, and is constitutive of reality. Language brings social objects into being.
People's responses to a questionnaire, or answers in an interview, are often theorised in terms of psychological constructs and motivations (they hold homophobic attitudes, they are jealous) or sociological features (people's attitudes reflect their age, geographic location, and/or racial and cultural background).	Because language is active, language (or discourse) and its effects are the focus of research. Research identifies patterns in language use, the meanings that surround and constitute particular social objects (such as homosexuality), and the effects of particular patterns of meaning. It is through discourse that homosexuality gains shape and texture and a social reality.
	With discursive approaches, the focus is on language use per se and the effects of particular patterns of language, rather than on the psychological or sociological motivations behind language use. Language use is theorised in terms of, for example, avoiding a particular inference (such as 'you are a homophobe') or designing an account to be persuasive.

the basic assumptions of mainstream psychology, as well as some of the assumptions of other qualitative methods. DA is often described as an approach to psychology rather than a method of data analysis, in that it provides us with an alternative way of thinking about and doing psychology. See Box 3.5 for a comparison of some of the key features of discourse analysis and mainstream psychology.

So what is the discourse that discourse analysts analyse? Discourse is defined in lots of different ways, but one common definition is that discourse refers to shared patterns of meaning that constitute social objects in particular ways (see Parker, 1990; Potter *et al.*, 1990). DA can broadly be described as founded on social constructionist or post-structuralist principles. But it is important to note that DA is not a homogeneous approach, and there are lots of different varieties of discourse analysis (see Willig, 2001, for an overview of two main types of discourse analysis – **post-structuralist/Foucauldian discourse analysis** and **discursive psychology**). Broadly speaking, DA research focuses on unravelling and dissecting particular patterns of meaning, such as different ways of speaking and writing about homosexuality, and the ways in which certain ideas about it are presented as acceptable (see Coyle, 2006). People may carefully craft how they speak about homosexuality to deflect accusations of homophobia, while still articulating views that, through careful analysis, can be shown to have negative effects (see Speer and Potter, 2000).

Elizabeth's (Peel, 2001a) groundbreaking study of **mundane heterosexism** (see Chapter 5) is a good example of a broader discursive approach. Her approach was more concerned with broader patterns of meaning in talk and their discursive effects, than with individual word choices and other features of interaction (such as intonation, pauses and emphasis; see Speer and Potter, 2000, for an example of a more 'fine-grained' discursive psychological approach to heterosexist talk).

Elizabeth analysed talk from lesbian and gay awareness training sessions and interviews with trainers and trainees. She identified three themes or 'types' of mundane heterosexism in the data, one of which was 'non-heterosexuality as deficit'. For example, one speaker compared a son coming out as gay to a son losing a leg in a motorbike accident. Elizabeth argued that the comparison between a gay son and a disabled son served to present non-heterosexuals as lacking or losing an aspect of their humanity when they come out and to present heterosexuals as normal, fully functioning individuals. Her analysis shows how ostensibly positive and 'caring' talk about non-heterosexuality (the speaker making the coming out/becoming disabled comparison was attempting to demonstrate a positive attitude to having a gay son) draws on and reinforces problematic heterosexist assumptions.

Discourse analysis is useful for critically examining prevailing cultural ideas, and mapping common ways of speaking and writing about particular issues, and the effects these have. Given the non-normativity of homosexuality, bisexuality and trans, there is much scope for using discourse analysis to examine how prevailing cultural ideas about homosexuality, bisexuality and trans are constructed, how negative views are justified, and how non-heterosexual and trans people negotiate, resist and challenge negative views (see Clarke and Kitzinger, 2005; Clarke *et al.*, 2004).

Participatory research

There is a wide range of participatory approaches to research that treat participants as 'experts' and encourage them to take a more active role in the research process, other than simply as sources of data (e.g., action research, memory work, co-operative inquiry, see Reason and Bradbury, 2001). Participants can be invited to help with generating research questions and to comment on research findings. Sometimes the researcher and participants may agree on and work towards a practical goal or outcome of the research process. This approach is intended as a challenge to the traditional hierarchical research framework, in which the researcher has power and control over the process and the participants. Participatory approaches have been used to study a wide range of topics including the experiences of lesbian and gay educators (Griffin, 1992), and those of **polyamorous** (see Chapter 8) women (Ritchie and Barker, 2005).

Participatory approaches are useful for exploring the experiences of socially marginalised groups, especially those about which little is known. These approaches are useful both when researchers are members of the group being studied (they can use their own experiences to enrich the research process) and when they are outsiders (because participants have greater control over the research process and can help the researcher to develop research questions). Outsider researchers may decide to collaborate with a co-researcher who is a member of the group, or enlist the help of an 'expert participant' to guide them through the research process. Participatory approaches are also useful for effecting social change; the changes that can be achieved can be deeply meaningful for the individuals and communities involved, if relatively small in scale.

Issues in doing LGBTQ psychological research

Now that we have identified the different approaches and methods used by LGBTQ psychologists, we consider some of the more general methodological issues that they encounter in conducting their research.

Defining, accessing and sampling LGBTQ populations

One of the most complicated aspects of doing LGBTQ psychological research is finding participants and constructing samples. In this section, we outline some of the challenges and dilemmas that researchers face when undertaking research on LGBTQ populations.

Defining the population

The first complex issue that LGBTQ researchers confront when doing research on LGBTQ populations is how to define the fundamental categories of 'lesbian', 'trans' and so on. Let's consider the example of defining the category lesbian. Imagine that you are conducting a study involving lesbians. How do you know that a woman is a lesbian? You could ask her to identify her sexuality. In so doing, you would have to trust that she is being accurate and honest about her sexuality. Furthermore, your study might include women who identify as lesbians but have never had sex or a relationship with another woman – would this be a problem? Another option is measuring women's sexuality, which of course raises the question, which component or components of sexuality would you attempt to measure? As we discussed in Chapter 2, sexuality has different components: our sexual desires and fantasies, the sexual practices we engage in, and how we identify and give meaning to our sexuality. So if you measured women's sexual experiences, you might not find out about their unfulfilled desires (which they might regard as more important in understanding the 'truth' of their sexuality). In addition, if you only asked about women's current or recent experiences you might get a very different picture of their sexuality than if you had asked about their entire sexual history.

Pioneers like Evelyn Hooker and June Hopkins spent a lot of time and resources on identifying their samples. Hooker, for instance, in her groundbreaking research on the adjustment of male homosexuals (discussed in Chapters 1 and 2), spent over two years isolating her sample of 'pure' homosexual and heterosexual men (men who only had sexual experiences consistent with their self-identity). Hooker questioned potential participants about their sexual experiences and desires and discounted men who were not pure or who reacted in a potentially suspect way to her questions. For example, 'heterosexual' men who vigorously denied having homosexual tendencies or who were disturbed by her questions were discounted (Minton, 2002). June Hopkins had potential participants rate themselves on the Kinsey scale and she used the women's ratings to allocate them to the homosexual group or the heterosexual group in her study, and to discount bisexual participants.

There is no simple answer to the question of who counts as a lesbian. Sexuality and gender identity categories have different meanings in different contexts and for different people. Furthermore, the notion of a 'true' lesbian relies on the belief in a fixed inner core of lesbianism organising a woman's sexual life (something that is impossible to measure, so we have to rely on reports of people's behaviour to make judgements about what this inner core might be). As we discussed in Chapter 2, LGBTQ psychologists who subscribe to a broadly social constructionist under-standing of sexuality find this notion of an 'inner core' problematic. Social con-structionists view sexuality as a product of social processes and interactions.

In our research, we have always recruited participants on the basis of self-identification, and this is how most researchers now recruit LGBTQ participants. Such an approach is thought to respect the meanings people give to their sexual and gender identities and practices. However, as British social scientist Julie Fish (2008) has pointed out, 'because many black and minority ethnic (BME) LGBT people may not use the term lesbian or gay to describe themselves, many have been excluded from research'. Fish indicates that researchers may need to use multiple and inclusive definitions of sexuality along the dimensions of desire, behaviour and identity to encourage the participation of some groups of LGBTQ people.

In research on non-heterosexuals, researchers often struggle to categorise bisexual identified people: should bisexual participants be allocated to the hetero-sexual group or the homosexual group, or should there be a separate bisexual group? In practice, bisexual participants are often either excluded from the study or allocated to the homosexual group, both of which are deeply problematic. Even research expressly focused on bisexuality has rejected bisexuality as a specific experience of sexuality. For example, a North American experimental study of bisexual men's arousal conducted by psychologists Gerulf Rieger *et al.* (2005) found that while bisexual men's self-reported sexual arousal conformed to a bisexual pattern, their (supposedly objective) genital arousal did not – some appeared homosexual and some heterosexual.

As we noted in Chapter 2, the category bisexuality represents a range of sexual practices that problematise the division of sexuality into homosexual and hetero-sexual (Hegarty, 1997). It is important to recognise the potential for differences between lesbians and gay men, and bisexual people (see Chapter 4). Although lesbians, gay men and bisexuals may share the experience of living outside of normative heterosexuality, unless research is explicitly examining this experience, it seems problematic automatically to group lesbians and gay men, and bisexual people (it can of course be equally problematic to group lesbians and gay men). Including trans people in research alongside non-heterosexuals also raises questions for researchers. Very often researchers use the label 'LGBT', but only refer to sexuality (and not gender identity). It is very easy to add trans people into the LGB 'melting pot', but most researchers fall short of considering the specifics of trans people's experiences and how they might differ from those of LGB people.

Issues in access and recruitment

Like most psychologists, we have all conducted research using samples of uni-versity and college students. Students are easy and economical to access (many psychology departments offer course credit in return for research participation); they are a highly visible population to researchers. In contrast, it is typically much more complicated to access samples of LGBTQ people. Such people are often described as a 'hidden' population because they are not immediately visible and accessible to researchers, and some members of LGBTQ communities are more 'hidden' than others. US social work educator and researcher Darrell Wheeler (2003) highlighted the existence of 'hard to engage' communities: those that may be reluctant to participate in research for a number of reasons. They may perceive little value in the research process or have questions regarding the researchers' motivation for conducting the research. They may be concerned about how their experiences will be represented and how the research findings will be used. They may be scared of being 'outed' and as a result of this being fired from their jobs or being rejected by their families. The history of research on LGBTQ communities shows such anxieties to be well founded.

US professors of social work William Meezan and James Martin (2003) have identified a number of hard to reach and difficult to engage communities (the following groups are of course not mutually exclusive and people may belong to more than one group):

- transgender and bisexual people
- those who do not identify with an LGBT community
- young people who are **questioning** their sexuality or who have not disclosed their non-heterosexuality to their parents

- older or non-white people
- poor and poorly educated people
- isolated people and people who live in rural areas
- people who engage in marginalised behaviour such as drug use and sex work.

One of the reasons why we know very little about these groups is because researchers have not gained entry, support or trust in these groups and because research on these groups has not been considered important (Wheeler, 2003).

So, how do LGBTQ psychologists access and recruit LGBTQ populations (and how do they recruit the least visible members of these communities)? The requirements of quantitative approaches and qualitative approaches are very different. Furthermore, researchers may use different sites to access smaller and larger samples, and if they do not have funding to pay a research assistant they may rely on more economical strategies. Common recruitment strategies, and ones that we have all used in our research, include the following:

- using the researcher's own professional and personal networks
- advertising for participants in the media (both the mainstream and the gay media)
- advertising for participants through LGBTQ organisations and groups, events, book shops, newsletters and so on
- The Internet.

One of the consistent weaknesses of these strategies that we (and other researchers) have experienced is that they tend to generate samples of white, educated, professional and middle-class people (characteristics that often reflect those of researchers, ourselves included). Accessing hidden and harder to engage groups may require different techniques.

Mignon Moore (2006), a US sociologist, has published a fascinating account of her attempts to recruit black lesbians for a research project on black lesbian families. Although Moore is a black lesbian, she had no experience of the community she sought to recruit participants from. She spent a year becoming acquainted with the community before beginning the process of data collection, attending social events and forming friendships with women in the community. Her view is that:

> There are populations that traditional methods of data gathering will not capture, and the black lesbian community is one such group. Public advertisements, notices, flyers at lesbian nightclubs, or postings at LGBT community centres largely go unnoticed or unanswered by gay populations of color, and studies that use these methods are not successful in recruiting significant numbers of nonwhites in their samples. (2006: 121)

Another limitation of common recruitment strategies is what is known as 'research fatigue' among LGBTQ participants. It is not that LGBTQ people are any less willing to participate than are heterosexual and non-trans people, but rather that LGBTQ issues are becoming increasingly popular topics for research across a wide range of disciplines. This is a good thing because, on the whole, LGBTQ issues have been under-researched; however, it also means that LGBTQ people who are easy to access (e.g., those who are most visible to researchers through their involvement in community activities) may have been saturated with requests to participate in research.

The 'insider advantage'

In the past it was believed that insiders could not conduct unbiased research with their own groups and only outsiders could notice what was important. As such, early affirmative researchers often remained silent about their insider status. For instance, a US priest turned sociologist, Laud Humphreys, who published a controversial observational study of men's same-sex sexual practices in public toilets (*Tearoom Trade*, 1970), did not acknowledge his homosexuality in his work. Humphreys noted that he performed the role of 'watch queen' (or 'look out') in order to observe the men's behaviour. Recent commentators have suggested that it is more likely that Humphreys was a participant-observer in the sexual activity in the public toilets and that he invented the role of 'watch queen' to protect his reputation and to avoid his research being dismissed as biased (Hollister, 2004). It is highly unlikely that an outsider would have developed a sympathetic study of men's same-sex sexual practices in **public sex environments (PSEs)** in the mid–late 1960s.

More recently, researchers have suggested that LGBTQ psychologists who are LGBTQ identified possess an 'insider advantage' when it comes to accessing and recruiting participants (LaSala, 2003). Currently, the balance has tipped in favour of the insider, and 'outsiders' are encouraged to reflect on their position and adhere to guidelines for good practice in order to conduct 'culturally sensitive' research on LGBTQ populations (McClennen, 2003; see also Wilkinson and Kitzinger, 1996b).

Being LGBTQ is thought to impart credibility and specialist knowledge that enables researchers to gain access to and secure the trust of potential participants. US psychologist Gayle Pitman (2002: 285) has described her experiences of accessing the lesbian and gay community in her research on women's body image:

> once the director of the GLBT Resource Centre knew I was 'family', I was granted full and unlimited access to her resources. Once gay, lesbian and bisexual students knew that I was a lesbian – 'the same' – they were much more willing to open up to me. And, in all likelihood, it was more than just being 'the same'; it was that we shared an understanding of oppression, and with that shared understanding was an unspoken agreement of support for one another.

The insider advantage is also thought to extend to data collection and analysis – the researchers' and the participants' shared language and knowledge facilitate the development of rapport and allow the production of deeper, more meaningful analyses. Although, some researchers who identify as LGBTQ may experience some degree of insider advantage, it is not enough simply to identify as LGBTQ to establish trust and rapport with participants. Just because people identify their sexuality or gender in similar ways, it doesn't mean that they have anything else in common, or that they have a shared experience of being LGBTQ. For instance, there is no guarantee that a white, middle-class, lesbian researcher can relate to the experiences of a black, working-class, lesbian participant. Celia Kitzinger, who conducted a groundbreaking interview-based study of lesbian identity, discussed her attempts to access a diverse group of participants and noted that her 'obvious **whiteness** and middle-classness' (1987: 88) limited the extent to which she was perceived as an insider by some of the women she approached. At the same time, Kitzinger noted that she 'came out' as a lesbian to all of the women she approached and several commented that they were willing to participate only because she was a lesbian. Other LGBTQ researchers have had similar experiences (e.g., Dunne, 1997). Some researchers are careful to identify themselves as members of LGBTQ communities in their recruitment materials (Hash and Cramer, 2003).

It is important to note that the concept of community has different meanings: it can be used broadly to refer to, for example, all lesbians or all bisexual people, or it can refer to specific, local lesbian or bisexual communities (people connected through social activities and friendships or political activism). Potential participants may not view an LGBTQ researcher as an 'insider' unless the researcher is a member of their local community. It is also important to recognise that LGBTQ researchers are not simply LGBTQ individuals; they are (or are likely to be perceived as) a professionals and experts. Much has been written about the hierarchical nature of the researcher–participant relationship, and the fact that researchers have more power and control in the research process relative to that of participants (see Wilkinson, 1998b). In general, researchers initiate the research process, determine the research question, decide on the methods of data collection and analysis, ask the questions (or administer the measures), analyse the data and write up the results, whereas participants just provide the data. All this means that the participant's perception of the researcher as an insider may be tempered by the researcher's expert role (see Clarke *et al.*, 2004). See Box 3.6 for a discussion of the advantages and disadvantages of being an 'insider' when researching LGBTQ communities.

We think heterosexual and non-trans researchers can (and should) conduct 'culturally sensitive' research with LGBTQ communities. There are numerous heterosexual and non-trans psychologists who work in the field and have made important contributions to understanding the lives and experiences of LGBTQ people and to positive social change for this group. Many feel that it is important to be open about their sexuality and gender. US counselling psychologist Nancy Asher (Asher and Asher, 1999) has written about her experiences of conducting a qualitative, interview-based study of lesbian women and body image from her standpoint as a heterosexual woman. She felt that it was important to disclose her heterosexuality at the start of each interview and acknowledge her status as a cultural outsider. Although she was anxious about how this information would be received, she found in practice that participants appreciated her disclosure and it helped to establish rapport. She wrote: 'Most important, it sent a message that I

Box 3.6 *Highlights: weighing up the 'insider advantage'*	
The potential advantages of being an insider	*The potential disadvantages of being an insider*
Insiders can use their own experiences to develop research questions and these questions may not occur to outsiders. They may find it easier to access potential participants, and have more knowledge about where to find their sample. People may be more open to participating in their research. Insiders can communicate empathy that establishes trust and honesty. They may be able to generate deeper insights and interpret insider norms and concepts more readily.	Insiders may fail to note what is unique and interesting about their own group. They may falsely assume that they understand participants' meanings. They may lack critical distance (and over-identify with participants), which limits their ability to interpret data. Social desirability bias and the fear of 'loss of face' might be heightened for a member of the researcher's own group(s). Participants may have concerns about anonymity or disclosing information to a member of their group(s).

was respectful of the participants' right to know who I was, why I was interested in them, and what I was willing to do to establish a forthright discussion' (p. 138).

Issues in sampling LGBTQ populations

Sampling is a complex issue in LGBTQ psychological research and has been described as the most important methodological issue in this area of psychology (Meyer and Colten, 1999). Throughout the history of LGBTQ research, studies have been based on atypical samples. As we noted in Chapter 1, in the pre-affirmative era samples were almost exclusively drawn from clinical or prison populations, and in the affirmative era samples have been drawn from sources such as gay and lesbian bars, LGBTQ student groups, and social/support groups within the LGBTQ community.

For psychologists doing quantitative and experimental research, the repre-sentativeness of a sample is a major concern. In order to make generalisations from a sample to the broader population, the sample must be representative of that population. Probability sampling is a way of ensuring representativeness. Within psychology there are two main forms of probability sampling: random sampling and stratified sampling. As its name suggests, random sampling means that a sample of individuals is picked at random (without reference to any other selection criteria), with each member of the population having an equal chance of being included in the sample. Stratified sampling, on the other hand, refers to a sample where individuals are selected to represent different predetermined subgroups within the population. So, for example, if we know that a given population comprises ninety men and thirty women and that 10 per cent of each group are individuals from working-class backgrounds, we would ensure that our sample reflects this gender and class breakdown. However, in the case of both random and stratified sampling it is necessary to know the parameters of the target population, and this is where things can get tricky for LGBTQ psychologists.

Although some research (primarily studies of homophobia) draws samples from the general population, most research within LGBTQ psychology focuses on the perceptions and experiences of LGBTQ people themselves. As we noted earlier, a major problem for researchers is that this particular population is relatively hidden and difficult to access. There isn't a register of LGBTQ people from which to generate a random sample, and almost without exception information about sexuality and gender identity is not routinely collected by employers, health services, and so forth. The difficulties of accessing LGBTQ populations are compounded by the fact that many LGBTQ people are not 'out', which means it is difficult to access diverse samples of LGBTQ people. Therefore it is virtually impossible to define this population in order to generate a random sample, and because the composition of the population is also unknown it is not possible to generate a stratified sample either.

Some researchers have suggested that one way to surmount the difficulties of generating representative samples of LGBTQ people is to include standard questions about sexuality and gender identity in research instruments and in national population censuses (D'Augelli, 2003). A small number of studies have extracted sub-samples of LGBTQ participants from large representative samples. For example, two general population studies of lesbian families have been conducted (one in the USA and one in the UK), extracting relevant data from general population studies of family functioning and child development (see Chapter 9). In the USA, psychologist and epidemiologist Susan Cochran and her colleagues have extracted data about non-heterosexuals from the US census (Cochran and Mays, 2000) and national surveys (Gilman et al., 2001) to investigate non-heterosexuals' physical and mental health.

There are a number of reasons why qualitative research tends to use rather different approaches to sampling from those used in quantitative research. For example, as we noted above qualitative researchers are generally concerned with 'situated meaning' and the contexts that shape the meanings people give to their experiences; as such they do not typically seek to make reliable and replicable generalisations about large populations. In addition, qualitative research requires a detailed engagement with the experiences and perspectives of individual participants. Qualitative research is typically conducted with relatively small samples (i.e., sixty participants would be a relatively large sample; six to thirty participants is a more common range). One of the most common sampling methods in qualitative research is purposive sampling, which selects participants on the basis of possessing relevant characteristics. Although sometimes there might be relevant pre-existing groups (e.g., a 'coming out' support group) from which to recruit participants, one common technique used to augment sample size is snowball sampling or 'friendship pyramiding' (Browne, 2005). This is where participants are identified from the researcher's personal or professional networks or from a pre-existing group and then from other participants. Contacts or participants might be asked to recommend people with particular characteristics or life experiences. For example, researchers might initially recruit participants through their personal network or through their local gay community and then ask these participants to recommend a friend who is not connected to the local community.

Principles for good research practice

Doing non-heterosexist and non-genderist research

In 1991, a group of LGB psychologists published guidelines for doing non-heterosexist research in the APA journal *American Psychologist* (Herek *et al.*, 1991). Since then there has been very little discussion of avoiding heterosexism in research within mainstream psychology. Although the work of LGBTQ psychologists has had some impact on research practices, you wouldn't need to spend long in your university or college library to uncover examples of heterosexist research and **genderist** research (i.e., research that discriminates against trans people). We think the 1991 guidelines, despite being almost twenty years old at the time of writing, still offer useful advice to researchers seeking to develop a non-heterosexist and inclusive research practice. We have adapted these guidelines to include trans and queer people. It is important to note that doing non-heterosexist research is not limited to research that is specifically focused on LGBTQ groups; all research, unless it is expressly concerned with the experiences and perspectives of self-identified heterosexuals, should avoid assuming heterosexuality. Non-heterosexist, non-genderist and inclusive research:

- is based on research questions that are inclusive of LGBTQ people and that avoid stereotypes and stigmatising LGBTQ people
- is not based on research questions that assume LGBTQ people's behaviours and practices can be explained solely in terms of their sexualities and gender identities
- is based on samples that are as representative as possible or include sufficient diversity
- avoids measures and data collection tools that assume heterosexuality or that participants are non-trans
- is conducted by researchers who are well informed about LGBTQ communities
- puts measures in place adequately to protect participants and does not have a negative effect on LGBTQ participants

- understands difference as difference, rather than as indicative of deficiency
- avoids heterosexist and genderist language
- acknowledges the limitations of research findings and anticipates potential misrepresentations of research findings
- disseminates research findings to participants and LGBTQ communities (and agencies that serve those communities).

Other researchers have made recommendations for conducting research with 'hard to engage' communities and with people outside of their own group(s) (McClennen, 2003; Wheeler, 2003); these recommendations add an important dimension to guidelines for good practice. Researchers conducting studies with hard to engage groups, or from the position of an outsider, should:

- reflect on their motivations for conducting the research and the ways in which the findings will be used (researchers must remember that they are not neutral and research is not necessarily benign)
- reflect on their understandings of social marginalisation issues (a sound awareness of these issues can facilitate a deeper appreciation of participants' contexts and a more meaningful interpretation of their situations)
- develop partnerships with members of the community being investigated and seek advice on the conduct of their research
- communicate effectively with the community (and avoid alienating and patronising language) and be clear about their ethical obligations
- avoid making assumptions about what it means to be a member of the community; they should learn about the community and, where appropriate, participate in community activities
- be prepared for objections to their research (from members of the community) and for the personal and professional risks associated with conducting LGBTQ research
- ideally produce research that leads to meaningful outcomes for members of the community.

For further information on good practice in researching LGBTQ communities see Box 3.7, which provides advice on conducting student research projects on LGBTQ issues.

Some heterosexual psychologists have taken the brave step of reflecting on and writing about the ways in which they have colluded with heterosexism in their research. New Zealand feminist psychologist Virginia Braun (2000) has written about the ways in which she unwittingly colluded with heterosexism in a qualitative focus group study of women's talk about the vagina. She identified a number of ways in which she and her participants articulated heterosexist assumptions. For example, talk about generic women became talk about heterosexual women, and therefore excluded lesbians. Questions about sex became immediately translated into questions about **heterosex** (specifically penis-in-vagina intercourse), and references to 'a partner' became a male partner. Braun also failed

Box 3.7 *Highlights: hints and tips on doing a research project in LGBTQ psychology*

- If you intend to recruit LGBTQ people to your study, think carefully about whether you will able to access an appropriate sample (if your research supervisor has no expertise in this area, they may not be able to advise you on recruitment methods). Do you have networks you can draw on to generate a sample? Do you know of organisations you can contact or events you can attend to find participants?
- Be prepared to spend more time recruiting LGBTQ participants than peers relying on student samples (and be prepared to be more creative!).
- If you approach an LGBTQ community organisation for help with recruitment, be respectful of people's time and resources. Such organisations often receive little or no funding and have limited resources, and often get lots of requests to help find participants for student projects. You should consider volunteering your time in exchange for help in finding participants.
- If you want to explore heterosexuals' views on an aspect of LGBTQ life, make sure you specifically advertise for heterosexual participants (you may be surprised otherwise!).
- Think carefully about whether you want to 'come out' to your participants (however you identify your sexuality or gender identity). Some participants may ask about your identity or ask questions about your motivation for conducting the study – what will you say?
- If you are LGBTQ identified don't assume that participants will view you as 'one of them'. 'Insider' status is strongly mediated by your position as a researcher and other aspects of your identity and background. At the same time, it's important not to overlook what might seem obvious to you and to the participants.
- You may want to consider adopting a participatory approach to your study, inviting participants to comment on your analysis, or you may want to recruit an 'expert participant' to guide you in recruiting participants, designing the study and producing the findings.
- If participants express distress as a result of participating, you must refer them to 'culturally appropriate' support services. It is your responsibility to ensure that services are open to LGBTQ people and are experienced in supporting this group.
- It is considered good practice to provide participants with a summary of your findings. If you conduct your project with the help of any LGBTQ organisations or groups, be sure to provide them with a summary of your findings.

overtly to challenge heterosexist assumptions and noted that her participants rarely did. Braun commented that she does not think her heterosexism is unusual among research conducted by heterosexual researchers that does not specifically aim to address lesbian experience. She argued that heterosexual researchers should confront their heterosexism, take responsibility for it and find ways to eliminate it. What Braun's paper highlights is the beguiling and 'common-sense' nature of heterosexist assumptions and the difficulties even the most ethically sensitive researchers encounter in conducting inclusive research.

Research ethics

The issue of protecting participants and conducting ethically appropriate research is especially pertinent to LGBTQ psychologists. One of the principal guidelines of the ethical codes developed by professional bodies such as the BPS, the APA and the APS centres on the avoidance of harm to participants. Meezan and Martin (2003) noted that LGBTQ research always occurs in a context in which LGBTQ people are socially marginalised and at risk of prejudice and discrimination. This means that there may be greater potential for harm to LGBTQ participants. Many would argue that research outcomes that support a pathologising model of homosexuality are ethically dubious. There are numerous examples of research that violates the 'avoidance of harm' principle, including some contemporary research that evaluates the effectiveness of conversion therapy (see Chapter 1). Although individual participants may not have experienced any harm as a result of completing the research, arguably seeking to prove the effectiveness of conversion therapy causes harm to the broader non-heterosexual community.

One particular harm that concerns many potential research participants relates to anonymity and the potential to be 'outed' through their involvement with the research, something that is a greater possibility in small communities. Rather than offering blanket assurances of anonymity, researchers in small communities should be more realistic about the degree to which they can protect participants and negotiate such issues with individual participants. Researchers who are members of the communities they are studying might encounter ethical dilemmas particular to their insider status. For instance, they might experience pressure not to publish (what could be perceived as) negative findings. They might also encounter the complexities of 'dual relationships' with participants (where the researcher is also the friend or colleague of a participant). Although ethical codes generally discourage dual relationships, in small communities they can be especially hard to avoid. Friends or colleagues of the researcher might experience pressure to participate and it can be very difficult to protect participants' privacy and confidentiality and keep the knowledge gained from the two relationships separate. There is also huge potential for causing harm when investigating 'deviant behaviours' (such as drug abuse, domestic violence and risky sexual practices). As we discussed above, researchers need to give serious thought to the potential for research findings to be used against LGBTQ communities.

Research ethics also include the issue of researcher safety, and the possibility for researchers to experience harm through the research process. Many LGBTQ researchers experience heterosexism in the course of their research and researchers with an interest in sexuality may be vulnerable to false and potentially damaging accusations of inappropriate behaviour.

There are also lots of examples of sound ethical practice, where researchers have worked hard to protect participants. If readers are planning to undertake a research project in LGBTQ psychology, we encourage you to reflect on the issues raised in this chapter and to exemplify good practice in researching LGBTQ populations.

Gaps and absences

- There is limited discussion of methodological issues within LGBTQ psychology (we drew heavily on related disciplines such as sociology when writing this chapter), which is mostly focused narrowly on sampling. We would like to see more exploration and reflection on the methodological aspects of LGBTQ psychological research and on why particular methods and approaches are useful for studying LGBTQ populations.
- The dominance of positivist-empiricism (particularly in the USA) means that qualitative approaches occupy a marginal position in the field. We give equal weight to qualitative and critical, and quantitative and experimental approaches in this book. We would like to encourage greater use of qualitative and critical approaches, more mixing of methods, and more methodological diversity in LGBTQ psychology.
- The dominance of positivist-empiricism also means that there is virtually no reflective discussion of the assumptions and benefits of quantitative approaches. Qualitative and critical researchers, by virtue of their departure from the norm, have been required to explain their rejection of mainstream psychology, the alternative assumptions that underpin their approach to psychology and the benefits of qualitative and critical methodologies. By contrast, adherents to the norm are not required to justify their position or explain their assumptions. We would like to see more critical reflection from mainstream psychologists and more open dialogue between quantitative and qualitative and mainstream and critical researchers.

Main chapter points

This chapter:

- Outlined the range of methods and approaches used by LGBTQ psychologists and considered the advantages of each for researching LGBTQ populations.
- Highlighted the challenges researchers face in accessing and sampling LGBTQ populations, particularly the least visible and most difficult to engage groups.
- Explored the potential advantages and complexities of being an insider researcher.
- Outlined guidelines for good practice in researching LGBTQ populations: both general guidelines and guidelines for researching hard to engage and socially marginalised groups.

Questions for discussion and classroom exercises

1.   Read Virginia Braun's (2000) article on heterosexism in focus group research then identify three ways in which you could avoid being heterosexist (and genderist) when collecting data for your own research.

2.   What are some of the main challenges that LGBTQ psychologists encounter in researching LGBTQ populations? How might these challenges be overcome?

3.   Find a recent LGBTQ psychological study and critically evaluate the research, focusing on the issues discussed in this chapter. For example: Are the goals of the research clearly explained and appropriate? How did the researchers access their participants? Is the sample limited (if so, what are the implications of this for the findings)? Does the research raise any particular ethical issues? Do the researchers discuss insider/outsider dynamics? Are the methods of data collection and analysis justified and appropriate? Do the researchers adhere to principles for non-heterosexist, non-genderist and inclusive research? Does the research contribute to positive social change for LGBTQ people?

4.   Compare and contrast the strengths and weaknesses of the different research methods used by LGBTQ psychologists.

5.   In what ways do you think the personal views or experiences of a researcher influence the research? Does this benefit or impair the research?

Further reading

Croom, G. (2000) Lesbian, gay, and bisexual people of color: a challenge to representative sampling in empirical research. In B. Greene and G. Croom (eds.), *Education, research, and practice in lesbian, gay, bisexual, and transgender psychology* (pp. 263–81). Thousand Oaks, CA: Sage.
In this chapter, US psychologist Gladys Croom explores the marginalisation of non-white LGBT people in psychological research and highlights the importance of self-examination on the part of white researchers engaged in research with non-white groups.

Fish, J. (1999) Sampling lesbians: how to get 1000 lesbians to complete a questionnaire. *Feminism and Psychology*, 9, 229–38.
In this article, British social scientist Julie Fish reflects on her experience of getting 1,000 lesbians to complete a survey on health.

Heaphy, B., Weeks, J. and Donovan, C. (1998) 'That's like my life': researching stories of non-heterosexual relationships. *Sexualities*, 1(4), 453–70.

A detailed discussion of the key methodological issues that emerged in a qualitative sociological study of the structure and meaning of non-heterosexual relationships.

Kong, T. S., Mahoney, D. and Plummer, K. (2002) Queering the interview. In J. F. Gubrium and J. A. Holstein (eds.), *Handbook of interview research: context and method* (pp. 239–58). Thousand Oaks, CA: Sage.
A historical account of the use of interviewing in research on homosexuality and a discussion of contemporary issues in interviewing research.

McDermott, E. (2004) Telling lesbian stories: interviewing and the class dynamics of 'talk'. *Women's Studies International Forum*, 27, 177–87.
In this article, British sociologist Elizabeth McDermott provides a fascinating account of the ways in which working-class and middle-class lesbian participants experience research interviews and the spaces they offer for telling lesbian stories.

Understanding social marginalisation in LGBTQ lives

4 Diversity

Overview

- Understanding diversity in LGBTQ communities
- Gender
- Bisexuality
- Trans and queer
- Social class
- Race
- Organised religion and spirituality
- Rural life
- Ability

Understanding diversity in LGBTQ communities

In this chapter we focus on the wide diversity that exists within LGBTQ communities, and the many different identities that LGBTQ people have. The chapter serves as a bridge between the opening three chapters, that together provide an overview of the field of LGBTQ psychology and its key theoretical, conceptual and methodological concerns, and the rest of the book, which focuses on key topics in LGBTQ psychology.

Focusing on the diversity of LGBTQ communities is important because it allows us to understand the limitations of applying one particular model of psychological research and practice across a range of groups of people. Although we primarily draw on research conducted with white, middle-class lesbians and gay men in this book, we are mindful of the fact that the experiences of this group do not represent the experiences of all LGBTQ people. Furthermore, it is not accurate to say that lesbians and gay men together form a coherent or unified group. In this chapter we highlight the breadth of experiences of LGBTQ people, drawing on the limited psychological research that is available, as well as on work from other academic disciplines and areas of research such as sociology, feminism and queer theory. We also emphasise the need for LGBTQ psychologists to examine the founding assumptions of the discipline of psychology (i.e., the norm of white, middle-class heterosexuality) and the negative impact of these assumptions on the knowledge claims of the discipline. Box 4.1 provides an example of how a failure to consider differences within LGBTQ communities has resulted in LGBTQ psychology research that perpetuates problematic social norms around race and culture.

Box 4.1   Key study: Damien Riggs (2007a) on recognising race in LGBTQ psychology

In this study, Damien examined how LGBTQ psychological research that includes racially diverse samples perpetuates problematic assumptions as a result of the 'whiteness' of psychological measures. In talking about 'whiteness', Damien discusses how the lives of white (and primarily middle-class, heterosexual) people are treated as the norm from which all other people deviate. In this sense, whiteness signifies a form of property possessed by white people that accords them considerable privilege. Importantly, Damien connects the existence of such privilege with the disadvantages that non-white people face. For example, in the context of Australia, white people live on land stolen from **Indigenous** people. In this sense, the relative privileges that white people enjoy in Australia come at the expense of Indigenous people, who continue to experience significant economic, familial, legal, political and social hardship as a result of **colonisation**.

In his examination of ten LGBTQ psychological papers that focus in some way on the experiences of differing racial and cultural groups (often comparing these groups), Damien identified four dominant ways in which LGBTQ psychology is shaped by the norm of whiteness, and the ways in which this disadvantages non-white people:

- *The assumption that only non-white people are racialised.* This was evident when racial categories were only used to refer to non-white people, and when white people's racial identities were left unnamed. This meant that white people were not seen as benefiting from whiteness, and non-white people were not seen to be disadvantaged as a result of the unequal distribution of resources in society.
- *The assumption that all non-white people are the same.* This was evident when disparate groups of non-white people were lumped into a generic category such as 'black'. Such an approach overlooks the unique experience of individual **racially marginalised** groups and does so via a blanket comparison of white and non-white people.
- *The assumption that race could be treated as a 'benign variable'.* This typically occurred when regression analyses were used to 'control' for the effects of race, so that other differences could be focused on. Such an understanding of race ignores the multiple and complex ways in which racial categories structure all aspects of our lives.
- *The use of generic models of identity and measurement.* This occurred when psychological tests normed on white populations were used with non-white people, and when categories developed within western countries (such as

'lesbian') were applied to individuals from countries where such labels have little meaning.

Together, these assumptions resulted in a failure to understand the unique experiences of a diverse range of groups of non-white people, and perpetuated a norm of whiteness against which all groups are compared. In this study, Damien highlights why **additive models of identity** are not sufficient to fully understand multiple identities. He also argues that it is not enough to simply add non-white people into LGBTQ psychology, but rather that LGBTQ psychologists need to fundamentally reassess the basic assumptions that shape the field.

In order to provide you with an understanding of diversity within LGBTQ communities, we outline eight overlapping areas of diversity. In reading this chapter you should consider the implications of each of these areas for one another (e.g., how may class and race intersect and shape non-heterosexual people's experiences of heterosexism?), and for the broader themes covered in this book (e.g., how may disabled LGBTQ people's experiences of romantic/sexual relationships differ from the relationship experiences of able-bodied LGBTQ people?). Throughout this book we use the concept of 'intersectionality' to highlight the need for LGBTQ psychology to explore the different ways in which people are located in relation to dominant social categories (see Chapter 11). We also use this concept to highlight the fact that different identities are experienced not in isolation from one another, but rather as overlapping categories that, in combination, produce particular experiences of the world. This is an important approach to understanding the lives of LGBTQ people, because if we only focus on sexual and gender identities and practices in isolation from other aspects of identity we limit our ability to engage with the complex and overlapping needs of LGBTQ communities in all their diversity.

We also want to encourage you to reflect on how certain groups *within* LGBTQ communities hold a more powerful position than other groups. LGBTQ communities are just as much a part of society as any other group – they contain people with a wide range of views, some of which do not always match up to the 'progressive' or 'radical' views that LGBTQ people are often assumed to hold. In examining diversity in LGBTQ communities, we ask how and why it is that some LGBTQ people experience a greater degree of privilege relative to other LGBTQ people who experience a greater degree of disadvantage. Understanding the intersections of privilege and disadvantage is a central theme of this chapter.

Gender

Victoria and Elizabeth (Clarke and Peel, 2007b) have argued that gender is often overlooked in research on LGBTQ people. In part this is because most

Box 4.2   Key study: Sarah Oerton (1998) on the 'gender empty' model of same-sex relationships

In this theoretical critique of research that characterises lesbian households as 'empty' of any processes and practices associated with gendering, British sociologist Sarah Oerton argued that, although less obvious, gender *is* important in these households. She noted that lesbian cohabiting couples have been seen as more egalitarian and as having a more democratic division of household labour than heterosexual cohabiting couples. As a result, inequalities based on gender difference have been seen as (potentially at least) absent in lesbian relationships.

However, in many cases, lesbians share the experiences of heterosexual women, in that women generally are more likely than men to take responsibility for certain kinds of household work and caring tasks. As such, Oerton posed the question 'can lesbians, insomuch as we too take responsibility for keeping the dust at bay and the food on the table, also be "housewives"?' (p. 76). She concluded by arguing that it is time for (some) lesbians to 'reclaim the long-discredited and much maligned identity of "housewife" as task doer and to come out, alongside their heterosexual sisters, as visible houseproud and caregiving women who routinely undertake important, challenging and demanding family, kin and household work' (p. 79).

LGBTQ psychological research focuses on lesbians and gay men, and it is assumed that because lesbians and gay men have sexual and emotional relationships with people of the same sex/gender, no gender differences exist in same-sex relationships. This assumption is often referred to as the 'gender empty' model of LGBTQ relationships (see Box 4.2). In addition, lesbians and gay men are often viewed as a homogeneous group, connected by a common sexuality. Such assumptions are problematic for the ways in which they:

- overlook potential gender differences in bisexual relationships (between women and men, *and* between same-sex partners)
- ignore the impact that gender norms have on trans people
- disregard the challenges to gender categories that people who identify as queer often present to dominant gender norms
- conflate the experiences of people of different genders in ways that neglect significant gender differences between people (i.e., when we refer to 'lesbians and gay men' as a group we overlook the different experiences of women and men living in male dominated societies).

These few examples (there are many more) demonstrate that acknowledging different experiences of gender is centrally important to understanding diversity within LGBTQ communities. We now consider some of these experiences of gender in more detail.

Feminist scholars have long identified how gender norms impact on the lives of all people, whether to the disadvantage of women or to the advantage of men (see Chapter 2). In LGBTQ communities, although the notion of 'community' is assumed to describe an inclusive and safe space for *all* LGBTQ people, it is often the case that such spaces reproduce the gender dynamics of the wider society, with men's voices and needs superseding those of women (see, for example, Humphrey, 2000). When the experiences of gay men are generalised to speak for the experiences of all LGBTQ people, or when LGBTQ research focuses primarily on the lives of gay men, we can see how gender differences, and the effects of living in male-dominated societies, shape LGBTQ communities and LGBTQ psychology.

Other examples of gender differences in LGBTQ communities are the disparities that exist between lesbian or bisexual mothers and gay or bisexual fathers. The International Lesbian and Gay Association (ILGA, 1998) reports that lesbian mothers (whether as single parents or in a couple) often experience considerable economic disadvantage as a result of the fact that women *on the whole* continue to be paid less than men, and have fewer opportunities for higher-paid jobs (see also Chapter 8). A two-parent lesbian household will therefore, on average, have a lower combined household income than either a two-parent heterosexual household or a two-parent gay male household. Similarly, gay fathers will often need to take time off work throughout the process of bringing biological children into their lives; however, this will most often be for a shorter period, and less detrimental to future employment options than the time taken off by lesbian mothers. This is just one example of the ways in which gender differences produce very real disparities in the economic security of lesbians and gay men.

It is also important to note that gay men are not 'outside' of gender; gender norms impact on gay men's lives as much as they do on other people's lives. For example, gay men are often assumed to challenge conventional norms around masculinity (through effeminacy and camp); however, US psychologist Gregory Simonsen and his colleagues (2000) found that their white, middle-class gay male participants were no freer than were heterosexual men from pressures associated with norms of masculinity. These pressures were connected with personal success, assertions of power, emotional detachment and work–family relationships. Gay men who felt pressure to conform to these forms of masculinity reported higher levels of anger, anxiety and depression compared to gay men who did not feel pressure to conform.

In her research with bisexual couples, Australian sociologist Kirsten McLean (2004) found that the acceptability of non-monogamy within bisexual relationships was often mediated by gender. Some partners were willing to negotiate open relationships, but within gendered limits. For example, some bisexual women who were in relationships with men were willing for their partners to have sex with other men but not with other women. Similarly, bisexual men who were currently in a relationship with a woman were willing for their female partners to have sex with other women but not with other men.

One particular area of concern relating to the presumption that LGBTQ relationships are not hierarchically gendered and therefore not structured around power differences relates to domestic violence. Research has increasingly found not only that domestic violence does occur within some lesbian or gay relationships (Renzetti and Miley, 1996), but that fear of homophobia often results in many LGBTQ people who experience abuse not reporting it (Burke and Follingstad, 1999). While patterns of abuse within same-sex relationships may differ from those within heterosexual relationships, it is nonetheless the case that violence *does* occur within LGBTQ communities, and the assumption that there are no power differentials operating in same-sex relationships often results in a failure to acknowledge such violence.

To summarise, gender functions in complex ways in LGBTQ communities. As a result, it is important to:

- recognise the different experiences of gender of LGBTQ people and not to treat lesbians and gay men (and BTQ people) as a homogeneous group, and instead consider the different ways in which gender shapes women's and men's experiences of non-heterosexuality
- understand that men within LGBTQ communities will typically stand to benefit from living in male-dominated societies, regardless of their experiences of marginalisation
- acknowledge that power differences (in relation to, for example, social class and income, race and age) do exist *within* lesbian and gay relationships and that LGBTQ people do not live outside of gender norms.

Bisexuality

The identity category 'bisexual' means many different things to people who identify as bisexual. For example, there are people who:

- are attracted to both women and men, and who are willing to enter into relationships on the basis of attraction to an individual person, rather than to a specific gender or sexuality (Gurevich *et al.*, 2007)
- are primarily sexually and emotionally attracted to people of the same sex, but who feel that the label 'bisexual' provides them with some protection against homophobia
- feel that the category 'bisexual' provides a better description of their identity than categories such as 'lesbian' or 'gay'.

In this book, we primarily understand bisexuality as a valid and often lifelong identity that does not represent a transitional phase between a heterosexual and a lesbian or gay identity. However, we do of course recognise that some lesbians or gay men refer to themselves as 'bisexual' in the process of coming out (see Chapter 7). In viewing bisexuality as a lifelong identity we are not suggesting that there is only one experience of bisexuality; some people experience bisexuality as a fluid and changing identity, and one that resists clear definition. Rather, our point is that bisexuality is a legitimate identity that for bisexual people represents their genuine attraction to a diverse range of individuals. The different meanings and experiences of bisexuality demonstrate the limitations of dominant identity categories to describe the experiences of bisexual people (Collins, 2004).

Bisexual people have often been marginalised in LGBTQ research and communities (Fox, 1995). For example, some lesbians and gay men have expressed concern that a focus on bisexuality and bisexual histories can serve to draw attention away from lesbian and gay experiences (Weiss, 2004). Some lesbian feminists have seen bisexuality as compromising the political commitment that many lesbian women make to challenging **patriarchy** (Ault, 1994). While we recognise the concerns of lesbians and gay men who have at times felt under threat by the category of bisexuality (either because of the ways in which it challenges the dichotomy of homosexuality/heterosexuality or because it throws into question lesbian feminist commitments to challenging patriarchy), we nonetheless respect and validate the experiences and voices of bisexual people. Another accusation levelled at bisexual people is that their sexual relationships or practices are inherently promiscuous and unstable. This type of accusation is increasingly countered by research on the lives of bisexual people. In bisexual relationships that *are* non-monogamous or **polyamorous**, research suggests that most bisexual people openly negotiate consent and have clear boundaries with their multiple partners (see also Chapter 8). Research also indicates that many bisexual people engage in committed monogamous relationships (with either different- or same-sex partners), in which their bisexuality is recognised and respected (McClean, 2004).

Of course, in refuting accusations of promiscuity, it is important that we do not fall into the trap of suggesting that all bisexual people are engaged in monogamous relationships. Part of the reason why notions of 'responsible non-monogamy' have been so important within some bisexual communities is that for many bisexual people the notion of a 'bisexual identity' is limiting. This is because bisexuality signals a commitment to moving beyond narrow binary categories of gender and sexuality that are typically bound up with discourses of monogamy (Klesse, 2007).

Challenging what has been termed 'biphobia' is important because research suggests that such marginalisation impacts negatively on the mental health of bisexual people. For example, bisexual people are constantly expected to defend their lives and 'come out' as bisexual when in a heterosexual relationship (Page, 2004). Conversely, some bisexual people may choose to remain 'in the closet' rather than disclose their bisexuality to other people and potentially face discrimination (McLean, 2008).

In sum, understanding the lives of bisexual people requires that we:

- recognise the multiple ways in which bisexual people define their identities
- comprehend and challenge the stereotypes that are perpetuated against bisexual people within mainstream society and within lesbian and gay communities
- acknowledge how binary models of gender and sexuality limit our understandings of the lives and experiences of bisexual people: bisexuality does not represent a 'failure to orientate' (Weiss, 2004: 43) to either one of the two dominant 'sexual orientations' (homosexuality or heterosexuality).

Trans and queer

To date, the experiences of trans and queer people have received little attention within LGBTQ psychology. One reason for this is that descriptions of these two groups of people are constantly changing in relation both to social norms and to the ways in which trans and queer people define themselves. Some of the groups of people who may identify as trans or queer include:

- people who do not subscribe to either of the two dominant masculine/feminine gender identities (e.g., butch lesbians, people who identify as 'genderqueer')
- **drag kings** and **drag queens**
- people who identify as androgynous
- people who cross-dress (some of these people may identify with the category transvestite)
- people who 'transition' from one sex/gender to the other through hormonal and/or surgical treatment.

When talking about queer and trans 'identities' it is important to understand the different ways in which gender and sexuality are understood across cultures. As we noted in Chapter 2, some researchers have suggested that the separation of sexual and gender identity (e.g., categorising people as trans *as well as* heterosexual, lesbian, gay or bisexual) may be largely a western phenomenon (McLelland, 2003). For example, US anthropologist Sharyn Graham (2004) reports on the experiences of people in South Sulawesi, Indonesia, who are 'male-bodied' but who do not identify as men, nor do they aspire to be women. Rather, they are identified as '**calabai**' (or '**calalai**' for those who are 'female-bodied'). These groups of people can often negotiate multiple relationships with (normatively identified) men and women in their lives, and potentially have children or enter into marriage relationships that are not seen as contradictory to their expression of gender and sexuality (see Chapter 11).

Using the term 'queer' as an identity category is one of the ways in which some people in western cultures have sought to rework or resist gender and sexuality categories. People who identify as queer may resist social expectations to adopt one clear gender or sexual identity, and may shift between and across norms surrounding gender and sexuality. This understanding of queer has also informed recent accounts of the lives of trans people, some of whom aim to develop a 'transgender identity', rather than embrace a gender identity and body coherent with their gender experience (Bockting *et al.*, 2004). Trans and queer identified people have been at the cutting edge of developments in new ways of talking about bodies and identities, such as in the creation of alternative pronouns to describe people who do not straightforwardly identify as either male or female (for example, 'zee' and 'hir'; see Clarke and Braun, 2009). Nonetheless, it is important to recognise that there are still many people who wish to adopt fully the bodily identity associated with their gender identity (Denny, 2004; Seil, 2004). Many trans people are also very clear about wanting to adopt a normative sexual identity after their transition (e.g., transwomen identifying as heterosexual women), though many trans people also identify as non-heterosexual.

As we noted in Chapter 2, trans and queer people have occupied a contested position within LGBTQ communities. Some lesbian feminists, for example, have rejected transgender people's identity claims and have suggested that transwomen are 'tools of patriarchy' in that they appropriate natal women's (women-only) spaces and communities and reinforce problematic stereotypes about femininity and masculinity. Furthermore, these processes are thought to be aided and abetted by a medical system that is focused on managing (natal) women's bodies (see Raymond, 1979). Other feminists (both natal women and transwomen) have emphasised the importance of valuing the lived experiences of trans people, and of developing trans-positive feminist analyses of the lives of trans people (Weiss, 2004).

As we also noted in Chapter 1, some lesbian feminists have also been critical of queer theory and queer activism (e.g., Jeffreys, 2004). However it is important to note that not all feminists are critical of trans and queer, and some feminists have made important contributions to understanding the lives of trans and queer people and trans and queer genders and sexualities (e.g., Johnson, 2007; Speer and Green, 2007). See Box 4.3 for a summary of British psychologist and key researcher Susan Speer's work on doctor–patient interactions in the **gender identity clinic**.

Box 4.3   Key researcher: Susan Speer on why I study trans

I began my research career with an interest in gender and sexuality prejudice, and how these forms of prejudice are 'done' in talk and interaction (Speer and Potter, 2000, 2002; Speer, 2002). Using discursive psychology and **conversation analysis** I explored, for example, how 'heterosexist' utterances do not have their negativity built into them, but rather become prejudiced or troublesome *in situ*, as their sense is produced and negotiated (Speer and Potter, 2000). I explored how speakers attend to 'heterosexism' in their talk and how they manage the potential for their remarks to be interpreted as prejudicial. I have also been interested in the social construction of gender and the interactional organisation of the process through which people come to identify others as male or female or make 'gender attributions' (Speer, 2005), and the ways in which (natal) men construct masculinity and situate themselves and others in relation to these constructions (Speer, 2001).

My interest in gender, sexuality and prejudice led me to a concern for transsexual identities, and how gender is constructed in the context of the gender identity clinic (GIC) (Speer and Green, 2008). In common with a number of other social and cultural theorists (such as the queer theorist Judith Butler, the sociologist Harold Garfinkel and the social psychologists Suzanne Kessler and Wendy McKenna), I believe that by studying the gender practices of trans people we can learn something broader about the construction of gender in society. I am also interested in the practical concerns of trans people and how the widely reported hostility and mismatch between the goals of patients and psychiatrists in the GIC are exemplified in the small-scale features of interaction. To explore these interests I have collected audio- and video-recordings of psychiatric assessment sessions and conducted interviews with psychiatrists and transsexual patients at the GIC.

Using conversation analysis, I have examined some of the fine-grained vocal and embodied techniques that patients use to persuade psychiatrists of the validity of their trans identity, and pass as 'true transsexuals' in their assessment sessions (Speer and Green, 2007). I have also explored psychiatrists' use of 'hypothetical' questions in assessment sessions: questions that invoke negative scenarios concerning patients' treatment (Speer, 2009; Speer and Parsons, 2006). I found that psychiatrists use these questions as a 'last resource' to confront patients with the potentially negative consequences of the decisions they are making. While psychiatrists find these questions to be beneficial, patients may perceive such questions as threatening, and become depressed or feel unsupported outside of the session. At the same time, many patients ultimately recognised the importance of being challenged when making such life-changing decisions. I hope my work will feed into improvements in the current treatment of transsexualism and gender identity disorder.

When engaging with the lives and experiences of trans and queer people, it is important to:

- recognise the many different groups of people who identify as trans or queer
- understand the cultural specificity of gender and sexuality categories and the challenges that trans and queer people make to western gender and sexuality norms
- acknowledge the varied ways in which trans people understand their bodies and identities.

Social class

Social class has a wide range of meanings. In some countries such as Australia and the USA it is typically understood as another word for 'socio-economic status' (i.e., the relative social position of individuals on the basis of differences in income). In other countries, such as the UK, social class has a much broader meaning, and relates to people's background, and their values, consumption practices and other behaviours (and as such, in some instances, social class has very little to do with income).

As we noted in Chapter 1, social class is often overlooked in discussions of LGBTQ psychology (Clarke and Peel, 2007b). Typically it is only mentioned when a sample is reported to be 'primarily middle-class', but such research tends not to discuss class as a factor, nor does it examine how class privilege may have shaped the lives of the (middle-class) participants. Moreover, when psychological research (including LGBTQ psychological research) has examined social class, it has rarely examined class in the broader terms outlined above, but instead has focused on differences in socio-economic status and their impact within LGBTQ communities. As such, this section focuses mainly on class in terms of socio-economic status, while also acknowledging the broader ways in which class is understood and impacts on the lives of LGBTQ people.

Some of the key findings that highlight the impact of inequities in socio-economic status in LGBTQ communities are from research on experiences of homelessness, specifically in relation to young LGBTQ people (e.g., Cochran *et al.*, 2002) and trans people (e.g., Sakamoto *et al.*, 2009). This research has shown how disparities in economic security result in some LGBTQ people experiencing much higher levels of mental and physical health problems than those who live in secure or stable housing. Homeless LGBTQ people are also vulnerable to abuse and are more likely to engage in activities such as prostitution or risky sexual behaviours, which can jeopardise their well-being.

An individual's socio-economic status is largely determined by employment options. Research on the employment options of LGBTQ people indicates that because of workplace heterosexism some LGBTQ people choose not to 'come out' to their employers or co-workers, and remaining **closeted** at work can be experienced as stressful (Hewitt, 1995). US-based economist Lee Badgett (1995) suggests that LGBTQ people who come out at work can be refused promotion, and even dismissed from their jobs, and can face hostility in the workplace. While many countries now have legislation aimed at protecting LGBTQ employees, research nonetheless continues to find evidence of hostility towards LGBTQ people in the workplace (e.g., Miller and Higgins, 2006), and the experience of hostility is often mediated by socio-economic status. For example, UK sociologist Elizabeth McDermott (2006) found in her research on coming out in the workplace that there were significant differences in the experiences of working-class and middle-class lesbian women. Perhaps unsurprisingly, women in more secure financial and social positions felt more able to challenge discrimination and to consider coming out a viable option.

Differences among LGBTQ people in relation to social class and socio-economic status indicate the importance of:

- recognising the impact of class differences *between* LGBTQ people (and particularly between partners in same-sex relationships), and the different ways in which LGBTQ people are positioned in relation to class
- understanding the effects of economic disparities on the health and well-being of LGBTQ people
- acknowledging how social class mediates experiences of coming out and discrimination in the workplace and in other arenas.

Race

As social theorists and biologists have long recognised, racial categories do not represent actual biological differences between groups. The mapping of the human genome has found, among other things, that differences *within* supposed 'racial groups' surpass differences *between* racial groups. This suggests that what have historically been understood as bodily markers of racial groupings are simply collections of body types that have occurred within particular locations: they do not represent specific or discrete racial groupings (McCann *et al.*, 2004). In addition to debunking racial categories, researchers have acknowledged that the values accorded to different 'racial groups' (such as in relation to supposed differences in intelligence or IQ) are the product of histories of colonisation and other forms of domination across the world aimed at subjugating one group of people to another (Richards, 1997). Futhermore, the claim that racial differences account for actual differences in the abilities of distinct groups of people has been found to be the result of the inappropriate use of tests on non-white populations. Tests normed on white populations are unable to measure adequately the abilities of non-white people (see Box 4.1).

Challenging the ways in which racial categories serve to justify discrimination is important, as past understandings of these categories have been based on incorrect interpretations of differences between people. Furthermore, these incorrect understandings have had very real and dangerous outcomes in the world. For example, racial categories were used to justify slavery in the USA, where African people were deemed to be less than human and subjected to appalling treatment. Racial categories were also used to justify colonisation, where certain groups of people considered it their birthright as members of a 'superior race' to appropriate the land of Indigenous peoples. Racial categories have also been used to justify acts of genocide, such as in Nazi Germany where Jewish people and members of other marginalised cultural and racial groups (including lesbians and gay men) were systematically killed.

Even though racial categories are socially and historically constructed, these categories shape the lives of LGBTQ people in very real ways. Racially marginalised people continue to be negatively affected by racism, regardless of the removal of racially discriminatory laws and the introduction of policies aimed at redressing discrimination against racially marginalised groups (Roberts, 2002). For example, US epidemiologist Tooru Nemoto and his colleagues (2004) found that, for many non-white trans people in the USA, racial discrimination results in restricted access to income (i.e., employers refuse to consider non-white applicants for a position or repeatedly turn them down for promotions). Restricted income can lead some people to engage in unprotected sexual intercourse in exchange for money. This can result in the transmission of HIV/AIDS and other sexually transmitted diseases (Nemoto *et al.*, 2004). If we view racial categories as the product of histories of oppression and violence, we can interpret the behaviours of certain groups of LGBTQ people (such as African American, Latina and Asian trans people who engage in sex work) as a response to racial discrimination and social marginalisation, rather than as representing pathology within these communities.

The ongoing legacies of colonisation, slavery and institutional racism detrimentally affect the mental health outcomes of **First Nation** LGBTQ people. For example, Native American lesbian, gay, bisexual and '**two-spirit**' people report the effects of dispossession from land on Native American communities as the greatest contributor to intergenerational trauma and the negative health outcomes it produces such as alcohol use and community violence (Balsam *et al.*, 2004).

It is also important to note that LGBTQ communities are not free from racism. **Dominant group** (typically white) LGBTQ people continue to experience more positive mental health than do LGBTQ people who are members of marginalised racial groups. Furthermore, some white LGBTQ people not only benefit from living in racialised contexts (where white people in general benefit from racial privilege – see Chapter 11), but also engage in racism against marginalised LGBTQ people (see Box 4.4). For example, Australian sociologist Ibrahim

---

Box 4.4   Key researcher: Beverly A. Greene on why I study ethnically and culturally marginalised LGBTQ people

I began my research in the USA on members of marginalised groups with an interest in the impact of race and racism, gender and sexism, and heterosexism/homophobia and LGB sexual orientation on psychological development and functioning. In its earliest incarnations the impetus for that work came as a result of its conspicuous absence during the course of my training. In my therapeutic practice I encountered clients whose needs had been completely neglected in the psychological literature and who in case conferences with colleagues were usually the focus of ignorance and bias.

In the course of constructing that early research it was clear to me that these issues of social marginalisation processes and social identities were connected to understanding privilege and disadvantage and more than one identity at a time. Much of my work has explored this issue in relation to counselling and psychotherapy (e.g., see Greene, 2004, 2005). 'Single identity' paradigms examined marginalised identities as separate entities in isolation from one another. These approaches failed to capture the complexity of the challenges to good mental health that I routinely observed in my LGB clients. Most clients who were LGB persons of colour complained that in their ethnic communities their LGB sexual orientation was not welcome, forcing them to deny that part of themselves. Similarly, in the broader LGB community they frequently faced racial discrimination and a lack of tolerance for their concerns about racial oppression.

At that time I was also aware of the many strengths that LGB people of colour had developed to manage and reframe racism as a social problem rather than their deficit and the ways these strengths could be used to negotiate the heterosexism in their lives. I found feminist psychotherapy theory helpful in framing social oppression as a significant contributing factor in creating mental health problems in women and, to my thinking, in members of other marginalised groups. I sought to expand feminist therapy approaches to encompass other forms of social marginalisation rather than focusing only on gender oppression.

That work also served to remind me that understanding the oppression of women required looking at women for all of their diversity, leading me back to my nascent ideas about developing paradigms that permitted us to view identity in more complex ways. This led to the evolution of my current work on the interrelated nature of social oppressions such as racism, sexism, classism and heterosexism and the ways they mutually reinforce one another, and multiple identity paradigms (e.g., see Greene *et al.*, 2008). The latter views each individual as having more than one identity in which some identities may be privileged and others disadvantaged. Each identity transforms and informs the other developmentally. This comes full circle in my understanding of LGB people of colour as having multiple identities, concerns and challenges.

Abraham (2009) reports that Lebanese Muslim queer people living in Australia experience considerable racism from within queer communities. This discrimination takes the form of explicit discrimination and rejection from white LGBTQ people and of a refusal to accept that some Lebanese Muslim people can identify as queer. These people (among many others) experience multiple levels of discrimination: they are often invisible as queer people in a heterosexist society and as Muslim people in (predominantly white) LGBTQ communities, and can be invisible as queer in Muslim communities.

When considering issues of race and culture within LGBTQ communities, it is important to:

- appreciate how ongoing histories of racism impact on all LGBTQ people, either to privilege some people or to disadvantage others
- understand the cultural construction of racial categories, as well as the very 'real' ways in which such categories shape the lives of LGBTQ people
- acknowledge the existence and effects of racism within LGBTQ communities.

Organised religion and spirituality

LGBTQ psychologists continue to play an important role in discrediting the research and clinical practices of 'conversion therapists' who claim to 'change' non-heterosexuals into heterosexuals (e.g., Riggs, 2004a; see also Chapter 1). LGBTQ psychologists have argued that conversion therapy is an ethically and morally suspect response to homosexuality. Some advocates of conversion therapy have claimed that LGBTQ people are distressed by their sexual identities, and that change is required (e.g., Nicolosi, 1991). What these advocates fail to acknowledge, however, is that for many LGBTQ people their distress is the product of living in homophobic societies, and, more specifically, living in particular contexts where certain religions condemn non-heterosexual identities and behaviours. LGBTQ psychologists have argued that what needs to change is not the sexual identities of LGBTQ people, but rather the groups of people and institutions (such as some religions) that deny the validity of LGBTQ identities. Or at the very least that such groups and institutions respect the rights of LGBTQ people to live free of persecution and discrimination.

Examining and challenging the claims of conversion therapists has been an important aspect of LGBTQ psychological research. However, it is also necessary to examine the *positive* experiences that LGBTQ people can have of organised religion and other forms of spirituality, and some LGBTQ people's desire to belong to communities of faith. There is considerable diversity among LGBTQ people who identify as religious, and within any given religion or spiritual practice there will be a range of positions held, such as:

- those who experience their religion as a generalised sense of 'faith' in the world
- those who are committed to a particular religious moral code
- those who live by the literal interpretation of a particular religious text (such as the Christian bible, the Qur'an in Islam, the Jewish Torah or the Hindu Bhagavad Gita)
- those who view religion as providing a sense of cultural connection but don't adhere to specific religious practices
- those who adhere to a combination of these (and other) understandings of religion.

For all of these positions, religion represents a place of safety from the discrimination that LGBTQ people face in their everyday lives. In his research on non-heterosexual Muslims living in Britain, sociologist Andrew Yip (2004) found that many of his participants experienced their commitment to Islam and their readings of the Qur'an as providing solace in the context of widespread hostility against Muslim people. Similarly, Abraham (2009) found that most of the queer Muslim Australians he interviewed experienced Islam as a source of strength in the face of multiple forms of discrimination. Some researchers have suggested that a sense of spiritual connection to others or to god may be important in times of crisis for LGBTQ Christians, such as at the height of the HIV/AIDS epidemic (Sherkat, 2002).

Yip's research draws our attention to an important distinction between the *texts and tenets* of a religion and the *cultural practices* of a religion. For many people the two are seen as inseparable, but for others the texts or tenets of a particular religion can be quite different from what is practised by its followers. If we take Islam as an example, UK social policy commentators Jivraj and de Jong (2004) note that there is considerable debate among scholars of Islam as to the differences between the Qur'an and the texts that surround it (that function to interpret the Qur'an into particular religious practices). The Qur'an has traditionally been interpreted as condemning same-sex sexualities (and in particular those between men, as have the scriptures that inform Christianity). However, alternative interpretations suggest that such prohibitions are placed on violent and non-consensual sexual relations, rather than 'condemning loving and mutually respectful relationships between men or between women' (Jivraj and de Jong, 2004: 6).

In regard to Christianity, US psychologists Eric Rodriguez and Suzanne Ouelette (2000) report that 75 per cent of Christian religions 'condemn homosexuals and homosexuality as being an abomination in the eyes of God' (p. 333). However, they also note that some religious groups actively affirm the experiences of LGBTQ Christians. Primary among these are the Metropolitan Community Churches (MCC), which have ministries across all five continents. The MCC actively teach about the lives of LGBTQ people in a religious context and MCC services are led by members of LGBTQ communities. MCC, in this sense, are identified as 'gay positive' rather than as 'gay friendly' churches. The latter is a place of worship that welcomes LGBTQ people but does not explicitly teach to and for LGBTQ communities.

Some LGBTQ people also engage in forms of spirituality outside of the dominant religions recognised across the world (Islam, Hinduism, Judaism, Buddhism and Christianity). For example, many lesbian and bisexual women identify with goddess-based religions such as Paganism and Wicca, which they believe offer an alternative to the male-dominated hierarchies that inform mainstream religions (Barrett, 2003). Gay men too have sought to engage in religious or spiritual practices that validate their desires for connectedness and to have their sexuality respected. For example, Radical Faeries are gay men who evoke pagan rituals as part of an earth-centred, anti-consumerist approach to being in the world (see Hennen, 2004). Recent research suggests that such 'earth-spirited' faiths are more inclusive of LGBTQ people than larger organised religions (Smith, 2007). There are also many indigenous forms of religious practice that celebrate the experiences of non-heterosexual people, although western understandings of Indigenous cultures typically enforce a dominant or colonising lens that fails to understand them on their own terms (see Chapter 11).

Psychological research has found that many Christian men and women reconcile the negative aspects of their religion with their non-heterosexual sexuality by altering their relationship to their religion. Rodriguez and Ouellette (2000) found that some gay and lesbian Christians focus on tangible ways of connecting spirituality and sexuality (such as through readings or attending church) rather than solely feeling a relationship to god.

Finally, it is important to note that although many LGBTQ people identify with particular organised religions or engage in a range of spiritual practices, many LGBTQ people also explicitly identify as atheist or humanist. For some people this may be a result of previous negative experiences of organised religions; for others, their reasons for rejecting religion may be no different from the reasons that members of the wider population have for identifying as atheist, rationalist or humanist.

To summarise, intersections of religion and sexuality in the lives of LGBTQ people requires us to:

- recognise that many LGBTQ people experience a commitment to organised religions or to a range of spiritual practices
- acknowledge that there is a diverse range of ways in which such LGBTQ people experience their faith
- understand that religions have a wide range of views on homosexuality (and different forms of a religion – e.g., orthodox or liberal – can have widely divergent views), and there is no one (correct) interpretation of how homosexuality is viewed within religious texts.

Rural life

As we noted in Chapter 1, most LGBTQ psychological research has, until recently, focused on the experiences of LGBTQ people living in urban centres (Greene, 2000). A growing body of research, however, has examined the specific experiences of LGBTQ people who live in rural or remote areas. Rural or remote areas are typically understood as areas constituted by a relatively low-density population, involving geographically dispersed communities that are located away from urban centres, and which often have a primary focus on agricultural economies (Rounds, 1988). Such geographical areas, particularly within the USA, are often organised around a strong commitment to (Christian) religion, with the church playing a central role in many rural communities. As such, some LGBTQ people living in rural areas may experience pressure to refuse an LGBTQ identity and identify instead as heterosexual (Willging *et al.*, 2006).

The social isolation associated with living in remote and rural areas (or even regional centres) can result in a lack of LGBTQ-specific support services. Moreover, those LGBTQ services that do exist may not be accessed by many LGBTQ people because of fears of further isolation or alienation from the broader community should their LGBTQ identity become known. In some areas, LGBTQ support groups are non-existent and meeting other LGBTQ people in safe ways can be very difficult. Research indicates that there is an increasing use of online spaces by rural-dwelling LGBTQ people in order to connect with other LGBTQ people and to access resources and support services (Haag and Chang, 1997). As Sonja Ellis (2007a) points out, however, the highly sexualised nature of many LGBTQ-specific online spaces means that some LGBTQ people living in rural settings who seek primarily non-sexualised interactions may not find online spaces particularly supportive (see also Chapter 8).

There are significant gender and racial differences among LGBTQ people in relation to access to services and safe spaces in which to meet other LGBTQ people. US epidemiologist David Knapp Whittier (1997) suggests that gay men or MSM often manage to create spaces where they can meet other men or access services (such as adult bookstores, public spaces and hotels). Lesbians or women who have sex with women (**WSW**) typically have less access to such spaces in rural and remote (and even in urban) areas.

Some LGBTQ people living in rural or remote areas may move to urban areas to connect with LGBTQ communities. This can be important for some young people, but can leave others vulnerable to abuse from people who take advantage of their relative lack of knowledge about urban LGBTQ practices (D'Augelli and Hart, 1987).

In summary, understanding issues of location in LGBTQ communities requires us to:

- appreciate the specific experiences and support needs of LGBTQ people living in rural and remote areas
- understand the complexities associated with using online spaces as a way to support LGBTQ people living in rural settings
- acknowledge the challenges faced by LGBTQ people who decide to move from rural to urban areas.

Ability

In most countries of the world, social spaces are typically geared towards the bodies of people with four functional limbs, and who possess adequate levels of hearing, sight, smell and touch and speech required to navigate such spaces. But not all people inhabit these particular bodily configurations. Recognising the differences between people in terms of their ability to move in social spaces (designed for able-bodied people) has led researchers in the field of disability research, such as the British social scientist Tom Shakespeare (1999), to make a distinction between impairment (i.e., a condition of the body or mind) and disability (the relationship between people with an impairment and the broader society in which they live that fails to acknowledge their needs). Recent 'queer-crip' research (e.g., Hall, 2003) has focused on how particular bodies are accorded more value than others, and how people often experience their level of ability as 'normal', rather than some people being 'abled' and some people being 'disabled'. Issues of ability cover a broad range of areas, including:

- physical abilities (including the use of limbs and the number of limbs)
- intellectual or learning abilities
- health abilities (including chronic illness)
- emotional abilities (including mental health issues).

All of us experience our bodies in a relationship to these forms of ability, and for many of us our range of abilities will change over our lives. For LGBTQ people who experience some form of impairment, their access to social spaces (including

LGBTQ-specific spaces) may be significantly limited by the failure of social spaces (and their inhabitants) to accommodate the diverse needs of all people. Because of the priority accorded to able-bodied norms, many LGBTQ people experience forms of vulnerability that result from:

- not being able to access non-discriminatory services (in a context where many community health services do not cater for the needs of LGBTQ people, and particularly the needs of LGBTQ people with a range of different abilities)
- a lack of supportive LGBTQ friendly or positive spaces (because of physical or emotional barriers such as a lack of ramps for wheelchair access that can result in actual physical exclusion, as well as feelings of exclusion from particular social spaces)
- a lack of information about sexual health or sexual practices (which leaves some people open to interpersonal abuse)
- limited access to employment options (which may curtail access to social spaces because of limited finances).

Heterosexism within hospital and residential care facilities can be detrimental to the lives of people who use these services. US disability advocate Corbett O'Toole (1996) highlighted some of the very negative consequences that arise from heterosexism directed against lesbian women who are 'differently abled'. These include 'withholding pain medication, ignoring call lights, staff being cool and detached, [and] staff turning other staff against patients' (p. 232). LGBTQ people living with impairments may experience difficulties in gaining support from other LGBTQ people. This may arise from:

- communication differences (for example hearing-impaired people may not readily have access to LGBTQ vernacular)
- bodily differences (some LGBTQ people can experience alienation if they are not perceived as embodying particular idealised 'types')
- health differences (many social support groups in LGBTQ communities require people to travel to services, which may not be feasible for people experiencing chronic health issues)
- some LGBTQ people treating the bodies of LGBTQ people with impairments as fetish objects (e.g., people who are attracted to people who have had a limb amputated)

Box 4.5 highlights a key study that examines the multiple forms of exclusion that gay men with intellectual disabilities experience in relation to care facilities and gay communities and social spaces.

Finally, it is only quite recently that research and public policy have begun to acknowledge not only that people of a range of abilities are sexually active, but that such activity is not solely heterosexual (Fraley et al., 2007). Research on sexuality and ability is increasingly examining the diverse ways in which people engage in sexual practices, and has often encouraged an emphasis on non-genital forms of sexual expression.

> **Box 4.5   Key study: Christopher Bennett and Adrian Coyle (2007) on gay men with intellectual disabilities**
>
> In their study, UK psychologists Christopher Bennett and Adrian Coyle interviewed ten men with mild intellectual disabilities who either identified as gay or thought they might be gay. Using interpretative phenomenological analysis (see Chapter 3) Bennett and Coyle explored five main aspects of these data:
>
> - *The experience of developing a gay identity.* This was similar to the experiences of gay men in general, but the men in the study were also focused on determining the origins of their gay identity. Some attributed their sexuality to the sexual abuse they had experienced from non-intellectually disabled men.
> - *The stigma of intellectual disability and being gay.* The men in the study reported experiences of discrimination by people in general about their intellectual disability and their gay identity, and also experiences of discrimination in relation to their intellectual disability from non-intellectually disabled gay men.
> - *Social isolation from gay communities.* Many of the men spoke of wanting to be a part of mainstream gay communities but feeling unwelcome there. For some men their isolation was the result of not knowing how to access gay resources; for others it was the result of fear about how they would be treated by other gay men.
> - *Sense of belonging.* Because of often feeling unwelcome in gay spaces, the participants reported feeling little sense of belonging to mainstream gay communities. This was exacerbated by having few connections to other gay men with intellectual disabilities and a lack of support in attending gay venues.
> - *Restrictions of being in care.* Some participants who lived in care homes felt that the lack of privacy impinged on their freedom to live as gay men. Some had been reprimanded for engaging in sexual activity with other men and others felt that this lack of privacy left them few options for meeting men and having their sexual and emotional needs met.
>
> These findings highlight the ways that multiple forms of identity result in different experiences for LGBTQ people. The participants may be seen to benefit from living as men in a male-dominated society, but this was greatly mediated by their gay identity and their experience of living with an intellectual disability.

Understanding the differing abilities and impairments within LGBTQ communities requires us to:

- recognise how bodily norms shape social spaces and limit the movement of some people
- understand the specific experiences of LGBTQ people living with impairments and their particular sexual and emotional needs
- acknowledge ableism within LGBTQ communities.

Main chapter points

This chapter:

- Demonstrated how social norms impact *on* and circulate *within* LGBTQ communities.
- Outlined the ways in which diversity within LGBTQ communities can result in particular groups of people experiencing marginalisation and the ways in which privilege and disadvantage occur in LGBTQ communities.
- Highlighted the multiple forms of identity that shape the experiences of LGBTQ people.

Questions for discussion and classroom exercises

1. Identify some of the sampling issues that can arise from attempting to access a diverse LGBTQ population (see Chapter 3). Design a method for sampling LGBTQ communities and recruiting participants that adequately accounts for the diverse experiences of LGBTQ people.
    How might your attempt to sample for diversity be hampered by discrimination and prejudice within LGBTQ communities?

2. Consider the experiences of a hypothetical individual which are shaped through three of the marginalised identities outlined in this chapter (e.g., a black, working-class, bisexual woman). How might each of her identities shape her experience of day-to-day life? How might the three identities together shape her life in ways that we would not appreciate if we only focused on her sexuality (or on one other aspect of her identity)?

3. There are two different, and competing, ways of meeting the needs of marginalised LGBTQ people within LGBTQ communities. The first is to expand and develop existing groups and services to create welcoming spaces for marginalised LGBTQ people (e.g., to make existing LGBTQ social spaces and community groups accessible to disabled LGBTQ people). The second is to create spaces expressly for particular groups of LGBTQ people (e.g., social groups for disabled LGBTQ people). Considering some of the different groups of LGBTQ people discussed in this chapter, discuss the benefits and limitations of each approach.

4. What are the limitations of the dominant binary approach to understanding gender within western societies? How does this limit the experiences of LGBTQ people? Which LGBTQ people in particular and why?

5. Read US feminist Peggy McIntosh's (1998) classic paper 'White privilege: unpacking the invisible knapsack'. Identify the ways in which white people are privileged in your community. Now identify the ways in which heterosexual people are privileged in your community. Now think

about the ways in which non-white and non-heterosexual people are *disadvantaged* in your community. Finally, reflect on the lives of people who experience both privilege and disadvantage (e.g., privilege as white people and disadvantage as non-heterosexual people) in your community. What would it feel like to experience simultaneously both privilege and disadvantage (perhaps you have personal experience you can draw on in answering this question)?

Further reading

Appleby, Y. (1994) Out on the margins. *Disability and Society*, 9(1), 19–32.
This article uses a social constructionist model of disability and lesbianism to explore the intersection of these two identities and disabled lesbian women's experiences of discrimination in an able-bodied, heterosexist society and of able-bodied discrimination within lesbian communities.

Barker, M., Bowes-Catton, H., Iantaffi, A., Cassidy, A. and Brewer, L. (2008) British bisexuality: a snapshot of bisexual identities in the UK. *Journal of Bisexuality*, 8(1/2), 141–62.
This article provides an overview of bisexual communities within the UK, and uses survey data, media analysis and focus groups to examine how bisexual people understand their identities and how bisexual people are represented in the wider culture. The article also highlights issues for future research on bisexuality.

Devor, H. (1993) Sexual orientation identities, attractions, and practices of female-to-male transsexuals. *Journal of Sex Research*, 30(6), 303–15.
In this article, Canadian sociologist Holly Devor explores transmen's experiences of relationships and sexual practices and highlights the intersections of gender and sexuality in the lives of gay transmen.

Han, A. (2006) 'I think you're the smartest race I've ever met': racialised economies of queer male desire. *ACRAWSA e-journal*, 2(2). Available at: www.acrawsa.org.au
This article provides an analysis of racialised differences within gay male communities, with a focus on how white gay men engage with and fetishise Asian gay men. Australian social scientist Alan Han examines how white gay men's relationships with Asian gay men draw on negative stereotypes of Asian men as effeminate, as well as the ways in which this stereotype shapes notions of desire within gay communities.

Taylor, Y. (2008) 'That's not really my scene': working-class lesbians in (and out of) place. *Sexualities*, 11(5), 523–46.
In this article, British sociologist Yvette Taylor explores working-class lesbians' views and experiences of the commercialised 'gay scene'. Taylor highlights the ways in which working-class lesbians both participate in and feel excluded from these spaces.

5   Prejudice and discrimination

Overview
- Sexuality and gender identity prejudice in context
- Sexuality and gender identity prejudice as anti-LGBTQ attitudes and behaviours
- Sexuality and gender identity prejudice as social marginalisation

Sexuality and gender identity prejudice in context

Since 2000, both in the UK and internationally, there has been unprecedented legal change outlawing discrimination on grounds of sexuality, including: lifting the ban on homosexuals in the military in some countries; the equalisation of the age of consent for sex between men in the UK; the repeal of **Section 28** of the Local Government Act in the UK; the extension of adoption rights to same-sex couples in the USA and the UK; protection from discrimination in the workplace in the UK; access to civil partnership and marriage in some countries (see Chapter 8 for a detailed list); and most recently, protection from discrimination in the provision of goods and services in the UK.

Similarly, there have been a number of positive changes in relation to gender identity. For example, in the UK, the 1999 Sex Discrimination (Gender Reassignment) Regulations – superseded by the Equality Act 2006 – outlawed discrimination against trans people in employment. Similarly, the Gender Recognition Act (2004) enabled trans people to have their acquired gender recognised; and in 2008 an Amendment to the Sex Discrimination Regulations made it unlawful to discriminate against trans people in the provision of goods, services, facilities and premises. Other countries vary in the degree to which trans issues are explicitly addressed in legislation. Typically, trans issues are subsumed under sex discrimination regulations.

However, this degree of positive social change may be contrasted with situations where LGBTQ people continue to be excluded from certain rights and social institutions, such as in the USA, where military policy still prevents 'active' homosexuals from serving in the armed forces and LGB people from disclosing their sexuality. Similarly, in Australia, LGBTQ people continue to be excluded from civil marriage and legal adoption (some states now have civil partnerships or relationship registers but these are not accompanied by rights); and the US Congress and State legislatures have repeatedly refused attempts to pass employment non-discrimination laws, and make provision for same-sex marriage.

Although in much of the western world LGBTQ people are afforded some level of equality, no fewer than eighty-five member countries of the United Nations (representing a wide range of cultures and faiths) still criminalise consensual same-sex sexual practices among adults, usually as 'unnatural acts'. While sex between males is more often criminalised than sex between women, in some countries both are explicitly legislated against and harshly punished. For example, in Iran, male homosexuality carries the death penalty and the punishment for lesbianism is one hundred lashes. Similarly, in Togo, Africa, the law states that 'impudent acts and crimes against nature with an individual of the same sex is punished with three years imprisonment and 100,000 – 500,000 (West African) Franc in fine' (www.ilga.org). In other countries, LGBTQ people are tortured, incarcerated, falsely arrested or even 'disappear', simply because of their sexuality and/or gender identity. So, although in some non-western countries gender and sexual diversity is acknowledged and in some instances legally protected, in many cases the basic human rights of LGBTQ people are not respected.

Sexuality and gender identity prejudice as anti-LGBTQ attitudes and behaviours

In the psychological literature there is a wide range of terms used to describe prejudice and discrimination against LGBTQ people. The term homophobia was coined by the US psychologist Kenneth Smith (1971) and popularised by the US clinical psychologist George Weinberg (1972: 4), who defined it as 'the dread of being in close quarters with homosexuals – and in the case of homosexuals themselves, self-loathing'. This became the basis for much psychological work that conceptualised homophobia as feelings of anxiety, disgust, aversion, anger, discomfort and fear towards lesbians and gay men (see Hudson and Ricketts, 1980). In the 1980s, the term '**internalised homophobia**' (Sophie, 1987) was introduced to describe negative feelings towards oneself as a lesbian or a gay man. Today the term homophobia is used inclusively to describe anti-gay and anti-lesbian (and sometimes anti-bisexual) prejudice and discrimination, and includes everything from negative attitudes towards lesbians and gay men and lesbian and gay issues to **hate crimes** based on sexuality.

In examining the LGBTQ literature, you will also find a number of other terms akin to homophobia such as 'homonegativism' (Hudson and Ricketts, 1980) and 'homosexophobia' (Levitt and Kassen, 1974), but these are not as widely used. More recently, the term homophobia has been criticised for not adequately encompassing prejudice and discrimination against bisexual and trans people. As a result, the terms biphobia and transphobia have started to appear but are not yet well established in the psychological literature. Although the term 'homophobia' is often used as an umbrella term for all forms of anti-LGBTQ prejudice, it does not adequately capture the ways in which the discrimination experienced by bisexual and trans people *differs* from that experienced by lesbians and gay men.

Although bisexuals and trans people share some issues of discrimination with lesbians and gay men (e.g., that they are not necessarily socially validated), they are also discriminated against because they do not fit commonly understood sexuality and gender norms. As we discussed in Chapters 2 and 4, owing to the dichotomisation of sexuality into a heterosexual–homosexual binary, bisexuality has been rendered invisible and therefore shrouded in suspicion and myth: a phenomenon known as monosexism or **mononormativity**. As a result, biphobia is manifest through negative stereotypes including that bisexuals are confused about their sexual identity; are really lesbians/gay men who lack the courage to come out; are promiscuous; have more than one partner at a time; and are obsessed with sex (Eliason, 2001; Rust, 1993). Likewise, the dichotomisation of gender into a male–female binary is equally problematic for trans (and intersex) people. Within most societies gender diversity is not tolerated and social structures perpetuate the erasure of gender fluidity and non-male/female identities (Monro, 2006). For example, in the English language there is no socially accepted term to refer to people who are not male or female, official documents (e.g., birth certificates and passports) require gender to be stated, with no room for fluidity, and spaces designated 'male' and 'female' (e.g., toilets) are daily reminders of the organisation of society around a two-sex model. In addition, trans people are often viewed as being 'really' lesbian or gay but as **transitioning** to the other sex to avoid being identified as lesbian or gay.

The terms 'biphobia' and 'transphobia' also provide a vehicle for describing prejudice against bisexual and trans people that originates in lesbian and gay communities as well as that perpetrated by heterosexuals; widely known as **'double discrimination'** (Ochs, 1996). Just as LGBTQ people may experience prejudice because they do not fit the taken-for-granted norms and conventions of heterosexual society, bisexual and trans people have sometimes been subject to prejudice for not fitting the norms of lesbian and gay communities. According to US lawyer Jillian Weiss (2004), lesbian and gay communities are characterised by a gender divide. That is, these communities are understood as comprising women who desire women as sexual partners (lesbians) and men who desire men as sexual partners (gay men). Within this framework, bisexuals – both men and women who desire both men and women as sexual partners – do not fit. Furthermore, because many lesbian women also identify with feminism and the women's movement, they see their lesbian identities as political: that is, as a stance against male privilege within society (see Chapter 2). Consequently, bisexual women are often viewed by lesbians as politically and emotionally *uninvested* in women's issues and as condoning male privilege through gratifying men's social, emotional and sexual needs (Rust, 1993, 1995).

Attitudes toward LGBTQ people and issues

As highlighted in Chapter 1, from the 1950s until the 1970s, the psychological study of LGBTQ people was dominated by research that portrayed lesbians and gay men as sick, abnormal or deviant (Kitzinger, 1987), and almost completely ignored bisexual people. In addition, while trans people were sometimes the subject of study, research at this time often pathologised trans people. It wasn't until the removal of homosexuality per se from the DSM in 1973 that psychologists began to explore the issue of prejudice and discrimination against lesbians and gay men. At that time, attitude research was already well established within psychology, providing a convenient framework within which to develop research on homophobia. Consequently, in the 1970s, a number of scales were developed to measure and assess homophobia. These measures treated homophobia as a personality trait that could be readily identified using a homophobia scale. As with any psychometric measurement, respondents in these studies would be asked to respond to a series of statements, such as 'I would not want to join an organisation that has homosexuals in its membership' (Lumby, 1976); 'The growing number of male homosexuals indicates a decline in American morals' (Millham *et al.*, 1976); or 'Homosexuals should be locked up to protect society' (Smith, 1971). Each item would then be coded and scored, and the scores added to give an overall homophobia score. The development of homophobia scales continued to proliferate into the 1980s, and in 1984 the US psychologist Gregory Herek produced what has become the most widely used homophobia scale: The Attitudes toward Lesbians and Gay Men Scale (see Box 5.1). Similar scales have been developed more recently to measure internalised homophobia (Szymanski and Chung, 2001), biphobia (Mulick and Wright, 2002) and transphobia (Hill and Willoughby, 2005; Tee and Hegarty, 2006).

Almost without exception, work on homophobia has employed surveys or questionnaires to measure levels of homophobia and is heavily dominated by research carried out in a North American context. Across the mainstream LGBTQ

Box 5.1   *Highlights: the Attitudes toward Lesbians and Gay Men Scale – short form (ATLG-S; Herek, 1984)*

- Just as in other species, male homosexuality is a natural expression of sexuality in human men.
- Lesbians just can't fit into our society.
- Lesbians and gay men should only be allowed to express their views as long as they don't offend or upset the majority.
- I think male homosexuals are disgusting.
- Lesbians are sick.
- Male homosexuality is a perversion.
- Male homosexuality is merely a different kind of lifestyle that should *not* be condemned.

- Society has a right to prevent lesbians and gay men who want to speak in schools from actively promoting homosexuality as equivalent to heterosexuality.
- State laws regulating private, consenting lesbian behaviour should be loosened.
- Homosexual behaviour between two men is just plain wrong.

psychological literature, there are numerous studies employing homophobia scales to investigate and document the attitudes of particular groups of individuals, such as psychologists, social workers, medical professionals, police officers and students, towards LGB people. In addition, a large body of work has focused on identifying predictors of homophobia. Homophobia research consistently reports that it is more common in men, those with conservative religious or political views, and those who lack personal contact with lesbians and/or gay men (e.g., D'Augelli, 1989). Similarly, a recent study (Nagoshi *et al.*, 2008) found that conservative religious and political views were highly correlated with transphobia.

Historically, the main purpose of identifying correlates with homophobia has been to identify people at risk of perpetrating homophobia. Education programmes can then be developed to target these 'at risk' groups. Diversity training is a strategy commonly employed in workplaces and schools to combat homophobia. Training tends to focus on three main goals: (1) the provision of 'facts' about LGB people; (2) the provision of contact with LGB people; and (3) drawing parallels between LGB people and other marginalised groups (Harding and Peel, 2007). Evaluations of such training show that it can be an effective tool for changing attitudes, although the extent to which this attitudinal change translates into practice remains largely unexplored (Peel, 2002). Correlational studies also enable the identification of risk-taking behaviours and the mental health indicators associated with homophobia. For example, correlational research on internalised homophobia has explored the likely effect of homophobia on LGBT people engaging in substance use (e.g., Amadio and Chung, 2004) or experiencing depression, anxiety and suicide (e.g., Igartua *et al.*, 2003). Such studies have also identified the personality factors which may result in an increased likelihood of internalised homophobia (Szymanski *et al.*, 2001).

In some social and cultural contexts where there is a pro-equality and anti-discrimination social climate, it has become less socially acceptable to express overt homophobic sentiments. A study carried out in Poland and the Netherlands demonstrated that when participants are asked to say something about a social group (e.g., LGBTQ people) in a situation that appears to have something to do with their attitudes towards that group (e.g., a focus group on LGBTQ issues), participants modify their responses to avoid making directly negative assertions (Maison, 1995). Consequently, data from studies that use homophobia scales are likely to produce a 'floor effect' (i.e., the majority of respondents scoring as 'not homophobic') even though in other settings the same people may freely express anti-LGBTQ sentiments.

In order to counteract these effects, some psychologists have attempted to develop more sophisticated scales, designed to identify more subtle forms of homophobia. One example is the Modern Homophobia Scale (Raja and Stokes, 1998), which comprises forty-six items designed to explore **institutional homophobia**, personal discomfort, and beliefs that homosexuality is deviant and changeable. Although the items are not substantially different from those of earlier homophobia scales, it comprises two subscales (the MHS-L and MHS-G) one of which focuses on attitudes towards lesbians and the other on attitudes towards gay men. This structure more readily facilitates comparisons between attitudes towards lesbians and attitudes towards gay men, which, with the exception of the ATLG (Herek, 1984), is not possible using earlier scales that treated lesbians and gay men as a homogeneous group.

In a small number of studies, attitudes towards lesbian and gay *issues* (rather than attitudes towards lesbian and gay *people*) have been used as a way of exploring homophobia. Based primarily in a European context, this work centres on exploring prejudice in relation to recent legal changes that have resulted in the institutionalisation of social equality for LGB people (e.g., see Ellis, 2002; Sotelo, 2000). These studies suggest that, in principle, the notion of equality for lesbians and gay men is well supported. For example, in Sonja's (Ellis, 2002) survey of 630 students across the UK, 96 per cent agreed with the statement 'a person's sexual orientation should not block that person's access to basic rights and freedoms'. However, this level of support somewhat diminished when respondents were asked about specific rights issues. In particular, respondents were unwilling to afford lesbians and gay men equal rights in relation to social issues such as getting married and having children, and having lesbian and gay issues represented in the school curriculum.

Although there is limited research on attitudes towards bisexuals, research consistently reports that anti-bisexual attitudes are prevalent. For example, in psychologists Patrick Mulick and Lester Wright's (2002) study almost half of the 224 undergraduate participants from a US university were deemed 'moderately' or 'severely' biphobic. The findings of the study also showed that biphobia was more prevalent among heterosexual students than among lesbian and gay students. This study is one of the few that explores attitudes towards bisexuals separately from attitudes towards lesbians and gay men. More commonly, attitudes towards LGB people are measured as a single entity as if LGB people were one homogeneous group (see Chapter 4). This approach is particularly problematic in that it assumes that if people are anti-gay they will also be anti-lesbian and anti-bisexual and therefore ignores the way in which gender norms and prejudices intersect with attitudes towards sexuality.

Some psychologists (e.g., Hill and Willoughby, 2005; Landén and Innala, 2000) have noted that attitude research tends to suggest that in principle people are pro-trans;

however, experimental research and anecdotal evidence appears to suggest otherwise. Anti-trans sentiments are prevalent in western society (but see Winter *et al.*, 2008 for a cross-cultural comparison), placing trans people at high risk of discrimination. For example, in 2006 a survey by Press for Change (www.pfc.org.uk) – a UK-based organisation which campaigns for the rights of trans people – showed that, despite legal protection, discrimination and harassment in the workplace still occurs. Of the 873 trans people surveyed, 10 per cent had been verbally abused and 6 per cent assaulted at work, and reports of verbal harassment were common. In addition, during and after transition, one in four had been made to use the toilets designated for their natal sex (Whittle *et al.*, 2007; see also Lombardi *et al.*, 2001). Transphobia also appears to be highly correlated with homophobia (e.g., see Nagoshi *et al.*, 2008).

Although essentialist work on attitudes towards LGBTQ people and issues has continued to thrive, the concept of homophobia (and by implication biphobia and transphobia) has at times come under criticism. In particular, lesbian feminist psychologists have been highly critical of the concept of homophobia because it individualises sexuality prejudice (Kitzinger, 1996b). That is, prejudice is constructed as a characteristic (or trait) of certain individuals who either are inherently prejudiced or have taken on board stereotypical misconceptions about LGBTQ people. As a result, the concept of homophobia ignores the ways in which attitudes might be seen as a reflection of prejudices that are embedded in the social and cultural fabric of society. Likewise, internalised homophobia has been viewed by some psychologists (e.g., Kitzinger and Perkins, 1993) as problematic because it pathologises the distress experienced by LGBTQ people as a private issue requiring individual adjustment, rather than as a political and cultural issue requiring social change. Lesbian feminists have also been critical of the ways in which homophobia scales equate a lack of prejudice with liberal values (see Chapter 2). Kitzinger (1987) argued from a social constructionist perspective that it is impossible to define objectively what counts as prejudiced and not-prejudiced (Kitzinger and Peel, 2005).

Anti-LGBTQ hate crime

A second strand of essentialist research centres on anti-LGBTQ behaviours. This body of work is about the victimisation of LGBTQ people, typically referred to as homophobic (or transphobic) hate crime. While statistical information about sexuality and gender identity prejudice is not routinely (if at all) collected by police and other law enforcement agencies, there is considerable research and anecdotal evidence that this discrimination occurs. The high-profile murder/manslaughter cases of Matthew Shepard, Tyra Hunter and Brandon Teena (in the US) and of David Morley and Jody Dobrowski (in the UK), and the 'Gay Gang Murders' (in Australia), are reminders that homophobic and transphobic hate crime is alive and well (see Box 5.2). A recent survey of 354 LGB people in Wales (Stonewall CYMRU, 2003) found that one in three respondents had been a victim of physical violence or bullying. Homophobic bullying in schools is also common (see Chapter 7).

Box 5.2   *Highlights: examples of homophobic and transphobic hate crimes*

- *Gay Gang Murders* (late 1980s and early 1990s). A series of murders and disappearances of (presumed) gay men from Marks Park (a known gay cruising area) bordering Bondi Beach in Sydney, Australia. These cases remained unsolved for more than a decade.
- *Brandon Teena* (d. 1993) was a natal female from Nebraska, USA, living as a transman who was raped and eventually murdered. Brandon's infamous hate crime case was the subject of the 1999 award-winning film *Boys Don't Cry*.
- *Tyra Hunter* (d. 1995) was a 24-year-old transsexual woman who was seriously injured when she was involved in a car accident. Medical personnel attending the scene made derogatory remarks and withdrew medical care after discovering her birth sex. She later died in Washington DC General Hospital.
- *Matthew Shepard* (d. 1998) was a 21-year-old gay student in Wyoming, US, who was 'befriended' by two men posing as gay men. They drove Shepard to a remote rural area where they robbed, pistol whipped and tortured him, then tied him to a fence and left him to die. He was discovered eighteen hours later by a cyclist but later died in hospital from severe head injuries. This case was the subject of another award-winning film *The Laramie Project*.
- *David Morley* (d. 2004) was a gay man (and a barman at the Admiral Duncan, a gay pub in Soho, London) who was attacked and kicked in the head by youths near Waterloo Station. He was taken to hospital where he later died. The post-mortem found that he had suffered forty-four injuries, and had died from a haemorrhage as a result of a ruptured spleen and broken ribs.
- *Jody Dobrowski* (d. 2005) was a 24-year-old assistant bar manager murdered on Clapham Common, South London. He was beaten and kicked to death because he was perceived to be gay. The post-mortem revealed that he had a swollen brain, broken nose, and extensive bruising to his neck, spine and groin. He was so badly disfigured that his parents were unable to identify him.

As with many types of victimisation, hate crime based on sexuality and gender identity is massively under-reported (Peel, 1999). This is often because the victims fear further retribution, and/or the risk of being 'outed'. Because of the way in which hate crime statistics are recorded, it is difficult to separate out cases based on sexuality from those based on gender (or indeed to separate out crimes against different groups of LGBTQ people). Furthermore, it is difficult to undertake cross-national comparisons because of the varying ways in which different countries present publicly available data. Nevertheless, there are some data available which can give us an indication of the scale of the problem. FBI statistics (www.fbi.gov) indicate that in 2006 a total of 1,415 offences based on 'sexual orientation' were reported to police in the USA. In the same year there were seventy-eight incidences of police-reported homophobic hate crime in Canada (Canadian Centre for Justice Statistics: www.statcan.ca). Although police statistics for homophobic/transphobic hate crime are not publicly available in the UK, many incidents result in court proceedings and/or prosecution. Between April 2006 and March 2007, the UK Crown Prosecution Service (CPS) dealt with 822 cases of homophobic/transphobic hate crime nationally. Of these, 478 resulted in a guilty plea and 124 further cases resulted in conviction after trial: in all, a 73.5 per cent conviction rate (www.cps.gov.uk). Perpetrators were typically young (aged 16–20) white males (www.homeoffice.gov.uk). Since crime statistics in Australasia are recorded by type of crime rather than by motive, it is not possible to determine the prevalence of sexuality/gender identity motivated hate crime in Australia and New Zealand.

You will notice that there is no specific mention of biphobic crime in these statistics. The main reason for this is that it is assumed that bisexuals would be targeted because they were presumed to be lesbian or gay (and therefore victims of homophobic crime) or trans (and therefore victims of transphobic crime). There is, therefore, an implicit (and misguided) assumption that individuals are not (or cannot be) targeted on grounds of being bisexual. The US data are the only statistics to be broken down by category, and in 2006 only 1.5 per cent of all reported sexual orientation hate crimes were anti-bisexual compared with 62.3 per cent anti-gay (male), 20.7 per cent anti-homosexual (gender not specified), 13.6 per cent anti-lesbian, and 2.0 per cent anti-heterosexual (www.fbi.gov). It is worth noting that while the UK hate crimes legislation includes transphobic incidents, trans is not used as a person or motive category in the FBI's hate crime statistics (Juang, 2006), nor is it in most other countries.

There is a well-established body of psychological research on homophobic hate crime. US psychologist Gregory Herek is the main researcher in this field, and he has undertaken a number of studies exploring incidences of hate crime. Herek's work suggests that there are significant differences in levels of homophobic hate crime depending on the sexuality of the victim. For example, in a recent survey (Herek, 2009) comprising 662 participants, gay men were significantly more likely (37.6 per cent) to report experiences of anti-gay hate crime than were bisexual men (10.7 per cent), lesbians (12.5 per cent) and bisexual women (12.7 per cent). It would also appear from an earlier survey (Herek et al., 1997) that there are gender differences in the locations where such incidences occur. This study found that homophobic hate crimes against women tend to occur in private settings (e.g., their home or the perpetrator's home) and hate crimes against men tend to occur in public settings (e.g., within the proximity of a gay venue). The perpetrators of both types of hate crimes are mainly men.

One of the challenges faced by both researchers and practitioners is determining what constitutes a *homophobic* hate crime. Just because a crime is committed against someone who is LGBTQ (or against their property), it is not automatically hate-motivated. Although it is reasonable to assume that crimes are motivated by anti-gay prejudice given the prevalence of this form of prejudice within society, Herek and colleagues (Herek *et al.*, 1997) explored how lesbians and gay men infer that the incidents they experienced were motivated by homophobia. On the basis of interview data they identified three criteria: verbal cues (i.e., the perpetrator made anti-gay or anti-lesbian remarks), visibility cues (i.e., the incident occurred in a gay-identified location or situation) or contextual inferences (e.g., the incident occurred while the person targeted was known to be away at a gay event).

While a considerable number of anti-LGBTQ hate crimes result in physical injury and even death, psychological trauma is the most common outcome. In an in-depth survey of 2,259 LGB women and men living in or around Sacramento, California, those who had experienced a homophobic assault or other crimes against the person within the last five years were significantly more likely to exhibit symptoms of depression, traumatic stress, anxiety and anger than those who had experienced crimes not based on their sexuality, or who had not been crime victims (Herek *et al.*, 1999).

In hate-motivated crimes, outsiders usually attribute blame to the perpetrator. However, in a recent US study by sociologist Christopher Lyons (2006) this was not found to be the case with homophobic hate crimes. Based on a survey of 320 students, homosexual victims were blamed more (on average) than were heterosexual victims. Typically, homosexual victims were blamed for exhibiting partner affection (e.g. holding hands), which was deemed as more provocative than the same actions from heterosexual victims.

Research on hate crimes is clearly very important and informative about how prejudice against LGBTQ people is enacted and about the psychological effects of such prejudice. However, because it focuses on overt forms of prejudice – that is, things that have happened or might happen (i.e., acts of aggression or violence, the expression of anti-LGBTQ sentiments) – and discrete incidences, it is less useful for understanding the wider impact that hate crimes have. As Celia Kitzinger (1996b: 11–12) highlighted, hate crimes can be understood 'not as a random, opportunistic, or particularistic attack [against individuals] but rather as the targeting of members of specific groups as *symbols* of that group' (our emphasis). In other words, the acts not only harm their victims, but also send a message of intimidation to the wider LGBTQ community. Therefore, the actions that LGBTQ people take to *avoid* victimisation, and the actions that heterosexual people take to avoid being labelled 'gay' or 'lesbian', are equally relevant to understanding homophobic, biphobic and transphobic victimisation as are the incidents themselves.

Perceptions of the social climate

Rather than focusing on attitudes towards LGBTQ people and issues, or on homophobic behaviour, some psychologists have concentrated their attention on LGBTQ people's *perceptions* of their environment and their experiences of homophobic, biphobic and transphobic prejudice. These studies form a third strand to the study of homophobia, and are commonly referred to as 'climate studies'. Anthony D'Augelli, the key researcher featured in this chapter, was the first to do work on this aspect of homophobia (see Box 5.3).

Box 5.3   Key researcher: Anthony R. D'Augelli on why I study the campus climate for LGB students

My professional training and the geography of my university led me to a career of research on lesbian, gay and bisexual (LGB) youth. Penn State University, located in central Pennsylvania, USA, is a small city of over 40,000 students, surrounded by mountains and forests. Most undergraduates love being at Penn State, far away from parents, in a community focused on their needs and wants. However, I learned in the late 1980s that not all students were content. LGB students experienced the university as a hostile place. I discovered this when I became the academic adviser to the campus LGB student organisation.

I am a clinical psychologist and a community psychologist, a background that conditions me to sensitivity both to mental health problems and to the social and community circumstances that produce the problems. Attending the meetings of the LGB group, I overheard quiet discussions of many problems. As the students spoke among themselves, I became increasingly concerned about their welfare. The problems they shared were serious – depression, anxiety, excessive alcohol and drug use, thoughts of suicide – and had started in the years before college. The cause was the stresses associated with being LGB. Many knew their sexual orientation as early adolescents but did not share feelings with friends or family, expecting disapproval or rejection.

Those who disclosed their sexual orientation ('came out') before college were the most troubled; some had been the target of persistent verbal abuse from peers, criticism from confused parents, and indifference from teachers who silently watched as homophobia targeted the few who told ... or who could not hide. The distance from the towns they grew up in encouraged them to be more open at Penn State, but the risks of openness were still serious. There was widespread harassment of open LGB students, much of it occurring in university housing under the authority of professionals. The academic community in which these young adults lived – in an isolated bucolic setting – was not helping them become LGB adults, but to become victims. This victimisation jeopardised their studies, leading to academic records that were poor reflections of their talent. The earlier worries about being singled out, the fears of being hurt, the terror that others would find out, followed them to college.

I was determined that this had to stop. I used my clout as a tenured academic staff member to help the group gain resources from the university and to instruct them how to demand equal treatment and protection. When senior university officials continued to turn their backs on the problem, I turned to the most powerful tool I had to change the lives of these students – research! Such was the beginning of a 20-year project of published research on the lives of LGB youth and young adults (e.g., D'Augelli, 1989, 1992; Grossman and D'Augelli, 2006; Hershberger and D'Augelli, 1995). Thinking back on these studies, I take pride in knowing that the research helped restore safety and normality to the lives of these young people. Research can indeed change the world and psychological research – mine and that of many others – has made enormous contributions to the lives of LGB people.

Climate studies focus largely on documenting perceptions of how 'safe' or 'LGBTQ-friendly' a particular setting is (usually colleges and universities or workplaces in the USA, e.g., Brown *et al.*, 2004; D'Augelli, 1989; Eliason, 1996). In the main, this body of research comprises survey-based studies undertaken in a single institution for the purposes of monitoring equal opportunities for LGBTQ students on campus. In most cases both staff and students (LGBTQ and heterosexual) have been surveyed about the campus climate for LGBTQ people.

Although the findings of these studies vary somewhat, all indicate that homophobia on campus is common. For example, in D'Augelli's (1989) study, 75 per cent of lesbians and gay men surveyed had experienced verbal harassment, 25 per cent had been threatened with physical violence at least once, and 17 per cent had sustained property damage. Similarly, US sociologist William Norris (1991) found that more than 80 per cent of (LGB and heterosexual) staff and students surveyed had overheard stereotypical or derogatory remarks about lesbians, gay men and bisexuals. However, studies that survey both LGB and heterosexual students and/or staff generally suggest that the campus climate is less hostile than is reported in studies with exclusively LGB samples. For example, only 57 per cent of employees in US psychologist Michele Eliason's (1996) study thought that anti-LGB attitudes were prevalent, and in a study by US sociologists Malaney *et al.* (1997) only 25 per cent of students surveyed thought anti-LGBT attitudes were prevalent on campus. A detailed examination of past studies seems to suggest that differences in findings are more a function of the samples used, the questions asked and differences in the types of institutions than 'real' differences in the occurrence of homophobia. In particular, the fact that samples primarily comprising heterosexual people report less experience of a homophobic climate is to be expected. Although homophobia is not exclusively aimed at LGBTQ people, it is these people who are most directly affected by it and therefore most likely to report it in surveys.

There are also a few small-scale UK and US qualitative studies looking at campus climate within specific settings such as residence halls (e.g., Evans and Broido, 2002; Taulke-Johnson and Rivers, 1999). Despite employing small samples these studies offer valuable insights into LGBTQ students' experiences in residence halls. The main finding reported in this type of study centres on the difficulty that LGBTQ people have in 'coming out' in this context. Although some report feeling supported by the sense of community in their particular corridor/flat, others encountered hostility that made their life at university unnecessarily difficult.

Sonja's more recent research on the experiences of LGBTQ students in UK universities indicates that homophobia on campus is still perceived by LGBTQ people to be a significant problem, and is mainly perpetrated by other students (see Box 5.4).

Box 5.4   Key study: Sonja Ellis (2008) on homophobia in a university context

Participants in this study comprised 291 LGBT students (57 per cent male, 42 per cent female; 1 per cent unspecified) from forty-two universities in the UK. Based on surveys used in other campus climate studies, the questionnaire comprised twenty-five questions covering four main aspects of campus climate: actual harassment/discrimination, perceptions of campus climate, campus climate and outness, and LGBT inclusiveness. Of the students surveyed, 23.4 per cent indicated that they had on at least one occasion been a victim of homophobic harassment/discrimination. Most of these incidents comprised derogatory remarks (77.9 per cent), and direct or indirect verbal harassment/threats (47.1 per cent). However, less common forms of harassment were also reported, including pressure to be silent about being LGBT (16.2 per cent). Typically these incidents were reported to have taken place in public spaces on campus, and in the majority of cases (76.5 per cent) were perpetrated by other students. Consistent with other campus climate studies, many of these incidents occurred in student accommodation.

Despite the incidence of harassment, the majority of participants (79.4 per cent) thought that LGBT people were unlikely to be harassed on campus, and 77.7 per cent said that they felt comfortable being out on campus. However, around half of the participants reported having deliberately concealed or avoided disclosing that they were LGBT to avoid intimidation or other negative consequences. Furthermore, only 39.2 per cent agreed or strongly agreed that 'the university thoroughly addresses campus issues related to sexual orientation/gender identity' and only 17.5 per cent agreed that LGBT issues are adequately represented within the curriculum. Those studying for degrees in psychology, social science, education and medicine were significantly more likely ($U = 3230$, $N = 203$, $p < .004$) than those studying in other disciplines to report that LGBT issues were not adequately represented within the curriculum.

The overall findings of this study suggest that although homophobia on campus is not an overwhelming problem, it is still a significant one: and one that universities themselves encourage by failing actively to address issues of homophobia, transphobia, biphobia and heteronormative bias.

Despite the limitations of existing studies, research since the 1980s consistently suggests that verbal harassment and threats of physical violence on campus are relatively common. Although actual incidents of violence are small in comparison, the experiential climate for LGBTQ students is one that often inhibits them from being open about their sexuality and/or gender identity and requires them to collude in their marginalisation. For example, most LGBTQ students report not feeling comfortable disclosing their sexual identity and many report deliberately making changes to their behaviour (e.g., avoiding known lesbian/gay locations, '**passing**' as straight, dissociating from known LGBTQ people) in order to avoid harassment and discrimination (Taulke-Johnson and Rivers, 1999). As with any form of (overt or covert) harassment and discrimination, such an unsupportive climate places LGBTQ students at increased risk of psychological distress. However, a recent study by British social scientist Richard Taulke-Johnson (2008) of gay male students suggests that, for some students at least, this perceptibly homophobic climate is viewed much more positively. For example, some participants in this study reported that anti-gay sentiments were often manifested as jokes, which they perceived as an indicator that their friends or housemates were comfortable with the idea that they were gay. Moreover, despite the dominance of a discourse of homophobia, intolerance and victimisation, Taulke-Johnson's participants:

> framed and experienced university as a space where in spite of the pervasive assumptions, expectations, norms and regulations of compulsory heterosexuality … they were able to explore and engage with their sexual orientation, develop emotional intelligence and social sensitivity, [and] skilfully negotiate boundaries and restrictions regarding the display and performance of their homosexuality. (p. 131)

So, for some young people university is not experienced as an unsupportive social climate in which to develop a sense of oneself as lesbian, gay, bisexual, trans and/or queer.

Sexuality and gender identity prejudice as social marginalisation

Heterosexism

As a direct result of criticism of the term 'homophobia' outlined in the section on attitudes, the term 'heterosexism' was introduced into the psychological lexicon. Unlike homophobia, which constructs this form of prejudice as primarily directed against lesbians and gay men, heterosexism more readily encompasses prejudice against all non-heterosexuals by shifting the focus to heterocentricity or heterosexual bias. The term heterosexism also more explicitly encapsulates the notion of social marginalisation in that it mirrors the words used to describe other forms of systematic marginalisation (e.g., racism, sexism, classism). Like racism, sexism and classism, the term heterosexism recognises the marginalisation of LGBTQ people as social rather than individual. This construct was popularised in the late 1980s by Gregory Herek (1990: 316) who defined heterosexism as 'an ideological system that denies … and stigmatises any non-heterosexual form of behavior, identity, relationship, or community'.

Herek suggested that heterosexism manifests itself in two main ways: 'cultural heterosexism' and 'psychological heterosexism'. Cultural heterosexism (or **institutionalised homophobia**) refers to heterosexual bias in societal customs and institutions (e.g., religion, education and the legal system), resulting in the erasure and denial of LGBQ existence, customs and history, and, by implication, the privileging of heterosexual experiences, customs and history. Psychological heterosexism, on the other hand, refers to anti-LGBTQ attitudes and behaviour – all the aspects commonly understood as homophobia. When psychologists use the term heterosexism they are usually adopting the much broader definition (comprising both cultural and psychological aspects) and are therefore interested in the wider social structures which maintain sexuality and gender identity prejudice. It is worth noting at this point that the terms homophobia and heterosexism are often used interchangeably in the psychological literature, which is very confusing! However, if a writer offers social explanations for prejudice and uses qualitative methods, and their work is concerned with subtle forms of prejudice, they are usually studying social heterosexism rather than psychological homophobia (e.g., see Clarke, 2005a; Ellis, 2001).

Theory and research on heterosexism are typically based within a social constructionist framework (see Chapter 2). Rather than documenting attitudes and acts, they are concerned with exploring how people *do* prejudice – that is, how prejudice is produced and reproduced in discourse and social interaction, and through cultural artefacts (e.g., images, official documents, institutional norms). It therefore focuses on anti-LGBTQ prejudice in the everyday business of living. Since this approach places a premium on social interaction, it more readily explains apparent shifts in attitude from one context to the next, and is more sensitive to identifying subtle forms of prejudice.

Psychology itself has been the subject of studies about heterosexism. In 1996, Celia Kitzinger highlighted the way in which lesbians are systematically excluded from psychology, with any inclusion amounting to little more than tokenism (see also Chapter 2). Kitzinger suggested that psychologists often make a passing reference to lesbian issues in order to appear inclusive, rather than systematically including lesbian perspectives throughout their work (Kitzinger, 1996a). Although specifically writing about lesbians, her analysis is also true of GBTQ inclusion. Over a decade later, little had changed. In a survey of a wide range of undergraduate psychology textbooks, British psychologist Meg Barker (2007) found that some did not mention LGB sexualities at all, and where they did, these mentions mostly comprised a separate, small section on 'sexual orientation' rather than systematic coverage throughout. In parts of the textbooks where relationships were discussed, the vast majority of images, examples and reported studies were about heterosexual couples. Furthermore, about half of the books failed to mention bisexuality, and in other books the word bisexuality was simply subsumed into the category 'lesbian and gay' with no discussion specifically about bisexuality. This analysis shows that LGBTQ perspectives are not simply marginalised within psychology, but in many cases are systematically excluded.

Heterosexism can also be seen in common practices within society. One such practice is the medical treatment of intersex infants (see also Chapter 2). In infancy these individuals are assigned a male or female gender. The primary criterion for determining whether an infant should be assigned as male or female is whether it is possible to construct a vagina which, in adulthood, could be penetrated by a penis or whether, in adulthood, the phallus will be long enough to penetrate a vagina. This is a clear example of heterosexuality – or more specifically, penis-in-vagina intercourse – being taken as the norm, with the added implication that bodies that do not fit the conventional categories 'male' and 'female' are not normal.

Discursive studies of prejudice (e.g., Wetherall and Potter, 1992) show that even people who claim not to be prejudiced often articulate prejudiced sentiments in their talk. The most obvious examples are typically prefaced with a disclaimer along the lines of 'I'm not prejudiced but …' which is followed by a justification such as 'I wish they (lesbians and gay men) wouldn't kiss in public'. In these instances the disclaimer is used to manage speakers' self-presentation to enable them to express (what might be construed as) a prejudiced sentiment, yet avoid being challenged as prejudiced. For example, in British psychologist Brendan Gough's (2002) study of the discursive reproduction of homophobia, one participant, Martin, positions himself as liberal ('I've always tolerated it') before launching an attack on gay marchers:

> If it's treated like conventional heterosexuality, you've got your partner and you keep it to yourself and it's not flaunted, I've always tolerated it but what annoys me is when you see these gay marches, they're all dressed up in these perverted leathers, whatever it is, bondage gear – if they wanna do that in their own home then that's alright, but I think they're getting themselves a bad name. (p. 226)

British psychologists Susan Speer and Jonathan Potter (2000) undertook a similar analysis of heterosexism in talk (and text) in relation to gender inequality in sport and leisure. The findings of their study showed that speakers were sensitive to the possibility of being heard as heterosexist and employed a number of strategies to avoid their talk being heard in this way. Incidences of heterosexism such as these are referred to as **mundane heterosexism**, a term coined by Elizabeth in her study of lesbian and gay awareness training (see Box 5.5).

It is clear then that heterosexism is commonly reproduced and reinforced in a social context where it is typically unchallenged. This is seen in everyday life. Imagine you are in a pub on a Friday evening with some friends, and in the course of a casual conversation a heterosexual man compliments his friend (another heterosexual man) on his new haircut and one of their friends jokes that they are 'in love'. Rather than challenge it, most people (including many LGBTQ people) would not notice the offensive comment and would possibly even laugh along, thereby colluding in heterosexism. This is an example of how heterosexism is

Box 5.5   Key study: Elizabeth Peel (2001a) on mundane heterosexism

Mundane heterosexism refers to everyday or subtle incidents of heterosexism, which are either unnoticed or unnoticeable because they are socially normative. Elizabeth's study of mundane heterosexism draws on data from diversity training about sexualities: 'sessions specifically aimed at heightening awareness of heterosexism and providing information about lesbians and gay men' (p. 544). The thirteen training sessions – conducted with a range of professionals including youth and social workers, clinical psychologists and NHS helpline staff – were recorded and analysed using a form of discourse analysis.

The analysis highlights some of the ways in which people *do* mundane heterosexism. One of the ways in which people do this is to suggest that reverse discrimination is occurring in some form (i.e., that there is prejudice against heterosexuals). For example, in the following excerpt (taken from a discussion of shared rooms in halls of residences), Nekesh makes the argument that social norms discriminate against lesbians and gay men, and exploits this to suggest that in fact it is heterosexuals who are discriminated against:

NEKESH: … if you have two people gay or lesbian they come and share a room together compare them to a male and female sharing a room together there is no difference. But we stop male and female sharing a room together.

BILL: I was gonna say that

NEKESH: But we don't stop two of the same sex therefore there is discrimination here against the heterosexual in a way.

This discourse works by assuming a false equivalence between lesbians/gay men and heterosexuals that ignores the fact that 'the rule' of room sharing doesn't take into account lesbians and gay men in the first place. This discourse is problematic because it ignores the structural inequalities that work to marginalise lesbians and gay men.

Another way in which mundane heterosexism is manifest is by refusing to acknowledge diversity and difference between LGBTQ people and heterosexuals. The argument that LGBTQ people are being divisive and depriving the rest of society of resources by having separate resources (e.g., health services, community centres, funding) is commonplace. Often this type of argument is used to suggest that LGBTQ people are complicit in their own marginalisation and works to deflect attention away from the source of prejudice and back on to LGBTQ people. It also ignores the way in which separate provision is a means of redressing inequality which exists between different groups.

socially produced, and the way in which everyone (even those who would not ordinarily consider themselves to be prejudiced) can be positioned in relationship to prejudice – even just momentarily! Not to laugh at the joke would feel socially awkward. Often LGBTQ people collude in heterosexism by 'passing'. To give an example from (one of) our experiences, in order to avoid discrimination, Sonja has sometimes failed to correct strangers when they have assumed that she has a male partner. Similarly, when she and her partner are in the company of family they have avoided acts of affection such as snuggling up on the sofa in order to manage the (perceived) homophobia of their families. By implicitly changing our behaviour in these and other ways, we also collude in heterosexism. Resisting heterosexism is of course not always a straightforward choice. Often the way in which social inter-action is structured makes it difficult to challenge taken-for-granted assumptions. For example, in the case of trans or intersex individuals, assumptions about gender are particularly problematic. In the western world, our language and culture are constructed around the notion that there are two (and only two) dichotomous categories of gender. Therefore, in everyday conversation it is difficult to think and talk about gender without invoking this binary. Similarly, we tend to construct bodies as unquestionably male or female, and gender identities as congruent with physiological sex. Trans as a category challenges these constructions by illustrating that gender identity and natal sex are not always congruent, while intersex calls into question the idea that bodies are only male or female.

Heteronormativity

Related to the idea of heterosexism is the construct of heteronormativity. This term was coined in 1991 by the US social theorist Michael Warner and has its roots in queer theory (see Chapter 2). Heteronormativity refers to the perceived reinforce-ment of certain beliefs about sexuality within social institutions and policies. These beliefs include things like the notion that sex equals penis-in-vagina intercourse, that 'family' constitutes a heterosexual couple and their children, and that marriage is a procreative institution and therefore should only be avail-able to 'opposite-sex' couples. From this perspective, heterosexuality is viewed as the only natural manifestation of sexuality. Heteronormativity may also be viewed as the practices and institutions which legitimise and privilege normative hetero-sexuality and the heterosexual relationships which epitomise this (Cohen, 2005).

Despite this, heterosexuality is not inherently heteronormative – it is possible to argue that some forms of sex and relationships between men and women actually challenge taken-for-granted heteronormative assumptions. This is the case with 'queer heterosexuals' (see Thomas, 2000). Conversely, some forms of non-heterosexual sex and relationships may conform to heteronormative assumptions as is the case with '**straight-acting queers**' (LGBTQ people who do not exhibit stereotypical appearances or practices). However, heteronormativity is not simply about sexual practices, but rather about the 'ways in which heterosexual privilege is woven into the fabric of social life, pervasively and insidiously ordering every-day existence' (Jackson, 2006: 108). Therefore, LGBTQ people are more readily included in society when their lifestyles mirror that of normalised heterosexuality (e.g., their appearance is gender conventional and their relationships are romantic, monogamous and committed). So, rather than simply focusing on heterosexist practices, the ways in which heterosexuality itself functions to reinforce gendered norms and constrain behaviour become the keystone for understanding how LGBTQ sexualities are marginalised through heteronormativity.

One of the main ways in which heteronormativity is socially produced is through the institutionalisation of heterosexuality. In 1980, US lesbian feminist Adrienne Rich wrote a classic article 'Compulsory heterosexuality and lesbian existence' in which she highlighted how heterosexuality is institutionalised as both normative and natural (and simultaneously marginalising other forms of sexuality). She claimed that heterosexuality is an institution designed to serve the interests of men, rather than being natural for most women. Rich argued that women are 'duped' into being heterosexual through the promotion of romance, the eroticisation of the male body, rape, and the censoring of lesbian pleasure. Heterosexuality is therefore viewed as compulsory in that women's social, emotional and sexual needs are subordinated to ensure men's privileged sexual and emotional access to women's bodies. Although today LGBTQ people enjoy greater visibility than they did when Rich wrote this paper, heterosexuality is still promoted and rewarded in ways that ensure that other forms of sexuality remain marginalised.

We don't need to search very far to find everyday examples of heteronormativity in action. For example, even a trip to the shop to buy a card will uncover this – couple relationship anniversary cards typically use heterosexual imagery, and even where the imagery does not immediately suggest heterosexuality, cards often include phrases such as 'to my wife … from your loving husband'. Furthermore, you will be hard-pushed to find a 'congratulations on your coming out' card in any high street store. As we go about our daily lives we are constantly bombarded with images of normative heterosexuality in the media, in books and in advertisements. For anyone who lives as a non-heterosexual, every conversation with someone new is likely to involve the decision whether to come out or not, as any discussion about partners, marriage or everyday lives invariably invokes the assumption that one's partner is of a different sex (and indeed that one is in a monogamous relationship). In contrast, the very existence of heteronormativity means that there is no social imperative (or need) to identify or 'come out' as heterosexual.

Using naturalistic data from telephone conversations, some researchers have explored 'heteronormativity in action'. In one such study, British **conversation analysts** Victoria Land and Celia Kitzinger (2005) explored the way in which lesbian speakers challenge (or sometimes fail to challenge) the heterosexist presumption in telephone conversations. Drawing on a set of 150 telephone calls, they found that in institutional calls (e.g., calls to the dentist, car insurance companies, plumbers) lesbian speakers frequently had to manage the presumption that they were heterosexual. Their study showed that lesbians encountered considerable interactional difficulty in managing their lesbian identities with strangers because coming out in conversation disrupts tacit assumptions about the world. In contrast, a study of telephone conversations with heterosexual speakers (Kitzinger, 2005) illustrated the way in which heterosexuals continually and routinely present themselves and others as heterosexual within ordinary conversations, which are not ostensibly about sexuality or relationships.

Another way in which heteronormativity has been studied is through the exploration of the way in which language is used to police sexual (and gender) identities and regulate heterosexual behaviour. Terms such as 'poof', 'dyke' and 'gay' are used as put-downs when a person is seen as not conforming to gender norms. In a UK study of teenagers, sociologist Sue Sharpe (2002) found that such language served an important function in enforcing gender conformity and ensuring that compulsory heterosexuality is maintained. Other studies of slang terms, such as slang terms for genitals (e.g., Braun and Kitzinger, 2001) and for sexual identities (e.g., Peel, 2005), have also made a significant contribution to our understanding of the way in which sexual identities are regulated.

Gaps and absences

- Empirical work on the nature and incidence of biphobia and transphobia is extremely limited.
- The field is dominated by work on homophobic attitudes, with relatively few studies of the way in which prejudice is manifested in social contexts.
- We know little about the experience of multiple oppression (i.e., how racism and classism intersect with and shape experiences of homophobia).
- Although there is a growing literature on LGB awareness training (e.g., Peel, 2009) and anti-homophobia education (e.g., Hillman and Martin, 2002; Simoni, 1996), there is a need for sustained research which explores ways in which homophobia, heterosexism and heteronormativity might be addressed in order to effect positive social change.

Main chapter points

This chapter:

- Provided a brief overview of the legal and socio-political discrimination faced by LGBTQ people.
- Introduced the term 'homophobia' and outlined research on attitudes towards LGBTQ people (homophobia studies), behaviours perpetrated against LGBTQ people (hate crimes) and perceptions of homophobia (climate studies).
- Outlined some of the criticisms of essentialist approaches to sexuality and gender identity prejudice.
- Introduced the terms 'heterosexism' and 'heteronormativity' and highlighted the ways in which studies using discourse and conversation analytical methods have shed light on sexuality and gender identity prejudice in everyday talk.

Questions for discussion and classroom exercises

1. Find some real-life examples of mundane heterosexism and/or heterosexual privilege (hint: some good places to look include sexual health services, media advertisements, women's fashion and beauty magazines, and men's magazines). Discuss how these forms of heterosexism could be prevented and managed.

2. What are the benefits and limitations of using homophobia scales to study prejudice against LGBTQ people and/or issues?

3. What are the similarities and differences between sexuality prejudice and other forms of prejudice (e.g., how is homophobia/heterosexism different from racism? How is prejudice against LGBTQ people different from prejudice against disabled people?)

4. Why do you think certain groups (e.g., men, those with conservative religious views) might be more homophobic?

5. What different forms of prejudice and discrimination might a trans person encounter on a typical day at university. How could these forms of prejudice and discrimination be challenged?

Further reading

Gough, B. (2002) 'I've always tolerated it but …': heterosexual masculinity and the discursive reproduction of homophobia. In A. Coyle and C. Kitzinger (eds.), *Lesbian and gay psychology: new perspectives* (pp. 219–38). Oxford: BPS Blackwell.
This chapter presents an analysis of how gender and sexuality are negotiated in men's talk, and highlights the importance of homophobic discourse in the construction of heterosexual masculinities.

Harding, R. and Peel, E. (2007) Heterosexism at work: diversity training, discrimination law and the limits of liberal individualism. In V. Clarke and E. Peel (eds.), *Out in psychology: lesbian, gay, bisexual, trans and queer perspectives* (pp. 247–71). Chichester: Wiley.
Focusing specifically on the work context, this chapter highlights the way in which 'equality' and 'equal opportunity' reflect liberal viewpoints that often reinforce rather than remove discrimination against LGBTQ people. This chapter also provides an excellent critical overview of diversity training.

Herek, G. M. (2004) Beyond 'homophobia': thinking about sexual prejudice and stigma in the twenty-first century. *Sexuality Research and Social Policy*, 1(2), 6–23.
This paper provides an overview of the history and application of the term 'homophobia' and highlights its limitations. A critical discussion of alternative terms (e.g., 'sexual stigma', 'heterosexism', 'sexual prejudice') is also included.

Mulick, P. S. and Wright, L. W. (2002) Examining the existence of biphobia in the heterosexual and homosexual populations. *Journal of Bisexuality*, 2(4), 45–64.
This paper reports on an empirical study that explores whether biphobia is distinct from homophobia. The study demonstrates the existence of biphobia in both the heterosexual and the lesbian/gay communities, which supports the notion that bisexual individuals may be subject to double discrimination.

Tee, N. and Hegarty, P. (2006) Predicting opposition to the civil rights of trans persons in the United Kingdom. *Journal of Community and Applied Social Psychology*, 16, 70–80.
This study explores support for and opposition to the civil rights of trans people. Using regression analysis, opposition to the civil rights of trans people is correlated with hetero-sexism, authoritarianism, a belief that there are only two sexes, a belief that gender is biologically based and several demographic variables.

6   Health

Overview

- What is LGBTQ health?
- Sexual health
- Mental health
- Physical health

What is LGBTQ health?

The US National Gay and Lesbian Task Force defined lesbian and gay (and we would add BTQ) health issues as 'diseases or conditions which are unique, more prevalent, more serious and for which risk factors and interventions are different' from heterosexuals (and we would add from non-trans people) (Plumb, 1997: 365). LGBTQ health research spans a number of disciplines outside psychology (public health, medicine, nursing, **epidemiology**) and, invariably, incorporates very wide, and indeed disparate, areas of research.

Historically, the bodies of LGBTQ people have been subjected to the medical gaze. Just one example is the research conducted by the Committee for the Study of Sex Variants during the 1930s in New York, which aimed to establish scientific ways of identifying and treating ('curing') homosexuality. Researchers assumed that there would be physiological differences that distinguished lesbians from heterosexual women: skeletons were X-rayed and genitals were inspected looking for signs of masculinity (Terry, 1990). It was thought that evidence of pathology was visible on the body. Stevens (1992: 91–2) neatly summed up the prevailing view during this period:

> Until the late 1970s, lesbians were characterized by the medical profession as sick, dangerous, aggressive, tragically unhappy, deceitful, contagious, and self-destructive … Their encounters with health care systems were fraught with the ideological construction of lesbianism as a sin, a crime, and a sickness.

Understandably, early gay affirmative health research placed a heavy emphasis on demonstrating the 'health' and 'normality' of LGBTQ people. By contrast, present-day research, as you'll see in this chapter, documents and engages with the health difficulties and illnesses that affect LGBTQ people. What constitutes 'good' or 'bad' LGBTQ health, however, not only is very complex and influenced by multiple factors, but also is closely connected to prevailing ideologies. In the contemporary West, for instance, the hegemonic discourse of individual responsibility for health/illness shapes the types, focus and interpretation of much health research that is conducted (Petersen and Lupton, 1996). Just turn on the television and see how many self-improvement programmes about lifestyle and behaviour change there are (*You are what you eat* to name just one)! Individualism and the **biomedical** – and indeed the **biopsychosocial** – **model** are interrelated (Stam, 2000). The biomedical model focuses on physical processes (such as the physiology of a disease), but even the biopsychosocial model, which is less reductionist, places more emphasis on the individualistic than on the 'social' aspects of health and illness. Most research addressing LGBTQ health and illness is informed by the biomedical or biopsychosocial model and there has been a push in some countries (e.g., the USA; Epstein, 2003) for LGBTQ people to be the subjects of biomedical research. However, the principles and approaches of **critical health psychology** (Murray, 2004b) – which, among other things, challenges the 'victim blaming' associated with individualism (Crossley, 2000) – are starting to be applied to LGBTQ health psychology (see Box 6.8; see also Chapter 2 for more information about critical psychology).

Since the late 1970s, disparities in health between LGBTQ people and the assumed-to-be-heterosexual and non-trans general population have been a central research focus, alongside documenting LGBTQ people's experiences with health care and health care professionals (see Box 6.1). Disparities have often been understood as a product of both societal and interpersonal anti-LGBTQ prejudice in health care settings and from health care professionals (Peterson, 1996; see also Chapter 10). A Canadian report starkly makes this point through comparing mortality statistics for non-LGB and LGB people, documenting 'the number of "pre-mature" deaths caused by homophobia' (Banks, 2003: 9). This report calculated that the number of LGB suicides caused by homophobia is 818–968 per year and that the number of LGB deaths per year from smoking is 1,232–2,599, from alcohol abuse is 236–1,843 and from illicit drug use is 64–74.

LGBTQ health issues are now firmly on the health care agenda in a number of western countries. For example, LGBTQ health information is provided through the US Centres for Disease Control and Prevention, and the British Department of Health has a Sexual Orientation and Gender Identity Advisory Group. However, although 'LGBTQ health' is a useful catch-all term and is widely used in the academic literature, by advocacy organisations and in the 'grey literature' (i.e., policy documents and technical reports), it is a bit of a misnomer. **Health inequalities** and people's experiences of health and illness are mediated by far more than sexuality: economic wealth or poverty, race and culture, education and myriad other social, physiological and genetic influences all play a part in understanding the health of non-heterosexual and trans people. The experience of illness is also heavily gendered; it is rare, for example, for biological men to experience breast

Box 6.1   Key study: Patricia Stevens (1992) on lesbian health care research

In her influential review, US nursing professor Patricia Stevens examined twenty-eight different studies: nine about health care professionals' (HCPs) attitudes towards lesbians (published 1978–91) and nineteen about lesbians' attitudes towards health care/HCPs (published 1973–90). The studies that focused on HCPs' attitudes included nurses, doctors, psychologists/therapists and psychology students. Only one study exclusively focused on black lesbian and bisexual women's views (Cochran and Mays, 1988), and Stevens could only find studies conducted in the USA. Key findings were:

Health care providers' attitudes

- Lesbianism was still considered an affliction by many HCPs.
- Significant numbers of doctors and nurses were uncomfortable providing care for lesbian patients, regularly refusing services to lesbian women.
- Many inappropriately associated high rates of HIV infection and transmission with lesbian patients.
- Nurses and doctors viewed lesbians as 'unnatural', 'disgusting', 'immoral', 'perverted' and 'criminal' and their interactions with lesbian patients evoked emotions such as 'pity', 'disgust', 'repulsion', 'unease', 'embarrassment', 'fear' and 'sorrow'.

Lesbians' health care experiences

- Lesbians believed HCPs were 'generally condemnatory toward and ignorant about them. They frequently interpreted health care provider behavior as hostile and rejecting and feared for their safety in health care interactions. Upon disclosure of their lesbian identity, they experienced many kinds of mistreatment' (p. 109), including rough physical handling, breaches of confidentiality and voyeuristic curiosity.
- The studies showed that HCPs' heterosexist assumptions were a major hindrance to effective therapeutic communication.
- Some women were inappropriately referred to mental health professionals.
- The health care settings that were seen as most hazardous were emergency services, inpatient hospital care, long-term care and surgery.
- Lesbians delayed seeking health care because of their fears and their poor health care experiences.

Are the findings of Stevens's review still relevant today? Unfortunately, evidence of heterosexism and homophobia in health care is present in more recent research exploring both HCPs' attitudes towards LGB patients and LGB people's views about health care services (Beehler, 2001; Eliason and Schope, 2001; Hinchcliff *et al.*, 2005 – see also Box 6.6). By comparison, a recent US survey of **female-to-male (FTM)** trans people found 70 per cent of the 122 respondents rated the quality of their health care as 'good' or 'excellent' (Rachlin *et al.*, 2008).

cancer and impossible for biological women to get prostate cancer. Health research is, therefore, often more segregated along gender lines than many other areas of LGBTQ psychology – and this chapter mirrors this division to some degree. Indeed, some argue that LG(BTQ) health research should be completely disaggregated, not only because different health issues affect different sections of these communities, but also to avoid a disproportionate focus on gay men's health (Wilkinson, 2002).

As the study of LGBTQ health has developed as a field of research, it has been increasingly recognised that various approaches to health (i.e., those that focus on positive health outcomes, those that examine the social contexts of health and illness, and those that acknowledge the incidence of poor health within certain LGBTQ communities) should be examined in conjunction with one another (e.g., Adams *et al.*, 2007). Also important to the study of LGBTQ health is the role that gay men and lesbians, in particular, have played in advocating for social change in relation to health: for example, by developing HIV/AIDS prevention programmes and setting agendas for meeting their health needs (Rofes, 2007; Wilton, 1997). In this chapter we cannot do justice to the vast and varied number of health and illness issues that affect LGBTQ people; we do, however, signpost key aspects of 'LGBTQ health' and navigate you through a wide-ranging set of literatures. Although we divide 'sexual', 'mental' and 'physical' health into discrete sections, it's important to recognise that all of these aspects of health mutually inform and affect each other. Therefore, although cervical cancer is typically considered under the banner of 'sexual health', cancer is a physical illness, and although disordered eating is seen as a 'mental health' issue, it can have physical health consequences. Similarly, smoking or substance (mis)use are (ill)health behaviours we consider in the 'physical health' section, but they can have mental and sexual health correlates.

Sexual health

In this section we focus on gay, lesbian and bisexual sexual health because the majority of the literature coheres around these identities. In terms of the sexual health of trans people, the limited research suggests that HIV and other sexually transmitted infections (STIs) are prevalent in trans communities: unprotected anal, vaginal and oral sex were identified as the most commonly reported risky behaviours in a US sample of 181 trans people (Bockting *et al.*, 2005). US-based clinical psychologist Walter Bockting and colleagues found that their participants indicated problems with sexual functioning (and discrimination and mental health problems), and it has been suggested that doctors should routinely include sexual health history taking in general health assessments with trans people (Feldman and Bockting, 2003).

Gay and bisexual men's sexual health

Research on gay, bisexual and men who have sex with men's (MSM) health has, from the 1980s onwards, been dominated by a focus on HIV/AIDS prevention (see Boxes 6.2 and 6.3). A review of the literature in the journal database

Box 6.2   Key researcher: Paul Flowers on why I study gay men's sexual health

I began studying gay men's sexual health as an undergraduate for my final-year research project. At around the same time I was doing voluntary work for a local HIV prevention and care charity. When I began to read the psychological literature regarding gay men and HIV prevention I was struck by the huge disparity between these two worlds. Health psychology theory and the application of traditional research methods seemed to actively construct gay men in ways that were so different from both my own experiences as a gay man and my experiences of working with other gay men.

One of the oddest things I struggled with was the way in which sexual conduct, so visceral and deeply interactive, could possibly be transformed into individual cognitions regarding 'health behaviour'. Clearly, HIV risk reduction was important and central to the survival of many gay men, yet to try and seek explanation and illustrate practical usefulness on the basis of the similarity of sexual conduct to something like vaccination behaviour seemed both short sighted and misguided. The need to breach these two worlds and to ensure that research is ultimately useful led me to engage with a wide range of research methodologies.

For me, working within a pragmatic research framework enables me to embrace a range of approaches from the idiographic and phenomenological, to large-scale quantitative behavioural surveillance (e.g., Flowers et al., 2002). Explaining and measuring the experiences of gay men in terms of their understandings of sex and sexual health offers an interesting and useful framework within which to study as an applied health psychologist. As a psychologist, exploring individual people's experiences in the context of their socio-cultural complexity lends itself to an insightful, educational and reflexive journey. I have been privileged enough to listen to people tell me about how their sexual conduct is deeply embedded in both their autobiography and their particular cultural frame. I have been shown how the scope of sexual decision-making is shaped by interactions with sexual partners, and the particularities of the location and time frame of sexual activity (e.g., Flowers et al., 2000). Through working with a host of HIV charities and statutory agencies I have a good understanding of how, in order to succeed, health promotion must engage with both the 'messy' aspects of sex, within its various cultural and temporal contexts, and the dilemmas of imposing the rationale of health therein.

In addition to researching HIV risk reduction, I have also become more and more interested in the challenges of living with HIV in an era of effective treatment and medicalisation. My voluntary work continues and now extends to include both policy and government work addressing HIV prevention, sexual health and HIV care.

Box 6.3   Key study: Paul Flowers and colleagues (2003) on the meaning of Scottish gay men learning their HIV status

In the West, the development of effective treatments for HIV (e.g., highly active anti-retroviral therapy – HAART) offer improved patient survival: a diagnosis of HIV has changed from a 'death sentence' to a 'life sentence'. HIV testing among gay men, from a biomedical perspective, is important to reduce 'the relatively high proportion of undiagnosed HIV positive gay men', increase 'access to appropriate medical care and ... reduce new HIV infections' (p. 180). Rates of HIV testing tend to be lower in the UK than in other countries (such as the USA and Australia). As such, British professor of sexual health psychology Paul Flowers and colleagues were interested in examining gay men's own understandings of HIV testing using IPA methodology (see Chapter 3).

Method

- Flowers *et al.* interviewed eighteen gay men, and a further nineteen gay men participated in focus groups.
- Participants were overwhelmingly white, their average age was mid-30s and they had diverse experiences of HIV testing. Some had never had a HIV test and some had tested once, or more. Twelve of the participants (32 per cent) were HIV positive, others were negative and some didn't know their status.
- Questions asked included: 'What are the advantages/disadvantages of having an HIV test?' and 'What are the current reasons why gay men do not want to get tested?'

Findings

1. *Reducing uncertainty: a reason to test for HIV.* An important reason for having a test was to achieve 'peace of mind'. For participants unsure of their status but expecting a negative test result, a negative test result was understood to reduce uncertainty. For those who had had a negative result it could suspend 'guilt' or 'worry' about prior risky sex, could motivate behaviour change or could lead to a sense of complacency about HIV risk taking.
2. *Coping with an uncertain future: a reason not to test for HIV.* For other participants the 'fear' of a positive test result could delay or dissuade them from testing. Their fear was largely based on their uncertainty about how they would cope with being positive.
3. *Living with uncertainty.* Some participants lived with the possibility of HIV infection in the back of their minds and remained 'blissfully ignorant' of their HIV status.

Flowers *et al.* concluded by suggesting that: (1) HIV testing cannot be understood solely from a biomedical perspective and gay men's decisions about testing are contextual and have multiple (and changing) meanings; and (2) HIV testing policy and service provision should be grounded in gay men's own beliefs about HIV testing.

MEDLINE (from 1980 to 1990) found that 56 per cent of LGBT health articles concerned HIV and STIs in gay and bisexual men (Boehmer, 2002). Although the continued emphasis on HIV/AIDS is to some extent understandable in countries where gay men continue to be over-represented in HIV transmission rates – and where research funding is (comparatively) easy to come by because it is high on the public health agenda – it has resulted in the neglect of other areas of gay and bisexual men's health. Whether HIV/AIDS is 'de-gayed' and seen as an 'equal opportunities' virus, or whether the connection between gay men and HIV/AIDS is emphasised is a contested issue that has ramifications for whether people are seen as 'homophobic' or not (Kitzinger and Peel, 2005). Celia Kitzinger and Elizabeth Peel (2005) found that when HIV/AIDS was discussed in LGB diversity training it was the gay male trainers who stressed the connection with gay men, while heterosexual trainees played down the connection – a very different scenario to the 1980s when AIDS was publicly conceptualised as a 'gay plague'. These findings draw attention to the importance of looking at talk about illness (and health) in its everyday context of use.

A focus on 'risk behaviours' and on gay and bisexual men as 'failing' to prevent HIV transmission has meant that HIV/AIDS research often has pathologising undertones where 'processes of risk construction are far from innocuous, [as] they provide a readily available framework of responsibility and blame which posits the burden of the epidemic increasingly upon the shoulders of the infected' (Flowers, 2001: 68). In response to this 'victim blaming', some research has moved away from a focus on individualised responsibility for health, and has instead undertaken an examination of the social correlates of gay men's health behaviours. A variety of psychosocial factors have been identified as influencing risky sexual behaviours (primarily unprotected anal intercourse or **barebacking**) amongst MSM including: self-esteem; social support; feelings of optimism and fatalism; the need for escapism; age; education; alcohol or drug use; the need to affirm gay identity; and the desire to seek intimacy (Flowers *et al.*, 1997a, 1997b; Hospers and Kok, 1995).

Research on HIV/AIDS shows how social disparities *within* gay and bisexual male communities make certain men more vulnerable to illness than others. For example, mainstream HIV/AIDS prevention programmes typically use the (supposedly) inclusive term MSM, which, in emphasising sexual behaviour over sexual identity, aims to decrease STIs. However, at the same time, mainstream HIV/AIDS prevention programmes often rely on white, western understandings of disease, sex and sexuality. This means that transmission rates among (primarily, racially marginalised) communities where particular understandings of sexuality (e.g., a 'gay identity') are less salient, or are irrelevant, may not be reduced by mainstream prevention programmes that fail to target or understand the needs of such groups (Cáceres, 2002). Research also indicates that socio-economic marginalisation can increase vulnerability to HIV among racially marginalised groups because racial and socio-economic marginalisation are often closely related (Nemoto *et al.*, 2004). These forms of social marginalisation can increase the likelihood of gay men engaging in sex for payment, as well as intravenous drug use, and therefore increase the likelihood of these groups of gay men experiencing HIV transmission (Peterson *et al.*, 2001). For example, research comparing white and African American gay and bisexual men has found that although both groups report having similar knowledge about HIV transmission, African American men are more vulnerable to HIV transmission for socio-economic reasons (Peterson *et al.*, 1992).

Researchers suggest the need to explore the social contexts in which health disparities between heterosexual and gay men occur (where the latter tend to be disadvantaged by social exclusion, discrimination and lack of services), and also to examine how we measure and understand sexual health (e.g., Meyer, 2001). Much of the current literature on 'barebacking' provides a good example of why it is important to examine how sexual health is measured, and the social contexts surrounding sexual health (e.g., Gauthier and Forsyth, 1999). This literature examines the behaviours of MSM who have unprotected anal intercourse and, in particular, the behaviours of men who do so without knowing their sexual partner's HIV status (therefore putting themselves at risk of HIV). Research on barebacking is often said to produce a 'moral panic' because it can seem as though large numbers of gay men are aiming to become HIV positive or at least that gay men are careless about their sexual health (Halperin, 2007). Such research contributes to the pathologisation of gay men, partly because it conceptualises health in terms of 'risk factors' and 'behaviour change', and frames 'good health' in moral terms (Barker *et al.*, 2007; Riggs, 2005). Not only does such an approach to understanding gay men's sexual health reinforce normative understandings of what it means to be 'healthy', but it also marginalises gay men's own accounts of morality, health and sexual practice.

One of the implications of the central focus accorded to HIV status in much research on gay men's sexual health is that HIV is understood as *the* organising principle around which gay men's identities revolve. While HIV is an important health concern within gay men's communities, it is typically treated as the *only* concern for gay men, and can become overemphasised both within research and among gay men. Research on barebacking, although important for its role in HIV prevention, can contribute to the marginalisation of HIV positive men, and can problematically normalise HIV among HIV negative men (Riggs, 2006a). Appreciating the complexity of gay and bisexual men's sexual health requires approaches that are mindful of social contexts and recognise men's own interpretations of their health and sexuality (see Box 6.3).

Of course sexual health is not solely about STIs and HIV/AIDS. Gay and bisexual men's sexual health is also about positive experiences of sex and how gay community norms and expectations impact on gay and bisexual men's sexual health. Sexual health, when viewed holistically, is not just about particular sexual behaviours, the amount of sex men have, and the prevention of STI transmission. Rather, it is about recognising how sexual health is the result of multiple health and demographic factors that together determine how particular MSM live and behave.

Lesbian and bisexual women's sexual health

Although there are a small number of studies that specifically focus on 'lesbian' sexual health issues (e.g., Bailey *et al.*, 2004; Evans *et al.*, 2007), the sexual health, and sexual health needs, of LBQ women and other 'women who have sex with women' (WSW) have been essentially ignored in the psychological literature. Within psychology (and the social sciences more broadly) there is a large body of theory and research on sexual health; however, this primarily centres on pregnancy and the transmission of STIs through heterosex.

The absence of research on non-heterosexual women's sexual health is mostly attributable to the heteronormative construction of sex and sexuality in the field of sexual health research, and in society more generally. This absence can also be attributed to the widespread (and false) assumption that STIs cannot be transmitted through woman-to-woman sex and that lesbians exclusively engage in non-risky sexual activities with other women, and therefore lesbian sexual practices constitute 'safe' sex. The notion of 'epidemiological irrelevance' is problematic, in that, by conflating sexual practice and sexual identity, it (wrongly) constructs lesbians as having no sexual health needs. It also ignores the fact that lesbians can get raped by men, or have sex with men through choice or for money (Lampon, 1995). Moreover, it assumes that STIs and other sexual health issues stem exclusively from sexual practices, ignoring the risks of transmission through intravenous drug use and self-insemination (see Chapter 9). By failing to discuss women's sexual health within a specifically non-heterosexual context, the needs of bisexual women and other WSW are rendered invisible. Moreover, since LBQ women vary considerably in their sexual practices, their sexual histories, the number, frequency and gender of their sexual partners, and their engagement in other potentially risky activities (e.g., IV drug use), it makes little sense to define sexual health needs in relation to sexual identity.

Medical research suggests that the transmission of STIs through woman-to-woman sex is low. However, low risk does not equate to *no* risk. Although woman-to-woman transmission of most STIs is rare, more than 10 per cent of women with exclusively female partners have a history of STIs (Bauer and Welles, 2001), and bacterial vaginosis (bacteria that cause vaginal discharge) is more common in WSW than it is in exclusively heterosexual women (Evans *et al.*, 2007; Hughes and Evans, 2003). In addition, genital warts (human papillomavirus (HPV)) and thrush (candidiasis) are also common in WSW (Bailey *et al.*, 2004; Marrazzo *et al.*, 2005). Despite the evidence that there is at least *some* potential risk from woman-to-woman sex, US studies of perceptions of risk and susceptibility among lesbian women suggest that few WSW believe themselves to be 'at risk' and most are ill informed of the potential risks posed by exposure to vaginal fluid (Dolan and Davis, 2003; Montcalm and Meyer, 2000). For example, using interview and focus group data, US sociologists Kathleen Dolan and Phillip Davis (2003) found that many women accepted the myth of *physical* immunity to STIs on the basis of being lesbian. In addition, many women constructed themselves as *socially* immune from infection on the basis of problematic assumptions of being able to trust their partners, of women being more trustworthy than men, and of the idea that honesty and communication could ward off infection. This seems to suggest that WSW have little awareness of their susceptibility to risk.

The notion of '**safer sex**' for lesbians is invisible in mainstream health promotion (MacBride-Stewart, 2004). Attempts to address 'lesbian' sexual health have failed to recognise the diversity in the sexual practices WSW engage in and the focus is almost exclusively on oral sex. For this reason, if it occurs at all, safer sex promotion centres on the use of dental dams (latex squares) during oral sex (cunnilingus). One of the problems with this approach is that dental dams are difficult to obtain (although some women use cling film or split condoms), and tend only to be promoted at LGBTQ events rather than through, for example, school-based education programmes. However, even where they are promoted, uptake is low and use appears only to increase with enhanced awareness of risk, and knowing other lesbians who have contracted STIs (Montcalm and Myer, 2000). At the same time, the promotion of dental dams can be complicit in the pathologisation of woman-to-woman oral sex by constructing it as inevitably risky or dangerous (MacBride-Stewart, 2004). For example, dental dams aren't promoted to heterosexuals who engage in the identical sexual practice and cunnilingus performed by a man on a woman is generally seen as a 'low risk' sexual activity.

The other area of lesbian sexual health which has been investigated is sexual health care practices, notably lesbian women's engagement in cervical screening and breast self-examination. The UK National Lesbians and Health Care Survey (Fish and Anthony, 2005; Fish and Wilkinson, 2000) surveyed 1,066 lesbians from 117 of the 122 UK postcode areas. The authors of the survey found that only 55 per cent of lesbians reported regular attendance for a cervical/pap smear test. The most common reason given by participants for non-attendance was 'not needing' a smear test because they hadn't had sex with men and/or they had been told by a health care professional that as a lesbian they did not need one. Both of these explanations are problematic. Although engaging in penis-in-vagina intercourse appears to be a significant risk factor in cervical cancer, focusing solely on this ignores other factors (e.g., smoking) that may put one at risk. Similarly, although we should be able to rely on health care professionals' advice, they (like many lay people) often assume that lesbians have never had (nor will have) sex with men and so are not at risk.

Mental health

Homosexuality and trans as mental illness

Historically, LGBTQ people were considered mentally ill simply because they were not heterosexual or did not conform to gender norms. As we discussed in

Chapter 1, although the diagnostic category 'homosexuality' was removed from the DSM in 1973 (and its successor 'ego-dystonic homosexuality' was removed in 1987) it wasn't until 1993 that homosexuality was removed from the World Health Organisation's International Classification of Diseases (ICD). However, it is worth noting that the category 'ego-dystonic sexual orientation' (in the ICD) and 'gender identity disorder' (in the DSM) have persisted; the latter is still widely used as a diagnostic category instead of 'transsexualism'. Gender identity disorder is extremely controversial in that it rests on the popular stereotype that trans people cross-dress or transition for sexual reasons (see also Chapter 7). In so doing, the notions of 'gender identity' and 'sexual identity' are conflated, which is unhelpful for understanding the lives of trans people and the distinctions between being trans and being LGB (Lombardi and Davis, 2006). The persistence of both 'ego-dystonic sexual orientation' and 'gender identity disorder' as diagnostic categories, and the history of homosexuality and trans as pathology in clinical diagnosis, mean that there is still much potential for LGBTQ people to be stigmatised in mental health settings.

Although few psychologists today would view LGBTQ people as mentally ill simply by virtue of identifying as LGBTQ, as we noted in Chapter 1, prior to the 1970s much psychological research focused on whether or not homosexuals were sick and how they could be cured (Morin, 1977). Because the discourse of 'homosexuality as pathology' was prevalent at that time, it was not uncommon for LGBTQ people to be incarcerated in psychiatric institutions or subjected to aversion therapy (lesbians tended to be locked up and gay men to be 'treated' with aversion therapy). Aversion therapy is a form of psychiatric/psychological treatment in which the patient is exposed to a stimulus while simultaneously being subjected to some form of discomfort. Such therapies included applying electric current via electrodes while men were shown pictures of naked men; chemical castration (use of hormonal drugs to eliminate sexual arousal); or injections of apomorphine to induce violent illness. Unsurprisingly, aversion therapy had a very high failure rate and often produced depression and suicide in patients. Ironically, it was therefore responsible for *causing* (rather than curing) mental illness.

Social stress and LGBTQ mental health

In contrast, more recent work on mental health has focused on social stress as the key mediator of mental health problems among LGBTQ people. In the general mental health literature, indicators of **subclinical** distress (e.g., affective disorders, anxiety and substance use disorders) have been found to be reactive to social stress (Dohrenwend, 2000). Therefore, widespread social stigma in relation to LGBTQ identities places LGBTQ people at higher risk of mental illness. However, the psychological literature on mental health has largely failed to recognise this (Nelson, 1994).

What is known about the mental health of LGBTQ people is limited, and mainly relies on a patchy collection of studies using self-report data from samples largely comprised of white, middle-class, US lesbians and gay men. In part this is due to sampling difficulties (see Cochran, 2001; see also Chapter 3). However, it is compounded by the fact that information about the sexual identity of clients is not routinely collected by mental health professionals. So, unless a client raises sexual identity as an issue, it is unlikely that the impact (if any) of sexual identity related issues on the person's mental health will be explored. The research literature in this field also focuses more heavily on (lesbian and bisexual) women than on men. This is largely a function of the gendered nature of engagement with mental health professionals – mental health clinics being the source from which samples are typically drawn – but also of the commonly held assumption that women are more susceptible to mental health problems than are men. This is reinforced by the fact that women are several times more likely to approach health professionals about potential mental health issues, and women are more readily diagnosed as suffering from depression and anxiety than men (Kerr and Emerson, 2003). Furthermore, the general literature around suicidality suggests that men are much more likely than women to succeed at committing suicide. Since it is often difficult in suicide cases to establish the factors that led to the suicide, and information about sexuality and gender identity is seldom collected, it is difficult to determine the extent to which sexuality and gender identity issues were factors. For all these reasons, what we know about the mental health of LGBTQ people is primarily derived from non-clinical populations and almost exclusively comprises indicators of subclinical distress rather than severe and persistent mental illness (i.e., that involving official clinical diagnosis and treatment).

Another problem is that almost nothing is known about the epidemiology of mental illness experienced by LGBTQ people from marginalised racial and cultural groups. The literature on such groups is scarce and relies heavily on anecdotal material from clinical settings. According to US psychologist Beverly Greene (1997), LGBTQ people from marginalised racial and cultural communities experience '**double jeopardy**': they are marginalised within their racial and cultural communities because they are LGBTQ and their 'lifestyle' is stigmatised and excluded within LGBTQ communities as a result of white ethnocentricity. A sense of never fully belonging in either community often results in feelings of isolation and estrangement, which may in turn lead to increased psychological vulnerability to mental illness.

Although much psychological (and medical) research uses samples of LGBTQ people in isolation, recent studies that compare LGB people and their heterosexual siblings (e.g., Balsam *et al.*, 2005; Rothblum and Factor, 2001), or unrelated heterosexual people (e.g., King *et al.*, 2003; Koh and Ross, 2006), consistently report that LGBTQ people are at greater risk of mental illness than their heterosexual counterparts. From a US survey sample of 524 lesbians, 143 bisexual women and 637 heterosexual women, Koh and Ross (2006) found that 56.7 per cent of lesbians and 53.2 per cent of bisexual women had been treated for depression, compared with only 42.1 per cent of heterosexual women, a highly statistically significant difference ($p < .01$). A large-scale Australian survey of

5,476 LGBT people found the prevalence of depressive disorders to be very high (Pitts *et al.*, 2006). In this study, 70 per cent of men and 80 per cent of women reported a lifetime prevalence of depressive disorders, with half of all participants having seen a counsellor or psychiatrist in the past five years. Although the reported incidence of depression varies considerably from study to study, depression is consistently reported as the most common diagnosis of mental illness among LGBTQ people, followed by anxiety. By and large, participants reporting depression and anxiety have been treated at a subclinical level (and have not been hospitalised), which seems to support the notion that social stress is an important underlying issue in the mental health of LGBTQ people. It is important to note that research on the mental health of bisexual and trans people is extremely limited. However, it would seem that bisexual women and trans people are particularly susceptible to mental health problems (Mathy *et al.*, 2003; Pitts *et al.*, 2009). Taken together, the incidence of mental health problems attributable to stress and prejudice is likely to be considerable.

Many studies on the mental health of LGBTQ people have also reported significantly higher levels of suicidality among LGBTQ youth than among the general population (see also Chapter 7). Although suicidal ideation (suicidal thoughts) is often used as a measure of suicidality, this construct is particularly problematic in that it is difficult to measure definitively. However, self-report studies consistently indicate that the incidence of attempted suicide and para-suicide (deliberate self-harm) among young LGBTQ people is considerably higher than it is for young heterosexual people (Roberts *et al.*, 2004). For instance, one UK study of 1,285 LGB people in England and Wales found that 31 per cent of the participants had attempted suicide (Warner *et al.*, 2004). This has also been found to be the case in non-western contexts (e.g., in Taiwan, Kuang *et al.*, 2003). Most studies estimate the rate of attempted suicide for heterosexual young people at around 10 per cent: young LGBTQ people are at least twice as likely to attempt suicide as their heterosexual counterparts (Roberts *et al.*, 2004).

LGBTQ people's interactions with mental health professionals

Research has also explored the extent to which LGBTQ people interface with mental health professionals (e.g., counsellors and therapists), what they think about the 'psy' professions and *how* therapy with LGBTQ people should be conducted (or not!). See Box 6.4 for further discussion of this and Box 6.5 for guidelines for conducting therapy with LGBTQ people. To date, no work has been conducted specifically on GBQ men's use of mental health services. However, one study indicates that men were less likely than women to report having been in therapy, but more likely to have experienced a psychiatric hospitalisation before the age of 18 (Balsam *et al.*, 2005). For women, on the other hand, there are a number of studies which focus on utilisation of mental health services. These studies report that more than 70 per cent of LBQ women have received outpatient treatment (e.g., counselling or therapy) for mental health problems

Box 6.4 *Highlights: therapy (and what type of therapy) or no therapy? That is the question!*

Given the lengthy history of the psychology, psychiatry and psychotherapy professions treating LGB(TQ) people inappropriately there has been a lot of debate about whether non-heterosexuals in general, and lesbians in particular, should engage with therapeutic professions when they are experiencing mental health difficulties. For instance, a debate was published in the journal *Feminism & Psychology* in the early 1990s, which explored anti-therapy and pro-therapy positions. British clinical psychologist Rachel Perkins (1991) argued, from a lesbian feminist perspective, that even psychological therapies that *aim* to be affirming and women-centred are anti-lesbian and anti-feminist because lesbian feminism and therapy are fundamentally incompatible. For Perkins, therapy is based on individualised and psychologised explanations and feminism is political and focused on patriarchy and women's oppression. She also argued that lesbians should foster and rely on their own communities to provide support in times of psychological need, rather than depend on psychological professionals and therapies (Kitzinger and Perkins, 1993). By contrast, US feminist therapist Laura Brown (1992) was optimistic about therapy for lesbians. She stressed the positive elements of a politically aware feminist therapy for lesbians and contrasted this with (problematic) non-feminist therapy for lesbians.

In contemporary discussions about therapy with LGBTQ people the issue isn't whether LGBTQ people should or shouldn't undergo therapy, but which therapeutic approaches are 'best', and what makes therapy 'gay affirmative'. The nature of the debate has changed, in part because more 'affirmative' therapy is available and more LGBTQ people themselves are practising psychologists and therapists, and also because non-heterosexuals are more likely to use psychotherapy or counselling services than are heterosexuals (Malley and Tasker, 2007).

(e.g., Razzano *et al.*, 2002; Robert *et al.*, 2004). Depression and relationship problems are frequently reported as the primary reasons for seeking support, again suggesting that problems with mental health are largely attributable to social stress.

The high use of mental health services among LGBTQ people, particularly women, is extremely problematic when put into the heterocentric (and sometimes even homophobic) context of therapy. Although therapy need not be seen as inherently problematic, a legacy of sexuality and gender identity pathologisation has meant that, in practice, mental health services are often ill equipped to address the mental health needs of LGBTQ people (see Box 6.6). For example, in a survey of 217 bisexual women and men, US private practitioner Emily Page (2004) found that respondents' experiences with mental health professionals were far from positive. Respondents reported that staff lacked knowledge of bisexual issues,

Box 6.5 *Highlights: guidelines for providing affirmative therapy to non-heterosexual and trans clients*

British social psychologist Darren Langdridge (2007b: 32) adapted guidelines for LGB (and we would add TQ) affirmative practice. For readers interested in pursuing a career as a clinical or counselling psychologist or therapist we have reproduced (a slightly modified version of) these guidelines (see also Davies 1996).

Therapists should:

- interrogate their own LGBTQ feelings
- not enter into therapeutic arrangements which imply that LGBTQ identities are pathological or undesirable
- recognise and work with the oppression all LGBTQ people have experienced
- work to deprogramme internalised stereotypes of LGBTQ people
- work to explore awareness of feelings, especially anger, amongst LGBTQ clients
- encourage the development of an LGBTQ support network
- support LGBTQ clients in engaging in consciousness-raising activities
- encourage LGBTQ clients to develop their own value system, mindful of the risk of relying on society's systems for self-validation
- work to lessen shame and guilt around LGBTQ thoughts and feelings
- use the weight of their authority to affirm LGBTQ thoughts and feelings.

and clients experienced invalidation and pathologisation of their bisexual identities, including the assumption that their bisexuality was connected to clinical issues when it wasn't, and the assumption that their bisexual attractions/behaviour would disappear when they regained their psychological health. A UK questionnaire study has examined what LGT people want from therapy and/or their therapist (Malley and Tasker, 2007). The study was based on a convenience sample of 637 mostly white London-based LGT people with a wide range of different incomes. Key findings included that: (1) therapists with knowledge of, and the confidence to discuss, issues of sexual identity were valued; (2) therapist disapproval of clients' sexuality was seen as a major negative factor; (3) the most common change that respondents would make in future therapy was seeking out a lesbian or gay male therapist; (4) generic factors such as 'understanding' and 'listening' were highly valued; (5) friends were highly valued as a source of support; and (6) a wide range of complementary therapies were seen as valuable.

In terms of mental health, it is not all 'doom and gloom' for LGBTQ people. Mental *health* research ironically often ignores mental health and focuses solely on LGBTQ mental health *problems*. However, it is also important to study the things that enhance LGBTQ people's psychological well-being. If we take gay men as an example, Australian research has found that a sense of belonging to gay communities can ameliorate feelings of isolation from the broader community and

Box 6.6   Key study: Alicia Lucksted (2004) on LGBT people receiving public mental health system services

Using qualitative methods, the project summarised in this paper aimed to explore the ways in which mental health services could better meet the needs of LGBT clients, especially those living with serious mental illnesses. Data for the study were collected from a range of sources, including relevant professional literature, networking, and interviews with thirty-five key informants (service users, advocates, community mental health workers, and professionals who provide services to LGBT people with serious mental illnesses) from across the USA.

Key issues in mental health provision for LGBT people included:

- *Exclusion of the seriously mentally ill.* Serious mental illness is not included within the remit of LGBT affirmative clinicians and programmes; LGBT community organisations often ignore the realities of LGBT people who suffer from serious mental illness.
- *Sexuality not addressed.* Sexuality is only discussed as a problem; there is an unspoken assumption that clients have, or should have, *no* sexuality.
- *Lack of knowledge and poor attitudes of staff.* High levels of ignorance; there are assumptions that 'LGBT people are either HIV positive, sexual predators, man-hating, swishy, butch, confused, sick, or other such stereotypes' (p. 31); and there is the view that being LGBT is 'no big deal'.
- *Peer intolerance.* There is disregard and discrimination from other clients in community and self-help groups.
- *Lack of information about LGBT community resources.* LGBT issues are ignored in treatment and discharge plans; there is lack of information about LGBT-affirmative services.

This study raises concerns about the needs and welfare of LGBT people with serious mental health issues. Lucksted highlights the vulnerability of this group, and therefore their dependency on mental health services, and calls for raised awareness of LGBT issues among service providers.

facilitate involvement in the broader community, both of which have a positive impact on mental health (McLaren *et al.*, 2008; see also Ellis, 2007a).

Physical health

In some ways physical health (beyond the confines of sexual health) has been a neglected topic in LGBTQ health research. Research on specifically trans and bisexual people's physical health is extremely limited, so this section will necessarily focus on lesbians, and gay men's physical health (although trans people can of course be lesbian or gay). What we do know about trans people's physical health is that there are physical health risks associated with hormone

Box 6.7	*Highlights: physical health concerns for transmen*

Transmen face a number of challenges, including the negative psychological consequences of discrimination (see Chapter 5); difficulties in meeting partners who accept their gender identity as men (see Chapter 8); and the immediate side-effects of treatment regimes. In addition to all of these challenges, recent research indicates that, for some transmen, long-term hormone therapy has significant cumulative effects on their health. Research on the physical health of transmen highlights both positive and negative side-effects of hormone therapy. Regarding the positive effects of hormone therapy, recent findings suggest that testosterone treatment can help to maintain or develop bone density, a significant factor in determining the likelihood of osteoporosis. However, this may only be the case for transmen who also undergo the removal of their ovaries, if not a complete hysterectomy (Turner *et al.*, 2004).

In terms of the negative effects of hormone therapy, general research on breast cancer suggests that there is an association between increased levels of androgens (such as testosterone) and breast cancer risk (Burcombe *et al.*, 2003; Andrews, 2008). This is especially pertinent for transmen who undergo hormone therapy for lengthy periods of time. For transmen who undergo a hysterectomy, while such surgery functions to lower levels of oestrogen (which research indicates reduces the chances of breast cancer), higher levels of testosterone (resulting from hormone therapy) will typically counter the benefit of reduced oestrogen. In addition, it has been suggested that elective mastectomies undertaken by transmen as part of their transition do not necessarily prevent future instances of breast cancer because of the above mentioned factors.

This research highlights the physical complexities of gender reassignment for trans people. While the psychological effects of transitioning may be positive for trans people (i.e., they may feel that their bodies finally match their gender identity), the physical effects can be long term and potentially life-threatening. Further research is required to understand how trans people make sense of these two conflicting outcomes, and how gender norms and the social requirement to have our bodily form match our gender identity impact negatively on trans people. Furthermore, it is important that transmen are made aware of the conflicting outcomes of hormone therapy and the fact that a mastectomy or hysterectomy does not necessarily prevent future instances of cancer occurring.

therapy (such as liver problems) (Lurie, 2005), and there may be a connection between feminising hormones and impaired glucose tolerance (i.e., increased risk of developing type 2 diabetes in 'overweight' transsexual women; Feldman, 2002; see also Box 6.7). In this final section we focus on the (ill)health-related behaviours of LGBTQ people and outline some problems with this individualistic approach; and discuss non-HIV related chronic illnesses.

Lifestyle 'choices', health-related behaviours and chronic illness

Like health research and health psychology more generally, a heavy emphasis has been placed on the lifestyle 'choices' and the health-related behaviours of LGB (TQ) people. (We have placed the term 'choices' in inverted commas because choices are always within constraints. You may, for instance, only want to eat organic fruit and vegetables or free range meat, but as these tend to be more expensive than the intensively farmed alternatives, you need more money to exercise this choice.) Research on gay men's physical health, for example, emphasises the importance of gender as a factor for determining health outcomes within LGBTQ communities. Like heterosexual men, gay men, it has been suggested, are less likely to engage in protective behaviours that facilitate positive health outcomes, and are more likely to engage in behaviours that increase the likelihood of developing illness and disease (Adams *et al.*, 2004).

In addition, LGB(TQ) people can be heavy users of alcohol (e.g., Hughes and Eliason, 2002), cigarettes (Ryan *et al.*, 2001) and recreational drugs (Skinner and Otis, 1996). In some studies, LGB people's use of such substances is significantly higher than heterosexuals' usage (Lee, 2000), and younger LGB people, in particular, seem to be more at risk of substance abuse (Savin-Williams, 1994). One study found that lesbians in some age brackets reported higher levels of marijuana and cocaine use, whereas gay men reported more use of inhalants (e.g., amyl or butyl nitrate, 'poppers'), hallucinogens and other illicit drugs than the 'general population' (Skinner and Otis, 1996). A recent Australian study found a third (33 per cent) of the lesbian and bisexual women surveyed had used illicit drugs within the previous six months (particularly cannabis, ecstasy and speed), compared to 17 per cent of the general population (Hyde *et al.*, 2007). Only a few studies of substance (mis)use in LGB populations have included sufficient numbers of people from marginalised racial and cultural groups for any conclusions to be made about their use of legal and illegal substances, compared to either heterosexuals from the same racial and cultural background or to white LGBT people.

Why does research evidence indicate that LGB people use health damaging substances more than heterosexuals? A number of suggestions have been put forward. The limited range of social networking options available to LGB(TQ) people (i.e., bars and clubs in urban areas) may shape LGB(TQ) people's consumption of substances like alcohol, nicotine and other recreational drugs. In other words, many LGB(TQ) people socialise in bars and clubs and these environments actively encourage substance use. Another explanation is that substance (mis)use may be a 'survival strategy' or a form of escapism from experiences of heterosexism, homophobia, biphobia and transphobia (Hiller *et al.*, 2004). We also suspect that when researchers 'look' for problematic health related behaviours they are more likely to find them. There has been a strong compulsion in the last few decades to demonstrate empirically that LGBT people *do* engage in health harming behaviours (*as* LGBT people, not because they are, for example, young, male and disenfranchised) in order to get 'LGBT health' onto the public health agenda.

It is important to raise awareness of LGBTQ people's health related behaviours in order to provide 'culturally appropriate' health services and support, but the narrow focus on individual health behaviours can, again, potentially lead to 'blaming the victim' and pathologising LGBTQ people. As a result, some LGBTQ health research has taken a critical health psychology approach that examines the broader social and cultural determinants of health. New Zealand critical psychologist Jeffery Adams and colleagues' exploration of gay men and alcohol consumption is a good example of this approach. Adams *et al.* (2007) focused on the socio-cultural context that shapes why and how gay men are encouraged to drink alcohol by examining how drinks companies specifically target gay male consumers in their advertising. They argued that high alcohol use is deeply embedded within gay culture. Adams *et al.* also suggested that advertising which targets gay communities may be complicit in the sense of social exclusion that some men experience. In addition, advertising plays a role in the incidence of body image problems among gay men because of its stereotyped representation of gay men's bodies as 'perfect' (e.g., toned, muscular).

Socio-cultural explanations for individual behaviour offer different solutions for reducing the problematic health behaviours LGBTQ people engage in. So, instead of, for instance, targeting alcohol reduction (or indeed smoking cessation or drug rehab) programmes at LGBTQ individuals or groups, within this broader socio-cultural framework, emphasis is on environmental prevention strategies. In the case of alcohol, alcohol-free LGBTQ community events and agreements between LGBTQ organisations and businesses to sell alcohol more responsibly are potential strategies to improve the health of LGBTQ people (Gay and Lesbian Medical Association (GLMA), 2001).

Diet and physical activity are other key aspects of health behaviour. Little is known about the diet and exercise behaviours of LGBTQ populations despite their importance to health and well-being. There is, however, some evidence which suggests that some segments of LGBTQ communities have higher rates of poor nutrition, of being overweight or obese and of having eating disorders. Thus far, research findings are highly gendered: simply put, lesbians tend to be overweight and gay men tend to be underweight (and prone to eating disorders; Siever, 1994). New Zealand research focusing on the Body Mass Index (BMI) of lesbians, for example, found 45 per cent to be over their 'ideal' weight, compared to 36 per cent of the 'general population' (Saphira and Glover, 2000). It had been suggested that lesbians 'opt out' of conventional notions of femininity and are therefore fatter, on average, than heterosexual women (Brand *et al.*, 1992). Other explanations include that some lesbians are on lower incomes and are therefore not able to afford healthy foods, or that they may gain psychological benefits from being large, such as feeling protected by taking up space (Wilton, 1997).

The Geneva Gay Men's Health Survey found that gay men (n=477) had significantly lower BMIs than a matched sample of the 'general' male population and were more likely to report paying close attention to food choices (Wang *et al.*, 2007). Younger gay men are more likely to be susceptible to eating disorders than older gay men, but again, this is mediated by gay men's sense of belonging to gay communities (Williamson and Spence, 2001). A focus on aesthetics and particularly bodily ideals in gay communities may promote eating disorders, but gay communities are not homogeneous. For example, it has been suggested that gay and bisexual men who identify as bears (and have hairier bodies, have beards/facial hair and are heavier/fatter) 'celebrate large bodies as more masculine' (GLMA, 2001: 245) and may experience significant risk factors associated with being overweight. Therefore lesbians and gay men can experience their weight and body/appearance in unique cultural ways that may involve a rejection of heterosexual norms.

Health related behaviours contribute to the development of many chronic illnesses (e.g., type 2 diabetes, heart disease), especially in later life, but the study of long-term physical illness has been a neglected aspect of LGBTQ health research (see Box 6.8). Illnesses that have been researched are typically connected

---

Box 6.8   Key study: Adam Jowett and Elizabeth Peel (2009) on LGBT people's experiences of chronic illness

British LGBTQ psychologist Adam Jowett and Elizabeth Peel have conducted a critical health psychology informed, predominantly qualitative, online survey of LGBT people's experiences of chronic illness(es). Data from 364 LGBT people, 190 (52 per cent) of whom reported they had chronic illness(es) were collected in 2008, mainly from the USA and the UK. The chronically ill respondents were living with fifty-two different physical illnesses; the most common were: arthritis (20 per cent), hypertension (20 per cent), diabetes (15 per cent), asthma (14 per cent) and chronic fatigue syndrome or ME (8 per cent). HIV/AIDS and cancer were jointly the eighth most prevalent illnesses (6 per cent). Mental health problems (most commonly depression) affected 10 per cent of those reporting chronic illness.

The analysis focused on four themes within the chronically ill participants' written comments:

- *LGBT communities: ableist or more accepting of difference?* Respondents reported viewing LGBT communities as 'HIV-centric', dismissive of illnesses outside of the realm of sexual health and mirroring the ableism of society in general. However, respondents also provided accounts of LGBT communities being more supportive than society as a whole, and more accepting of people's differences related to health and disability.
- *Isolation from LGBT communities and the desire to affiliate with other chronically ill LGBT people.* Respondents commented on the many different ways their illness(es) impacted on their everyday lives (including their illness(es) resulting in the ending of relationships, and difficulties in dating). Respondents with more severely disabling illnesses reported a sense of social isolation from other LGBT people and communities.

- *Heteronormativity within sources of information and support.* Few respondents (except some in the USA) had access to face-to-face groups for LGBT people with their illness. Some reported not feeling the need for such groups; others represented general illness related support groups as constituted predominantly of heterosexual people and as potentially homophobic environments. Some respondents described other forms of support (e.g., written information, illness related charity websites) as heteronormative in their assumption that the user is heterosexual.
- *Homophobia/fear of homophobia from health care professionals.* Some respondents recounted experiences of homophobia from health care professionals; one such respondent stated that 'homophobia is still an ever present reality' within health care services. These negative experiences mainly took the form of health care professionals verbalising their anti-LGBT views. Some reported that their health care providers were not aware of their sexual identity (and that their sexuality was not relevant to their health care); others reported not feeling safe to disclose their sexuality to health care professionals, fearing it might negatively affect their care.

The authors concluded by suggesting that LGBTQ psychologists could usefully draw on critical health psychology principles and frameworks to explore non-heterosexuals' lived experiences of chronic illness. They also argued that there continues to be a need for specifically targeted support groups and services (virtual or otherwise) for LGBT people with chronic illnesses.

to sexual health or functioning: colon and rectal disease (Lipton, 2004) and prostate cancer (Santillo and Lowe, 2005) among gay men, and cervical and breast cancer among lesbians (Fish and Wilkinson, 2000).

Chronic illnesses that do not construct LGBTQ people as sexual beings have been especially overlooked (but see Axtell, 1999) and provide a fruitful area for future research.

Gaps and absences

- Robust public health statistics about the incidence of illness and disease in LGBTQ groups, and the inclusion of sexuality and gender identity as routine demographic information in population-based health surveys.
- Although critical health psychology research has engaged with gender, little critical psychological research has focused on non-heterosexuality and trans.
- Research on trans and bisexual health and illness.
- Mental health service use patterns of GBQ men and racially and culturally marginalised LGBTQ people.
- Experiences of LGBTQ people suffering from psychiatric disorders.
- The application of 'mainstream' health psychology models (e.g., the theory of planned behaviour) to LGBTQ people or to LGBTQ health issues.

Main chapter points

This chapter:

- Located research on LGBTQ health in historical context.
- Outlined key health research perspectives and highlighted reasons for health inequalities between heterosexual and LGBTQ people.
- Overviewed LGB(TQ) sexual health research and key mental health issues for LGBTQ people.
- Explored health related behaviours and lifestyle choices related to LGBTQ health, and touched on (non-HIV related) chronic illnesses.

Questions for discussion and classroom exercises

1. Imagine you are a health psychologist trying to promote LGBTQ health and well-being. Design a health promotion poster aimed at a non-heterosexual or trans group. What message will you convey? What images will you use on your poster? Where will your poster be displayed in order to reach the target audience?

2. Discuss the advantages and disadvantages of both the biopsychosocial and the critical health psychology perspectives on LGBTQ health. Which do you prefer, and why?

3. Find a recent journal article that reports a health psychology study and answer the following questions: Is the sexuality of the participants taken into account? Why or why not? Is gender considered beyond 'male' and 'female'? Can you think of any ways that this health issue/illness might affect LGBTQ people?

4. Discuss the statement 'there is no such thing as an LGBTQ illness'. What criteria can you use to decide whether something is an LGBTQ illness or not? Which criteria do you favour, and why? What are the theoretical and applied implications of labelling an area of health or a particular disease a lesbian, gay, bisexual or trans 'issue', or of not labelling it as such?

Further reading

Cochran, S. D. (2001) Emerging issues in research on lesbians' and gay men's mental health: does sexual orientation really matter? *American Psychologist*, 56 (11), 931–47. This US-based article provides an excellent overview and critique of the literature on LG (BTQ) mental health.

Epstein, S. (2003) Sexualising governance and medicalising identities: the emergence of a 'state-centered' LGBT health politics in the United States. *Sexualities*, 6(2), 131–71.
In this interesting and critical article, US sociologist Steven Epstein provides a detailed account of grassroots activism/political lobbying for LGBT inclusion in public health initiatives and also critiques this 'state-centred' approach to LGBT health.

Fish, J. (2006) *Heterosexism in health and social care*. Basingstoke: Palgrave Macmillan.
British social scientist Julie Fish's book provides an accessible introduction to a wide range of LGBT health and social care issues (see chapter 2 especially). In the second part of the book she outlines her empirical investigation of lesbians' health care experiences.

Lombardi, E. (2001) Enhancing transgender health care. *American Journal of Public Health*, 91(6), 869–72.
This short US-based article outlines some of the health care issues for trans people and provides suggestions for improving trans health.

Wilton, T. (2000) *Sexualities in health and social care: a textbook*. Buckingham: Open University Press.
Chapters of particular interest in this introductory textbook by British sociologist Tamsin Wilton include chapter 4 (Science and sexuality: the medical model and its implications), chapter 6 (Sexual health), chapter 7 (Writing sexual orientation into health) and chapter 10 (Sexuality and health promotion).

LGBTQ experiences across the lifespan

7 Young people, coming out and identity development

Overview

- Young people, sexuality and gender identity
- Models of LGBTQ identity development
- Sexual fluidity
- Disclosure to family and friends
- LGBTQ young people in school
- Exploring identity and finding a community

Young people, sexuality and gender identity

Identifying as LGBTQ can occur at any stage of the lifespan. However, the vast majority of research has tended to focus on young people. For this reason, this chapter will predominantly focus on identifying as LGBTQ as it applies to young people.

Much of the work on identity development in relation to sexuality (e.g., Savin-Williams, 2005) and gender identity (e.g., Grossman *et al.*, 2006) suggests that LGBTQ young people can be recognised from an early age by characteristics such as childhood feelings of 'difference' and gender atypical behaviour, appearance or interests. Moreover, Gender Identity Disorder (GID) of childhood is believed to be more strongly associated with homosexuality than with trans in adulthood (deVries *et al.*, 2007). The reality is that LGBTQ people represent as diverse a range of backgrounds and experiences as is the case for all people. Often the scripts of 'childhood difference' and 'gender atypicality' are a product of the research questions asked and the social imperative to construct sexual and gender identities coherently. In other words, because lesbians are assumed only to be sexually attracted to women, and gay men only to men, they are assumed not to have (had) sexual experiences with, or feelings for, people of another sex. Likewise, because gender is assumed to be innate, trans people are expected to have experienced their gender as incongruent from an early age. It is therefore common for people to present their own sexuality and gender identity in such a way as to include information which is consistent with commonly held assumptions about that identity and to omit information which is not. For instance, telling the story 'I've always been lesbian', 'I was born gay' or 'I always felt like a woman trapped in a man's body' (or vice versa).

Almost without exception, psychological theory and research on LGBTQ identity development is premised on the notion that young people who are not out or who resist coming out are either 'in denial' about their sexuality or gender identity, or are not able to come out but want to. However, as Ritch Savin-Williams (2005) highlights, with increasing visibility of diverse sexualities, young people attracted to the same sex appear less willing to adopt labels for their sexuality and gender identity. Whereas there may be a number of reasons why young people don't or are reluctant to use labels such as 'lesbian' or 'gay' (e.g., they are not out; they don't feel that they fit the label; they have not engaged in same-sex sexual practices), many young people today reject labels 'in defiance of social identity labels which would suggest the primacy of sexuality in their personal identities' (Cohler and Hammack, 2007: 48). For every young person who identifies as LGBTQ, there are many more who do *not* identify as LGBTQ but are attracted to people of the same sex and/or engage in same-sex sexual practices. Some may later come to identify as LGBTQ, while others who currently identify as LGBTQ may later drop those labels. Others still will continue to engage in a range of sexual behaviours, including same-sex practices, yet resolutely identify as heterosexual. Likewise, work on people from marginalised racial and cultural groups suggests that young people from these groups tend to resist using sexual identity labels, perceiving them as westernised constructs which don't apply to them (e.g., see Chan, 1996). Therefore, sexuality and gender identity is often a poor criterion for researching the experiences of, and issues affecting the lives and development of, young **people with same-sex attractions** and those who are trans. This level of diversity suggests that the 'choice' to come out (or not) is quite complex. It also calls into question the relevance of coming out for all LGBTQ young people.

A related issue is that many young people today experience their sexuality as fluid. Whereas some young people will have no clear sense of their sexual selves, but are seeking this, and may even be exploring different identities and practices, for others, same-sex attractions and relationships are not considered to imply anything permanent about their sexuality (Savin-Williams, 2005). For these young people attractions are viewed as fluid beyond what might be expected by sexuality and gender identity labels and they pursue sexual partners relatively independently of sex/gender. Although some young people identify as LGB, for many others same-sex attractions, desires and behaviour are viewed as a form of 'sexual freedom' or 'sexual choice' – a trendy 'add-on' to otherwise conventional heterosexuality (Diamond, 2005). For a number of young people **sexual fluidity** may facilitate identity exploration; for others it makes coming to identify as LGB a difficult (or even confusing) path to navigate.

Another problem with much of the existing psychological research is that it commonly compares LGB young people with heterosexuals as if they were two distinct populations. However, the sexual experiences of LGB young people are markedly similar to those of their heterosexual peers, including a diverse range of sexual experiences with people of the same and a different sex. To characterise LGB young people as a homogeneous group conceals this diversity and fails to recognise important differences between people in relation to factors such as gender, class and culture (Savin-Williams, 2001).

For trans young people, gender identity development can be even more complex. While some young trans people may experience their gender as fairly rigid or fixed (just different from their natal sex), others may experience their gender as fluid or changing. Gender fluidity extends beyond behaviour and interests to the experience of multiple, and sometimes contradictory, gender identifications. For example, some young people describe themselves as *feeling* like a 'girl' on one day and a 'boy' on another, or even that neither term describes them accurately. However, there is little opportunity for young people to engage in gender identity exploration, in a society which is rigidly structured around two, and only two, sex/gender categories (i.e., male/female and masculine/feminine) and where gender diversity is seldom embraced. The lived experience of gender fluidity presents a challenge to dualistic ways of thinking about gender, and this is something which has remained largely unexplored in psychological research.

What is clear is that the socio-political landscape has changed considerably since the 1980s, and research has struggled to keep up with the impact of these changes on the identity development and sexual practices of contemporary LGBTQ young people. Owing to a relative lack of high-quality research on LGBTQ young people, the field has been dogged by limited samples, and (often) poor research design, resulting in a somewhat patchy and partial picture of the identity development and experiences of LGBTQ young people. Furthermore, research on LGBTQ young people has tended to be hyperfocused on the negative aspects of identifying as LGBTQ. This may in part be because researchers want to effect positive social change, but in so doing the field is impoverished by a lack of understanding of the strengths and resilience of LGBTQ young people (Savin-Williams, 2001). The lived realities and experiences of LGBTQ young people today are profoundly different from those of even a decade or so ago, and there is also considerable variability cross-nationally and cross-culturally. The vast majority of existing research on LGBTQ young people looks extremely dated and does not reflect the sexual and gender diversity we have just described. Moreover, it represents an overwhelming bias towards a white western perspective and towards sexuality over gender identity. As much as possible within this chapter, we have drawn from recent studies. However, as you engage with the theories and research presented here, we encourage you to bear in mind the limitations of the samples and other methodological issues which may impact on the findings.

Models of LGBTQ identity development

Identifying as LGBTQ (sometimes known as 'coming out to self') has typically been constructed by psychologists as a process through which people pass in coming (personally) to define their sexuality/gender identity. Like other developmental psychological processes using an essentialist approach (see Chapter 2), it has been theorised through the creation of stage models. From 1979 until the mid-1980s several stage models of 'homosexual' identity development were published (e.g., Cass, 1979; Coleman, 1982; Troiden, 1979). Vivienne Cass's (1979) six-stage model of 'homosexual identity formation' – the most frequently cited model – was the first to be published and is the archetype on which most subsequent models have been based. Cass, an Australian psychologist, developed the model during several years of clinical work with lesbians and gay men (see Box 7.1).

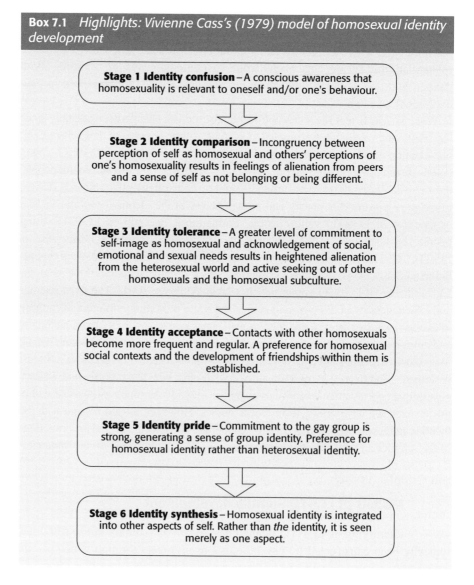

Box 7.1   *Highlights: Vivienne Cass's (1979) model of homosexual identity development*

Stage 1 Identity confusion – A conscious awareness that homosexuality is relevant to oneself and/or one's behaviour.

Stage 2 Identity comparison – Incongruency between perception of self as homosexual and others' perceptions of one's homosexuality results in feelings of alienation from peers and a sense of self as not belonging or being different.

Stage 3 Identity tolerance – A greater level of commitment to self-image as homosexual and acknowledgement of social, emotional and sexual needs results in heightened alienation from the heterosexual world and active seeking out of other homosexuals and the homosexual subculture.

Stage 4 Identity acceptance – Contacts with other homosexuals become more frequent and regular. A preference for homosexual social contexts and the development of friendships within them is established.

Stage 5 Identity pride – Commitment to the gay group is strong, generating a sense of group identity. Preference for homosexual identity rather than heterosexual identity.

Stage 6 Identity synthesis – Homosexual identity is integrated into other aspects of self. Rather than *the* identity, it is seen merely as one aspect.

By the mid-1980s there were a number of models describing the process of coming to identify oneself as lesbian or gay, and there are four main elements common to all of the models: (1) an awareness of homosexual feelings; (2) exploration of homosexuality; (3) taking on board a lesbian/gay self-identity; and (4) integrating one's lesbian/gay identity into one's broader sense of self. Each of the models is underpinned by what Cohler and Hammack (2007) call the 'narrative of struggle and success'. That is, coming to identify as lesbian or gay is constructed as normative, but entwined with the challenge of managing stigma in order to emerge with a secure and positive sense of one's sexuality. However, because sexuality has typically been conceptualised as a simple heterosexual/homosexual binary, these models do not take seriously the notion of bisexuality, and because their focus is exclusively on sexuality – ignoring the intersections of gender and sexuality – the development of trans identity is absent. It is also worth noting that to date there does not appear to be a parallel model of heterosexual identity development.

In the 1990s, bisexuality began to appear on the psychological agenda. Following the models established within lesbian and gay psychology, early work on bisexual identity development also adopted a process-based stage model approach. The most widely cited model is that devised by US sociologist Martin Weinberg and colleagues (1994); see Box 7.2. Whereas identifying as lesbian or gay was characterised by the rejection of the label 'heterosexual' in relation to oneself, bisexuality involves the rejection of *both* the category 'heterosexual' and the category 'lesbian'/'gay'. For this reason, it would be expected that identifying as bisexual brings with it related, but different, challenges from identification as lesbian or gay. The main difference between this model of identity development and models of lesbian and gay identity development lies in the final stage of the model. Weinberg suggests that, rather than attaining a secure sense of self as bisexual (which is the case in models of lesbian and gay identity development), identifying as bisexual is characterised by ongoing uncertainty about one's sexuality. Work by Canadian psychologist Maria Gurevich and colleagues (2007) reinforces this, but interprets this 'uncertainty' to reflect a resistance to and questioning of the label 'bisexuality', and striving to find a suitable alternative.

As already highlighted, trans identity development has tended to be ignored in the psychological literature because the focus has been on 'causes' and treatment of transsexualism and GID rather than on the lived experience of trans people and the development of identity as trans. However, some work exploring the process of trans identity development has been undertaken by British clinical psychologists Clair Clifford and Jim Orford (2007). Clifford and Orford collected data from twenty-eight trans women and men (nineteen MTF and nine FTM) in the UK, recruited through trans and LGBTQ networks. In Clifford and Orford's research, eight people participated in semi-structured interviews and provided detailed accounts of their experiences of identifying as trans. A preliminary model was developed on the basis of these interviews. A different group of twelve trans people were provided with a diagrammatical representation and description of the model and a list of questions to consider. Their

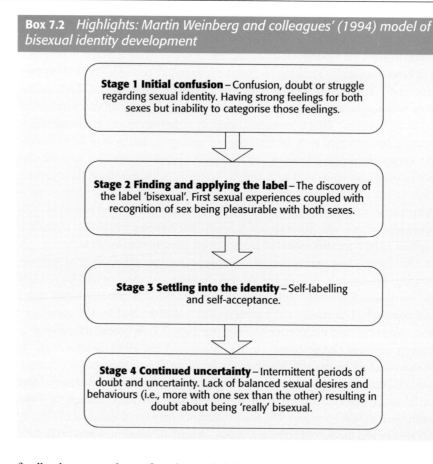

Box 7.2   *Highlights: Martin Weinberg and colleagues' (1994) model of bisexual identity development*

Stage 1 Initial confusion – Confusion, doubt or struggle regarding sexual identity. Having strong feelings for both sexes but inability to categorise those feelings.

Stage 2 Finding and applying the label – The discovery of the label 'bisexual'. First sexual experiences coupled with recognition of sex being pleasurable with both sexes.

Stage 3 Settling into the identity – Self-labelling and self-acceptance.

Stage 4 Continued uncertainty – Intermittent periods of doubt and uncertainty. Lack of balanced sexual desires and behaviours (i.e., more with one sex than the other) resulting in doubt about being 'really' bisexual.

feedback was used to refine the model (some categories were collapsed; others were split into two or more categories). Finally, a further group of eight participants were invited to comment on the refined model. The model consists of three main phases, as illustrated in Box 7.3.

Despite their popularity, stage models of sexuality development have been heavily criticised. As well as the conflation of identity development with identity disclosure (and, in the case of trans, with a physiological change of sex), one of the main problems with a stage theory approach is that it assumes that sexuality is innate and that through introspection people can come to discover their 'true' identity. In short, coming to identify as an LGB person is seen as a journey of self-discovery, whereby individuals come to shed their 'false' identity as heterosexual and correctly identify as LGB. Conversely, if there were stage models of trans identity development based on similar assumptions as those underpinning stage models of lesbian/gay identity development, transitioning would be seen as a journey whereby a person sheds a false identity as 'male' (if born male) or 'female' (if born female) and correctly identifies either as 'gender variant' or as other than their natal sex. This approach assumes that sexuality and gender identity are fixed and fails to account for (potential) fluidity in those identities.

Box 7.3 *Highlights: Clair Clifford and Jim Orford's (2007) model of trans identity development*

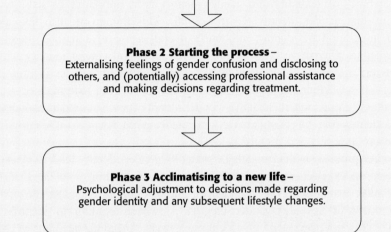

Phase 1 Developing an awareness of being different –
Managing internal feelings of gender confusion.
Developing a full awareness that one's internal (psychological)
gender is different from the physical body.

Phase 2 Starting the process –
Externalising feelings of gender confusion and disclosing to
others, and (potentially) accessing professional assistance
and making decisions regarding treatment.

Phase 3 Acclimatising to a new life –
Psychological adjustment to decisions made regarding
gender identity and any subsequent lifestyle changes.

In addition, social context is seen largely as a backdrop against which self-reflection occurs. As a consequence, the role of social context (e.g., family; peers; community) and historical processes (e.g., the women's and gay liberation movements; the AIDS/HIV crisis) in facilitating or impeding development is not explicitly included in the models (as stage model theorists themselves have acknowledged, e.g., Cass, 2005). Socio-historical factors may be responsible for considerable differences in experiences of identity development between cohorts. For example, a gay man coming out in the UK in the 1940s when socio-political attitudes were very conservative and gay male sex was illegal would have had a markedly different experience from a young gay man coming out today when the socio-political climate is much more liberal, and LGBTQ people have greater freedom of self-expression. Similarly, a young person living in a (**socio-centric**) non-western society may have a different experience of identifying as trans from a young person living in a (individualistic) western society.

A third major criticism has been the rigidity of these models, in that they assume that developing an LGBTQ identity is a linear, sequential and unidirectional process. Although proponents of the models suggest that individuals may vary in the degree to which they follow the sequence of stages, the structure of the models themselves implies that people pass through the stages in a set order. People who do not pass through all the stages are viewed as having failed to complete the developmental process. There are, however, many people whose path to sexuality and gender identity development does not fit this rigid framework. For example, longitudinal work with women suggests that reconsidering and (re)discovering (or reconstructing! – depending on what theoretical approach you take) different sexual identities is an important, and indeed common, part of many women's more fluid sexual attractions, practices and relationships (Diamond, 2006). The stage model approach therefore lacks a sense of the possibility of moving within and between different identities and stages, where the instability of sexuality and gender identity is as normative as stability of sexuality and gender identity (Griffin, 2000). This framework also favours a liberal integration of identity into one's overall sense of self, and therefore problematises alternative constructions of sexuality and gender identity which may assert the primacy of sexuality (i.e., where sexuality/gender identity are politicised; see Kitzinger, 1987). Similarly, for those from marginalised racial and cultural groups where sexuality/gender identity may be compartmentalised, sexual identity may be constructed as separate from other aspects of identity (see 'disclosure to family and friends' below).

Another problem is that models of sexuality/gender identity tend to place an emphasis on experiences (e.g., sexual practices; association with the LGBTQ community; transitioning) as the catalyst and/or defining characteristic of the development of sexuality/gender identity. However, coming to identify as LGBTQ does not necessarily involve these aspects. Anecdotal accounts of coming out often report LGB people having come to identify as such without having ever had a same-sex relationship or sexual experience and/or having interfaced with an LGBTQ community. When considering trans identity development it is important to note that not all trans people explore the possibility of transitioning, and not all those who do actually undergo transition. Adolescents diagnosed with gender dysphoria may have a strong and persistent wish for reassignment, be ambivalent about it, be confused or change their mind (de Vries *et al.*, 2007). For this reason, the identity development process for some trans people will simply comprise 'transgender emergence' (Lev, 2004): the process of realising, discovering, identifying and naming one's gender identity. Transgender emergence differs markedly from coming out as LGB in that trans is not as widely understood, and the use of gender pronouns (i.e., 'he', 'she') don't make trans identities visible. Consequently, trans people often struggle to find a way to articulate their gender identity (Lev, 2004). In an interview study with sixty-five MTF trans participants (aged 24–68 years), US sociologist Patricia Gagné and colleagues (1997) found that in addition to childhood events which marked their cross-gender feelings as wrong, the main catalysts for participants identifying as trans were discovering that there was an identity label for their feelings and that there were others who had similar experiences.

Finally, stage models construct the coming out process as inherently negative. They all imply that identifying as LGBTQ is fraught with personal struggle and lack of self-acceptance. For example, Coleman (1982: 471) stated that 'the awareness of same-sex interests and feelings is usually a slow and painful process'. While this may be the experience of some LGBTQ people, the process of identifying as LGBTQ is hardly universal in the way that the models might suggest. Stage models therefore serve to perpetuate assumptions of LGBTQ pathology and undermine the attempts of contemporary LGBTQ psychologists to promote more positive models of sexuality/gender identity. In essence, stage models over-simplify the process of sexuality/gender identity development and are inadequate for capturing the complex process of coming to identify as LGBTQ.

In the main, the LGBTQ psychological literature on coming out suggests that the typical pattern of sexuality development begins with an awareness that one is not heterosexual, followed by same-sex sexual experience (which acts as confirmation), and culminates in disclosure of an LGBTQ identity to family and friends. However, recent research by US psychologists Shira Maguen and colleagues (2002) found considerable variation in the developmental paths of LGB people surveyed. For a significant minority of participants, first same-sex sexual experience occurred simultaneously with awareness of LGB identity, whilst 33 per cent disclosed their sexuality prior to having any same-sex sexual experience. Maguen and colleagues also found significant differences in developmental pathways as a function of sexuality and gender identity. Of those respondents reporting having had sexual experiences, only 14 per cent of gay men as opposed to 45 per cent of lesbians and 46 per cent of bisexuals (male or female) had their first sexual contact with someone of a different sex. For lesbian participants this initial different sex encounter was followed a year or two later by a first same-sex encounter.

Sexual fluidity

In contrast to the essentialist constructions of sexuality and gender encapsulated in models of sexuality and gender identity development, some research has suggested that sexual attractions, experiences and identities are subject to change over time, a phenomenon known as sexual fluidity (or sexual plasticity). Until relatively recently, psychology has lacked a way of talking about individuals whose sexual attractions, experiences and identities have changed rather than remained stable. Although the term 'bisexuality' has often been used to describe notions of sexual fluidity, we suggest that it inadequately captures the diversity and complexity of individual sexual trajectories (and also potentially conflates the experiences of bisexual people with those of people who identify as gender fluid, two categories that may be both distinctly different and at times overlapping). As understandings of sexuality have increasingly moved away from a dichotomous approach, it has become more common to encounter people who see no contradiction in moving between relationships with men, with women or with both. For these people sexual attraction, behaviour and identity have more to do with the characteristics of the person or the relationship itself than they do with gender (Diamond, 2003; Peplau, 2001). As highlighted at the beginning of this chapter, for many young people this is the dominant framework employed in thinking about their sexuality and gender identity, and is largely the reason for their resistance to adopting sexuality and gender identity labels (Savin-Williams, 2005).

For example, the notion of sexual fluidity described above appears to be more readily adopted by women than it is by men (e.g., see Baumeister, 2000). However, this does not presuppose that most women's sexual identities and practices *will* change over time. Some women may exhibit such changes, but others will adopt patterns of heterosexuality or lesbianism that remain stable across time (Peplau and Garnets, 2000). At least in the West, sex differences in sexual fluidity may be largely attributable to the different ways in which men and women are socialised to interact with those of the same sex. In particular, women are socialised to privilege emotional and affectionate (but not sexual) aspects of relationships with other women, which opens up the potential for unexpected experiences which blur the boundaries between love, romance, friendship and sexuality (Thompson and Morgan, 2008). Men, on the other hand, are socialised to maintain strict emotional and affectionate boundaries, which clearly demarcate the differences between friendships and sexual relationships.

Among young people terms such as 'lezzie' and 'poof' are used as a put-down for those who do not conform to heteronormative notions of gender and sexuality. Primarily, for this reason, and because it is associated with the unpopular 'F' word (feminism), young women appear reluctant to use the label 'lesbian' to describe themselves. While some may identify as bisexual and retain this identity for life, others may adopt the label 'bisexual' as a temporary alternative to lesbian. However, a recent proliferation of newer and 'safer' alternatives (e.g., 'mostly heterosexual'; 'heteroflexible'; 'bicurious') allows young women to keep their heterosexual label while simultaneously experimenting with same-sex attractions and desires (Thompson and Morgan, 2008). Despite a concerted effort to explore sexuality and gender identity development in (young) women, there is a paucity of comparable work exploring how young men construct their sexual identities or of any in-depth explorations of the ways in which discourses of masculinity militate against sexual fluidity in young men.

Regardless of the identity labels that individuals may or may not choose to use, much psychological theory and research has focused on sexual fluidity: that is, change in attractions and behaviour across time independent of the way in which individuals define themselves. This approach dates back to the early work of Alfred Kinsey and colleagues (see Chapter 1). Building on Kinsey's work, Fritz Klein operationalised the Kinsey Scale by developing a measure of sexual fluidity: the Klein Sexual Orientation Grid (Klein *et al.*, 1985). This measure was designed to explore a range of aspects of sexuality including individuals' same- and other-sex attractions, behaviours, fantasies, preferences and identities across time (past, present and ideal). Recent research using this scale (e.g., Amestoy, 2001; Weinrich and Klein, 2002) has empirically demonstrated that sexuality is not a one-dimensional construct. For example, in a study of 250 postgraduate students in the USA (Amestoy, 2001), participants' labels for sexual attraction, sexual practices and self-identification were consistent with their current sexuality, but considerably less consistent with their sexuality in the past. Only three participants (all Asian American) demonstrated total consistency across time (past, present, ideal) and aspect of sexuality (behaviour, fantasy, preference, self-identification).

The construct of sexual fluidity offers a way forward from the very rigid ways of thinking about sexuality typically espoused by psychologists. For example, one of the main problems with an essentialist approach to sexuality and gender identity is that it means accounting for (or discounting) experiences that are incongruent with one's sexual or gender identity. For this reason, it is not uncommon to hear heterosexually defined people accounting for previous same-sex encounters as 'experimentation', 'a phase' or even 'practice for heterosex'. Likewise, it is not uncommon to hear lesbians and gay men constructing previous heterosex in terms of repression/denial or the following of social conventions. It is also common in lesbian and gay coming out stories for people to construct previous heterosexual experiences in a negative way (e.g., as unfulfilling; as not proper sex) or even to omit such experiences altogether, and to present their same-sex experiences as overwhelmingly positive. Since identity categories can be contested, people employ these rhetorical devices in order to construct their sexual identity as both authentic and above question. This is clearly illustrated in the accounts of lesbians coming out after an extended period of heterosexuality (see Kitzinger and Wilkinson, 1995; Rickards and Wuest, 2006).

In most cases, research about sexual fluidity has relied on data from one-off samples where adults have been asked to recall retrospectively their past sexual attractions, behaviours and identities. While there is considerable evidence of sexual fluidity among young people, sexual identity development is best understood by studying change across time. Although such studies are fairly uncommon, US psychologist Lisa Diamond has recently published a study that explores the sexual identity development of seventy-nine women over a ten-year period (see Box 7.4).

Box 7.4 Key study: Lisa Diamond (2008) on female bisexuality from adolescence to adulthood

Across the psychological literature there is considerable debate about whether bisexuality is a temporary stage of denial, transition or experimentation, a sexual orientation category characterised by attraction to both men and women, or a capacity for sexual fluidity. Each of these models encompasses a different perspective on change over time in sexual attractions, behaviours and identities. Lisa Diamond's (2008) study is the first to study temporal change in sexuality longitudinally.

In this study, Diamond interviewed a sample of seventy-nine non-heterosexual women approximately every two years over a ten-year period. Participants were aged 18–25 at the initial interview and recruited from LGB community events, youth groups and university-based groups located in and around New York.

By the end of the study, 67 per cent of participants had changed their identities at least once since the initial interview, and 36 per cent had changed their identity more than once. The study found little evidence to support the model of bisexuality as a transitional stage in that those initially identifying as 'bisexual' or 'unlabelled' were more likely to switch between these labels than to settle for 'lesbian' or 'heterosexual' labels. The overall number of women adopting the labels 'bisexual' or 'unlabelled' remained relatively consistent (at 50–60 per cent) throughout the study, and after ten years 80 per cent of participants had adopted one of these labels at some point during the study. Therefore the shift was predominantly *towards* rather than away from these identities, running contrary to the model of 'bisexuality' as a transitional identity.

The study did, however, provide clear evidence for bisexuality as a distinct orientation and as a capacity for fluidity. 'Bisexual' and 'unlabelled' women reported consistently lower percentages of same-sex attractions than did 'lesbian' women, and largely the same pattern of same-sex and other-sex attractions as they had reported at the outset. Furthermore, those who changed to a 'lesbian' identity did not show significant increases in their same-sex attractions over time, and those who switched to a 'heterosexual' identity did not show significant decreases. Although the balance of same-sex to other-sex attractions/behaviours may vary as a function of interpersonal and situational factors, the findings suggest that bisexuality may be interpreted as a (relatively) stable attraction to both sexes.

Changes in attractions and behaviour over time were observed in both 'lesbian' and 'bisexual/unlabelled' women, which supports the notion of sexual fluidity. By the end of the study, 60 per cent of 'lesbians' had had sexual contact, and 30 per cent romantic involvement, with a man, and this explains why transitions to 'bisexual/unlabelled' identities were more common than transitions away from them. Overall, women's identity changes reflected their own shifting experiences and provided a way of resolving the contradictions between a lesbian identity and their other-sex attractions/behaviour. These 'post-coming-out' identity changes challenge the taken-for-granted assumption that sexuality questioning is resolved as soon as an individual initially identifies with a category. Rather, sexuality and gender identity would appear to be much more susceptible to re-evaluation than is suggested by essentialist models of sexuality and gender identity development, which posit that people have fixed sexual identities that are consistent throughout their lives.

Disclosure to family and friends

For LGBTQ young people, the disclosure to family and friends of a non-heterosexual or trans identity is often experienced as an important developmental milestone. Disclosure typically signifies exiting conventional heterosexual and gendered social expectations and making a commitment to a LGBTQ identity.

This process can be experienced as very stressful for the individual as well as for their family and friends, but to date it has not received much research attention. Where it has been investigated, studies overwhelmingly focus on negative parental responses and consequently little is known about young people who have (relatively) positive experiences of coming out (Gorman-Murray, 2008).

Research in the US suggests that young people today are more likely to disclose their LGBTQ identity than were young people in previous generations (Savin-Williams, 2005). While this may in part be due to an (arguably) more 'gay affirmative' societal climate, young people today also receive much greater exposure to issues of sexuality (including LGB sexualities) than in the past. It is therefore more common for young LGB people to disclose their sexuality in secondary/high school, around the age of 16 (Clarke and Broughton, 2005; Maguen *et al.*, 2002).

Disclosure of a trans identity to family and friends has not (to date) been a subject of research. However, because trans can be more stigmatised in society, disclosing a trans identity is potentially more difficult for a young person than disclosing an LGB identity. For instance, in US sociologists Gagné and colleagues' (1997) study, the sixty-five MTF trans participants reported disclosing their identity to their parent(s) out of a sense of obligation and most experienced difficulty in doing this.

With regard to disclosure itself, the research is remarkably consistent in highlighting that young people typically discuss their same-sex inclinations with their peers prior to disclosure to parents. In Savin-Williams and Ream's US (2003) study, of those who had told both parents in heterosexual-headed families, 54 per cent had indicated that they told their mother first, while 35 per cent told their mother and father simultaneously. Although there is the potential for a range of responses from parents, few participants in this study felt that the quality of their relationship with their parents had changed as a result of their disclosure. However, this study and others which explore parental responses to coming out have tended to draw on very limited samples. It might therefore be the case that there is more variation in coming out experiences than has been captured in research to date. For example, anecdotal evidence suggests that the disclosure of an LGBTQ identity has for some young people resulted in physical abuse or being thrown out of home.

Parental and sibling responses to coming out can all have a significant bearing on the young person's subjectivity as an LGBTQ person. For example, in Andrew Gorman-Murray's (2008) analysis of Australian coming out stories, affirmative parental and sibling responses facilitated the coming out of LGB young people and changed their perceptions of the family home as a wholly heteronormative environment. However, the ability of families to respond positively to a family member's coming out depends heavily on characteristics of the family itself. Using family stress theory as a framework, US psychologist Brian Willoughby and colleagues (2008) reviewed empirical evidence on parental reactions to disclosure of sexuality. Their review identified three main factors on which responses to coming out as LGB were contingent: family-based resources to manage the disclosure (e.g., positive relationships among family members; strong problem-solving abilities), pre-existing beliefs and attitudes about same-sex attraction and practices, and other family pressures at the time of disclosure.

In a study of parents of trans adolescents, British clinical psychologist Bernadette Wren (2002) found that parents often had an inkling of their child's gender identity issues prior to disclosure. Consequently, within the family, gender identity issues were handled with enormous care. While some of the parents Wren interviewed did not receive the news positively (seeing it as a sign of immaturity or an indicator of other difficulties), many were accepting of their child's atypical gender identity. However, even those who were accepting went to great lengths to justify their acceptance to Wren in the interviews on grounds of biological causation (their child was born with a gender problem), unconditional love (that a parent should love their child no matter what) and continuity (that their child was the same person that they knew and loved prior to disclosure).

In choosing to come out or not, LGBTQ young people have to consider who to come out to and how to come out, as well as weighing up the perceived costs and benefits of doing so. Studies of the disclosure of an LGB (e.g., Hillier, 2002; Lasser and Tharinger, 2003) or trans (e.g., Gagné *et al.*, 1997) identity consistently show that LGBTQ people are acutely aware of the potential stigma associated with non-heterosexuality and trans and the potential consequences (good or bad) that their disclosure might bring for themselves and for their parents. In these studies, young people reported assessing their environment (home, classroom, peer group) by gathering information about attitudes and actions towards LGBTQ people in order to determine to whom it might be 'safe' to come out, and whether disclosure to that person might result in an 'unsafe' person finding out. However, in some cases the decision to tell or not was taken out of their hands. For example, in Hillier's (2002) study some respondents reported their coming out being pre-empted by parents who either asked directly if they were 'gay' or unwittingly encountered evidence of their child's non-heterosexuality (e.g., finding love letters; finding them in bed with a same-sex lover). Likewise, some teenagers with GID actively live as the sex they consider themselves to be (rather than their natal sex) yet choose not to disclose (Holman and Goldberg, 2007), running the risk that their trans status will be discovered by others (e.g., in the changing rooms at school).

Despite the lack of research on the social and psychological benefits of disclosure to family and friends, it is commonly assumed that affirming one's identity as LGBTQ is a positive step. However, explicitly coming out to family and friends is not always viable or even safe. For example, the initial findings of the Safra Project (www.safraproject.org) show that for many Muslim LBT women coming out (or being 'outed') may result in negative reactions from family and friends (e.g., complete rejection; intensified pressure to get married; domestic violence). Similarly, for those who are financially and emotionally dependent on their families, the loss of support systems through coming out may affect matters such as housing, education and employment. Therefore, the gains of coming out do not always outweigh the potential losses or risks. For many members of marginalised racial and cultural groups, maintaining a close relationship with family and the family's respect in the community is valued very highly. Consequently, LGBTQ young people within these communities have to manage carefully the cultural values and expectations of their family and wider community in relation to their identity as LGBTQ. For this reason, many LGBTQ young people from racially and culturally marginalised groups maintain impermeable boundaries which segregate their LGBTQ life from other aspects of their life.

One of the problems of research on disclosure to family and friends is that it focuses solely on initial disclosure, ignoring the way in which for LGBTQ people disclosure is an ongoing phenomenon rather than a one-off event (e.g., see Kitzinger, 2000b). Moreover, while LGBTQ people may choose to come out in some instances they may also choose not to in others. For the most part, coming out in these mundane situations has been overlooked in psychological research. However, as Victoria Land and Celia Kitzinger (2005) highlight, because disclosure of an LGBTQ identity disrupts commonly held assumptions about the social world, disclosure (particularly in institutional settings) is interactionally difficult. Considerable identity management work is therefore done by LGBTQ individuals when they correct (or pass up opportunities to correct) the assumption that they are heterosexual (see also Chapter 5).

LGBTQ young people in school

Exploring one's sexuality, developing a sense of self and coming out (or not) are central to the sexuality and gender identity development of young people in adolescence. However, successfully negotiating this developmental task is unnecessarily complicated for many LGBTQ young people because the social contexts within which they find themselves (i.e., home, school) provide inadequate social support in relation to their sexuality and/or gender identity development.

Research in the UK (Hunt and Jensen, 2006; Ryan and Rivers, 2003), the USA (Ryan and Rivers, 2003), Australia (Hillier *et al.*, 2005) and New Zealand (Nairn and Smith, 2003) consistently reports that schools are particularly problematic places for LGBTQ young people. In particular, homophobic bullying by other students (and in some cases teachers) means that many LGBTQ young people spend a significant proportion of their day in an environment which is detrimental to their learning as well as to their health and well-being. A British survey of 1,145 LGBTQ young people (Hunt and Jensen, 2006) found that 65 per cent of respondents had experienced homophobic bullying in school. Almost all respondents had heard words and phrases such as 'dyke', 'poof' and 'you're so gay' used in a derogatory way, and of those who had been bullied, 92 per cent had experienced verbal homophobia, 41 per cent had been physically bullied and

17 per cent had received death threats. LGBTQ young people also frequently report being ostracised or excluded by peers. These incidences contribute to the creation of a hostile climate which leads to the alienation of LGBTQ young people (see Box 7.5).

Box 7.5   Key researcher: Ian Rivers on why I study homophobic bullying

In 1987, a study was published in the *Journal of Personality* that purported to show that young men who were victims of bullying at school experience difficulties in forming lasting intimate relationships in adulthood. As I intended to do my honours dissertation on the very same topic not only was this study of great interest to me but, as I read on, I was intrigued by the sampling frame used by the author. Like many other studies, the author surveyed American college undergraduates. However, in his analysis and write-up he only included those students who identified as heterosexual, setting aside those (some 13 per cent) who had identified otherwise. I conducted various literature searches to see if a follow-up study had been conducted with this small group to determine whether or not they exhibited similar findings and I was surprised to find that, despite a clear gap in our knowledge, no such follow-up had been conducted. My research agenda was set.

When I took up my first post as a lecturer in 1993, I was lucky enough to have a Dean of Faculty who gave me a small budget to conduct an exploratory study. Her reasoning for giving me this money was simple: 'I suppose they (lesbians and gay men) get bullied too.' From a budget of £500 grew the first study of homophobic bullying and its long-term correlates (Rivers, 2001). Over a period of three years I collected data from 190 former victims of bullying who recounted their experiences at school, providing me with evidence of the long-term and systematic abuse they experienced. Participants were then asked to complete further questionnaires that focused on long-term correlates (depression, anxiety, post-traumatic stress, relationship satisfaction, suicide ideation and bullying in the workplace). Finally, I conducted a series of interviews.

A decade later and this study has yet to be matched. There are larger and more comprehensive prospective and retrospective surveys of homophobic bullying, but none it seems captures the sadness, anger, frustration and torment that pervade this first study. I continue to study homophobic bullying because I have watched how my own research (e.g., Rivers, 2000; 2001) has been used by policy makers to move the UK from a position of ignorance to one of complacency. Does ticking a box in a school inspection really mean that schools are now safe? I continue with my work because I see policies drawn up which fail to understand the subtleties of my own and other studies. Do victims of homophobic bullying really fail to achieve academically at school? I never said so. Finally, I continue with this work because I am constantly in search of a better way to measure homophobic bullying and to assess its long-term effects.

Although there is widespread incidence of homophobic bullying in schools, it is reported that little if anything is done to address the issue. In the UK, fewer than 6 per cent of schools have a bullying policy that specifically addresses homophobic bullying, despite a government directive (DfEE Circular 10/99) which notes that head teachers have a legal responsibility to 'prevent all forms of bullying – including that related to sexual orientation' (Warwick *et al.*, 2001: 133). Similarly, despite significant investment in programmes aimed at promoting acceptance of gender and sexuality diversity and the reduction of homophobia in Australian schools, there is little evidence that these interventions have had any impact (Hillier *et al.*, 2005). Since teachers fail actively to promote sexual and gender diversity, infrequently address homophobic bullying when it occurs, and in some cases perpetrate prejudice themselves, it is hardly surprising that homophobic bullying in schools is under-reported and that LGBTQ young people do not feel supported.

This is compounded by the lack of engagement with LGBTQ issues and concerns in curriculum content. In the UK, fewer than 30 per cent of LGBTQ young people have ever been taught about lesbian and gay people or issues in class (Hunt and Jensen, 2006), while in Australia it is reported to be fewer than 20 per cent (Hillier *et al.*, 2005). Furthermore, in directly relevant subject areas such as Personal, Social and Health Education (PSHE) in the UK and Personal Development, Health and Physical Education (PDHPE) in Australia, LGBTQ issues and concerns are seldom discussed. Similarly, while information and advice about **different-sex relationships** and safer heterosex are freely available, information about same-sex relationships and safer same-sex sexual practices are non-existent.

Although LGBTQ people may be bullied for reasons other than their sexuality/gender identity, the problem of specifically homophobic, biphobic and transphobic bullying should not be underestimated. The targets of the bullying may not necessarily be LGBTQ, because one of the purposes of homophobic bullying is reinforcing gender conformity and the construction of heterosexuality as the norm (Sharpe, 2002). For example, girls whose appearance or behaviour is not stereotypically feminine ('butch girls') and boys whose appearance or behaviour is not stereotypically masculine ('effeminate boys') may also be subject to homophobic bullying. While its effects are often felt more acutely by LGBTQ young people, it creates a climate of prejudice which is experienced by all young people regardless of sexuality or gender identity. Although much homophobic bullying centres on name calling – i.e., using terms such as 'poof' and 'lezzie' as put-downs – some forms of bullying are much more serious. Such incidences include physical violence (being hit, punched or kicked); sexual assault; and theft of, or damage to, property.

As a result of homophobic, biphobic and transphobic bullying many LGBTQ young people develop strategies to avert victimisation. There is significant evidence to suggest that some resort to absenteeism to avoid being bullied (see Carragher and Rivers, 2002; Rivers, 2000) and many engage in 'visibility management'. US psychologists Jon Lasser and Deborah Tharinger (2003) define visibility management as the ongoing process by which LGBTQ adolescents make careful, planned decisions about whether they will disclose their sexuality and gender identity, and to whom, and how they will monitor their self-presentation to avoid being identified. This may include modifying one's dress, speech and body language or dating individuals of a different sex, to ensure that they conform to gender stereotypes and can 'pass' as heterosexual. (Interestingly, recent research indicates that dress and appearance are important factors in the formation of LGB identities for young people, see Clarke and Turner, 2007.)

However, one of the biggest challenges facing LGBTQ young people in the school setting is a lack of support from teachers. In some cases, there is evidence of teachers actively and passively supporting negative attitudes and even participating in acts of physical, verbal and emotional aggression (Rivers, 2000). In addition, LGBTQ young people frequently encounter teachers who are confused about, unable or unwilling to address their needs. Although in the UK this may in part be due to the legacy of Section 28, a Canadian interview study (Mishna *et al.*, 2008) of people who work with LGB young people (e.g., teachers, counsellors, social workers) indicated that the main reasons for not addressing homophobic bullying were a denial that LGB young people exist, not viewing homophobic bullying as a serious problem, and a fear of being victimised themselves.

A recent survey of LGBQ young people in UK schools (Hunt and Jensen, 2006) suggests that in schools which affirm that homophobic bullying is wrong, where teachers respond to homophobic incidents, and where pupils are taught positively about lesbian and gay issues, LGBQ young people are significantly less likely to have been bullied, and more likely to feel safe and happy in school. Although not included within the sample, it would seem likely that this would apply to young trans people as well. In the absence of school-based support, community-based LGBTQ youth groups have sought to promote emotional well-being and provide a space in which young people can safely meet and come to understand themselves and their sexuality/gender identity (Crowley *et al.*, 2007; Warwick *et al.*, 2001). However, in the main these initiatives are located in a few large cities, and therefore are not readily accessible to the majority of LGBTQ young people.

The psychosocial effects of homophobic bullying and lack of social support for LGBTQ young people are cause for concern. For example, Canadian psychotherapist Faye Mishna and colleagues (2008) indicated that homophobic bullying typically resulted in both psychological effects (e.g., low self-esteem, anxiety and depression) and social effects (e.g., being 'silenced', feeling alienated from peers). LGBTQ young people appear to be significantly more at risk of suicidality and are over-represented in statistics for alcohol and substance abuse, absenteeism (truancy) and dropping out of school (Rivers, 2000). Despite the limitations of work in this area (e.g., small samples in localised settings) it can confidently be concluded that there *are* negative outcomes of homophobic, transphobic and biphobic bullying and a school climate that is unsupportive of LGBTQ issues/concerns. However, there is limited information about the extent to which LGBTQ young people are 'at risk' and which LGBTQ young people are particularly vulnerable.

Exploring identity and finding a community

As we have highlighted, opportunities at school and at home to discuss LGBTQ issues can be extremely limited. There are also few safe social spaces in which to explore sexuality and gender identity. For example, although there are – in larger towns/cities, at least – 'gay' nightclubs, these can be highly sexualised (and noisy!) environments. They are therefore far from ideal social contexts for the development of emotional and social aspects of sexuality and gender identity; and provide little opportunity to establish social and support networks and to seek information. For these reasons it is common for LGBTQ young people to seek alternative sources of support and friendship.

Historically, as we noted above, the main way in which young people have met other LGBTQ young people has been through community-based LGBTQ groups (e.g., coming out groups; LGBTQ youth groups). Such groups have served an important function in supporting young people through the coming out process, being a source of information, and providing a point of contact for connecting with the wider LGBTQ community. Although these groups continue to thrive in some places, they are often unfunded and staffed by volunteers, so may not be readily available or even accessible to many LGBTQ young people. As well as typically being located in large urban areas, in-person attendance requires a certain level of independence and outness; and, in most cases, to have reached a minimum age such as 14 or 16.

For many LGBTQ young people, the advent of the Internet has revolutionised the ability to explore sexuality and gender identity, seek information and support, and connect with other LGBTQ people. Research in the USA and Australia (e.g., Hillier and Harrison, 2007; Thomas et al., 2007) has explored the role of the Internet in the identity development and coming out of LGB young people (see also Chapter 8). One of the main advantages offered by the Internet is the ability to seek out information and connect with others while maintaining anonymity. This is particularly important for young people who are still exploring their sexuality as well as for those who don't feel safe to come out in their immediate social and familial environment. The Internet provides a space in which young people can feel more confident to be themselves, and where they can explore what it is like to be LGBT through practising disclosure, building online friendships, and even engaging in cybersex without risking their anonymity. It also provides an important function as a repository of information about LGBTQ issues such as coming out and safer sex – information which is largely non-existent elsewhere.

In particular, chat rooms have been found to provide an effective social tool for overcoming emotional (e.g., shyness; fear) and social (e.g., geographical location; living with parents) barriers. In this respect, chat rooms appear to provide a central role in the coming out process by aiding self-discovery, reducing anxiety about LGBTQ life, receiving social support, entering LGBT communities, and searching for potential partners. In many cases, young people have reported using such forums as a way to develop new social circles which subsequently developed into offline friendships and relationships.

Trans people are particularly vulnerable to isolation and social exclusion. For young trans people, the Internet offers additional potential in that it does not involve face-to-face contact, so there is the opportunity to interact with people without the complication of physical cues. This is illustrated in the following excerpt where Billy (FTM trans) describes his experiences of using the Internet to connect with other trans people:

> I can be myself. I can think before I type so I don't screw things up as I find it hard to talk to others. I can communicate with people around the world who are in a similar situation to me. I can communicate as myself, a boy and learn of other people's experiences. The fact that I am (ugh) biologically female is no matter (neither). My face nor voice is projected so the only thing they get is what is on my mind. (quoted in Hillier *et al.*, 2001: 56)

It would seem then, that the very aspects of internet chat rooms that are often viewed by parents and teachers as problematic because of the potential for vulnerable young people to be exploited are those which provide a liberating opportunity, especially for trans people. Furthermore, as Australian social scientists Lynne Hillier and Lyn Harrison (2007) highlight, LGBTQ young people demonstrate a great deal of agency in choosing how far to take friendships and relationships established online. This of course does not mean that LGBTQ young people are not at risk of becoming victims of predatory adults (sexual or otherwise), but because they are already exposed to identity-related risks in the physical social world they appear to have a more acute awareness of the potential risks of the virtual world. However, issues such as these have not been well researched, so it is difficult to establish the extent to which there is a match between actual and perceived risk in both physical and virtual contexts.

Although the Internet is widely used by young people, it is important to remember that access will vary considerably. For example, according to the Office for National Statistics (ONS) only an estimated 57 per cent of households in the UK have access to the Internet, which means that a sizeable minority of young people (including LGBTQ young people) will not easily be able to access Internet-based communities and information. Furthermore, even for those who do have access at home, in most instances this is via a PC shared with other family members, which may considerably limit the extent to which they feel able to access LGBTQ specific information.

Gaps and absences

- There is very limited information about the experiences of trans young people in identifying as trans and coming out to others.
- Psychologists have paid little attention to the way in which sexuality and gender intersect with other factors (e.g., race, culture, religion, ability, socio-economic

status and social class) and the impact of these other factors on the process of identity development and disclosure.

- Virtually nothing is known about the experiences of LGBTQ young people who have left education (either working or unemployed) and the issues specific to that particular group.

- Most research on coming out as non-heterosexual has focused on younger people; less is known about coming out later in life (but see Chapter 10).

Main chapter points

This chapter:

- Outlined some classic models of LGBTQ identity development and critiqued the stage model approach to coming out.
- Discussed sexual fluidity as it applies to young people and more generally across the lifespan.
- Overviewed the experiences of LGBTQ young people in disclosing their sexuality/gender identity to family and friends.
- Explored the school experiences of LGBTQ young people with particular reference to homophobic, biphobic and transphobic bullying.
- Reviewed the ways in which LGBTQ young people explore their identity and find community.

Questions for discussion and classroom exercises

1. Are the experiences of LGBTQ young people inevitably negative? What evidence is there to suggest that LGBTQ young people have positive experiences of being/becoming LGBTQ?

2. When did you first recognise that you were heterosexual/lesbian/gay/bisexual/trans/queer? How did you know? What explanation (if any) do you have for your sexuality and gender identity?

3. Could you ever envisage your sexuality and gender identity changing at some point in your life? What leads you to draw the conclusion that you do? What theoretical assumptions about gender/sexuality are your conclusions based on?

4. Imagine you have been asked to design an anti-homophobic, -biphobic and -transphobic bullying campaign for your local schools. What information would it include? How would you raise awareness of homophobic, biphobic and transphobic bullying in schools? What measures would you introduce to combat such bullying?

5.   What are some of the advantages and disadvantages of theorising LGBTQ identity development in terms of a series of stages? Try devising your own model for one or all of these identity categories. How would it improve on existing models?

Further reading

Gagné, P., Tewksbury, R. and McGaughey, D. (1997) Coming out and crossing over: identity formation and proclamation in a transgender community. *Gender and Society*, 11(4), 478–508.
Drawing on data from interviews with sixty-five MTF trans people, this paper examines the coming-out experiences of transgendered individuals, and the extent to which trans identities provide challenges to the binary system of sex/gender.

Griffin, C. (2000) Absences that matter: constructions of sexuality in studies of young women's friendships. *Feminism and Psychology*, 10(2), 227–45.
This article reviews research on young women's friendship groups in western societies, arguing that much of this work has relatively little to say about the sexual and erotic dimension of such relationships and the construction of young women's sexualities. It also explores the way in which research on young women's lives often overlooks the possibility of same-sex female desire, and also lesbian (or bisexual) existence, thereby assuming that young women are always already heterosexual.

Maguen, S., Floyd, F. J., Bakeman, R. and Armistead, L. (2002) Developmental milestones and disclosure of sexual orientation among gay, lesbian and bisexual youths. *Applied Developmental Psychology*, 23, 219–33.
This research paper presents findings from a US questionnaire study of coming out, disclosure and self-esteem for LGB young people. The findings suggest diverse individual trajectories of coming-out experiences and highlight the need for greater attention to individual differences in sexual identity development.

Rivers, I. (2002) Developmental issues for lesbian and gay youth. In A. Coyle and C. Kitzinger (eds.), *Lesbian and gay psychology: new perspectives* (pp. 30–44). Oxford: BPS Blackwell.
This chapter offers a good overview of the issues encountered by lesbian and gay youth in coming to identify as lesbian/gay and in negotiating the social aspects of living as a lesbian/gay adolescent.

Savin-Williams, R. C. (2001) A critique of research on sexual-minority youths. *Journal of Adolescence*, 24(1), 5–13.
This paper reviews psychological research on LGB young people and offers a critique of this body of work.

8   Relationships

Overview

- Legal recognition of same-sex relationships
- Comparing same-sex and different-sex relationships
- Sexual practices
- Beyond the normative couple

There are a number of stereotypes about LGBTQ relationships. These include the idea that non-heterosexual people are unable to form intimate relationships and that they live lonely lives; that same-sex relationships are unstable or mimic traditional heterosexual roles; and that gay men and bisexuals have multiple sexual partners (and that this is a negative thing). As you will see in this chapter, the research on same-sex relationships shows that these stereotypes are not true, and that often they reflect normative assumptions about what constitutes 'good' relationships. 'Same-sex' couples comprised of bisexual and trans people in relationships with people of the same sex/gender have been largely ignored in the psychological literature to date. Therefore this chapter focuses mainly on lesbian and gay relational experiences.

Legal recognition of same-sex relationships

As same-sex relationships have been historically marginalised, partnership rights have become an important political goal for lesbians and gay men (but see Kandaswamy, 2008). Elizabeth Peel and socio-legal scholar Rosie Harding conducted an online survey with 1,538 LGBTQ people from twenty-seven countries and found that 94.5 per cent agreed that same-sex couples should be able to marry 'just like' different-sex couples (Harding and Peel, 2006). The absence of legal recognition has had negative consequences for LGBTQ people. The US case of Sharon Kowalski is one example. Sharon and her partner Karen Thompson had lived together for four years when, in 1988, Sharon suffered a severe head injury as a result of a car accident. Karen wanted to care for Sharon at home, but Sharon's parents put her in a nursing home and prevented contact between the two women.

After a nearly ten-year legal battle, Karen was finally permitted to bring Sharon home (Townsend, 1998). Examples such as this demonstrate why legal protection for same-sex relationships is an important issue in the lives of many LGBTQ people.

In recent years one of the most important social changes for same-sex couples (particularly middle-class gay men and lesbians) has been the introduction of legal recognition of their relationships in most western democracies (Peel and Harding, 2008). There are a few exceptions: the USA and Australia at a federal level, Greece, Ireland and Italy. The type of legal recognition varies. In 2008, nine jurisdictions had full marriage equivalent to heterosexual marriage. Many jurisdictions have other similar forms of legal recognition, including civil partnership (CP) in the UK (Box 8.1).

Kitzinger and Wilkinson (2006: 177) argue that equal access to marriage, irrespective of gender, is important because it 'would mean that categories like "male" and "female", and "lesbian"/ "gay"/ "bisexual" etcetera do not have to be

---

Box 8.1 *Highlights: legal recognition of same-sex relationships internationally*

Laws are changing rapidly in this area so more countries may have same-sex marriage, or similar laws when you read this! More responsibilities and rights are attached to marriage and various forms of civil unions than to domestic partnership or cohabitation. The dates listed are the year that the legislation came into force. As you'll see, Denmark was the first country in the world to bring in partnership rights in the late 1980s.

Marriage

The Netherlands (2001), Belgium (2003), Canada (2005), Spain (2005), South Africa (2006), Norway (2009), and the US states of Massachusetts (2004), Iowa (2007) and California (2008).

Civil union, civil partnership or registered partnership

Civil Union – US states of Vermont (2000), Connecticut (2005), New Jersey (2007), New Hampshire (2008), Tasmania, Australia (2004), New Zealand (2005), Rio Grande de Sul, Brazil (2004), two parts of Mexico: Mexico City (2006) and Coahuila region (2007).
Civil partnership – Britain and Northern Ireland (2005).
Registered partnership – Denmark (1989), Sweden (1995), Iceland (1996), Greenland (1996), The Netherlands (1998), France (1999), Germany (2001), Finland (2002), Luxemburg (2004), Andorra (2005), Czech Republic (2006), Switzerland (2007).

Domestic partnership or co-habitation rights

Hungary (1996), South Africa (1999), US states of Hawaii (1997), California (2000), Maine (2004), Washington (2007), Oregon (2008), and the District of Columbia, Washington DC (2002), Portugal (2001), Austria (2003), Croatia (2003), some regions of Italy (2004), Slovenia (2006), Australia: relationship registries in Victoria and New South Wales (2008), and civil unions (with no formal rights attached) in Tasmania (2004) and the Australian Capital Territory (2008).

continually reproduced. What's needed is not "same-sex marriage" or "gay marriage", just equal access to marriage (and to civil partnership) for everyone regardless of gender and sexuality.' They also point out that the current legal situation in the UK is unfair to trans, intersex and bisexual people because the definition of marriage – as restricted to one man and one woman, and two men or two women for CP – shores up gender boundaries and reinforces binary notions of sex/gender and sexuality.

Legal segregation on the basis of gender and sexuality can cause people difficulties in their everyday lives, especially if they are trans, or if they identify as polyamorous and have more than one relationship at a time. UK-based sociologist Christian Klesse (2006b) suggests that the current British legal context forces people living in non-monogamous bisexual relationships into a difficult position. First, they need to choose between which (if any) of their partners they wish to be in a legally recognised relationship with and, second, if they marry their different-sex partner that relationship is privileged over their same-sex relationship(s). See Box 8.2 for information about how law can cause problems for transsexual people in relationships.

Effects of legal recognition on same-sex relationships

There is a small, but growing, body of empirical research about legal relationship recognition (e.g., Clarke *et al.*, 2006; Porche and Purvin, 2008) hinged around questions like:

- What, if any, effect does legal recognition have on relationships?
- How does legal recognition for same-sex couples impact on the wider society?
- Are there differences between legally recognised same-sex couples and heterosexual married couples?
- Are there differences between legally recognised and non-legally recognised same-sex relationships?
- How do same-sex couples negotiate conventional understandings of relationships in their everyday lives?

Qualitative studies exploring same-sex couples' views about legal recognition have found that the everyday reasons for partnership recognition include: love;

Box 8.2 *Highlights: implications of the Gender Recognition Act (2004) for married transsexual people*

The way in which the Gender Recognition Act (GRA, 2004) intersects with the different levels of legal recognition offered to different-sex and same-sex relationships in the UK is a good example of how society regulates gender and sexual identities in a manner that privileges heteronormativity. The GRA offers transsexual people full legal recognition of their change of gender, so a male-to-female (MTF) transsexual person can register as a woman in English law and a female-to-male (FTM) transsexual person can legally register as a man. When a person applies for and receives their gender recognition certificate, they are entitled to a new birth certificate reflecting their acquired gender. The person is then able to have a civil partnership with a person of the same gender as her or his acquired gender, or marry someone of the 'opposite' gender to his or her acquired gender.

But what happens if the person was already heterosexually married before they registered their new gender? A few cases have hit the British headlines:

Dian Parry, a 66-year-old Welsh reverend, is a step away from being legally recognised as a woman but this would mean annulling her forty-five-year marriage to Anita and entering into a civil partnership. Annulling their marriage, a spokesperson said to a regional newspaper, *Wales on Sunday* (1 January 2006), 'is like a physical break for people who have been married for years'. Dian is being forced to choose between her gender and her marriage.

A 31-year-old finance manager from Edinburgh underwent sex reassignment surgery in 2003 and is petitioning the European Court of Human Rights because she can only be legally recognised as a woman by divorcing her wife of six years. The couple said to a national newspaper, the *Sunday Times* (30 October 2005): 'We feel trapped. When we married we made a public commitment in front of our friends and family to stay together for better or for worse and have no intention of breaking that promise … This legislation breaches our human rights because it is plain interference by the state in our private lives … A civil partnership is not the same as marriage.'

protecting already established mutual responsibilities (e.g., the non-birth mother's role in lesbian parented families); encouraging recognition of the relationship from family members; legal and financial rights; and the importance of a public statement of commitment (Clarke *et al.*, 2007; Shipman and Smart, 2007).

US LGBTQ psychologist Esther Rothblum and her colleagues have conducted quantitative questionnaire research comparing three groups: (1) same-sex couples in civil unions; (2) same-sex couples not in civil unions; and (3) the heterosexual married siblings of civil union couples (e.g., Rothblum *et al.*, 2006). They obtained copies of all the Vermont civil union certificates issued in the first year civil unions were made available (2000–1) and sent this population of same-sex couples letters asking them to take part in a questionnaire study. As they were comparing three groups they decided to limit the sample to the first 400 civil union couples who were willing to nominate friends and siblings to participate as well. More of their results are discussed in the next section of this chapter, but in terms of comparisons between lesbians and gay men in civil unions with those not in civil unions they found some differences. Lesbian couples in civil unions were more open about their sexual identity, reported more contact with their mothers and were more likely to consider themselves married than lesbian couples not in civil unions. Gay men in civil unions had more children (17 per cent compared to 9.7 per cent), and were more likely to consider themselves married, initiate contact with their partner's mother and to state that their partner's father made them feel like part of the family than gay men not in civil unions. Gay men not in civil unions were more likely to report that they had seriously considered ending their relationship. It appears, then, that same-sex couples in legal unions have closer relationships with their **families of origin** as well as their families in-law, and in some ways appear more like heterosexual married couples.

Comparing same-sex and different-sex relationships

The central tradition in relationships research has been comparative studies of lesbian/gay and heterosexual relationships. This research has documented both similarities and differences between same-sex and heterosexual couples. There has been, however, an emphasis on similarities, especially in early research which concentrated on proving that same-sex relationships are just as good as heterosexual ones, and challenging myths about same-sex relationships. Core topics within the comparison paradigm include the division of domestic labour, relationship satisfaction and quality, and money management. We now explore two of these topics – the division of domestic labour and relationship satisfaction (for a discussion of money management, see Burns *et al.*, 2008; Clarke *et al.*, 2005).

Within the context of heterosexual marriage, although some heterosexual men are increasingly involved in household labour, on the whole heterosexual women retain responsibility for household labour (deciding what needs to be done, when) and carry out more domestic chores than men (Dryden, 1999). By contrast, research has found greater parity in lesbian and gay relationships, with most couples reporting that they share household labour. Gay male partners tend to specialise in particular domestic duties (e.g., one partner does the cooking and the other washes the dishes); whereas lesbian partners tend to do the same tasks equally often (Kurdek, 2007; see also Chapter 9).

The greater commitment to equality in lesbian and gay male couples and families has been explained by structural and ideological factors (Patterson *et al.*, 2004). In heterosexual relationships, men still earn, on average, more than women, spend more time in full-time paid employment, and have occupations with greater status, than their female partners (Equal Opportunities Commission, 2006). It is easy to think that there are not any gender differences between women and men these days, but in Britain in 2005, for instance, the gap between men's and women's earnings was 17.1 per cent for full-time workers and 38.4 per cent for part-time workers. Ninety per cent of men with children under 5 were in employment compared to 55 per cent of women (Equal Opportunities Commission, 2006). These structural issues, for various reasons, are used to justify the reduced amount of unpaid labour that heterosexual men undertake in the home.

By comparison, most lesbians and gay men are in dual-income relationships (Peplau and Fingerhut, 2007). Some researchers argue that lesbian couples tend be in occupations of similar levels of prestige and have an ideological commitment to contributing equally to unpaid labour in the home (Dunne, 1997). This ideological commitment to equality in lesbian relationships and families is strongly mediated by opting out of conventional (heterosexual) gender norms pertaining to the ways in which women and men are supposed to relate to their partners and their children (Dunne, 2003). The UK-based sociologist Gillian Dunne (1998: 292) argues that it is important to look at the ways in which same-sex partners negotiate divisions of labour because: 'knowledge of what can be achieved in these situations provides alternative models for evaluating the effectiveness and fairness of dominant heterosexual practice and for identifying barriers that hinder the development of greater equality between the sexes'. Therefore, in terms of division of labour, same-sex relationships typically compare favourably to different-sex relationships, and there might even be scope for same-sex relationships to provide an egalitarian model for heterosexual relationships.

However, as we briefly noted in Chapter 2, some researchers have questioned whether the 'equality norm' for same-sex couples is an artefact of particular research methods, agendas and populations. In other words, it is important to consider how a reliance on samples of white, middle-class couples in which both partners have similar backgrounds can shape the research findings (Carrington, 1999; Gabb, 2004). US sociologist Christopher Carrington (1999) conducted a study of fifty-two same-sex couples in San Francisco, using ethnographic observation and interviews. He found that three quarters of the couples had a specialised pattern of household labour with one partner doing *more* of the household tasks. Although couples were committed to egalitarianism (as many different-sex couples are), Carrington identified discrepant accounts of housework, with gay men taking the credit and lesbians giving credit to their partners for domestic labour. He concluded from this that same-sex couples hide unequal divisions of labour to protect the gender identity of partners who have transgressed cultural expectations by doing more or less housework than is 'expected' of their gender.

Relationship satisfaction and relationship quality research generally shows that there are few differences between lesbian, gay and heterosexual couples and that the processes that regulate relationship functioning are applicable across these different types of relationships. In their classic *American Couples* study, sociologists Philip Blumstein and Pepper Schwartz (1983) found that arguing about money, intrusion of work into the relationship, spending too much time apart and non-monogamy were all related to poor relationship quality in heterosexual, lesbian and gay couples. Like their heterosexual counterparts, lesbian and gay couples typically benefit when partners are similar in background, attitudes and values (Peplau and Fingerhut, 2007).

Using psychometric measures of psychological adjustment, personality traits, relationship style and conflict resolution, US-based psychologist Lawrence Kurdek (2004) found there were no differences between fifty-three lesbian couples, eighty gay male couples and eighty heterosexual couples with children on half the measures. Most of the differences he found indicated that the gay and lesbian partners functioned better than the heterosexual partners in the sample. Lesbian and gay couples fared less well on perceived levels of social support, which means there may be less 'social glue' to keep same-sex couples together through times of difficulty in the relationship than for heterosexual couples. In terms of relationship formation, again the pattern is similar across sexualities. See Box 8.3 for more information about how LGBTQ people form relationships.

Box 8.3   *Highlights: love in cyberspace*

How do LGBTQ people meet to form relationships? Traditionally, pubs and clubs, the gay press, and events (such as Pride or Mardi Gras) and other specific social spaces for LGBTQ people (such as youth groups), were the only safe environments in which non-heterosexual and trans people could meet each other. Nowadays dating is increasingly virtual: LGBTQ people find love in cyberspace through friendship and dating websites like Gaydar, Gaydargirls, PolyMatchmaker, BiCupid and TransPassions. 'Cybersexuality', it is argued, is 'a sexual space midway between fantasy and action … creating sexual communities' (Ross, 2005: 342). For socially marginalised groups, such as LGBTQ people, the Internet has the potential to remove barriers associated with geography, age, social class, culture, disability and so on. Moreover, as LGBTQ people continue to have relatively few opportunities in real life (IRL) to meet each other without fear of negative social consequences, the (often anonymous) Internet has grown rapidly as a venue for meeting partners, responding to personal ads, using chat rooms and engaging in cybersex. However, British psychotherapist Martin Milton (2006: 306–8) raises a note of caution about the ways gay men, for example, can relate to each other on the Internet and in chat rooms, because these forums:

> allow a set of assumptions along the line of the promise of 'what you want, when you want it' – in fact one popular site uses this very catch phrase … Who doesn't like the idea that you can have whatever you want *and* you can have it when you want it? … [But] under the guise of 'I am sorry but "it" doesn't do it for me' … it seems we are able to insult, berate, reject and psychologically traumatise others … We might feel that we have done

> something very positive when we say 'Sorry, not into that' … Would people feel so smug if they realised that, in effect, they have just told the vulnerable youth taking his first steps at coming out, that he needn't bother?

Although the Internet is an especially popular forum for LGBTQ people to interact and potentially form relationships (whether they are casual, sexual, long-lasting or platonic), little research has been carried out in this area. The existing research tends to focus on MSM. US researchers Allen Thomas *et al.* (2007) conducted a small-scale qualitative study with young gay men (aged 19–26). The analysis of the young men's coming out stories indicated that their online experiences facilitated greater self-acceptance of their sexuality. Social work researcher Mark Henrickson (2007) reported that Asian-born New Zealanders were more likely than other groups to use the Internet for their first and continuing contact with LGB communities. Male participants used the web more than did female participants to facilitate sexual contact regardless of age, income or relationship status. However, in a study of the use of chat rooms by gay men in Sweden, Ronny Tikkanen and Michael Ross (2000) found that discrimination and social exclusion does occur between LGBTQ people in online spaces. They also found that the demographics associated with Internet use continue to be skewed towards younger, more affluent LGBTQ people. Furthermore, Australian research indicates that online spaces for young LGBTQ people are highly racialised, with white gay young men being the norm which all other groups are compared with or differentiated from (Fraser, 2009).

    The general consensus of mainstream psychological research in the comparative paradigm has been summed up as follows: 'despite external differences in how gay, lesbian and heterosexual couples are constituted, the relationships of gay and lesbian partners appear to work in much the same way as the relationships of heterosexual partners' (Kurdek, 2005: 253). However, this research has been criticised for de-emphasising differences between same-sex and heterosexual relationships. If we look again at the research of Rothblum and colleagues on civil unions, we see some differences between the couples in their samples. For example, the lesbians in their study (whether or not they were in a civil union) reported sharing household tasks and finances more equally than their heterosexual siblings even though they shared a similar background (Rothblum *et al.*, 2006).

    Researchers have often highlighted the similarities between same- and different-sex couples and have commonly failed to consider potential sources of power imbalance *within* same-sex relationships because 'emphasising sameness' supposedly demonstrates the 'normality' of same-sex relationships. Yet this approach can be heteronormative or may pathologise LGBTQ relationships that deliberately (or inadvertently) do not mirror heterosexual relationship practices. For example, lesbian relationships have been seen to be too intimate and 'enmeshed', suffering from 'fusion' and 'merger' because the boundaries between women are too blurred, and so women lose their individuality (e.g., Krestan and Bepko, 1980). But this idea is based on a heterosexual way of relating which considers higher levels of 'separateness' between the people in the relationship as the norm (opposites attract!), and lesbians' departure from this norm is considered problematic. It seems that both emphasising similarities and emphasising differences are important. Stressing similarities across sexualities can be positive if it means lesbian and gay relationships are less stigmatised and myths are dispelled (see also Chapter 9). Focusing on differences can also be a way of celebrating the unique and important contribution same-sex relationships can make to our understanding of human relationships more generally (Dunne, 1997).

Sexual practices

Sexual relationships and practices are a significant part of most adults' lives. It is important to point out that although lesbians and gay men tend to be associated with particular sex acts (oral sex for lesbians; anal sex for gay men; Peel, 2005), sexual practices do not map onto sexual identities – heterosexuals too practise oral and anal sex and bondage, domination, sadism, masochism (**BDSM**). Research on LGBTQ sexual practices is patchy, partly because of the ethical dilemmas associated with undertaking research on sex related topics (Klesse, 2007), and also because of a shift away from focusing on sexual practices in order to challenge the pathologisation of LGBTQ people as 'perverts' (Halperin, 2007). Typically, those sexual practices considered more acceptable (both within LGBTQ communities and by society in general) are those that occur between coupled, monogamous LGBTQ people in the privacy of their homes. Laws across many countries, and the public opinion that often accompanies (or indeed shapes) them, deem such a private, monogamous view of LGBTQ sexual practices as largely acceptable. LGBTQ sexual practices that are more publicly visible or that don't approximate monogamous coupledom are often viewed as problematic or even as dangerous (e.g., sex between men in **public sex environments (PSEs)**).

Unsurprisingly then, sex in relationships has been another popular topic for comparative research. Within same-sex and different-sex relationships there is a great deal of variability in the amount of sex people have and a general decline in the frequency of sex in relationships over time. In Solomon *et al.*'s (2005) study, married heterosexual women reported having more sex (two or three times a month, on average) than did lesbians (closer to once a month, on average). Heterosexual and gay men did not significantly differ in frequency of sex, but over half of the gay men had experienced sex outside their primary relationship compared to only 15.2 per cent of the married heterosexual men. This pattern mirrors the findings of research more generally – gay male couples have more sex than other couples; lesbians report having the least sex (Blumstein and Schwartz, 1983). Heterosexual couples and lesbian couples tend to have more sexually exclusive relationships than gay men (and some bisexual people) who tend to be more sexually open and non-monogamous. But the meaning attached to monogamy is different across couples; it is positively related to relationship satisfaction for lesbian and heterosexual couples, but less so for gay male couples (Kurdek, 1991a).

Lots of value judgements are made in relationships research: the notion of 'promiscuity' is a good example. How much sex people have, and (of course) with whom, is culturally value-laden and the label 'promiscuous' – as applied to gay men, bisexuals or younger heterosexual women who are actively interested in sex – is not seen as a positive thing! Nevertheless, research evidence seems to suggest that gay men *do* have more sex than other groups. However, the notion of 'promiscuity' is highly problematic and we need to ask who decides how much sex is too much sex. Not gay men, because if standards for quantity of sex were determined by the average amount reported by the majority of gay men, then everyone else would be having too little! Another way to think about this is to focus on the issue of safety rather than quantity of sex: if people are practising safer sex does it matter how much sex they are having? From a liberal perspective the answer is 'no' but from some religiously informed and cultural perspectives the answer would be 'yes'. So the moral dimensions of relationships research are always bubbling away in the background and are inescapable regardless of the research methods used.

Despite the binary between 'good' (private, monogamous) LGBTQ sexual practices and 'bad' (public, non-monogamous) sexual practices, LGBTQ people engage in a range of sexual practices that blur this boundary. It is not the case that all LGBTQ sexual practices are intentionally transgressive; however, they are often viewed this way because of their difference from the heterosexual norm. Some LGBTQ people engage in sexual practices that *are* intended to be transgressive – they are intended to evoke resistance to social norms or they aim to explore alternative understandings of sexual identities and practices (e.g., BDSM).

Gay sexual practices

Historically, sex in public places and sex in venues designed for sexual encounters (e.g., gay saunas) have played an important role in providing gay men with opportunities to meet one another. Although it may be argued that men who have sex with men (MSM) have often been restricted to seeking sex in these places because of limited alternative options, the use of public spaces and sex venues has also allowed MSM opportunities to develop their own sexual communities (Frankis and Flowers, 2005).

Diversity in sexual practices exists not only among LGBTQ people, but also within each individual subgroup of LGBTQ communities. For instance, research highlights the range of sexual identities adopted by trans people. US sociologist David Schleifer (2006) has explored the sexual practices of gay trans men. As sex reassignment surgery (particularly phalloplasty) for trans men lags a long way behind sex reassignment surgery for trans women, trans men often engage in sexual and other types of intimate relationships with people who recognise and celebrate their chosen gender identity, regardless of their physiology. Schleifer suggests that gay trans men may hesitate to enter into sexual relationships if they feel their sexual identities as gay men won't be respected. For some of Schleifer's participants, vaginal intercourse between trans gay men (with vaginas) and natal gay men can often meet the sexual needs of both parties, without undermining their gay male identities.

It is also important to recognise how racial differences impact on sexual practices. Although positive interracial sexual relations occur between a range of LGBTQ people, some people hold negative stereotypes about other racial/cultural groups, such as white US gay men expecting African American gay men to be sexually aggressive (McBride, 2005), or white gay men in general expecting Asian gay men to be sexually passive (Han, 2006).

Lesbian sexual practices

Various suggestions have been put forward for why lesbians have less sex, particularly in the context of long-term relationships, known colloquially as 'lesbian bed death'. There has been considerable debate among lesbians and lesbian psychologists about the extent to which 'lesbian bed death' exists. One theory is that gender socialisation leads women to ignore sexual feelings and not initiate sex and this effect is amplified in intimate relationships between women (Nicols, 2004). Another argument is that because sex is often conceived solely in terms of penis-in-vagina intercourse, any research that uses the generic term 'sex' might not adequately capture lesbians' sexual experiences, which are much wider and more diverse than penetration. This means that the criteria on which lesbians are judged to have 'less sex' should be challenged (Peplau and Fingerhut, 2007). Therefore, on the one hand, it can be argued that it is heterosexist and patriarchal to view low levels of sexual activity among lesbians as 'unhealthy'. But on the other hand, others have argued that settling for a sexless norm in long-term lesbian relationships is problematic because it reinforces cultural notions that women are not sexual beings (Iasenza, 2002). In terms of what lesbians actually *do* sexually, a (predominantly) London-based survey completed by 1,218 lesbians found 90 per cent reported engaging in oral sex, vaginal penetration with fingers and mutual masturbation, 53 per cent reported vaginal penetration using a sex toy, and 85 per cent also reported sexual activity with men (Farquhar *et al.*, 2001).

Lesbians adopting a 'sex radical' approach have emphasised individual women's rights to engage in sexual practices and to not be labelled 'promiscuous' or 'dupes of patriarchy' (Gordon, 2006). Moreover, they have highlighted the fact that power in sexual relationships need not be considered inherently oppressive, but may be viewed as productive of new forms of sexual engagement.

Despite these varied accounts of lesbian sex provided by different groups of women, two recent studies indicate that many white, middle-class women emphasised a desire for caring relationships over casual sexual encounters, and that non-monogamy is the exception, rather than the rule, within many lesbian communities (Gordon, 2006; Bullock, 2004). Historical shifts in lesbian identities have often resulted in changing norms within lesbian communities about sexual practices (Gordon, 2006), such as the emergence of a distinction between 'butch' and 'femme' lesbians (see Box 8.4). Lesbian psychologist Nichols (1987) highlighted the shifting ways in which lesbian women adopt identities that do not necessarily mirror their sexual practices, and that the assumption of a 'butch' identity is not necessarily related to engaging in 'masculine' sexual practices.

Box 8.4   *Highlights: Who's the man and who's the woman? Butch–femme and top–bottom*

Students often ask us how gender is 'played out' in same-sex relationships. For lesbians in particular, the notions of 'butch' and 'femme' were historically – and to a lesser extent currently – important ones. ('Top' and 'bottom' are terms more closely associated with gay men and refer to the insertive and receptive partner in anal sex respectively.) As British cultural theorist Sally Munt (1998: 4) has commented: 'The two most public lesbian genders are butch and femme. Whether as the singular categories butch and femme, or as the "co-dependent" entity butch/femme, these lesbian genders have facilitated lesbian sex, lesbian desire, for decades.' Butch–femme identities were especially prominent in working-class lesbian communities in the US in the 1950s and 1960s. Lesbian relationships could 'survive' the hostile anti-LGB climate by 'mirroring' heterosexual relationships (Faderman, 1991). Nowadays in western societies, butch–femme is not the central organising principle of most lesbian relationships.

The concepts of butch–femme and top–bottom are apparent in non-western cultures as well, but with different meanings and different names. For example, in Brazil (and in other Latin American countries), the position taken in sexual intercourse is a core construct in understanding both gender *and* sexuality – so those who penetrate are defined as masculine (*macho*) and those who are penetrated are defined as feminine (*bicha* or *viado*; see also Chapter 2). As US-based anthropologist Serena Nanda (2000: 46) writes:

> a male who enters into a sexual relationship with another male does not necessarily sacrifice his masculinity, so long as he performs the penetrating, active, masculine role during sexual intercourse … he does not regard himself as a homosexual and is not regarded as one by society … the sexually receptive partner is expected to enact other aspects of the feminine gender role: to behave and/or sound and/or dress in ways appropriate to women.

Therefore, in Brazil, the notion of top–bottom is a foundational principle of gender/sexuality relations.

Butch–femme relationships between women are found, for instance, in the West Sumatran Minangkabau – an Islamic ethnic group in Indonesia that is matrilineal (land and property are passed down from mother to daughter). *Tombois* (the butch partner) see themselves as men, not lesbians, and they are viewed as transgressive because of the cultural pressure on women to marry men and have children in order to perpetuate the matriline (see Blackwood and Wieringa, 1999).

BDSM – bondage, domination, sadism, masochism

Heteronormative and homophobic accounts of LGBTQ sexual practices have historically constructed them as pathological or perverse. As we suggested earlier, this has at times led to the silencing of, and lack of research on, particular sexual practices such as BDSM (Langdridge and Barker, 2007). BDSM is practised by non-trans and trans people and heterosexual and non-heterosexual people. Traditionally, these sexual practices have been understood through the binary lenses of masculine/feminine, dominant/submissive and active/passive, and these binaries have been tied to particular identities (e.g., masculine people are dominant and active, feminine people are submissive and passive). Research on gay SMers (i.e., gay men who embrace a sado-masochistic sexual identity) suggests that many men do not have exclusive preferences for either sadism or masochism, and that their preference may vary according to the context, their own desires in the moment, and the particular sexual partner(s) they engage with (Chaline, 2005). Research on anal sex between gay men similarly suggests that the meanings attached to the role of the insertive or receptive partner in anal intercourse are not always tied to particular identities (i.e., insertive partners are dominant and receptive partners are passive). Rather these roles are adopted by individual men because they are experienced as pleasurable (Kippax and Smith, 2001).

Beyond the normative couple

Many LGBTQ researchers have taken issue with the normative model of the life-long, monogamous couple relationship. For instance, Ringer (2001: 138) stated that 'much of the knowledge that we have gained about same-sex relationships through research is based on normative heterosexual assumptions and values that view relationships as necessary, consisting of two people, and permanent. Are these assumptions equally appropriate for gay, lesbian, or bisexual relationships?' As we have seen, there is a lot of research about same-sex *couples*, but as Hostetler and Cohler (1997: 200) noted, 'the experience of singlehood – across the life course or at any given time – has been almost entirely neglected'. Singledom can be looked at in two ways: as an involuntary state because of the inability to find a partner, or as an ideological choice or purposeful decision to remain single for a variety of reasons including wanting to be more autonomous and self-determining (Sandfield and Percy, 2003). Either way, the very limited research in this area tends not to view being single as especially positive, with reports of lesbian and gay male couples having fewer sexual problems and greater well-being than single lesbians and gay men. Gay men are more likely to be single at any given time than are lesbians, who are more likely to be in couple relationships at rates similar to heterosexuals (Hostetler and Cohler, 1997).

There is also the issue of LGBTQ people who are in, or were in, heterosexual relationships. People's relationships change and develop over time and most LGB people have experience of different-sex relationships. Some lesbians and gay men get heterosexually married before coming out as lesbian or gay and some stay married. A heterosexual marriage may not be all that it seems to the outside world (e.g., a 'marriage of convenience' between a gay man and a lesbian) and for some non-heterosexual people, heterosexual marriage might be a necessary option – particularly in cultural contexts when open LGBTQ identities are especially frowned upon. For some people, especially those with cultural backgrounds or religious beliefs that place a very heavy emphasis on the importance of hetero-sexual marriage and kinship (for instance, South Asian communities in the UK), it may be impossible to live outside of a heterosexual framework, even though they are attracted to people of the same sex or even self-identify as LGBQ. For others, living within a same-sex relationship comes at a high price. British psychologist Alison Rolfe (2008) conducted an in-depth interview study with eight couples and individuals who were choosing *not* to have a civil partnership. She found that cultural prohibitions were a factor for some couples. A mixed race gay male couple (one Middle Eastern, one white British) talked of their fears of 'honour killing' (that is, the punitive murder of a family member by the family when they believe dishonour has been brought on the family) if they were to have a civil partnership. As 'David' said, 'in the public acknowledgement [of our gay relation-ship], immediately it becomes a life threatening act' (Rolfe, 2008). This is an extreme example, but nevertheless we can see why for some people the price of openly living in a same-sex relationship is too high to pay.

There are many kinds of relationship other than the monogamous, same-sex couple and there have been a number of challenges to the centrality of 'the couple', including research about: non-monogamous and polyamorous relation-ships; **families of choice**; adult friendships between LGB(T) people and friend-ships between LGB(T) people and heterosexuals. We now briefly discuss each of these areas of research in turn.

Polyamorous relationships

Polyamory, or 'poly' for short, is an approach to intimate relationships that assumes that having multiple love/sexual relationships and/or partners is possible and acceptable – see Box 8.5. British psychologist Meg Barker (2005) explains that the term 'polyamory' originated in the 1960s to refer to responsible non-monogamy. There are various types of polyamorous set-ups, including people having one or two 'primary' partners and other 'secondary' ones, triadic

Box 8.5   Key study: Ani Ritchie and Meg Barker (2006) on the construction of polyamorous language in a culture of compulsory monogamy

British media and culture scholar Ani Ritchie and psychologist Meg Barker have explored the language polyamorous communities use to claim identities, define relationships and describe feelings. Taking a social constructionist perspective, they argue that by creating a new language around poly lifestyles, mononormativity can be challenged and poly identities and communities can be legitimated.

Their analysis used text from web-based discussion groups, community message boards, email lists and polyamory websites (e.g., alt.polyamory and bi-org/uk-poly). One of the advantages of using these data was that it enabled 'track[ing] the emergence of new words, making it possible to pinpoint the conception and use of specific terms' (2006: 587). They particularly focused on the terms of British poly communities, especially a London-based social network known as 'LondonPolyBis' (London Polyamorous Bisexuals). When focusing on the terminology used they were guided by the question: 'what is achieved by the use of this language, and what power is there in telling a story using these terms over previous ones?' (p. 589).

Their key findings were that:

- Many people in poly relationships feel constrained by existing language surrounding relationships, particularly notions of infidelity, adultery, unfaithfulness, affairs and cheating.
- The term 'ethical slut' is used positively to reclaim the word 'slut' and (despite its typical association with women) is applied equally to women and men and seen as a strategy of resistance in virtual (safe) spaces.
- The conventional language of coupledom is challenged in various ways. For example, rather than labelling a man's additional female partner(s) as 'the other woman' or 'the mistress' – neither of which respect the relationships between a poly person's partners – the word 'metamour' is used (this word is also used for other male partners). 'Paramour' refers to the unmarried partner of a married poly person.
- Jealousy is closely connected to poly relationships, but some poly people have rewritten the language of jealousy in order to facilitate new experiences of the emotion. The term 'wibbly' has been coined to refer to feeling uncomfortable or insecure about a partner's other relationship(s). Thus, 'wibbling' can be a way of expressing anxiety and asking for reassurance without the negative connotations of jealousy.
- The term 'frubbly' has been coined to describe positive feelings and taking joy in a partner's relationship with other partner(s).

Ritchie and Barker conclude by emphasising the potential of language to shape people's experiences, they write: 'In "making up" words the polyamorous communities we have considered are actively rewriting the language of love, relationships and emotions in a way that enables them to experience a better fit between spoken/written language and lived experiences' (p. 598).

relationships (a relationship between three people) or quads (e.g., two couples involved with each other). Some poly people live together in 'tribes' and are either sexually exclusive within that grouping ('polyfidelity') or open to sexual relationships outside of the tribe. Those in poly relationships aim 'to get past the limitations of monogamy and erode set binarisms, including the myth that being part of a closed dyad is the only authentic form of love ... polyamory can be seen as a new word for non-monogamy that turns a negative into a positive' (D'Onofrio, 2004: 165). Researching 'poly' relationships is a way of examining dominant constructions of intimate relationships because poly entails open refusal of standard ideals of monogamy and fidelity (Barker, 2005).

Often poly people identify as bisexual and form relationships with both men and women (Ritchie and Barker, 2006). As we noted above, non-monogamy is also common among gay men (Bettinger, 2005). Gordon (2006) suggests that it is typically more socially acceptable for men, as opposed to women, to engage in non-monogamy. This has implications for lesbian, bisexual and trans women who choose a non-monogamous lifestyle and who may potentially experience social exclusion from lesbian, bisexual or trans communities on the basis of this choice.

US communications researcher Jeffrey Ringer (2001) conducted in-depth interviews with thirty gay male couples, asking them to tell the story of their relationship from the day they met. Ringer was interested in the gay men's relational ideologies and found that non-monogamy was a key practice that the couples in his study engaged with in a number of ways. For example, the couples:

- agreed that one partner could have sex outside the relationship but would then have to discuss it immediately with the other partner
- encouraged the forming of a relationship with another sexual partner and enabling this person to become a friend of both partners because the couple had the view that 'no two people can completely fulfil each other's needs'
- allowed partners to have sex with others but only when they were out of town
- aimed to become non-monogamous after a few years of monogamy to solidify the primary couple relationship
- recognised that it was inevitable that their partner would 'cheat' because 'that's the way men are' but not wanting to know or talk about it when it happened.

Ringer (2001: 148) concluded that, because of the normativity of monogamy or mononormativity, 'maintaining an alternative ideological configuration of a relationship requires continuous maintenance'.

In sum, although openly polyamorous and non-monogamous relationships are in general rarer than monogamous ones, they allow us to examine alternative ways of organising personal relationships and to challenge mononormativity. Non-monogamy and poly relational practices are also used by heterosexuals to enact their sexuality outside of the boundaries of heteronormativity – to queer heterosexuality (Thomas, 2000).

Friendship

The boundaries between friendship and sexual/romantic relationships are complex in a non-heterosexual context and LGBQ people are likely to stay friends with former sexual partners (Weinstock and Rothblum, 1996). LGBTQ friendships are an under-researched area in part because the language that we use often trivialises the significance of friendship:

> If a sexual relationship is a 'primary relationship', does this mean that friendships are 'secondary'? If a sexual partner is a 'significant other', are friends 'insignificant others'? And what about the questions, 'Are you two together, or are you just friends?' when we are both 'together' and 'friends' and there is no 'just' about it? (Kitzinger, 1996c: 296)

There are lots of ways we can look at friendships: What importance does friendship have in LGBTQ lives? Who are LGBTQ people friends with, and why? What role does sexual attraction have in LGBTQ people's friendships with other LGBTQ people and heterosexuals? Jacqueline Weinstock, a US developmental psychologist, has examined lesbian and gay male friendships in adulthood and found that both lesbians and gay men tend to be friends with their *own* group more than with each other (Weinstock, 1998). Lesbians, especially, are understood to develop and maintain friendships with ex-lovers more than gay men and heterosexuals (Weinstock, 2004). Although 'enmeshment' in lesbian relationships (mentioned above) has been seen from a heteronormative standpoint as a problem, it can be a good thing when it helps lesbians maintain ties with each other when relationships change from being romantic/sexual to being platonic (Fitzgerald, 2004). See Box 8.6.

Box 8.6   Key study: Jacqueline Weinstock (2004) on maintaining friendships when lesbian relationships change

The nature of boundaries between friendships and sexual relationships seems to be gendered. Many women become involved with each other sexually through a close friendship, whereas for gay men friendships are likely to be formed through an initial sexual encounter (Weeks *et al.*, 2001). In one US study of lesbian and gay friendships, lesbians were twice as likely as gay men (34 per cent compared to 17 per cent) to report that their best friend (who they were not in a relationship with) was a former lover (Nardi and Sherrod, 1994). Weinstock outlined ten different stories (four she regarded as problematic, six she felt signalled adaptation in the context of marginalisation) that offer explanations for why lesbians maintain friendships with their ex-partners.

Problematic stories

1. Lesbians' lover and ex-lover relationships are bound too tight and enmeshed.
2. Lesbians can't let go, can't move on; lesbians' staying friends after a break-up reflect difficulties with separation.

3. Lesbian lover relationships are not legitimate so members of a couple do not place demands on how one partner should interact with the other's ex(es).
4. Lesbian social networks and communities are smaller, partners are drawn from those communities, and therefore intrusive social networks including exes are accepted.

Stories of adaptation in the context of marginalisation

5. Isolation and lack of formal relationship recognition means ex-lover relationship patterns are positive adaptations to the social context.
6. The shared experience of marginalisation encourages the maintenance of close connections with other lesbians, including exes.
7. Lesbians as women have been socialised to have good 'relationshipping' skills and so care more about close relationships.
8. Friendships are an essential part of developing and maintaining non-heterosexual identities and therefore friendships with exes are important to maintain in a heterosexist society.
9. Sustaining friendships across different sexualities (e.g., lesbians' friendships with heterosexual women) can be challenging and this may increase lesbians' commitment to staying friends with exes.
10. Lesbians' friends are seen as family and therefore this encourages preserving friendships through changes in the nature of the relationship.

Weinstock coined the term FLEX, which stands for 'friend and/or family connections among lesbian ex-lovers' (p. 200), to recognise 'our willingness and ability to be flexible in our intimate relationships, supporting shifts in form and function even as we maintain our important connections'.

US social anthropologist Kath Weston (1991) has critically explored the notion of 'friends as family' among lesbians and gay men. She argues that by claiming friends as kin, the traditional framework that places (biological) family at its centre is both reinforced and undermined; it is undermined because building families of friends can also be a challenge to traditional notions of family. Based on their interview research with ninety-six non-heterosexual women and men, British sociologists Jeffrey Weeks, Brian Heaphy and Catherine Donovan (2001: 4) differentiated 'families of origin' and 'families of choice'; the latter being 'flexible, informal and varied, but strong and supportive networks of friends and lovers, often including members of families of origin'. Weeks *et al.* are less critical of non-heterosexuals using the language of kinship to describe their networks and point out that 'friendships are more than mere crutches for those who society barely acknowledges ... they offer the opportunity for alternatives that challenge the inevitability of conventional family life' (p. 53). Families of choice are especially important for those

LGBTQ people estranged from or ostracised by their families of origin (Israel, 2005).

Another aspect of friendship is those *across* different sexual identities (Price, 1998). US communications researcher Lisa Tillmann-Healy (2001), for example, looked at the friendships she and her husband had with gay male friends, focusing especially on how their heterosexism was reduced through having these friendships. However, barriers have been identified in close relationships between lesbians and gay men and heterosexuals. From their focus group study of US lesbian and heterosexual women, O'Boyle and Thomas (1996) found lesbians were concerned that heterosexual women may be wary of any physical intimacy they expressed or of conversations about sexual relationships. Therefore, lesbians tended to restrict these behaviours with their heterosexual female friends. Similarly, heterosexual women with lesbian friends reported less personal disclosure and discussion of their sexual relationships than with their heterosexual women friends. Difference can be overcome in relationships across various sexualities (and indeed other axes of difference), but an awareness of heterosexism and a positive stance on LGBTQ issues is crucial for heterosexuals' friendships with LGBTQ people.

Gaps and absences

- Like most research in LGBTQ psychology, most relationships research has focused on gay men and lesbians, so there is a need for more research on bisexual and trans people's relationships. Similarly, most of the existing research is based on samples of white, middle-class gay men and lesbians; more emphasis should be placed on understanding the relationships of working-class and non-white people.
- Most relationship research has been conducted in the USA and in other western countries; as such, more research is needed looking at same-sex relationships in non-western contexts.
- There has been a heavy emphasis placed on cohabiting monogamous couples. We need to learn more about couples who choose not to live together and/or who are non-monogamous or in polyamorous relationships.
- Very little research has focused on the break-up of intimate relationships. The reasons lesbians and gay men give for ending their relationships seem to be similar to those of heterosexuals (Kurdek, 1991b), but the ending of legally recognised same-sex relationships is a new, and as yet unexplored, area of research.
- Little research has looked at interracial or interfaith same-sex couples.
- Very little research has focused on the experiences of single or celibate LGBTQ people.
- Although there has been a recent flurry of interest in domestic violence in same-sex relationships (e.g., Turrell, 2000; Halpern *et al.*, 2004), in general very little

is known about how power operates in same-sex relationships because of the emphasis on relational equality in much existing research.

Main chapter points

This chapter:

- Discussed the legal recognition of same-sex relationships through marriage and civil partnership.
- Explored what we currently know about the effects legal recognition has on same-sex relationships.
- Outlined research that compares and contrasts same-sex and heterosexual relationships and provided some critiques of the comparison paradigm. In particular, we highlighted the ways in which same-sex relationships are influenced by gender, race, culture, social class and other forms of difference.
- Signposted some of the key issues in relation to LGBTQ sexual practices and highlighted the diversity in LGBTQ sexual practices.
- Problematised the notion of 'the monogamous couple' as the mainstay of relationships research and identified other forms of adult relationships worthy of exploration, such as friendships and non-monogamous relationships.

Questions for discussion and classroom exercises

1. Academics and members of LGBTQ communities have vigorously debated the pros and cons of legal relationship recognition for same-sex couples and LGBTQ communities, and the different forms legal recognition might take. What benefits might LGBTQ communities and individuals obtain from relationship recognition? What costs might there be?

2. 'Equality in relationships is a myth.' Construct an argument (using evidence) both to support and to refute this statement in relation to same-sex relationships.

3. What are 'heterosexual norms' for relationships and how are they applied to LGBTQ people's relationships in psychological research?

4. What might be the differences and similarities between online and 'in real life' LGBTQ relationships? Does cyberspace really transcend axes of marginalisation (like race, culture and disability)? If so, how and why? If not, why not? In what ways is the Internet constituting and (re)defining LGBTQ relationships?

5.   Identify the most important people in your life. Who would be in your family of choice? In what ways is this different from your family of origin? How may your family of choice (and family of origin) change over your lifetime?

Further reading

Hines, S. (2006) Intimate transitions: transgender practices of partnering and parenting. *Sociology*, 40(2), 353–71.
This article uses three case studies to explore experiences of intimacy (relationships and parenting) and the importance of emotional support and care in the context of gender transition. British sociologist Sally Hines argues that transgender experiences should be more fully incorporated into analyses of intimacy.

Kitzinger, C. and Coyle, A. (1995) Lesbian and gay couples: speaking of difference. *Psychologist*, 8, 64–9.
This short article focuses on the differences between lesbian and gay couples and heterosexual couples in a non-pathologising way. British LGBTQ psychologists Celia Kitzinger and Adrian Coyle discuss cohabitation, sexual activity and (non)exclusivity, equality and sex roles, and the social context as key areas of difference, and argue that heterosexually derived models and assumptions need to be avoided in order to research same-sex relationships appropriately.

Kitzinger, C. and Wilkinson, S. (2004) The rebranding of marriage: why we got married instead of registering a civil partnership. *Feminism & Psychology*, 14(1), 127–50.
This article outlines British lesbian couple Celia Kitzinger and Sue Wilkinson's reasons for having a Canadian marriage rather than a civil partnership in the UK. They argue that everyone – regardless of gender and sexuality – should have equal access to marriage *and* that radical critiques of marriage are needed.

Peplau, L. A. and Fingerhut, A. W. (2007) The close relationships of lesbians and gay men. *Annual Review of Psychology*, 58, 405–24.
This review article outlines the key findings of empirical research about same-sex couples in the USA. The review draws on research using mainly mainstream psychological methods and covers topics like: relationship formation; division of household labour and power; love and satisfaction; and conflict and partner violence.

Weeks, J., Heaphy, B. and Donovan, C. (2001) *Same sex intimacies: families of choice and other life experiments*. London: Routledge.
An interesting theoretical and empirical sociological account of same-sex intimate relationships based on interviews with ninety-six non-heterosexual people. Focus on chapter 1 (families of choice), chapter 2 (life experiments), chapter 3 (the friendship ethic) and chapter 5 (partnership rites).

9 Parenting and family

Overview

- Paths to parenthood for LGBTQ people
- Comparing lesbian-, gay- and trans-headed families with heterosexual-headed families
- Moving away from a 'proving otherwise' agenda
- Looking inside LGBTQ families

Paths to parenthood for LGBTQ people

Until relatively recently, one of the most widely held stereotypes about lesbians and gay men was that they do not have children. Research on lesbian, gay and trans parenting has been underway since the early 1970s and a considerable body of knowledge has developed since then, so we know that this stereotype is not true! Although many non-heterosexuals choose not to parent, and one of the things they value about being non-heterosexual is a perceived freedom from social pressures to have children (Stacey, 2006), many non-heterosexuals are parents. Because of the difficulties of generating representative samples of non-heterosexuals that we discussed in Chapter 3, it is impossible to provide precise statistics on the numbers of non-heterosexual parents. However, a number of studies have found that around a third of lesbians and about 10 to 20 per cent of gay men are parents (there are no figures for the numbers of bisexual parents). Some psychologists have argued that these figures under-represent rates of parenting among marginalised racial and cultural groups. The suggestion is that members of these groups are less likely to identify with categories such as 'lesbian' and 'gay' and are more likely to be involved in heterosexual relationships, and as such are more likely to be parents (Bell and Weinberg, 1978). It is estimated that up to one third of trans people attending a gender identity clinic have children (di Ceglie, 1998), and some conception clinics have reported small numbers of trans people and their partners requesting their services (see Box 9.1).

Most research on LGBTQ parenting has concentrated on lesbian families and, more specifically, on white, middle-class lesbian families (Gabb, 2004). There are a number of personal accounts that address, for example, parenting as a bisexual man (Anders, 2005), parenting as a black lesbian mother (Lorde, 1987), being a

Box 9.1 *Highlights: transsexualism and parenting*

As Paul De Sutter, a medical doctor at a fertility centre in Belgium, noted, 'until recently, transition to the desired gender and reproduction seemed to be mutually exclusive for transsexual people. To many, loss of reproductive potential seems the "price to pay" for transition' (2001: 612). Hormonal and surgical treatments lead to the irreversible loss of reproductive potential; however, modern reproductive techniques mean that transsexual women could be given the option of sperm freezing prior to medical treatment, just as (natal) men undergoing treatment for cancer would be. A recent study of 121 transsexual women by De Sutter and colleagues (2002) found that most respondents favoured being given the option to freeze sperm.

In the past, many psychiatrists viewed a complete break with the past as a male and losing the possibility to 'father' a child as psychological necessities for a successful transition to the female role. In fact, people with children were sometimes excluded from treatment. Fortunately, most psychiatrists and psychologists agree that loss of fertility is no longer a necessity for successful transition. Moreover, the Standards of Care for the treatment of Gender Identity Disorder recommend that people should be counselled about the loss of their reproductive potential. De Sutter (2001) suggested that it is likely that more trans people will seek to become parents post-transition because people are increasingly diagnosed and treated at an earlier age.

white lesbian adoptive parent of a black child (Thompson, 2000), and being a trans parent (Cook-Daniels, 2000). However, empirical research on such parenting experiences is minimal. This means that lesbian parenting will be the main focus of this chapter, but we will refer to research on GBTQ parenting where it exists.

There are numerous paths to parenthood for LGBTQ people, just as there are for heterosexual and non-trans people. In the past, and sometimes still today, most non-heterosexuals became parents through heterosexual relationships (Tasker and Patterson, 2007). These parents are usually referred to as **divorced lesbian mothers/gay fathers** and many continue to co-parent with their former partner and family relationships may involve a complex network of both heterosexual and same-sex past and present relationships. Lesbians and gay men may also choose to become parents after coming out as lesbian or gay; **planned lesbian/gay families** most often consist of a **birth mother/father** and a **co-parent** or **social parent**. The term co-parent does not necessarily imply a secondary role; some lesbian mother families may divide child-care equally, whereas others may adopt a more traditional pattern of breadwinner/primary parent (Patterson, 1995). It is also important to note that although **queer nuclear families** are common (Folgerø, 2008), some planned non-heterosexual families contain more than two parents.

Increasing numbers of lesbian couples and single women choose to become pregnant through **donor insemination** (as we noted above, this is also a path to parenthood for some trans people and their partners). Some women choose to have an 'unknown' donor (they will tell the child basic information about the donor), others choose to have a 'known' donor, who is involved in family life to a greater or lesser extent. A small number of gay men become parents through **surrogacy** arrangements. These gay men are reported to choose surrogacy because they want a biological connection with their child and want to raise a child from birth (Lev, 2006). By contrast, some non-heterosexuals choose parenting relationships where there is no biological connection and children have spent time in another family, namely adoption and fostering (see Box 9.2).

Box 9.2   *Highlights: adoption and fostering in LGBTQ communities*

Many non-heterosexuals consider fostering or adoption a primary option for creating a family. As Ryan (2007) notes, there is a dearth of research on lesbian and gay adoptive parents and children. What little research there is shows that lesbians and gay men experience heterosexism in the adoption and fostering assessment process, even though official attitudes towards same-sex adoption and fostering have become increasingly positive in the last decade or so (Riggs, 2004b). For this reason the assessment process can be very stressful and negatively impact the mental health of potential adopters (Ross *et al.*, 2008). Non-heterosexuals are often expected to 'educate' social workers about non-heterosexual lives and show that they will provide children with 'opposite-sex' role models (Hicks, 2005a; Riggs, 2007b). Black participants in British research reported experiencing both heterosexism and racism from social workers (Hicks and McDermott, 1999). Damien (Riggs, 2007b) argues that the assessment of lesbian and gay foster-care applicants should focus on the specific experiences of lesbians and gay men and resist the heterosexualisation of lesbian and gay families.

A small number of studies have examined family functioning in lesbian and gay adoptive families. Bennett (2003) explored parental perceptions of attachment in fifteen lesbian couples who had adopted internationally. In this qualitative study, it was reported that all of the children developed bonds of attachment to both mothers, but 80 per cent of the children had primary bonds to one mother, even though child-care and domestic responsibilities were shared equally. In a comparative study of lesbian and gay and heterosexual adoptive families, Leung *et al.* (2005) found no negative effects for children adopted by lesbian and gay parents. Older children and children with more pre-adoption foster placements are commonly associated with higher levels of post-adoption difficulty; in lesbian and gay families, these children experienced higher levels of family functioning.

Ryan (2007; see also Riggs, 2009a) argues that research on lesbian and gay adoptive family life has often focused on deficits and problems at the expense of strengths and resources. He found that lesbian and gay adoptive parents demonstrated high levels of parental skills and their children were reported to have high levels of strength. In contrast to calls for proof of 'opposite-sex' role models, Mallon (2006) argues that the gender-sameness of lesbian and gay families has unique advantages in relation to adoption and fostering. For example, young girls who have been abused by their fathers and/or other adult men may have a better opportunity to develop positive parent–child relationships in an all-woman, lesbian household.

Because many non-heterosexuals parent outside of established norms, there are no widely agreed terms with which to designate non-heterosexual family forms and relationships. Nonetheless biology features heavily in the terms that have developed over the past few decades, and some researchers have been critical of this (Gabb, 2004). It is important to note that many of the terms mentioned above are heavily contested and individual non-heterosexual parents might reject many or all of these terms and prefer to be known simply as 'mum', 'dad' or 'parent'.

Negative assumptions about LGBTQ parents

The law plays a significant role in non-heterosexual and trans people's freedom to become parents (see Box 9.3). Researchers have suggested that public attitudes

---

Box 9.3   *Highlights: LGBTQ parenting, the law and equality*

Understanding how law and social policy shape LGBTQ people's freedom to become parents is rather difficult. This is partly because so many different areas of law and social policy impact on parenting and family and the law changes constantly. In general, LGBTQ people seek the following parenting rights:

- the right to equal treatment in relation to child custody
- the right to adopt and foster children as a couple or as a single person on a par with heterosexual and non-trans people
- the right to access conception services on a par with heterosexual couples and non-trans people or to arrange private inseminations
- the right of social parents to be fully acknowledged as parents of their children
- the right to access relationship recognition such as same-sex marriage on a par with heterosexuals.

The extent to which non-heterosexual and trans people have gained these rights varies massively from country to country (and within federal countries such as the USA and Australia, from state to state). To give an example of a country that has adopted more progressive legislation, in Britain, same-sex couples and single non-heterosexuals have the right to adopt and foster children. A recently passed law means that lesbian couples and single women have access to conception services on a par with heterosexual couples. Sexuality per se is no longer a factor in custody disputes involving lesbian mothers; however, gay fathers and trans parents still face negative assumptions about their parenting. Same-sex couples have access to civil partnership (see Chapter 8), and the law awards automatic parental status to social parents (in lesbian couples) in civil partnerships. For women using assisted conception services, the social parent is also automatically regarded as a legal parent. In these circumstances social parents can list their name on their child's birth certificate. In private insemination arrangements where the couple are not in a civil partnership, if a child is born, the biological mother and **sperm donor** will be treated the same as an unmarried heterosexual couple. This means that the donor may attempt to acquire parental rights, even if he originally agreed with the mother(s) to act as a sperm donor and not as a father.

may be the greatest deterrent to LGBTQ people achieving equal parenting rights. Research on attitudes towards lesbian and gay parenting has produced mixed results. Some studies have found negative attitudes to lesbian and gay parents. Lesbian and gay couples are viewed as more likely to create a dangerous environment for children than heterosexual couples (Crawford and Solliday, 1996). The children of lesbian and gay parents are viewed as more likely to experience confusion over their sexual orientation and gender identity, more likely to be homosexual and more likely to experience stigma and teasing than the children of heterosexual parents (Morse *et al.*, 2007). However, a study of US college students found that most participants were willing to be friends with children of lesbians (King and Black, 1999), and a study of trainee school-teachers found less homophobic attitudes and more comfort with lesbian and gay families than was anticipated (Maney and Cain, 1997).

Research has also examined discussions of lesbian and gay parenting in the media and the arguments that are used to justify opposition to lesbian and gay parenting (see Box 9.4). This research shows that lesbian and gay parenting challenges a range of normative ideas about family and child development, including the notion that healthy child development depends on complementary gender roles (see Clarke, 2006; 2007). In line with the 'gender inversion' theory of homosexuality (see Chapter 1), lesbians are often viewed as too masculine, and gay men as too feminine, to be good parents or gender 'role models'. Negative assumptions about trans parenting also often hinge on trans people's gender identities and the negative effects these might have on their children's psychological development.

Box 9.4   *Highlights: media 'myths' about lesbian and gay parenting*

Victoria Clarke (2001) has identified six common arguments used against lesbian and gay parenting in newspaper and magazine reports and in television talk shows and documentaries: (1) it is sinful – 'God made Adam and Eve, not Adam and Steve!'; (2) it is unnatural (and abnormal); (3) it is selfish and ignores 'the best interests of the child'; (4) children are denied appropriate role models; (5) children are at risk of becoming confused about their gender and sexuality and growing up lesbian/gay; and (6) children are at risk of being bullied because of prejudice about homosexuality.

Whereas the first two arguments are straightforward 'moral' arguments, easily dismissed as expressing homophobic sentiments, the latter four, which focus on the welfare of children, are more complex. Arguments about bullying, in particular, are often used by speakers who explicitly disclaim prejudice against lesbians and gay men. For example, 'I've got nothing against lesbian and gay couples having children, I'm just worried about the effects of bullying on their children.' Such arguments require non-heterosexuals to adapt to and accommodate heterosexism by not parenting. Making a similar argument in relation to race – black people shouldn't have children because of racism – highlights the offensiveness of arguments about homophobic bullying.

Victoria and her colleague Celia Kitzinger have also analysed how lesbian and gay parents and their allies deal with such arguments. Lesbian and gay parents tend to emphasise the importance of family processes – that 'love makes a family' – and the ordinariness of life in lesbian and gay families. Lesbian and gay parents are 'just parents', they don't 'live on planet lesbian' (Clarke and Kitzinger, 2005) or make 'gay breakfast' (Clarke and Kitzinger, 2004), lesbian and gay families are 'just the family next door'. The children of lesbian and gay parents often feature on television talk shows to 'prove otherwise' (Stacey, 1996) about lesbian and gay parenting. Girls dressed in pink and boys in blue and adult-children who identify as heterosexual are greeted with rapturous applause on such shows. All of these strategies problematically normalise lesbian and gay families: they are defensive and apologetic, seeking to fit lesbians and gay men into existing understandings of family and parenting and denying their (sexual) difference. Normalising discourses of lesbian parenting ultimately collude in heterosexism (Clarke, 2002b).

Comparing lesbian-, gay- and trans-headed families with heterosexual-headed families

Affirmative research on lesbian parenting began in the early 1970s and focused on challenging negative assumptions about the psychological effects on children of growing up in a lesbian family. One of the most important early studies was conducted by the British developmental psychologist, and key researcher (see Box 9.5), Susan Golombok and colleagues (1983). This study was a comprehensive comparison of thirty-seven children aged 5 to 17 years in twenty-seven lesbian mother families with thirty-eight children in twenty-seven single heterosexual mother families. These were volunteer samples recruited through gay and single parent organisations and publications. The authors collected data from the mothers, the children and the children's teachers using standardised interviews and a wide range of other measures. They examined numerous aspects of children's development, behaviour and relationships and the mothers' adjustment and attitudes. They found that most of the children of lesbian mothers had spent at least two years in a heterosexual home before living in a lesbian household and these children had more contact with their fathers than children in heterosexual mother households.

In this, and other early lesbian mother studies, 'psychosexual development' or 'sexual identity development' was used as an umbrella term for the development of gender identity, sex-role behaviour and 'sexual orientation'. There was no evidence of 'inappropriate' gender identity for any of the children. The children's sex role behaviour was measured with two scales, and on both scales the boys showed behaviour that was 'characteristically masculine' and the girls showed behaviour that was 'characteristically feminine', and there were no significant

Box 9.5   Key researcher: Susan Golombok on why I study lesbian families

In 1976 I read an article in *Spare Rib* magazine. The picture on the cover was of three women and their children, and the caption read 'Why could one of these women lose custody of her child?' The answer was that the mothers were lesbian, and one of them was facing a custody dispute that would inevitably end with the loss of her child – simply on the grounds of her sexual orientation. The article asked for a psychologist to volunteer to carry out an independent study of lesbian mothers and their children. At the time I was a postgraduate student in the field of child development wanting to carry out socially relevant research and this seemed like the perfect project for me. I responded to the request and soon began a series of studies that are continuing to this day.

The first study focused on children's social, emotional and gender development – the main areas of concern in child custody cases – comparing children in lesbian families with children raised by a single heterosexual mother (Golombok *et al.*, 1983). It was found that children in lesbian families did not differ in emotional or behavioural problems, or in the quality of peer relationships, from children in heterosexual homes. In addition, no differences in gender role behaviour were found between children in lesbian and heterosexual families for either boys or girls.

But that wasn't the end of the story. Only school-age children had been studied, and it was argued that 'sleeper effects' may exist – that children in lesbian families would experience psychological problems when they grew up. In order to address this, the children in the original study were followed up in their mid-20s (Tasker and Golombok, 1997). We found them to be well-adjusted adults. Interestingly, we also found them generally to have a positive relationship with their mother's female partner, unlike their counterparts from the comparison group who grew up with a stepfather. And contrary to the assumptions that have prevailed over the years, the large majority of young adults raised in lesbian homes identified as heterosexual. Other studies followed, including an investigation of children raised in lesbian families from birth to examine the consequences of father absence from the outset (Golombok *et al.*, 1997), and an investigation of a general population sample of lesbian mother families to avoid the possible biases associated with volunteer samples (Golombok *et al.*, 2003), both studies producing very similar findings to those of the earlier research.

In the twenty-first century a lesbian sexual orientation is no longer a reason to deny a mother the custody of her children, and lesbian women now adopt children and have children through assisted reproduction. It is because psychological research has helped challenge prejudiced beliefs and tackle the injustice that has damaged lives that I study lesbian families.

differences between the two groups. With the pubertal and post-pubertal children, 'the two groups did not differ on sexual orientation and the pattern in both seemed typical for the age group' (p. 564). Most lesbian mothers had no clear preference in relation to their children's sexuality and did not pressure their children to adopt atypical sex roles. There were no significant differences between the groups in terms of the children's emotional difficulties, their behaviour at home and at school, and their peer relationships. Most children in both groups provided evidence of good peer relationships.

Other early studies were based on comparisons between lesbian and single heterosexual mother families and reached similar conclusions, emphasising the lack of differences between these two types of families. This led many researchers and professional bodies (including the APA) to resolve that 'there is no evidence that the development of children with lesbian and gay parents is compromised in any significant respect relative to that among children of heterosexual parents' (Patterson, 1992: 1025).

A number of criticisms have been made of these early studies, including:

- Only school-age children had been studied, but 'sleeper effects' may exist whereby children in lesbian families may experience problems when they reach adulthood (Golombok, 2007).
- Most of the children studied had spent their earliest years in a heterosexual household before making the transition to a lesbian family, so findings could not be generalised to children raised by lesbian mothers from birth (Golombok, 2007). It is also important to distinguish the impact of parents' sexuality from the impact of factors such as divorce, re-partnering and heterosexism (Stacey and Biblarz, 2001).
- Only volunteer or convenience samples had been studied, which may have produced an atypical account of the adjustment of children in lesbian families (Golombok, 2007).
- Because 'samples tend to be exclusively white, predominantly well-educated, and upwardly mobile' (Hill, 1987: 215; see Box 9.6) lesbian mothers, we know very little about the experiences of non-white and working-class lesbian mother-headed families and trans-, bisexual- and gay male-headed families.

Box 9.6   Key study: Marjorie Hill (1987) on the child-rearing attitudes of black lesbian mothers

Hill argued that the 'principal difference between lesbian mothers and heterosexual mothers is that lesbians present an alternative to the present traditional family structure … For the lesbian mother herself, there are no set guidelines to follow. The universal concerns and problems associated with parenthood … may be compounded by being a lesbian. At the same time, having to choose guidelines frees the lesbian mother to make parenting a more creative endeavor' (p. 215). Hill expected the child-rearing attitudes of lesbian mothers to reflect the research finding that lesbians are 'more independent, more candid, resilient, and self-sufficient than their heterosexual counterparts' (p. 216). Hill compared twenty-six black lesbian mothers and twenty-six black heterosexual mothers recruited from black women's groups. The women completed questionnaires on their child-rearing practices, the perceived and expected sex roles of their children and their degree of permissiveness in relation to sex education. Key findings included that:

- Heterosexual mothers demanded adherence to rules more frequently than lesbian mothers.
- Lesbian mothers demonstrated more tolerance of children's sexuality than did the heterosexual mothers – lesbian mothers were more permissive about modesty and sex play and exhibited greater openness in giving information about sex.
- Lesbian mothers viewed male and female children as more similar than did heterosexual mothers.
- Lesbian mothers expressed more traditionally masculine role expectations of their daughters than did heterosexual mothers.
- Lesbian mothers did not place a higher value on independence.

One interpretation of the failure to support the hypothesis that lesbian mothers value independence more than heterosexual mothers is that independence is important to black women regardless of sexuality. Hill suggested that the lesbian mothers' greater flexibility, permissiveness and less traditional ideas about gender may be an outgrowth of their alternative lifestyle, the fact that 35 per cent of the lesbian sample were highly educated and the fact that many of the lesbians were politically aware and active in the gay community. Hill acknowledged that the finding that lesbians have more masculine role expectations of their daughters could be viewed negatively, but she chose to interpret it as positive and helpful. She also pointed out that just as it may not be possible to generalise from research on white lesbian mothers to other racial groups, it may not be possible to generalise from her sample to all black lesbian mothers: 'Just as motherhood is complex, so are blackness, femaleness, and gayness' (p. 220; see also Cahill, 2003).

Longitudinal research

Subsequent research has sought to address some of these criticisms and absences. Fiona Tasker and Susan Golombok (1997) conducted one of the first longitudinal studies of children in lesbian mother families. They followed up twenty-five young adults raised by lesbian mothers and a comparison group of twenty-one young adults raised by heterosexual single mothers from the Golombok *et al.* (1983) study. The young adults were an average age of 23. Tasker and Golombok found that the children raised by lesbian mothers continued to function well in adulthood and did not experience any negative effects from their upbringing. Some of the key findings included that children in lesbian families were no more likely to remember having been teased or bullied during adolescence than children from heterosexual single mother families. However, there was a tendency for children from lesbian families to be more likely to remember having been teased about being lesbian or gay (perhaps because these events were more salient). Children from lesbian families described their relationship with their mother's partner more positively than children who had been raised by a divorced heterosexual mother and her new male partner. Children from lesbian mothers were no more likely to report experiencing sexual attraction to someone of the same sex. However, children from lesbian families were more likely to have had a same-sex relationship (6 versus 0 from heterosexual mother families) and were more likely to have considered the possibility of a same-sex relationship (14 versus 3). The minority of children who were negative about their experiences of growing up in a lesbian family tended to come from poorer backgrounds and to live in communities hostile to homosexuality.

Children raised in lesbian families from birth and general population samples

Comparative studies of lesbian and heterosexual families with children conceived by donor insemination have been conducted in the USA (Chan *et al.*, 1998), the UK (Golombok *et al.*, 1997), Belgium (Brewaeys *et al.*, 1995) and the Netherlands (Bos *et al.*, 2003). The evidence from all of these studies largely confirms the findings of earlier research – children in lesbian families do not differ from their peers in heterosexual families in terms of psychological well-being or gender development. The only clear difference to emerge from these studies is that social mothers in lesbian families are more involved with their children than are fathers in heterosexual families (see Short *et al.*, 2007).

US psychologist Raymond Chan and colleagues (1998) argued that child development is more strongly related to family processes and interactions (such as parenting stress and conflict between parents) than to issues associated with family structure (such as the number and gender of parents in the home and parents' sexuality). As US psychologist David Flaks and colleagues (1995) noted, such a conclusion – that neither father presence nor parental heterosexuality is crucial for healthy child development – is controversial within developmental psychology because it challenges widely accepted psychoanalytic and social learning theories of child development. Flaks *et al.* (1995: 113) argued that:

> Because such theories rely on traditional family structures to define the factors that promote children's development, they are not able to account easily for successful outcomes in non-traditional families, particularly those in which there is no opposite-sex parent in the home. Evidence … which suggests that well-adjusted children of both sexes can be raised in families of varying configurations, will hopefully provide an impetus for a reevaluation of the parental qualities most important for optimum child development.

The criticism that early studies were based on volunteer or convenience samples has also been addressed in more recent research. A research team in the USA (Wainright *et al.*, 2004) and one in the UK (Golombok *et al.*, 2003) have conducted studies of general population samples of children raised by lesbian mothers. Both of these studies showed that children were functioning well and their adjustment was not generally associated with family type.

Trans parenting

Research on the psychological adjustment of children in trans parent families is very limited. In Chapter 1, we discussed a groundbreaking study by the British-based psychiatrist Richard Green (1978), which assessed the adjustment of children being raised by lesbian mothers and transsexual parents. This study found that of sixteen children with transsexual parents, none had gender identity problems and all reported gender typical activities and interests. All of the post-pubertal children reported heterosexual fantasies and relationships. In 1998, Green published another study of eighteen children of transsexual parents. None of the children met the DSM-IV criteria for GID and no clinically significant cross-gender behaviour was reported (other studies have found very little evidence of cross-generational cross-gender behaviour; Freedman *et al.*, 2002). Three children were selective in informing peers about their transsexual parent; three experienced some (transient and resolved) teasing; the remainder reported no problems. Green concluded that children are not adversely affected by their parent's transsexualism and children's best interests are served by having contact with their transsexual parent.

The authors of a US study reported similar findings (White and Ettner, 2007). This study also found that children who were younger at the time of their parent's transition tended to have a better relationship with their parents and less adjustment difficulties (see also Israel, 2005). One decision that families encounter is what name to use for the parent post-transition (see Box 9.7). One third of the

---

Box 9.7   Key study: Sally Hines (2007) on transgender practices of parenting

Although cross-dressing and cross-gender-identifying women and men have always been parents, self-identifying as a trans parent is a recent social development. British sociologist Sally Hines has published one of the few explorations of experiences of parenting within the context of gender transition, based on interviews with seven transgender parents. Central concerns of the participants were when and how to tell children about their forthcoming transition and balancing self-identity with emotional care for children. Many parents stressed the importance of open dialogue to help children adapt to the changes initiated by their gender transition.

Hines discussed the case of Dan, the single parent of a 9-year-old son. Dan decided to get married and have a child because he 'thought it would make it go away' (p. 137), but being a parent did not stop him questioning his gender. Dan initially viewed transitioning as something that would disrupt his relationship with his son, but eventually realised that he needed to transition in order to be a good parent. Dan's son found the situation hard to understand at first, but Dan's openness enabled his son to understand more fully the process of gender reassignment. Dan suggested that his son call him by a version of his new first name ('Danny'), rather than reversing the parenting nouns of 'mum' and 'dad', to help his son come to terms with his gender transition.

Hines reported that children whose parents transition from female-to-male found the process easier to adapt to because their parents were more able to present androgynously before transitioning than were male-to-female parents. Dan always wore a shirt and tie to work before transitioning, so his son benefited from greater cultural acceptance of female androgyny. The head teacher of Dan's son's school also smoothed the process of transitioning by speaking to the son's classmates in a way 'that really bound them together in a protective network' (p. 144). Hines argued that this highlights the significance of the reactions of important others such as teachers, children's peers and other children's parents. The relationship between a child's parents can also significantly impact on how a child adapts to the gender transition and the child's well-being.

children in this study used their parent's first name in public, one third continued to use the **pre-transition** parental title (these children were most embarrassed by the transition), and the remaining third used a nickname, 'aunt' or 'uncle', or the **post-transition** gender congruent parental title. White and Ettner note that it was not possible for them to tease apart the effects of divorce and the effects of transition, because their study did not include a comparison group of children who had experienced parental divorce.

British-based psychiatrist Domenico di Ceglie (1998) argued that many factors influence a child's reaction to a parent's transition, including the way in which **gender reassignment** is managed by the parents and explained to the children, the impact of the transition on the relationship between the child's parents, the attitudes of other family members and the support offered to the child, and the responses of the child's peers and the wider community.

Gay parenting

There is also very little research on gay parenting, and most was conducted in the 1970s and 1980s, and is now rather dated. This research has been mainly conducted within sociology and has focused on topics like gay father social identities (Bozett, 1981; Miller, 1979). These relatively small-scale qualitative studies showed that, in spite of public stigma, most gay fathers over time achieved integration of their gay and father identities (identities assumed to be antithetical) and a sense of psychological well-being. Other sociological studies have explored the experiences of married and divorced non-heterosexual fathers (Dunne, 2001), mapping out their varied parenting circumstances and their relationships with their ex-wives. A more recent study by US sociologist Judith Stacey (2006) has explored gay men's narratives of parental desire and decision-making. She constructed a 'passion for parenthood' continuum and most of the fifty men in her study occupied an intermediate zone, in which life circumstances or more passionate partners could recruit or divert these men into or away from parenting.

Some men regarded themselves as predestined parents and often pursued parent-hood against enormous odds, whereas others regarded themselves as 'born to be child-free'. Stacey noted that although this is the dominant stereotype of gay male culture, only a minority of her participants were opposed to parenthood.

In terms of psychological research focusing on fathers, a study by US psychol-ogists Jerry Bigner and R. Brooke Jacobsen (1989a; 1989b) is one of the few pieces of research to have compared divorced gay and heterosexual non-resident fathers. Bigner and Jacobsen (1989a) compared thirty-three gay fathers and thirty-three heterosexual fathers on the 'Value of Children' scale, a measure of the motivations for parenthood, and found few differences between gay and hetero-sexual men. The differences that emerged included that gay fathers were more inclined to indicate that having children enhances masculinity, and provides entry into adulthood and acceptance in the heterosexual community. Another early US study (Robinson and Skeen, 1982) compared the sex role orientation of thirty gay fathers and thirty gay non-fathers and found that gay fathers were no more masculine than gay non-fathers, which suggests that the link between masculinity and gay fatherhood is a stereotype rather than a reality.

In terms of gay fathers' parenting skills and behaviours and the extent of their involvement with their children, the Bigner and Jacobsen (1989b) comparative study found that gay men reported similar levels of intimacy and involvement with their children as did heterosexual fathers. However, gay fathers tended to be more strict, more responsive to children's needs, more consistent in providing reasons for appropriate behaviour to children and less likely to parent in a conventional male sex role style than heterosexual fathers. Bigner and Jacobsen suggested that gay fathers may have felt more pressures to be competent parents than hetero-sexual fathers and to demonstrate a blending of the qualities conventionally associated with mother and father roles.

A US study of forty-eight white gay male step-families refused comparison with heterosexual step-families on the grounds that 'comparing with dominant culture step-families would promote a deficit-comparison conceptualisation of these families' (Crosbie-Burnett and Helmbrecht, 1993: 256). This study found that for all family members (biological father, stepfather and children) family happiness was related to stepfather inclusion in the family and to a positive step-parenting relationship. As might be expected, the study also found that children were more closeted than adults about their gay-headed family and got little in the way of social support from friends or relatives. The British Gay and Bisexual Parenting Survey (Barrett and Tasker, 2001) asked fathers to rate the extent to which their children experienced difficulties; the mean ratings were all low, but the most significant problems were tension because of keeping a family secret, being teased or bullied, and feeling different.

Other studies have found that children of gay fathers expressed concerns about being ostracised by their peers, but actual instances of homophobia were relatively rare (Bozett, 1988; Miller, 1987). Bozett (1988) interviewed nineteen children (thirteen girls/women, six boys/men, aged between 14 and 35) of fourteen gay fathers. He found that the children used different social control strategies in relation to their fathers to manage how others perceived them. These strategies included boundary control, which may focus on the father's behaviour (asking him to stop holding hands with a male partner) or others' behaviour (for example, not bringing friends home to keep them from encountering their father). The use of these strategies helped the child to manage the embarrassment they felt. Bozett found that most gay fathers were extremely sensitive to their children and often went to great lengths to conceal their sexuality to protect their children. In addition, most children were able to work out whom they could safely tell about their father's sexuality. Bozett concluded that children might need help to recognise that much of their stress is related to social attitudes to homosexuality, rather than to their father's homosexuality per se. Studies of lesbian families have reported similar findings (Vanfraussen *et al.*, 2002).

With regard to the sexuality of children with gay male and bisexual fathers, US psychologist Michael Bailey and colleagues (Bailey *et al.*, 1995) asked gay and bisexual fathers whether their adult sons were heterosexual, bisexual or gay and 9 per cent of sons were considered gay or bisexual. As with the Tasker and Golombok (1997) findings about the sexuality of the children of lesbian mothers, this finding has been widely debated, with sympathetic researchers emphasising that most children were heterosexual, and anti-gay scholars treating this finding as evidence of some degree of parent–child transmission of homosexuality.

Research is beginning to examine the experiences of planned gay father families (see Box 9.2 above) and gay male sperm donors. For example, Damien has found that gay men are more likely than heterosexual men to act as sperm donors in response to the needs of lesbian friends or because of a desire to become a parent (Riggs, 2008). Gay male sperm donors also reported to undertake a considerable degree of 'emotion work' when acting as sperm donors, both in terms of the practicalities of co-ordinating donations and in terms of negotiating sperm donation in the context of their partnerships and heterosexist institutions such as conception clinics (Riggs, 2009c).

Moving away from a 'proving otherwise' agenda

Just as LGBTQ psychological research more generally has moved away from a 'proving otherwise' research agenda (that is, one concerned with proving the psychological health of LGBTQ people), research on parenting has begun to move away from a focus on the psychological health of children in lesbian and gay families. Although comparative research on lesbian parenting has been instrumental in challenging the negative treatment of lesbian mothers, it has also been highly controversial. We now discuss some of the main criticisms of comparative research.

Comparative research is defensive

As US sociologists Judith Stacey and Timothy Biblarz (2001: 160) noted, the political stakes of lesbian and gay parenting research are high: 'Because anti-gay scholars seek evidence of harm, sympathetic researchers defensively stress its absence.' Stacey and Biblarz examined findings from twenty-one studies of lesbian and gay families published between 1981 and 1998 (eighteen studies of lesbian parents and three of gay male parents). They argued that both anti-gay and sympathetic scholars' research is premised on heteronormative assumptions (that healthy child development depends on parenting by a married heterosexual couple): 'even the most sympathetic proceed from a highly defensive posture that accepts heterosexual parenting as the gold standard and investigates whether lesbigay parents and their children are inferior' (p. 162). Predominant research designs place the 'burden of proof' on lesbian and gay families – they must show that they are no less healthy and functional than heterosexual families. Moreover, by treating negative assumptions about lesbian and gay parenting as worthy of investigation, the validity of the assumptions and the heteronormative model of family that they underpin are (perhaps unwittingly) reinforced (Clarke, 2002a).

Comparative research reinforces problematic social norms

Following on from this criticism, feminist scholars, in particular, have expressed concern about the ways in which comparative research reinforces heteronormative understandings of gender and sexuality (e.g., Pollack, 1987). Girls are 'sugar and spice and all things nice' and boys are made of 'slugs and snails and puppy dog tails', and romance should only blossom when 'boy meets girl'. Authors of comparative research measure the extent to which children conform to culturally normative definitions of gender identities and gender roles. Evidence of cross-gender identification or unconventional gender behaviour is interpreted as a 'bad outcome' for the children of lesbian and gay parents, rather than as a positive sign of breaking down gender stereotypes and experiencing gender in new and liberating ways.

Comparative research treats difference as problematic

Stacey and Biblarz (2001) argued that authors of comparative studies downplay evidence of differences between the children of lesbian and heterosexual mothers in the arenas of gender and sexuality. They alleged that while interpretations of findings are often technically accurate, they deflect attention away from the differences that the study actually reports. Moreover, most studies use conventional levels of significance on very small samples, which increases the likelihood of finding no differences. Stacey and Biblarz concluded their review of the literature with the argument that: 'contemporary children and young adults with lesbian or gay parents do differ in modest and interesting ways from children with heterosexual parents' (p. 176). In particular, children appear to be less convention-ally gender-typed and more open to same-sex relationships. They argued that these differences are not caused by parental sexuality but are perhaps indirect effects of parental gender. Many gender theories would predict that children with two same-gender parents, particularly with two mothers, would develop in less gender-conventional ways than children with two heterosexual parents. Indeed, more recent research has found that lesbian mothers encourage their sons to have more sensitive and caring attitudes than the stereotypical male (MacCallum and Golombok, 2004).

This downplaying of difference in relation to gender and sexuality contrasts sharply with lesbian feminist accounts of lesbian mothering and the ways in which lesbian mothers, in accordance with their feminist principles, seek to challenge, what they perceive as, damaging gender norms (see Clarke, 2005b). For example, lesbian feminist Jess Wells (1997: x–xi), when comparing lesbian families with heterosexual or 'patriarchal' families, wrote that:

> lesbian households are raising a new generation of men who will be significantly different from their counterparts from patriarchal families … Patriarchal families teach girls what they cannot do and teach boys what they cannot feel … Lesbian families teach their sons to embrace the full range of their emotions. No one in a lesbian household says, 'Take it like a man' or 'Big boys don't cry.'

Furthermore, some lesbian feminists have written about the pride they feel in their sexuality and the positive experience of being lesbian, and about wanting their children to experience the benefits of living outside of heteronormativity. Lesbian feminist Baba Copper (1987: 239), in a piece on the radical potential of lesbian mothering of daughters, wrote that:

> Another heteromyth which needs radically defusing is the notion that lesbian mothers must maintain neutrality in relation to the future sexual preference of their daughters … we are lesbians, and it is a fundamental expression of self-love to want our daughters to grow up reflecting our woman-identified choices.

Some lesbian feminists have also highlighted the damage done to the queer children of queer parents by the implicit message that their sexuality represents a failure on the part of their parents.

Feminists, sociologists and critical psychologists have been critical of the problematic treatment of difference in comparative research (e.g., Hicks, 2005b). Just as early gay affirmative researchers have been criticised for assuming that difference equals deficiency, a similar charge has been levelled at the authors of comparative studies. The liberal 'lesbian mothers are just like heterosexual mothers' message of comparative research ignores lesbian mothers' experiences of heterosexism and their attempts to create and live family in ways that differ from the nuclear norm (Clarke, 2002b).

Comparative research polices the lives of lesbian mothers

Critical psychologists have called attention to the **regulatory role of psychology**, that is, the way in which psychological knowledge supports normative and dominant practices and behaviours. For example, in the original Golombok *et al.* (1983) study, gender-role behaviours were defined as those *regarded by the culture* as masculine or feminine. Although they acknowledged the existence of cultural norms around gender, they did not offer any critique of these norms, and as such provided implicit support for such norms. The 'just the same as' message of comparative research supports a distinction between 'good lesbian mothers' and 'bad lesbian mothers' (Clarke, 2008). Good lesbian mothers keep their sexuality private, separate from and subordinate to their role as mothers; they ensure their children have male role models and remain neutral about their children's sexuality. By contrast, bad lesbian mothers express pride in their sexuality, are engaged in feminist and lesbian communities and activism (in the words of judges in lesbian mother custody cases in the 1970s and 1980s, these women are 'missionary' and 'militant' about their sexuality), and encourage their children to break free from gender stereotypes. This distinction between unacceptable and acceptable behaviour and attitudes has damaged the lives of many lesbian mothers. In relation to custody disputes, for example, women have felt compelled to play the part of the good lesbian mother and to downplay any aspects of their lived experience that departs from the confines of this role. Non-conforming (and even conforming) women have been penalised by harsh restrictions on their relationships with their children and their women partners.

Beyond comparison?

In light of these criticisms, a number of scholars have called for less defensive research on lesbian and gay parenting. One argument is that LGBTQ psychologists should focus on the distinctive elements of lesbian and gay families (such as more egalitarian relationships between parents) and examine the positive effects these might have on children's development. For example, some more recent comparative research has explored the 'degendering' of parenting in lesbian mother families by comparing the division of child-care and domestic labour in lesbian mother families and heterosexual (single mother and/or two-parent) families (Fulcher *et al.*, 2008). Many of these studies have shown that lesbian mother families divide child-care and domestic labour more equally than heterosexual couples. Moreover, one US study has found that a more equal division of child-care and domestic labour within lesbian couples is associated with higher levels of parental satisfaction and child adjustment (Patterson, 1995).

Other critics of comparative research, like Stacey and Biblarz (2001), urge LGBTQ parenting researchers to take a new direction in order to exploit the rich opportunity presented by same-sex parenting for examining the interactions of gender, sexuality and family structure on parenting and child development. Such research would acknowledge the strengths *and* vulnerabilities of LGBTQ parenting and would reflect a more genuinely pluralist approach to family diversity (rather than ranking families in relation to the 'gold standard' of married heterosexual parents). Stacey and Biblarz argue that lesbian feminist claims that lesbian mother families raise sons to be 'boys who cry', that is, to experience rather than repress emotion, and raise girls to realise their full potential, are testable hypotheses with important theoretical implications. In addition, Stacey and Biblarz argue that existing findings suggest some important avenues for future research. For example, the finding that children in lesbian and gay families contend with a degree of social stigma but show no differences in psychological well-being suggests the presence of some compensatory processes in these families. Exploring how lesbian and gay families help children cope with social stigma might generate some interesting findings. Finally, some critical researchers propose abandoning comparative research altogether and focusing instead on a new research agenda that foregrounds the lived experiences of non-heterosexual families and the effects of social marginalisation on these families (Clarke, 2002a).

LGBTQ psychological research on parenting and family has started to acknowledge that family has lots of different meanings for LGBTQ people, and is moving away from an exclusive focus on queer nuclear or biparental (Gross, 2006) families to explore the variety of ways in which LGBTQ people do family such as families of choice (as discussed in Chapter 8), polyamorous families (see Pallota-Chiarolli, 2006) and multiparental families (where there are more than two parents) (see Gross, 2006).

Looking inside LGBTQ families

Since the 1990s, a whole new body of research has developed on LGBTQ families, which focuses on the everyday experiences of these families. Instead of comparing the development of children in lesbian- and gay-headed families and heterosexual families (that is, responding to the concerns of the wider society), researchers have focused on the lived experiences of LGBTQ families, 'bringing forth the voices and experiences of this marginalized population' (Litovich and Langhout, 2004: 415). Most studies are relatively small scale, qualitative, interview-based projects that focus on white, middle-class, planned lesbian families (with birth or adopted children) living in western countries. However, research in this tradition is beginning to examine a wider variety of parenting and family experiences, including those of gay-headed families (Gianino, 2008), lesbian and gay foster carers (Riggs, 2004b; 2007b), and lesbian-headed families in non-western countries (Lubbe, 2008).

LGBTQ families are viewed as on the cutting edge of a key social shift rather than as on the margins to be compared to a central norm (Benkov, 1995). Researchers in this tradition tend to use a more fluid language around family – a key phrase is 'doing family' (rather than 'the family'). In contrast to the essential notion of 'the family' as a discrete social institution is the idea of family as a verb (something we do) rather than a noun (something that is, or that we are) (Morgan, 1999). It is important to note that although LGBTQ families attempt to 'do family' differently, they cannot completely live outside of dominant understandings of family (Perlesz et al., 2006).

This literature has addressed a number of topics including: children's experiences of heterosexism (Litovich and Langhout, 2004); how lesbian families negotiate the school environment (Lindsay *et al.*, 2006); lesbian mothers' experiences of 'living well' in the context of heterosexism (Short, 2007); the ways in which lesbian families negotiate their identities through symbols and rituals (Suter *et al.*, 2008); and lesbian mothers' decision-making about sperm donors (Touroni and Coyle, 2002). Researchers in this tradition are also conducting longitudinal studies – for example, one study in the USA is following the experiences of seventy-eight lesbian mother-headed families (Gartrell *et al.*, 2006).

Let us now consider an example of one of these studies. US psychologist Abbie Goldberg (2007a) highlights the importance of understanding processes unique to the structure of LGB families. One such process for the children of LGB parents concerns disclosure: adult children of LGB parents face constant decisions about how open to be in relation to their unique family structure. She interviewed forty-two adults (aged between 19 and 50, with a mean age of 30; thirty-five women and seven men; most identified as heterosexual) with one or more LGB parents. Some participants had always known their parents were LGB and had been raised in an atmosphere of open communication about their parents' sexuality. These participants felt that open and early communication helped prepare them for the many questions they faced about their family from peers and others. Other participants had known since childhood (although some parents had never officially disclosed or discussed their sexuality): some recalled responding relatively positively to their parents' disclosure, others were initially negative (of these many grew up in homophobic environments). Participants whose homes were characterised by secrecy felt less prepared to handle questions from others.

Many participants reported feeling pride in their parents' sexuality. Some were initially vocal about their families, encountered negative reactions, felt less positive about their parents' sexuality, and then went on to reclaim their sense of pride. Some participants came out about their families because they felt a strong desire to defend their families and the LGB community and to educate others, and some used this information as a 'litmus test' to gauge whether they wanted to get to know someone or not. Some felt a strong need to be honest and open (these participants had grown up in relatively closeted families), some disclosed to preempt negative reactions, and finally a small minority did not disclose.

Goldberg noted some tensions and contradictions in the participants' accounts: some participants who reported that they tended to be private about their family also reported being prompted to disclose in the face of homophobia. In addition, participants who described themselves as very open also reported that at times they remained silent about their parents' sexuality (e.g., when it felt unsafe to disclose).

In another report, Goldberg (2007b) explored the participants' perceptions of how growing up with LGB parents influenced them as adults. The participants felt that they were more tolerant and open-minded (see also Saffron, 1998) and had more flexible ideas about gender and sexuality. Goldberg and colleague Katherine

Allen (2007) have also examined lesbian mothers' perceptions of male involvement in their families during the transition to parenthood. They found a spectrum of perceptions and intentions regarding male involvement and identified three groups of women: deliberate, flexible and ambivalent. Deliberate women thought male involvement was very important and intended to make special efforts to ensure their children had contact with men. Flexible women thought male involvement was important but did not intend to go out of their way to ensure it. Finally, ambivalent women did not intend actively to pursue male involvement.

This is just a flavour of a growing body of research that prioritises the voices and experiences of lesbian families. We hope this chapter has shown that while there is a substantial literature on LGBTQ (and especially lesbian) parenting, there is still much to find out about life in LGBTQ-headed families.

Gaps and absences

- Most research is based on samples of white lesbian mothers who are comparatively highly educated, mature and professional, and live in relatively progressive urban centres. Furthermore, there is a tendency to treat LGBTQ families as homogeneous and to overlook differences between individual families. As such our knowledge of the diversity of LGBTQ family life is limited.
- The range of LGBTQ family forms explored in research remains narrow and most research focuses on two-parent families, and overlooks single parents and multiparental families.
- No study has systematically investigated how children respond to the loss of contact with an LGBTQ parent who is denied custody or visitation rights or how LGBTQ parents respond to the loss of contact with their children.
- The conceptualisation of sexuality in existing research is unsophisticated – little is known about the sexuality of participating parents other than their self-identification as lesbian or gay (Tasker, 2005). Furthermore, as Stacey and Biblarz (2001) pointed out, most studies measure sexuality as a dichotomy rather than as a continuum, so we can only speculate about how a more nuanced conceptualisation of sexuality might alter the findings reported.

Main chapter points

This chapter:

- Outlined the many ways in which LGBTQ people become parents and the existence of widespread negative assumptions about LGBTQ parenting that often hinge on the risks of children developing 'faulty' gender and sexual identities.

- Summarised the findings of research that compares lesbian-, gay- and trans-headed families with heterosexual families, which has centred on disproving concerns about LGT people's poor parenting and the negative effects on children of growing up in a LGT-headed family.

- Summarised criticisms of comparative research, which highlight the defensive and reactive stance of this research.

- Explored an emerging body of research that prioritises the experiences and voices of members of LGBTQ families, and the ways in which they live out their lives and negotiate their family and personal identities in a heteronormative social context.

Questions for discussion and classroom exercises

1.   Imagine how the children of LGBTQ parents experience the (typical) school environment (if you are a child of LGBTQ parents or a LGBTQ parent you might like to share your experiences of schooling). Then imagine you are an educational psychologist advising a school on how to create an inclusive environment and manage homophobic, biphobic and transphobic bullying. What measures would you introduce to the school? How would you raise awareness of family diversity?

2.   What evidence is there that LGBTQ-headed families are similar to heterosexual-headed families? What evidence is there that LGBTQ-headed families are different from heterosexual-headed families?

3.   What challenges do the findings of psychological research on LGBTQ-headed families present to traditional theories of child development?

4.   Consider the costs and benefits of comparative research discussed in this chapter. On balance, would you urge psychologists to continue with or to abandon comparative research? What are the reasons for your choice?

5.   US social work educator Elena Marie DiLapi (1989) constructed a motherhood hierarchy to reflect the social value accorded to different types of mothers. She argued that (white, middle-class, married) heterosexual women are the 'most appropriate' type of mother and lesbians the 'least appropriate', with teenage, disabled, black and working-class mothers occupying the second-tier of 'moderately appropriate' mothers. Do you think this hierarchy is an accurate reflection of contemporary society? Does it reflect the values of your community? Where on the hierarchy would you place some of the other types of

parents discussed in this chapter such as trans, bisexual and polyamorous parents?

Further reading

Anderssen, N., Amlie, C. and Yitterøy, A. (2002) Outcomes for children with lesbian or gay parents. A review of studies from 1978 to 2000. *Scandinavian Journal of Psychology*, 43, 335–51.
An excellent review of the predominantly comparative psychological literature on lesbian and gay parenting, which highlights some of the limitations of existing knowledge.

Folgerø, T. (2008) Queer nuclear families: reproducing and transgressing heteronormativity. *Journal of Homosexuality*, 54(1/2), 124–49.
This article provides an analysis of how queer families both transgress and reproduce heteronormative assumptions about childhood, fatherhood, motherhood and family.

Hicks, S. (2008) Gender role models … who needs 'em?! *Qualitative Social Work*, 7(1), 43–59.
This article critically examines the use of socialisation theory and, in particular, the notion of 'gender role models' in relation to assessing lesbian and gay applicants for foster care and adoption.

Paechter, C. (2000) Growing up with a lesbian mother: a theoretically-based analysis of personal experience. *Sexualities*, 3(4), 395–408.
Professor of education Carrie Paechter explores her experiences of growing up with a lesbian mother.

Perlesz, A. and McNair, R. (2004) Lesbian parenting: insiders' voices. *Australian and New Zealand Journal of Family Therapy*, 25(2), 129–40.
An Australian study that provides a good example of listening to the voices of lesbian mothers and exploring *their* accounts of the challenges and benefits of lesbian parenting.

10 Ageing and old age

Overview

- Age, ageing and ageism in LGBTQ communities
- Styles of ageing
- Issues in health and social care in old age
- Bereavement and death

Age, ageing and ageism in LGBTQ communities

Stereotypes of older LGBTQ people

Older LGBTQ people are a 'hidden' section of the LGBTQ population: 'the most invisible of an invisible minority' (Blando, 2001: 87). Popular images of LGBTQ people tend to be of younger people dancing the night away in a 'gay club' or marching in feather boas and hot pants in a Mardi Gras parade! Beyond middle age, it would seem that LGBTQ people simply disappear. British social scientist Stephen Pugh (2002: 160) writes that 'The disappearance of older lesbians and gay men [and BTQ people] may seem somewhat analogous to a science fiction tale in which everybody over a given age suddenly vanishes as if to avoid tarnishing younger people.'

Gerontology (the study of ageing and old age) began to focus on older LGBTQ people, and particularly older gay men, in the 1970s. However, gerontology as a whole remains resolutely heterosexist and this is partly why, although research on old age and ageing within LGBTQ communities is increasing, we know comparatively little about older LGBTQ people. This chapter will be informed by work in psychology as well as work in gerontology, sociology and other related disciplines in order to provide as complete a picture as possible of old age and ageing within LGBTQ communities.

Within LGBTQ communities, negative stereotypes of older people abound. A common image of older gay men is one of: 'Loneliness, isolation, sexlessness, poor psychological adjustment and functioning, fearful anxiousness, sadness and depression and sexual predation on the gay young who reject their company and exclude them from a "youthist" gay culture' (Wahler and Gabbay, 1997: 9). US psychologist and key researcher Douglas Kimmel (1978) dismissed the sexually predatory stereotype of older gay men when he found that they actually have little contact with younger gay men (see Box 10.1). The notion that older gay men are sexually predatory is based on offensive and faulty assumptions about the links between gay men, promiscuity and paedophilia.

Box 10.1   Key researcher: Douglas C. Kimmel on why I study gay ageing

In 1975 my textbook *Adulthood and aging* had received excellent reviews and I secured tenure at City College in New York City. Since 1973 I had been quietly involved with the emerging Association of Gay Psychologists, which met during the annual convention of the American Psychological Association (APA). With the security of a tenured academic position, I decided to put my two interests together and study older gay men. In part, I was motivated by the power of the stigma imposed by a grudgingly tolerant attitude of some straight and gay friends: 'It may be OK to be gay when you are young, but wait until you are old and alone!' It seemed important to challenge that view if the burgeoning gay liberation movement was to succeed. Moreover, we needed role models since few of us had 'gay grandparents' at that time.

I developed an open-ended questionnaire for a lengthy interview and no grey haired man at any gay meeting was safe from being asked to be interviewed. Eventually I found a dozen men who were willing to let me transcribe the interview. The resulting data were very rich, leading to three scholarly articles (Kimmel, 1977a, 1978, 1979) and one popular one published in a gay magazine, *Christopher Street* (Kimmel, 1977b). The central finding was the great diversity among the older gay men – in every respect. The basic conclusion was that being an older gay man did not inevitably mean loneliness and, in fact, the men often found advantages to being gay in terms of planning for old age and developing many skills that helped them cope with the challenges that can face any older person; most also were sexually active.

An important fortuitous meeting resulted from my research when I was invited to discuss the idea of a programme of services for older gay men and lesbians. We went on to gather our friends for an organising meeting in 1977 of the group that became SAGE in New York city (presently known as Services and Advocacy for GLBT Elders). I played a leading role in SAGE during the early years.

During the 1980s Clarence Adams and I studied older African American gay men, again finding diversity rather than stereotypic patterns of ageing (Adams and Kimmel, 1997; see Box 10.4). I was also involved in APA activities on gay and ageing issues. Then, working with Linda Garnets on an invited Master Lecture at the APA Convention and on an edited book, *Psychological perspectives on lesbian and gay male experiences* (Garnets and Kimmel, 1993), I came to know Evelyn Hooker, the pioneer researcher on homosexuality.

In 2006, Tara Rose, Steven David and I co-edited *Lesbian, gay, bisexual, and transgender aging*, a work that sheds some early light on ageing issues among bisexual and transgender persons.

The stereotype of older gay men and lesbians as lonely and miserable may also apply to older bisexual and trans people, but as with other areas of LGBTQ psychology, we know very little about the experiences of these latter groups. Therefore, this chapter will largely report the experiences of older gay men and lesbians. As the charity Age Concern England (ACE) (2007) notes, regardless of the sexual identity that trans people identify with (ACE estimates that roughly equal numbers identify as heterosexual and as non-heterosexual), older trans people have some issues in common with older LGB people. ACE suggests that older trans people also experience a unique set of issues relating to their trans status. Older trans people have been described as an 'emerging population' with distinctive needs (Witten, 2003); see Box 10.2.

Box 10.2   Key study: Tarynn M. Witten and Stephen Whittle (2004) on transpanthers

According to gerontologist Tarynn Witten and legal scholar Stephen Whittle:

> for the first time in this modern historical period, we are faced with an aging 'trans' community with a wide range of health and social care needs conjoint with their diverse sexed and gendered bodies and identity. Moreover, this community contains many cohorts of individuals, each with their own specialised needs and who, as they age, will need various degrees of specialised attention beyond that of the 'normative' aging process. (2004:2)

Witten and Whittle identify some of the key issues faced by older trans people, including: violence and abuse, unemployment and poverty, legal and social discrimination, limited social support and social isolation, and unmet health and social care needs. They provide some case studies to illustrate the intersection of these issues in the lives of individual older trans people. For example:

> James, a trans man of 71 who had undergone chest reconstruction but not genital surgery, was in the stages of early Alzheimer's. He was placed within a local authority care home where every other client was female. The staff at the care home was very uncomfortable with meeting his bodily needs … They had also taken to not passing on his post which include a support group magazine, deciding that he was not able to read and understand it. A local volunteer visitor contacted a support group after discovering James very distressed … the volunteers found a local gay men's resident home which providing nursing care and would accept James … Being in a 'men's' home, James became much happier. (p. 7)

Witten and Whittle argue that there is an ongoing failure to acknowledge the diversity within the trans population: 'To ensure respect, dignity and to adjust support to meet the individual need, it is imperative that the mythology of the trans body be erased and replaced with reality' (p. 12). The trans community is made up of a wide range of people with different versions of sexed and gendered bodies; diversity arises in relation to the complexities of personal identity as well as in relation to body modifications.

Witten and Whittle contend that older trans people have coped with the challenges of a difficult life, including social stigma, poverty and health concerns, and it is vitally important that they are not re-stigmatised as they enter old age. Witten and Whittle urge health and social care providers to respect the diversity of trans people's bodies.

In a review of the literature on ageing, US psychologist James Reid (1995: 227) concluded that 'the available literature suggests that the stereotypes of lonely, alienated, and despondent older lesbians and gay men are incorrect. Rather, what emerges is picture [*sic*] of older gay men and lesbians who are active, selectively engaging in activities and interests of their choosing'. The literature on gay and lesbian ageing that has developed since the 1970s has 'refused to use research on heterosexual ageing as its benchmark' (Harrison and Riggs, 2006: 42) and has rejected the comparative agenda pursued in other areas of LGBTQ psychological research such as parenting and relationships. Instead, research has focused expressly on the experiences of ageing and old age within gay and lesbian communities and has sought to understand how older gay men and lesbians *as* gay men and lesbians negotiate the ageing process.

Multiple marginalisation and cohort effects

Many researchers argue that older LGBTQ people experience 'double discrimination' or 'double jeopardy' because they face heterosexist assumptions in the wider society, and ageist assumptions both in LGBTQ communities and in the wider society. Ageism, or age-related assumptions that impact negatively on older people's everyday lives, is a common experience of all older people (Pugh, 2002). The recognition of ageism as a system of social marginalisation is relatively recent. Butler (1987: 22) defined ageism as 'a process of systematic stereotyping of, and discrimination against, people just because they are old, just as racism and sexism accomplish this for skin colour and gender'. Stereotyping results in the assumption that all older people are the same: all older people are slow, forgetful and living in the past, they smell, they moan, they are old-fashioned and conservative and a burden on society.

Older people are also imagined to be uninterested in sex (although the advent of new pharmaceuticals such as Viagra troubles this notion somewhat) and sexually unattractive and/or inactive. Sex is often assumed to be the territory of the young. There is something of a double standard here, however, in that older men can be viewed positively (particularly when they are wealthy and powerful), whereas older women are just old. The assumption that older people are asexual means that any expression of their sexuality is viewed as a problem to be managed or treated. It also means that the possibility that some older people might be non-heterosexual has been unrecognised or ignored (Price, 2005).

Ageism may be heightened within the gay community. As British social scientist David Clover (2006: 43) notes, 'the visible gay community is generally considered to have an emphasis and focus on youth, the gay media rarely portraying images of older men, and gay venues often favouring and attracting a younger clientele'. The sociologists Brian Heaphy, Andrew Yip and Debbie Thompson (2004) have conducted the first major British study of ageing and old age within non-heterosexual communities using focus groups, interviews and a postal survey (with a total of 316 lesbian, gay and bisexual participants aged between 50 and 70+) (see Box 10.3). They found that 35.3 per cent of women and 69.5 per cent of men felt there was a lot of ageism in non-heterosexual communities. Thirty-four per cent of women and 53.7 per cent of men felt less welcome in gay spaces as they got older. In Clover's (2006) small-scale qualitative study of older gay men, a minority reported feeling lonely and isolated, and the difficulties

---

Box 10.3   Key study: Brian Heaphy and colleagues (2003) on relationships and social support in later life

One of the topics covered by Heaphy *et al.*'s major British study of 316 LGB people aged between the fifties and the eighties is relationships and social support. Almost 60 per cent of the women in their sample were in couple relationships (all same-sex) compared to roughly 40 per cent of the men (nine of sixty-one were in different-sex relationships). In general, the younger the participant, the more likely that they were in a relationship. Couple relationships were highly valued by the participants and a majority thought that couple relationships had become increasingly important as they aged. At the same time, there was broad agreement among the participants that it was increasingly difficult to meet partners as they aged. A large proportion of the participants lived alone (41.2 per cent of the women and 65.2 per cent of the men), and this percentage increased with age. Participants in relationships tended to live with their partners, but this was more likely among the women (48 per cent) than the men (26.8 per cent).

Early research on ageing suggested that older non-heterosexuals are particularly likely to be distanced from their family of origin. Heaphy *et al.* found that 34.3 per cent of the women and 22 per cent of the men were distanced from their family of origin because of their sexuality, but the majority (62.9 per cent) felt that their relationships with their family of origin were important. Relationships with children were significant for many of the participants: 42.2 per cent of the women and 24.2 per cent of the men were parents.

In line with earlier research, friendships were important to the participants: 96.1 per cent of the women and 93.9 per cent of the men considered friendships important. Most participants felt that friendships became more important as they got older. Many participants described their friends as 'the most important people' in their lives. Participants were more likely to turn to friends for emotional support than to their family of origin, but most expected partners and care professionals to provide instrumental care as they aged. Access to non-heterosexual communities had been a 'lifeline' for many participants, especially during 'critical moments' such as a bereavement or relationship break-up. Fifty per cent of the women and 48.3 per cent of the men were currently involved in non-heterosexual groups or organisations. However, ageism was a significant factor for participants who attempted to access non-heterosexual communities. Heaphy *et al.* commented that: 'While non-heterosexual communities offer support and resources for some of their members as they approach and experience old age, they do so more unevenly than has been suggested in much of the theoretical and empirical work' (p. 898).

of meeting people were felt to be exacerbated by ageism in the gay community and a lack of social opportunities for older gay men. One of the participants in Clover's study commented that: 'if you're not a boozer and you're not a clubber, where do you go to meet gay men? ... there's just nothing else' (p. 45). In the Heaphy *et al.* (2004) study, a large proportion of the older gay men felt uncomfortable or unwelcome in gay bars, where some of the men felt their ageing bodies marked them as undesirable.

The notion of 'double jeopardy' of course overlooks the fact that some older LGBTQ people are also socially marginalised in relation to, for example, race and gender. Some researchers have used the concept of 'triple jeopardy' (Auger, 1990; Norman, 1985) to capture the experiences of older LGBTQ people who also face social marginalisation in relation to race or gender but we prefer the concept of multiple marginalisation. Multiple marginalisation acknowledges the intersections of social marginalisation *and* privilege in relation to gender, age, race, culture, ability and social class, among other things, for all older LGBTQ people. Another dimension of marginalisation/privilege for older LGBTQ people is whether they live in rural or urban settings. In most urban settings there are LGBTQ networks, which allow people to socialise and provide emotional support; in larger metropolitan areas, older LGBTQ people are more likely to find LGBTQ-positive services. Research indicates that older LGBTQ people who live in rural settings can be very isolated (Auger, 1990). There is also some evidence to suggest that older trans people are particularly vulnerable to the effects of social isolation and diminished social support networks (Witten, 2003).

As Pugh (2002) notes, one of the difficulties of writing about older LGBTQ people as a group is the temptation to treat older people as a homogeneous group, with common interests and similar lives, but older LGBTQ people are not a socially cohesive group (see Box 10.4). US psychologist Douglas Kimmel (1977a; 1978; 1979), one of the first people to conduct research on older gay men, found considerable differences between older gay men, as did Professor of Sexuality and Anthropology Gilbert Herdt and colleagues (1997), in their study of the lives and needs of older lesbians and gay men living in Chicago. For instance, they found that marriage (and having children) dramatically affected the life course of their participants and the timing of significant events such as coming out as lesbian or gay: people who married tended to come out an average of ten years later than those who did not marry. Herdt *et al.* (1997: 238) concluded that 'there does not appear to be one, normative life course for older gays and lesbians ... there appears to be a variety of life course trajectories, which are substantially influenced by one's gender, cohort, marital and coming out histories, and friendship networks'.

Another dimension on which older LGBTQ people differ is 'cohort effects'. Cohort effects refer to the distinct political and economic experiences that separate generations and have a lasting impact (Pugh, 2002). Non-heterosexual and trans people's lives have been shaped by the historical period in which they have grown up and developed. Pugh argues that cohort effects are crucial when considering the lives of older gay men and lesbians (and, we would add, BTQ people) because

Box 10.4   Key study: Clarence Lancelot Adams, Jr. and Douglas C. Kimmel (1997) on the lives of older African American gay men

US-based psychologists Clarence Adams and Douglas Kimmel conducted one of the first empirical studies of older African American gay men – based on a sample of twenty men (aged between 39 and 73, with an average age of 56) living in New York. Open-ended life-history interviews were the major source of information. The interview data were analysed using grounded theory, and Adams and Kimmel discussed a number of themes including: relationship with family of origin, involvement with the African American and gay communities, historical effects and discrimination.

Most of the men maintained ties with their families of origin and most families knew the men were gay and their reactions were generally not hostile. Nine of the men were involved with gay social organisations, and, with two exceptions, these organisations were African American lesbian and gay social groups, which were reported to have a long history.

Participants indicated that the dynamics of interracial social relationships within gay communities are complex. Some of the men preferred to avoid social contact with white men. One participant commented that: 'I seek out Blacks who have a Black consciousness. I get very distressed when I deal with Black gay men who spend a lot of time with White gays' (p. 144). Some men only had sexual contact with other African Americans. One participant said: 'I feel a sense, being a Black person in a White setting of, "What are you doing here?" – that kind of attitude, unless you are with a White lover. And even the few friends of mine that have a White lover, they have that kind of problem' (p. 145).

Most of the men were not involved in non-gay African American organisations, perhaps because of a lack of comfort as a gay man with these groups. All of the men felt the lesbian and gay movement was a positive change, even if the changes were mainly for 'White boys in jeans' (p. 147).

The men experienced age discrimination in the gay community and in the broader society; they also experienced anti-gay discrimination, but both of these types of discrimination were less important in the lives of the men than racial discrimination. When asked if there is racial discrimination in the gay community, one participant commented: 'Absolutely. When I attend a gay benefit I am the fly in the plate of milk … I assume there is as much bias in the gay community as elsewhere' (p. 148). Another participant said that: 'Being Black, gay, and old is a heavy load' (p. 145).

Adams and Kimmel concluded by highlighting the diversity of experiences within their sample and calling for further research on older African American gay men and on other racial and cultural groups of older gay men and lesbians.

they inform issues such as self-identification, associations with other gay men and lesbians, and the circumstances in which same-sex relationships were formed and endured. For example, during the era of the criminalisation and pathologisation of homosexuality, and because of their individual circumstances, some gay men and lesbians opted to live openly, whereas others got married and lived overtly as heterosexual, while conducting secret same-sex relationships. Pugh (2002: 166) asks: 'In family histories, how many uncles and great uncles remained bachelors, thereby hiding their gay sexuality?' The criminalisation of homosexuality created an imperative for secrecy and discomfort with publicly acknowledging sexuality, which may linger on for some older gay men and lesbians.

Non-heterosexuals who came out after homosexuality was de-criminalised and depathologised may feel more comfortable with publicly acknowledging their sexuality and may carry this attitude through with them into old age. Heaphy and Yip (2003: 4) note that 'new and different possibilities were to open up for lesbian and gay identity in the wake of the women's and gay liberation movements of the 1960s'. Some of their participants reported that these movements offered opportunities to redefine and reinvent themselves in some way. In the 1960s, many men and women embraced 'gay' and 'lesbian' as labels of self-identification. A strong identification with sexuality politics provided people with a vocabulary and framework for constructing an empowered sense of self. However, Heaphy and Yip (2006) found that the perceived possibilities for creating and living non-heterosexual lives post-1960s varied widely. Some of their participants still felt unable to reject the pressure to live a heterosexual life and many had a strong sense of the risks associated with living openly as non-heterosexual. Heaphy and Yip commented that: 'While significant opportunities for non-heterosexual "re-invention" and "self-creation" have emerged over the past forty years, the degree to which these are, or can be, taken up by older men and women are uneven' (2006: 6). Similarly, Herdt *et al.* (1997: 237) concluded that: 'the positive gains won by the gay rights movement may have differentially impacted the lives of our respondents, depending on their age and life-course experiences'. Witten (2002) argues that cohort effects are also visible in the trans population, with many elderly transsexuals choosing not to reveal their natal sex because of fear of stigma, unlike younger adults who constitute the majority of the out and politically active trans population.

Defining age

So what counts as 'older'? Given the existence of popular sayings such as 'you're as old as you feel', how are the boundaries between middle age and old age determined? Gerontologists have tended to draw distinctions between older adults on the basis of chronological age (Reid, 1995). To quote Reid (1995: 216): 'Typically, "middle age" is thought of as occurring between the ages of 35 and 55. Late life is divided into periods of "young old" (65 to 75 or 80) and "old-old" (75 or 80 to about 90), and "oldest-old" (90+).' These categories highlight the fact that older adults are not a homogeneous group: some may be employed, whereas others may be retired; some may live independently in their own homes, whereas others may live in sheltered housing or residential homes and require care.

Unfortunately most research has focused on the 'young old' and neglected the experiences and perspectives of the 'older old' (Lee, 2008). Like all 'hidden' populations, obtaining exact figures for the number of older LGBTQ people in the population is notoriously problematic. In England, ACE (2006) estimates that every fifteenth potential user of a service for older people is a lesbian or gay man.

Research has examined the meanings attached to 'old age' and 'ageing' by LGB people. The concept of 'accelerated ageing' has been used to capture how some people self-identify in relation to age. The argument is that the emphasis on youth and the body beautiful, particularly in gay male communities, leads some gay men to identify themselves as old long before their heterosexual counterparts. Gay men in mid-life might feel disregarded and unattractive, feelings reflected in the saying, 'nobody loves a fairy after they're forty'. However, findings are contradictory, with some studies providing little support for the concept (Bennett and Thompson, 1991). More recently, Heaphy et al. (2004) found that 45 per cent of their sample defined old age as being in the seventies or older, while 23.3 per cent nominated the sixties and older. Participants of all ages tended to refer to themselves as older in relation to their sexual identities. Many men, in particular, reported that youth-oriented non-heterosexual cultures made them feel conscious of their age. Heaphy and colleagues argue that the meaning of old age is as fluid for non-heterosexuals as it is in the wider culture, where interpretations of age are thought to be becoming increasingly flexible and personal.

Coming out or transitioning in later life

Although many people understand themselves to be non-heterosexual earlier in life, some people come out as non-heterosexual in later life (see also Chapter 7). Auger (1990) noted that many lesbians 'come out' after the age of 50, often from heterosexual marriages or after they have been widowed. It is important to remember that coming out is not a one-off event, but an ongoing process, with each new relationship or social event involving decisions about coming out. Some early research on older LGBTQ people conducted in the 1970s and 1980s found that their perspectives on publicly acknowledging their sexuality had been shaped by earlier experiences of heterosexism and homophobia during more conservative social eras (Pugh, 2002). More recently, Heaphy et al. (2003) found that most participants were totally out to their friends (95 per cent), a majority were out to at least some family members, more often siblings than parents (69 per cent), and about half (51 per cent) were out to some neighbours. At the same time, not all of the participants were ageing with a confident and open approach to their sexuality. Just over a third of the men, particularly the older men, (37 per cent) and just under a quarter of the women (23 per cent) had hidden their sexuality throughout their lives. Heaphy et al. argue that these figures highlight the resilience of internalised sanctions against homosexuality and of the perceived risks of being open about their sexuality.

Although most people start to question their gender identity earlier in life, it is quite possible for older people to be questioning this (ACE, 2007). Older people can transition: people have transitioned successfully in their sixties, seventies or eighties. In some respects transitioning in later life may be easier because as people age many become more gender neutral in their physical appearance, so it takes very little for people to be seen as a member of their preferred gender. However, as people age hormone therapy and surgery are higher risk and it may be difficult to be healthy enough to undergo full gender reassignment. Because hormone therapy and gender reassignment surgery only became widespread in the 1960s and 1970s, it is only recently that doctors have been able to assess a cohort of people who have been living post-operatively in their new gender for over twenty years. The long-term prognosis for trans people is positive; however, new health risks are still being discovered (ACE, 2007; see Chapter 6).

Styles of ageing

The notion of 'gay ageing' was first written about in the late 1960s (Weinberg, 1969), and since then a lot of research on ageing in non-heterosexual contexts has examined how gay men and lesbians psychologically managed the ageing process. Some early research on ageing suggested that gay men's and lesbians' experiences of heterosexism and homophobia equipped them to adjust positively to the ageing process (Francher and Henkin, 1973; Kimmel, 1978). Berger (1980: 238) used the concept 'mastery of crisis' in relation to gay ageing:

> There are aspects of the homosexual experience that facilitate adjustment to ageing … the coming-out period is a major life crisis, which, when resolved, provides the individual with a stamina unavailable to many others. Today's older homosexual had to resolve a crisis of independence at a young age and at a time less tolerant of sexual nonconformity. He knew he could not rely on the traditional family supports that heterosexuals take for granted. Whereas older homosexuals are as likely as heterosexuals to be alone in old age, they are better prepared for it, both emotionally and in terms of support networks of friends.

Some researchers have also identified unique challenges associated with non-heterosexual experiences of ageing, including a lack of self-acceptance as gay or lesbian, not being 'out', and not being involved with the wider lesbian and gay community (Wahler and Gabbay, 1997). Indeed, self-acceptance is thought to be a critical factor in successful gay ageing. LGBTQ people who are 'out of the closet' are thought to experience ageing differently from those who are still 'in' (Auger, 1990). Some research has also identified benefits attached to ageing as an older LGBTQ person. For example, Jeanette Auger's (1990) research on older lesbians in Canada found that many of them experienced the pleasure of growing old without the expectations and pressures placed on heterosexual women. In Heaphy et al.'s (2003) study, the women often commented that the privileging of youth was less of an issue in lesbian communities than it was for heterosexual women in mainstream cultures.

Gerontologists developed the concept of 'successful ageing' (alongside 'pathological' and 'normal' ageing) to describe positive adaptation to the ageing process and the associated changes in physical, emotional/psychological and social circumstances (Reid, 1995). Researchers have developed models of successful ageing in relation to lesbians and gay men. Friend's (1991) model of successful gay and lesbian ageing emphasised the achievement of a positive and open gay or lesbian identity. Friend (1991: 108) described 'affirmative' older gay men and lesbians as those who achieved 'a high level of self-acceptance and psychological adjustment, even within the hostile historical periods in which they were raised'. Less optimal outcomes involved internalising the negative beliefs and attitudes of the wider society. 'Stereotypical' older gay men and lesbians internalised the homophobia of the wider culture, felt shame about their sexuality and kept their sexuality secret. The 'passing' older gay man or lesbian responded to the homophobia of the wider culture by entering heterosexual relationships and passing as heterosexual. In Friend's model, successful ageing requires psychological attributes such as 'crisis competence'.

Clover (2006) argues that most early research from North America depicts older gay men and lesbians as healthy and happy, psychologically well adjusted, self-accepting, and adapting well to the ageing process. We must be cautious in making generalisations from these early studies, however, because they were generally based on small, convenience samples of white, middle-class, well-educated, urban-dwelling gay men, who were mainly in their forties and fifties and participated actively in the gay community, and so do not reflect the diversity within non-heterosexual communities (Clover, 2006; Heaphy et al., 2003). Clover also notes that research in the 1970s and 1980s, like other early gay affirmative research, was very much focused on challenging negative stereotypes of older gay men.

As you can imagine, more recent writing on ageing in non-heterosexual contexts has been highly critical of concepts such as 'successful ageing'. Pugh (2002) argues that such concepts reinforce the widely held assumption that ageing is a negative process that requires adjustment. Pugh also argues that the most important factor in so-called 'successful ageing' is income and access to financial resources (rather than psychological ones). Other more concrete factors include education (which is related to income), health and the presence of a life partner. Notions such as 'successful ageing' have been important in challenging the negative stereotype of older gay men and lesbians as lonely and miserable. However, such constructs place the burden of responsibility for 'successful ageing' on individual people and their psychological resources and fail to take account of the huge importance of material, physical, cultural and social factors in determining how older LGBTQ people navigate the ageing process (Heaphy et al., 2004).

Heaphy et al. (2003) found that the participants in their study who had the lowest incomes rated their finances as their most significant concern about ageing. Many lesbians in their study had diminished opportunities to achieve financial security in old age through pensions and savings because they had been mothers and carers. Some participants also felt that homophobia in the workplace had resulted in a lack of career progression and had impacted on their financial security. It is important to note that theories about 'successful ageing' create norms and imperatives that may be at odds with older people's experiences and life course, and their wishes and desires for their life. It is also important not to lose sight of the fact that, as Adelman (1986: 11) noted in a book on older lesbians, 'the most important factor for determining psychological well-being in lesbians in late life is the level of homophobia in society'.

Issues in health and social care in old age

The existing research on the health and social care experiences of older LGBTQ people highlights three themes: (1) heterosexism and homophobia in services for older people; (2) LGBTQ relationships in the contexts of aged care facilities; and (3) the specific health needs of some LGBTQ people.

Heterosexism and homophobia in services for older people

Research indicates that many older LGBTQ people will have experienced a 'lifetime exposure' to discrimination (Chandler et al., 2005). Such exposure affects the levels of trust older LGBTQ people are willing to place in social and health services. Clover (2006) found that older gay men viewed health services with caution because of experiences or expectations of discrimination or poor treatment. Fear of differing treatment was more common than actual experiences of discrimination. Similarly, in the Heaphy and Yip (2006) study, most participants expressed a lack of confidence and trust in health professionals. Among participants who were open about their sexuality in their interactions with health professionals, 45 per cent of the women and 22 per cent of the men reported experiences of prejudice and discrimination. Participants in both studies felt that health professionals operate according to a heterosexual assumption.

Heterosexism and genderism occur in very mundane ways in health and social care, such as in 'admission questions which enquire about wives or husbands, photographs with heterosexual images, and staff who are not trained to handle gender-variant residents' (Chandler et al., 2005: 16). US gerontologist Tarynn Witten (2002) has suggested that health and social care can be more complex for transgender people than for people who are transsexual and post-operative: apparent mismatches between gender presentation and genital anatomy can result in difficulty in obtaining (appropriate) health and social care. Witten discussed the cases of a number of transgender and pre-operative transsexual people who were denied medical care (unrelated to their trans status) when their gender incongruity was revealed.

In relation to homophobia in health and social care, Röndahl, Innala and Carlsson (2004) found that in their Swedish sample 36 per cent of their nursing staff participants would refrain from nursing LGBTQ people if that option were available. They suggest that this may be changing among younger trainee nurses; however, because of the attitudes of some established nursing staff, existing services may fail to meet the needs of older LGBTQ people. Anecdotal evidence also abounds as to homophobia in aged care facilities. Raphael (1997, cited in Cook-Daniels, 1997) tells of 'an older resident of a nursing home whom staff refused to bathe because they didn't want to touch "the lesbian"'. Cook-Daniels (1997) outlined how a 'social worker reported a case where the home care assistant threatened to "out" her older gay male client if he reported her negligent care' (p. 40). Brown (1998: 113) quoted an older, disabled lesbian woman:

> I am a woman paralysed after a stroke from the neck down. How can I ask my home carer, employed to facilitate my 'independent living', to switch on *Dyke TV* (Channel 4, 1995) when I do not wish to reveal my sexual orientation because the carer has already let me know that their opinion that Beth Jordace's death on *Brookside* (Channel 4, 1995) was better than she deserved because she was a lesbian?

These examples of homophobia highlight the age-specific power imbalances that shape the lives of older LGBTQ people in interactions with service providers, and how this can negatively affect their health and well-being.

LGBTQ relationships in the contexts of aged care facilities

Little attention has been paid to LGBTQ relationships in aged care services, particularly to those relationships that do not conform to social norms. Consider, for example, older LGBTQ people who have previously been married, and who continue to enjoy ongoing friendships with their ex-spouses. These friendships may serve as immensely important sources of support, but they may also be misread by health care providers as signifying the heterosexuality of LGBTQ people, thus contributing to the invisibility of their sexualities. By contrast, LGBTQ people who are involved in long-term relationships with more than one partner can encounter negative attitudes from health care professionals. Health care professionals may not regard older people as potentially sexually active, and may view the practice of having multiple sexual or emotional partners as 'inappropriate' behaviour for older LGBTQ people.

LGBTQ people have much strength as a result of living in a context of discrimination. For example, LGBTQ people often develop families of choice and other support networks (see Chapter 8). However, the independence that LGBTQ communities encourage can be problematic for older LGBTQ people as they become increasingly reliant on others for help and their support networks cannot meet these needs.

When older LGBTQ people can no longer meet their own support needs or when their own support networks are reduced, some may decide to enter into supported living arrangements. The degree to which such older LGBTQ people can control their circumstances will often depend on factors such as their socio-economic status. In many countries, including the USA and Australia, there have been moves towards LGBTQ-specific aged care facilities, but only certain groups of (primarily white, middle-class) LGBTQ people can afford to access these services. Other older LGBTQ people who can no longer live independently are likely to be forced into mainstream services that may provide little support or recognition for LGBTQ people. This lack of support may be exacerbated by the increased outsourcing of social and health care services to private organisations, many of which are run by religious groups. Most participants in the Heaphy *et al.* (2004) study viewed residential care and nursing homes as an undesirable option because of threats to their identity and ways of living. As one participant commented, 'to go into a residential home as a gay person, your life would be hell' (p. 892).

The specific health needs of some LGBTQ people

As we have discussed throughout this book, LGBTQ people are far from a homogeneous group, and individual people (and groups of people) have specific health needs. For example, as we noted above, trans people have unique needs that are negatively impacted by inappropriate health services. In addition to issues of heteronormativity and homophobia, trans people may also experience transphobic responses from health care providers (Age Concern England, 2007). The use of language that denies trans people's gender identities, or that adopts outdated or pathologising understandings of trans people, contributes to the marginalisation of older trans people. Older trans people can also present to services with health needs that are the result of early surgery or hormone therapy, which may have been inadequate and as such contribute to some older trans people's dissatisfaction with, or mistrust of, health care providers. Sex reassignment surgery conducted decades ago can continue to be problematic both in a physical health sense and in relation to some older trans people's sense of self and identity.

Another group of LGBTQ people who require specific attention in services for older people in the west are those living with HIV. As HIV medication makes it increasingly possible for HIV positive people to live longer, the issue of managing the ongoing side-effects of medication becomes important, with the likelihood that older HIV positive people will require specific services. In the context of aged care facilities, workers need not only to understand HIV management programmes, but to recognise how anti-HIV positive prejudice functions, and how this impacts on the lives of older HIV positive people. When older HIV positive people live with HIV and chronic illnesses that increase their support needs and reduce their independence, social support services must be able to meet these needs appropriately (Chesney *et al.*, 2003). As Witten (2003: 18) notes, HIV/AIDS is a significant problem in the trans population, so 'it is not unreasonable to assume that the transgender population will have a growing number of individuals who are on age-related prescriptions … simultaneously on hormones, and in need of HIV/AIDS drugs all at the same time'.

Bereavement and death

Within psychology, there is a large body of work on the social aspects of bereavement and death. However, the majority of this work focuses on (heterosexual) widowhood; that is, the loss of a legally recognised spouse. As highlighted in Chapter 8, the ability to marry or enter into a legally recognised same-sex partnership is by no means universal. Although some same-sex couples have entered into legally recognised partnerships, this is a relatively new phenomenon, and may not necessarily be afforded an equivalent social status to heterosexual marriage within society. The loss of a partner within such a union, therefore, may not be experienced in the same way as the loss of a partner within a socially legitimate heterosexual relationship. Writing on same-sex partner bereavement (e.g., Shernoff, 1998; Whiple, 2006) primarily relies on anecdotal accounts from lesbians and gay men or therapists working with clients who have lost a partner in the context of a same-sex relationship. These anecdotal accounts typically report same-sex partners being denied the right to execute decisions (about life support, life-saving operations, funeral arrangements) for their dying or deceased partner, and having to face lengthy court battles to remain in their previously shared house, or to secure access to their partner's financial resources and personal belongings. In addition, by law there are only specific relationships that are recognised when registering a death. For example, in the UK this must be a legal spouse, a relative, the deceased's executor or other legal representative – any other person is simply registered as a 'person present at death'. Therefore, unlike a 'spouse' or 'relative', there has been no capacity for a same-sex partner to register his/her partner's death in the capacity of 'partner' until the introduction of civil partnership (Age Concern England, 2005). In Box 10.5 you will find a case study which illustrates some of these issues.

For older non-heterosexuals, the issue of invisibility poses a particular problem. As we noted above, despite changes in societal attitudes and increasing legal recognition, having identified as non-heterosexual in a climate where homosexuality was particularly stigmatised, or even illegal, many older non-heterosexuals have 'chosen' to stay closeted, maintaining their anonymity in order to avoid discrimination. This together with ageism in the LGBTQ community has contributed significantly to their isolation and invisibility. This invisibility raises specific issues for non-heterosexuals when faced with the death of a partner. In particular, older (and other closeted) LGBTQ people often refer to their same-sex partner as a 'friend' (or 'room-mate'), terms which imply a less significant relationship than would be understood by terms such as 'partner' or 'spouse'. As a result such relation-ships – particularly where the couple did not share a single residence – evoke less empathic responses than is typically the case with spousal and (different-sex) partner bereavements.

Box 10.5   *Highlights: Francis's story from Sonja Ellis's interview study of contemporary issues in the lives of LGB people in the UK (see Ellis, 2007a, 2007b, for details of the study)*

[My partner John] died when I was 39 and it was really very devastating for me, I wasn't out to my parents, I wasn't out at work, although I had to come out to some extent just to get time off. I was out to a few friends, but not … my older friends … so it was a very lonely time … I had a house of my own, John had a house of his own, we were in our thirties, I couldn't have imagined selling my house and moving in with him or vice versa and explaining that away when you're in your thirties to your parents … when John died … I was faced with these things that you read horror stories about. I didn't inherit any of John's stuff, he was on a life support machine, and I didn't have any rights about that being turned off or not.

At the funeral I didn't know whether I was supposed to go with his parents to the front row, or go with them in the funeral car, and it was even more difficult to raise that 'cos I thought either I should know that, they would expect that I should know whether the answer was yes or no, in fact the answer was no I think.

I didn't have any say in the funeral, it was an extraordinary experience, as there were about 150 people at John's funeral … most of them knew that I was his partner and knew us as a couple, or if they didn't know us as a couple they knew John had a partner called Francis, and yet I wasn't mentioned at the funeral … the vicar went round [to his mother and stepfather's place] … he asked them at one point 'Is there anyone you'd like me to mention? Anyone special?' and his mum and stepfather said 'no', but he was aware that the sister looked a bit surprised at this, but nothing was said, so he was picking up vibes but couldn't say anything, so … he chose as his reading the story of David and his lamenting for Jonathon, which would pass over the heads of anyone who didn't know John was gay but was glaringly obvious to anyone who [did]. I found it very comforting …

I'd met his mother a few times, got on alright with her and kept in contact with her, but his stepfather hadn't known he was gay until he was taken ill with the heart thing a few weeks before he died.

It was months later … I suddenly thought, well he was a therapist for the NHS, if we'd been in a heterosexual married couple wouldn't I have a got a widow's pension or something? You don't get anything like that, I got a few clothes and one or two things from the house as I helped them go through his stuff, but it was clear the financial stuff was up to the father and mother to sort out … it just irritated me that I wasn't even considered really, I was a proper partner … I got on with his mother, I still do, but I'm not sure if at the bottom she viewed it as the same as a marriage, her daughter's marriage.

LGBTQ persons and 'disenfranchised grief'

Because same-sex relationships are often not legitimated in the same way as different-sex relationships, bereaved LGBTQ people are more likely to lack adequate social support networks. For some, support from family may be limited or family members are not equipped to understand the LGBTQ-specific nuances of partner bereavement.

One of the key assumptions of mainstream psychological work on death, dying and bereavement is that grief is openly acknowledged, socially sanctioned and/or publicly shared (Leming and Dickinson, 2002). However, in the case of same-sex partner bereavement this is not necessarily the case, particularly for older LGBTQ people. As a result, those bereaved from the loss of a same-sex partner may be particularly susceptible to what Kenneth Doka (1989) called 'disenfranchised grief' (see Box 10.6).

Whenever disenfranchised grief occurs, the experience of grief is intensified and it is more likely that normal sources of social support are lacking. Leming and Dickinson (2002) suggest that disenfranchised grievers are often barred from

---

Box 10.6 *Highlights: disenfranchised grief and LGBTQ people*

Disenfranchised grief (Doka, 1989) occurs when one or more of the following are present:

The relationship to the deceased is not socially recognised, because outsiders are unaware that the relationship exists (e.g., the couple were not 'out') or choose not to acknowledge its existence.

The loss is not acknowledged by others as being a genuine loss, because a same-sex relationship is not seen as a serious (or 'proper') relationship and therefore is viewed as less significant than a heterosexual marital relationship. Also, because many LGBTQ people do not parent children the loss is seen as less detrimental than the loss of a mother or father in a heterosexual relationship.

The grievers are unrecognised. Since many LGBTQ people value other LGBTQ persons as their 'chosen family', those closest to them may not be recognised as legitimately bereaved because they do not fit the usual definition of close family. This can sometimes be problematic if a LGBTQ person requires bereavement leave. Also, the bereaved partner from a same-sex relationship who is not out to his/her employer may experience similar issues.

The death is not socially sanctioned. When people feel ambivalent, awkward and/or uncomfortable about the cause of death, they may be unable or unwilling to provide the necessary support. Disenfranchised grief may therefore be compounded for LGBTQ people who are the survivors of a partner who died, for example, by suicide.

contact with the deceased during the dying process, are frequently excluded from rituals and support systems, and typically experience practical and legal difficulties after the death. Anecdotal evidence certainly suggests that for many lesbians and gay men this is the reality when faced with the death of a same-sex partner (Walter, 2003).

Much of the work on the loss of a same-sex partner arose out of a heightened awareness of gay partnerships and bereavement brought about by the AIDS epidemic in the 1980s. Research on gay men and the AIDS crisis demonstrated that death and bereavement affect LGBTQ people and their families and friends not only in old age but also at other stages of the life course (see Box 10.7).

Box 10.7 *Highlights: pregnancy loss bereavement for non-heterosexual women*

There are many different types of bereavement, not all of them associated with old age. Loss of a pregnancy through miscarriage, stillbirth or neonatal death is a very common cause of grief (early pregnancy loss occurs in up to a third of all confirmed pregnancies, Cosgrove, 2004), but one that is surrounded by a 'culture of silence' (Layne, 2003). There is a 'heterosexist monopoly' (Wojnar and Swanson, 2006) in reproduction and pregnancy loss research; lesbian and bisexual women's experiences are invisible – in reality practically *no one* fits the dominant narrative of the heterosexual, blissfully happy, consumption-driven, medically uneventful pregnancy. As US feminist psychologist Lisa Cosgrove (2004: 117) writes: 'heterosexist assumptions – and beliefs about who has the right to be a mother and thus whose loss "counts" – not only inform research agendas, but these assumptions have also silenced the voices of poor, single, or lesbian mothers, and nontraditional couples who experience pregnancy loss'.

Just one empirical study, to date, has focused exclusively on non-heterosexuals' experiences of pregnancy loss bereavement. US nursing academic Danuta Wojnar (2007) conducted a phenomenological study based on interviews with ten white US lesbian couples (she interviewed each partner separately and also conducted a joint interview with each couple). All the couples had experienced miscarriage as a couple within the previous two years and had lived together for on average 8.7 years. Five couples used known donor insemination and five used unknown donor sperm. The gestational age at miscarriage ranged from one to twenty weeks and it had taken her participants from one to five years to get pregnant.

Wojnar identified the central theme 'we are not in control' from these women's accounts, alongside 'we work so hard to get a baby' and 'it hurts so bad: the sorrow of miscarriage'. All the participants in her study had planned and wanted their babies (about 50 per cent of heterosexuals' pregnancies are unplanned) and described the process of conception as a stressful emotional rollercoaster – more akin to the atypical experience of heterosexual women who experience infertility than the usual heterosexual conception. She found that, unlike some heterosexual mothers, lesbian birth mothers generally bonded with their unborn child very early in pregnancy, and miscarriage was described as an unanticipated and painful experience. As one participant said: 'I don't think anybody can really explain how unbelievably devastating it is to lose something you want so badly and work for so hard' (p. 482). She found that birth mothers typically grieved their loss openly while social mothers kept their sadness more private and felt that they needed to be strong for their partners. Some participants expressed frustration about family and friends' lack of recognition of the social mother's grief and for many this lack of recognition was a hurdle they needed to overcome as a couple (see also Chapter 9).

Gay men and the AIDS crisis

In terms of death, dying and bereavement, the 1980s was a devastating time for gay male communities as the full impact of the AIDS epidemic hit. Throughout Europe and North America, cohorts of gay men experienced the deaths of one or more lovers, friends or acquaintances. Although gay men were by no means the only people dying of AIDS at the time, the number of deaths was far higher for this group than for heterosexuals or other non-heterosexual people. Unfortunately, this statistical trend was quickly grasped by groups with a vested interest in condemning homosexuality and who claimed that AIDS was divine retribution for homosexual acts. As a result, there was a resurgence of a homophobic climate that inevitably impacted on the bereavement of gay men and their friends and families, and allies from LGBTQ communities.

AIDS-related bereavement in gay communities is far more complex than is suggested by psychological models of bereavement. At the time, deaths from AIDS were typically premature deaths of relatively young men, following a lengthy and progressively debilitating illness. Therefore, as well as individual losses (i.e., of partners and close friends), the multiple losses of gay men because of AIDS meant that gay men saw their community and thus their primary support system diminish (Springer and Lease, 2000). Because of the pace of the epidemic, there was often not time for those bereaved to work through one loss before another occurred or was imminent, resulting in individuals collectively suffering what practitioners called 'bereavement overload'. A positive outcome, however, was that the fragmentation and destruction of natural social networks mobilised a need to develop specifically AIDS-focused bereavement initiatives, many of which still function today (Maasen, 1998).

Most lesbians have not been directly affected by the AIDS epidemic because they are one of the groups at least risk of HIV infection (see Chapter 6). However, lesbian communities were central to providing care and support to many gay men, and joined gay men in solidarity against discrimination. For this reason lesbians too were often affected by AIDS losses.

Gaps and absences

- Most research has been conducted in the USA (with a handful of studies conducted in Canada, the UK and Australia). As such we know very little about the lives of older LGBTQ people outside of the USA, and virtually nothing about the lives of older LGBTQ people in non-western countries.
- Most research is based on convenience samples of white, middle-class gay men living in large cities; therefore, we know very little about LBTQ ageing. We also know very little about the lives of older LGBTQ people who are socially marginalised in relation to race, culture, gender, social class and ability, and who live in rural or isolated areas. There is little understanding of how LGBTQ people negotiate intersections of privilege and marginalisation in old age.
- Much research has focused on how people manage their sexual identities in old age; Heaphy *et al.* (2004) argue for the need to go beyond 'identity' and explore others factors such as the relational and community contexts that shape how older LGBTQ people experience ageing.
- Age is not consistently defined in the literature and there is an emphasis on the experiences and perspectives of the younger-old. As such, we know very little about the older-old and LGBTQ people who live in care homes or who experience deteriorating health.
- Studies are mainly descriptive and based on a limited range of methods; there is an over-reliance on interviews as a method of data collection.
- There is a need to assess the impact of recent legal changes (such as, for example, the introduction of the Civil Partnership Act and the Gender Recognition Act in Britain) and social changes on the lives of older LGBTQ people. Heaphy *et al.* (2004) argue that older non-heterosexual people (and, we would add, trans people) can provide valuable insights into the personal consequences of social change.
- Research on ageing has yet to engage with challenges to the notion of fixed categories of sexual identity; it tends to rely on such categories, rather than acknowledge the complexities in how people experience their sexuality.

Main chapter points

This chapter:

- Outlined the multiple marginalisation experienced by older LGBTQ people and the emphasis in early research on challenging stereotypes of older gay men and lesbians as lonely and miserable.
- Explored different 'styles' of ageing and the argument that non-heterosexual people's experiences of negotiating heterosexism and the coming out process equip them to age 'successfully'.

- Summarised LGBTQ people's distinct needs and concerns in relation to health and social care provision, and the heterosexism, homophobia and transphobia that LGBTQ people often experience from health and social care professionals.
- Outlined issues around bereavement and explored the way in which, for some LGBTQ people, same-sex partner loss may be considered a form of 'disenfranchised grief'.

Questions for discussion and classroom exercises

1. You have been invited by your local aged care facility to raise awareness of the needs and concerns of older LGBTQ people among staff, residents and visitors. How will you do this? What will be the main issues addressed by your campaign?

2. How might the experience of coming out as non-heterosexual and/or trans in later life be different from the experience of coming out in your teens or early twenties?

3. How would you raise awareness of and challenge ageist attitudes within LGBTQ communities?

4. In what ways are the health and social care needs of older LGBTQ people the same as those of older heterosexual and non-trans people? In what ways are they different?

5. In what ways are experiences of bereavement in non-heterosexual and trans communities different from experiences of bereavement in the wider society?

Further reading

Barker, J. C. (2003) Lesbian aging: an agenda for social research. In G. Herdt and B. de Vries (eds.), *Gay and lesbian aging: research and future directions* (pp. 29–72). New York: Springer.
This chapter focuses specifically on research on lesbian ageing and outlines an agenda for future research.

Clover, D. (2006) Overcoming barriers for older gay men in the use of health services: a qualitative study of growing older, sexuality and health. *Health Education Journal*, 65(1), 41–52.
This article examines gay men's use of health services and the barriers they face to accessing affirmative health provision.

de Vries, B. and Blando, J. A. (2003) The study of gay and lesbian aging: lessons for social gerontology. In G. Herdt and B. de Vries (eds.), *Gay and lesbian aging: research and future directions* (pp. 3–28). New York: Springer.
An accessible overview of the literature on lesbian and gay ageing.

Heaphy, B. and Yip, A. K. T. (2003) Uneven possibilities: understanding non-heterosexual ageing and the implications of social change. *Sociological Research Online*, 8(4), www. socresonline.org.uk/8/4/heaphy.html.
This paper provides more information on one of the most recent and significant studies on ageing in non-heterosexual communities.

Walter, C. A. (2003) *The loss of a life partner: narratives of the bereaved*. New York: Columbia University Press.
Chapters 5 and 6 explore gay men's and lesbians' experiences of partner loss.

Conclusion

11 The future of LGBTQ psychology

Overview

- Beyond the 'usual suspects'
- Intersectionality and privilege
- Applications of LGBTQ psychology
- Future directions

Beyond the 'usual suspects'

Until relatively recently, most research in LGBTQ psychology has relied on samples of primarily white, middle-class lesbians and gay men living in western countries such as Britain and the USA. There is now an emerging body of research documenting the experiences of LGBTQ people from a wider range of backgrounds. Although this is an important development in LGBTQ psychological research, and one that signals more adequate engagement with the diversity within LGBTQ communities, there remain issues in relation to the representativeness of the field that require attention.

One of these issues is the beliefs and values that have shaped the field of LGBTQ psychology. Not only has much of the knowledge that we have about LGBTQ people been derived from samples of the '**usual suspects**' (i.e., white, middle-class, coupled lesbians and gay men), but this knowledge has primarily been produced in a framework of 'white, middle-classness': the theories, the models of identity and the methods of analysis that LGBTQ psychologists draw on are primarily based on white, middle-class beliefs and values. As we highlighted in Chapter 4, there are many social and cultural frameworks or identities through which the lives of LGBTQ people are shaped: race, religion, gender, ability, geographic location and, of course, sexuality. In this final chapter, drawing on Damien's (Riggs, 2007a) work on racial norms (see also Chapter 4), we examine how norms of whiteness have shaped LGBTQ psychology. Obviously we recognise that many different identity categories shape the lives of LGBTQ people, but a focus on race provides us with a relatively straightforward example of how ingrained particular ways of seeing the world are within the field of LGBTQ psychology. The example of race also highlights the need to be critical of the social norms that underpin the work of LGBTQ psychologists.

Of course some researchers have already begun the process of reflexively engaging with the social norms underpinning LGBTQ psychology. For example, as we discussed in Chapter 9, psychologists such as Victoria (Clarke, 2000, 2002a, 2006, 2008) and Damien (Riggs, 2007b) and researchers in other disciplines such as sociology (e.g., Hicks, 2005b; Stacey and Biblarz, 2001) have critically examined the heteronormative assumptions about sexuality, gender and difference that have shaped much comparative research on same-sex parenting. Celia Kitzinger's (1987) critique of the liberal founding assumptions of early 'gay affirmative' psychology is another example of this type of critique; as is lesbian feminists' critique of the heterosexist assumptions that have formed the basis of much feminist psychology (Kitzinger, 1996a; Peel, 2001b), and Peter Hegarty's (2007b) recent examination of the use of discursive and conversational analytic methods within LGBTQ psychology. However, on the whole, LGBTQ psychologists have less often engaged in much by way of reflexive critique (other than, of course, to highlight the heterosexism of psychology), unlike psychologists in related disciplines such as feminist psychology, who have engaged in thorough-going critiques of, for example, the male bias underpinning psychology. For instance, in her classic book *The Mismeasure of Women*, US feminist psychologist Carol Tavris (1993) argued that because most psychological models and theories have been normed on the experiences of men, women are typically and problematically seen as 'different' or 'inferior'.

Although there have been some analyses of whiteness from within LGBTQ psychology (e.g., Greene, 2000; Riggs, 2007a; Tafoya, 1997), much analysis of whiteness has been undertaken by scholars outside of psychology working in disciplines and areas such as cultural studies, sociology, literary studies, queer theory, and the developing area of critical race and whiteness studies (see Riggs, 2007d, for an overview of this research). For example, US professor of English Greg Thomas (2007) provides a critical reading of western categories of gender and sexuality and the racial norms that inform them, both in the work of African American scholars and in literary representations of African people. Thomas argues that western binary models of gender overlook the fact that relationships between African people prior to slavery and colonisation were structured in highly different ways from relationships between people living in colonial nations. As a result, he argues that it is nonsensical (and potentially offensive) to use western gender and sexuality categories to account for the historical (and contemporary) experiences of African people. Doing so, he claims, can result in the inability to see individual differences within African communities on their own terms.

Another problem with western binary categories of gender and sexuality relates to attempts to understand the experiences of people who do not identify as 'heterosexual' within First Nations or Indigenous communities. In her examination of the terms used to describe the experiences of Navajo **nádleehí**, US anthropologist Carolyn Epple (1998) argued that words such as 'two-spirit', 'gay', **berdache** or 'alternate gender' are all premised on a western binary model of gender, rather than on a Navajo worldview. Epple proposed that the ways in which western researchers read the identities of First Nation and Indigenous people forces their bodies into a western framework, where particular markers (such as forms of dress, ways of movement, terms of reference) are taken as symbolising the same things across cultures, rather than having potentially different meanings across cultures. For example, she notes that the wearing of a dress by a person born with a penis may, in western cultures, mean that the person wishes to 'become a woman', or that they have a sexual fetish for women's clothing. However, in non-western cultures, it may mean something entirely different (i.e., the dress itself may not be seen as gender-specific or clothing may have no relationship to gender identity). Anthropological research conducted with Samoan **fa'afafine** suggests similarly that western concepts of gender and sexuality and the use of terms such as 'woman' or 'gay' to describe the experiences of fa'afafine overlook the cultural specificity of their experiences of **embodiment** and identity (Worth, 2001).

Criticisms such as these of applying western categories of gender and sexuality to non-western people and cultures highlight the importance of LGBTQ psychologists engaging with the racialised (and other social) norms that shape our field. These criticisms also indicate the need to develop research frameworks in which a diverse range of participants can be represented. Furthermore, it is important to interrogate the reliance on the 'usual suspects' within LGBTQ psychology *and* the assumptions underpinning the theories and methods used by LGBTQ psychologists. For example, Indigenous psychologists in Australia such as Tracey Westerman (2004) have demonstrated that IQ tests are normed on the values and beliefs of white people. Correcting this problem requires more than simply applying IQ tests to people who aren't 'usual suspects'. Rather, it requires psychologists to rethink the limitations of the concept of 'IQ' and the cultural specificity of IQ measures, and to recognise the varied ways in which different groups of people understand their own capacities. In Box 11.1 key researcher Esther Rothblum reflects on the future of LGBTQ psychology in the USA and the need for US psychologists to embrace a plurality of research methods and approaches in order to achieve the goal of representing a diverse range of LGBTQ people.

> **Box 11.1   Key researcher: Esther Rothblum on her vision of LGBTQ psychology in the future**
>
> Imagine the reaction you would receive if you told your friends, colleagues and lecturers that you had interviewed eight extraterrestrials and submitted the results for publication in a psychology journal. That is a bit what the field of lesbian and gay studies was like when I first began conducting research. Once in a while, an article would appear in a psychology journal based on a few case studies of gay men and sometimes an even smaller number of lesbians (there was little research on bisexuals). The authors were psychologists who had

come across these individuals in their therapy practices and exoticised and pathologised their personalities. In short, the first wave of LGB samples was not so much science as science fiction.

My own research has focused on research methods and challenges when studying LGBT individuals. I have compared LGB people to their heterosexual siblings (e.g., Rothblum *et al.*, 2006), and compared transgendered people to their conventionally gendered siblings (Factor and Rothblum, 2008). I've shown that when it comes to preoccupation with weight and dieting, it is people who are sexually involved with men (heterosexual women and gay men) who are more affected than people who are sexually involved with women (heterosexual men and lesbians; Rothblum, 2002). I've argued that focusing research on members of LGBTQ communities is important, and different from large population studies of people that include small numbers of individuals who have same-sex sexual partners and who may not identify as LGB (Rothblum, 2007). From these findings there are three key areas that I believe need ongoing consideration in the future of LGBTQ psychology:

Language and identity. In the future, researchers will have to take into account the ever-changing language about sexuality and gender identity over time and across cultures. Thus, old terms like 'invert' and new terms like 'queer' complicate research on sexuality and gender identity because inclusion criteria differ across place and time. People who are bisexual are less inclined to use labels for self-identity (Rust, 2000), possibly explaining the relatively small numbers of bisexuals found in research. New theory and writing from the trans movement will increase our understanding about the intersection of gender identity with sexuality.

New research methods. I would encourage researchers to write about (and journal editors to accept for publication) theoretical issues in the application of research methods for use with LGBTQ samples. Too often researchers are forced into a specific methodology (by their supervisors/academic advisors, funding bodies, and manuscript reviewers) simply because such methods are the status quo among the general population. Similarly, publishing anecdotal articles, pilot studies or results of a few interviews with LGBTQ people on new topic areas can be extremely useful in generating discussion among mental health practitioners, policy makers and researchers. Sometimes the most interesting parts of large, standardised, questionnaire studies are to be found in the comments written in by participants at the end of the questionnaire. Such qualitative impressions should be written up, and luckily there are now a number of LGBTQ journals across academic disciplines for submission of qualitative research.

End of homophobia and transphobia. Finally, a time may come when LGBTQ people are so assimilated into mainstream society that it will be difficult to conceptualise sexuality and gender identity as distinct categories. This will necessitate new methods for a new age.

Intersectionality and privilege

One response to the limitations outlined above, and one that we have discussed throughout this book, is to focus on the intersections of identities. The concept of intersectionality derives from the work of Kimberlé Crenshaw (1991), a US legal scholar and black feminist theorist. She coined the term to capture the overlapping marginalities that shape the lives of some of the most vulnerable people in society, and the ways in which differences between people intersect in institutional arrangements, social practices and cultural discourses. For example, when people go about their lives they are never just a 'lesbian' or a 'transman', but rather they experience their lives as a 'black, middle-class lesbian in a couple relationship' or a 'single, white, working-class heterosexual transman'. These multiple identity categories produce a relatively coherent experience of self, and are not experienced in isolation from one another. As such, the concept of intersectionality opposes an 'additive model' of identity, which understands people's experience of the world to be shaped by the summing of the different aspects of their identities (e.g., 'black + working class' = more oppressed than 'white + working class'; see Clarke and Braun, 2009). In an examination of the implicit whiteness of much queer theory, US cultural theorist Ian Barnard (2003) suggests that one of the problems associated with additive models is that they always take socially normative categories as the basis for comparison. For instance, within an additive model, the identity 'Chicana (Mexican) lesbian' is treated as an identity that differs from the norms of whiteness and heterosexuality. Instead, Barnard asks us to consider how the category 'Chicana lesbian' may be an identity in and of itself – it is likely to be experienced as such by Chicana lesbians (see, for example, Espin, 1995).

Our discussion of intersectionality throughout the book has been less about examining different 'axes' of identity in isolation, and more about exploring the complex and intersecting ways in which identity categories *simultaneously* produce experiences. As such, we need to consider how, for example, racial categories are always sexualised (e.g., the colonial stereotype of the 'virginal white woman'), and how social class is always gendered (e.g., the assumption that working-class men are all 'rough' and 'butch') and so forth. As Greg Thomas (2007: 68) argues in regard to identity categories: 'There are never, ever merely girls and boys, men and women, without race and class. Analytically speaking, there are instead a legion of genders and sexualities, so to speak; and they cannot be reduced to the anatomy of any one white racist elite.' Engaging in intersectional analysis requires that we understand individual identities on their own terms, rather than imposing a particular cultural framework on the lives of diverse groups of people.

Importantly, understanding intersectionality involves examining the ways in which different identities produce unique individual experiences of privilege and/or disadvantage. The concept of 'privilege' refers to the benefits or advantages that accrue to particular groups of people as a result of social hierarchies around, for example, gender, race and class (e.g., men experience privilege in a male-dominated society). Privilege and disadvantage are intimately related; the former is normally productive of the latter (see Chapter 4). The concept of privilege is important not because it allows us to 'pin the blame' on those groups of people who experience privilege, but rather because it allows us to understand and analyse the behaviours of people that reflect and produce privilege. When we understand the relationship between privilege and disadvantage, we can see that a male-dominated society (for example) is orientated towards the needs or values of what is deemed to be 'masculine' and this results in relative privilege for all men. By viewing privilege in its social context, we can see not only how this benefits men (albeit in highly different ways according to their other intersecting social locations), but also how it disadvantages women, regardless of the intentions of individual men or women. Consider the example of a young heterosexual couple who are committed to equality and about to have their first child. They don't want to use child-care and also don't want to reproduce the conventional roles of 'stay-at-home mum' and 'working dad', but because the man earns more than the woman (as is generally the case), it makes economic sense for the man to continue working and the woman to stay at home and care for their child. The man might want to be an active parent but because he has to get up early to go to work his partner is generally the one who tends to the baby in the night. Because the woman spends more time caring for the child she becomes more knowledgeable about the child's needs and routine – and thus the traditional roles of men and women are reproduced in spite of the couple's intentions and desires.

As another example, when we talk about 'racial privilege' or 'white privilege', we are not accusing those of us who identify as white of being racist, or as seeking out privilege. Rather, these terms allow us better to understand the benefits that white people experience when living in a white-dominated society. Damien Riggs, in collaboration with the feminist psychologist Precilla Choi, examined how identifying as both white and gay produces a particular identity at the intersection of these two categories that results in experiences of both privilege (i.e., as a white person in a white-dominated society and a man in a male-dominated society) *and* disadvantage (i.e., as a gay man in a heteronormative society) (Riggs and Choi, 2006). Understanding the dual nature of privilege and disadvantage does not mean that we have to weigh up which experience has a greater impact on our place in the world (e.g., 2 parts privilege minus 1 part disadvantage = more privileged than disadvantaged), but rather it means that we can develop more complex and nuanced accounts of people's experiences in the world.

Finally, in order to understand pluralities in relation to gender, sexuality, race and class (and so forth) we need to go beyond simply acknowledging the cultural specificity of the categories typically used in LGBTQ psychology research and the broad range of conceptualisations of identity that exist across many cultures. We must also develop accounts of how dominant-group members experience them-selves *as* dominant-group members. In other words, although much existing research in LGBTQ psychology has focused on the 'usual suspects', it has typically not explicitly analysed how race and social class (for example) shape the lives of white, middle-class LGBTQ people. Although the limitations of samples consisting of the usual suspects are usually noted, such samples are not explicitly examined for what they can tell us about the experiences of white, middle-class LGBTQ people and their racial and class identities (Greene, 2000). To counter this, some researchers, including Damien Riggs (2006b), have attempted expressly to examine the experiences of white, middle-class LGBTQ people *as* white, middle-class LGBTQ people. While this approach produces yet more research on white, middle-class people, it is important to examine race and class in the lives of white, middle-class LGBTQ people and how the identities of this group of people are formed in a relationship to both privilege *and* disadvantage.

In Box 11.2, UK psychologist Adrian Coyle, a key researcher in the field of LGBTQ psychology, argues that it is vital that we move beyond a focus on the lives of the 'usual suspects' and on sexuality as a primary lens, and consider the interactions of different social positions in the lives of all LGBTQ people.

Box 11.2   Key researcher: Adrian Coyle on his vision of LGBTQ psychology in the future

Thinking about future directions for LGBTQ psychology is interesting but challenging. When I entered the field as a PhD student in 1986, I am not at all sure that I could have envisaged the developments in LGBTQ possibilities and experiences that have occurred in parts of the western cultural world following hard-won socio-political advances and changed social contexts, with consequent implications for LGBTQ psychology. If I were exploring my PhD topic of gay identity today, the questions I would ask (and the ways I would conceptualise 'gay identity') would be quite different in light of these changes. Of course, legal and social acceptance and validation of LGBTQ life structures are far from universal. This means that some of the questions that were explored in the early years of LGBTQ psychology are just as pertinent today in many parts of the world. However, LGBTQ psychology now has a broader theoretical and methodological knowledge base from which to ask these questions and to make sense of the answers obtained. For example, today it would be difficult to claim to have adequately examined 'sexual identity' without considering how it interacts with other social positions such as gender, race, class and religion. Indeed, many LGBTQ psychologists would now query the idea of a stable, homogeneous 'sexual identity'.

The diversity of LGBTQ psychology today is remarkable: traditional 'scientific' approaches involving measurement and experimental designs exist alongside research approaches which focus on how LGBTQ issues are negotiated in and through social interaction, especially in people's talk. In some places, one approach is more dominant. For example, in Britain, LGBTQ psychology has become associated with 'radical' qualitative approaches. There are some risks in this. If the advocates of one approach view other approaches as having little value or legitimacy, LGBTQ psychology could fragment into isolated sub-domains. Whatever possibility the area might have of influencing policy and practice in relation to LGBTQ issues would be lost: what policy maker or service provider would want to be guided by a rabble of conflicting voices? What I hope will happen instead is that scholars within LGBTQ psychology will routinely recognise that different theoretical and methodological approaches have something valuable to contribute to the emergence of increasingly complex and complete pictures of LGBTQ lives. The result could be a rich patchwork of insights that are useful for different audiences, even if the elements do not fit together tidily. This might sound idealistic but there is a lot at stake. Our diverse resources potentially place us in a strong position to do justice to new psychological questions in relation to LGBTQ experiences, to examine established questions in new ways and to produce useful knowledge for the benefit of LGBTQ people.

Applications of LGBTQ psychology

The findings of LGBTQ psychological research are applicable across the discipline of psychology. LGBTQ psychology is not simply a critique of hetero-normativity in psychology, nor is it just an account of the lives of LGBTQ people (although it is those things too). It also provides us with very practical ways of creating change in the world, understanding people's lives, and reflecting on the ways in which psychological and social norms can be detrimental to the lives of diverse groups of people. We now consider a few examples of LGBTQ psychological research, drawing on our own work – both published studies and our current projects – and the research of other LGBTQ psychologists, which highlight the relevance of LGBTQ psychology for key areas of psychology and the wider social contexts of law, policy and social change. These key areas of psychology include core areas of the psychology curriculum such as social and developmental psychology, applied areas like clinical and counselling, health, and educational psychology, and areas of psychology that intersect a number of different concerns such as the psychology of the family and relationships, workplace and leisure, and the media. This is not to suggest that our (or anyone else's) research is definitive, but it will give you an idea of the breadth of application of LGBTQ psychology research, and how our own research connects with and references the histories of research in the discipline.

Social psychology

One of the central concerns of social psychological research has been measuring and understanding the attitudes of one group of people towards another group and developing ways to combat negative and prejudicial attitudes. We all work within the field of social psychology, as do many other LGBTQ psychologists (indeed LGBTQ psychology is often viewed as synonymous with social psychology, Coyle and Wilkinson, 2002). Social psychological research has been vitally important in documenting the existence of homophobia and heterosexism, and understanding how these forms of marginalisation function, and the impact they have on the lives of lesbians and gay men. For example, Gregory Herek's work on homophobic hate crimes influenced the decision of the US Government to include 'sexual orientation' in hate crimes legislation (e.g., Herek *et al.*, 1997), and Ian Rivers's work on homophobic bullying has influenced the development of policies on homophobic bullying in UK schools (e.g., Rivers, 2001).

We have all conducted research exploring homophobia and heterosexism – we have used both mainstream (Ellis, 2002a; Ellis *et al.*, 2002) and discursive and qualitative approaches (Clarke, 2002b; Ellis, 2002b, 2004a, 2004b, 2004c; Peel, 2001a, 2009; Riggs, 2006a, 2006c) to examine the operation of homophobia and heterosexism within the wider (heterosexual) society. We have also (discursively) examined how lesbians and gay men resist and challenge heterosexism (Clarke and Kitzinger, 2005) and the success (or otherwise) of attempts to educate heterosexuals about the lives and experiences of lesbians and gay men (Kitzinger and Peel, 2005).

It is essential that such work continues (and expands to include a focus on biphobia and transphobia), so that we can continue to find effective ways to challenge the social marginalisation of LGBTQ people. It is also important to explore attitudes *within* LGBTQ communities towards various aspects of LGBTQ lives, and not to assume that LGBTQ people are homogeneous and all hold similar views. For instance, Damien Riggs and colleagues have examined attitudes within lesbian and gay communities to lesbian and gay parenting (Riggs *et al.*, 2009).

Developmental psychology

This is another key area of psychology in which LGBTQ psychologists have made crucial interventions. As we discussed in Chapter 9, LGBTQ psychological research on lesbian parenting has had a significant positive impact on custody cases involving lesbian mothers and has been influential in lifting the ban on lesbian and gay fostering and adoption, and broadening the understanding of family, in many countries. Key researchers such as US psychologist Charlotte Patterson (2008) and British psychologist Susan Golombok (2000) led the way towards an inclusive approach to developmental psychology by publishing texts that feature LGBTQ families and parents. Research on lesbian and gay parenting has also highlighted the heteronormative assumptions underpinning many mainstream theories of child development. Both Victoria (Clarke, 2001, 2002a, 2002b, 2008) and Damien (Riggs, 2006c, 2008) have critically examined the construction of lesbian and gay parenting within psychology and the wider society. Although Victoria and Damien recognise the important political contributions made by mainstream work on lesbian and gay parenting, they have argued that even this 'affirmative' research is underpinned by heteronormative assumptions about gender and sexuality.

Clinical and counselling psychology

There is still much work to be done to remedy the legacy of the pathologisation of non-heterosexual and trans people within clinical psychology for much of the last century. As we noted in Chapters 1 and 6, LGBTQ psychologists have developed models for affirmative practice with LGBTQ clients (Milton and Coyle, 2003; Langdridge, 2007b) and have been at the forefront of challenges to biased and non-affirmative psychological practice (including conversion therapy) with LGBTQ clients (Clarke and Peel, 2007c). LGBTQ psychologists have also examined LGBTQ people's experiences of therapy and counselling (Malley and Tasker, 2007) and the processes and practices of counselling and clinical psychology training (Coyle *et al.*, 2001; Moon, 2007). Damien has built on this important work in recent collaborative research on heteronormativity in psychological practice (Fell *et al.*, 2008), which has developed tools for challenging heteronormativity among trainee and practising psychologists.

Educational psychology

LGBTQ psychologists have made significant contributions to the field of educational (school) psychology, and to teaching and learning in psychology more broadly. LGBTQ psychologists have developed inclusive curricula for degree-level psychology teaching (APA, 1998), and have critiqued the heterosexist and genderist foundations of many mainstream psychological theories and models. Psychologists have also examined LGBTQ students' and academics' experiences of higher education (HE), both in order to document these experiences, which are often invisible because of the 'hidden curriculum of heteronormativity' within HE, and to find ways to improve LGBTQ people's experience of HE and make it more inclusive (Hodges and Pearson, 2008). For example, Sonja (Ellis, 2009) has surveyed LGBT students on their experiences of HE in the UK. Victoria, in collaboration with Virginia Braun, has interviewed LGBTQ (and heterosexual) academics in a number of different countries about their experiences of coming out in the classroom and managing heteronormativity, and LGB students in the UK and New Zealand about the positive and negative aspects of their experience of higher education (see Clarke and Braun, 2009). Among other things, this research aims to develop practical suggestions for avoiding heterosexist and genderist assumptions in all forms of teaching and learning at university (Clarke and Braun, 2006). Damien (Riggs, 2009b, 2009c) has added an extra dimension to this work, by exploring the importance of an intersectional lens through which to teach about non-heterosexual lives.

LGBTQ psychologists have also intervened in school-based education. For instance, Damien (Lovell and Riggs, 2009; Riggs and Augoustinos, 2007) has explored how school books model particular understandings of difference and diversity that treat the experiences of white middle-class heterosexual people as the norm. Finally, LGBTQ psychologists have made important contributions to the development and evaluation of inclusive education and training programmes in a wide variety of contexts, including lesbian and gay diversity training in the workplace (Harding and Peel, 2007; Peel, 2002).

Health psychology

As we have documented throughout this book, LGBTQ people face considerable disadvantages that negatively impact on their health. LGBTQ health psychology research renders visible the disparities in health outcomes between heterosexual and non-trans people and LGBTQ people, and draws attention to the specific health needs of LGBTQ communities. For example, LGBTQ health researchers and activists have been key advocates for generating funds for researching HIV/AIDS within LGBTQ communities and have contributed significantly to what we know about the disease across all populations. Both Elizabeth and Damien are actively engaged in LGBTQ health research (see Peel and Thomson, 2009). For instance, Damien (Riggs, 2006) has explored what accounts of seroconversion among gay men (i.e., a change in the status of one's blood from, in this instance, HIV negative to HIV positive) tell us about how gay men understand their relationships to others, to gay communities and to their health. Damien has also examined the experiences of gay male sperm donors (Riggs, 2009c). This research provides insight into the specific health and emotional needs of this group of men. For example, it highlights the emotion work that men engage when negotiating sperm donation and the need for reproductive health clinics to examine and challenge instances of homophobia and heterosexism in the delivery of their services.

As we noted in Chapter 6, LGBTQ people's experiences of chronic physical illness (other than HIV/AIDS) has been a neglected area of research. Liz Peel and Adam Jowett's (Jowett and Peel, 2009) groundbreaking research on LGBT people's experiences of chronic illness highlights some of the barriers LGBTQ people face when living with a chronic illness. Similarly, Elizabeth's current research on experiences of pregnancy loss among lesbian and bisexual women (Peel and Cain, 2008) highlights a neglected area of research and the barriers same-sex couples face in dealing with pregnancy loss. Such research has huge potential to impact positively on the delivery of health care services to LGBTQ communities.

Psychology of family and relationships

LGBTQ psychologists working in the domain of family psychology have made significant contributions to understanding the structure and processes of the families and relationships of LGBTQ people. They have also challenged the heteronormative underpinnings of much psychological research on family and relationships, and the commonplace assumption that all families and relationships are heterosexual. Although LGBTQ people are sometimes viewed as 'outsiders' to family life, and LGBTQ families and relationships are perceived as bad for children, the work of LGBTQ psychologists has demonstrated the central and positive roles that family and relationships play in the lives of LGBTQ people. LGBTQ psychologists like Victoria and her colleagues Maree Burns and Carole Burgoyne (Burns *et al.* 2008; Clarke *et al.*, 2008), Damien (2007b) and Elizabeth and Rosie Harding (2006; Peel and Harding, 2008) have demonstrated the creative ways in which LGBTQ people navigate heteronormative assumptions about family and relationships.

LGBTQ psychologists have also intervened in important debates about the legal recognition of same-sex relationships (Clarke, *et al.*, 2006, 2007; Harding and Peel, 2007; Peel and Harding, 2004) and have argued that law and social policy need to take account of the ways in which LGBTQ people live their lives, rather than assuming that LGBTQ relationships and families can be forced into heteronormative models. The work of LGBTQ scholars has played an important role in the ever increasing legal recognition of same-sex families and relationships, and LGBTQ psychologists now have a new task – understanding the form and function of new social institutions like civil partnership and same-sex marriage, and the new rites and rituals that are developing around them. Elizabeth and Victoria are currently undertaking qualitative interview and survey research on civil partnerships in the UK, focusing on people's reasons for entering into a civil partnership, the reactions of their family and friends to their civil partnership, and how the actual civil partnership and any associated ceremony or celebration unfolds (e.g., Peel and Clarke, 2007).

Psychology of work and leisure

Two growing areas of concern within LGBTQ psychology are the work and leisure of LGBTQ people. Research on the workplace has primarily focused on experiences of homophobia and heterosexism within the workplace (Harding and Peel, 2007; Kitzinger, 1991), and how some LGBTQ people negotiate a heteronormative work environment and achieve success in their careers (Rostad and Long, 2007). LGBTQ psychologists have also been at the forefront of challenges to heterosexism in the workplace more broadly. LGBTQ psychologists have developed and evaluated lesbian and gay diversity training programmes for a variety of different professions/ places of work (Kitzinger and Peel, 2005; Peel, 2002, 2005).

We know surprisingly little about the lives of LGBTQ people outside of the workplace or school and college/university (other than, of course, in relation to their families and relationships), and the ways in which LGBTQ people engage in sport and leisure. Most research to date has focused on sport and exercise. LGBTQ psychologists have examined, for example, the experiences of lesbian athletes and coaches, heteronormative sports climates and stereotypes of female athletes (Krane and Kauer, 2007). Research has also focused on gay male athletes and their experiences of coming out to their sporting peers (Gough, 2007). This research highlights the challenges faced by non-heterosexual sportswomen and men in a world infused with ideals of **hegemonic masculinity** and heterosexuality; and in which sportswomen who display qualities associated with masculinity (such as aggression, strength and confidence) are (negatively) assumed to be lesbian.

Psychology of the media

Psychologists have long been concerned with the media, and the ways in which the media depict particular groups of people and things (such as violence), and the impact of these depictions on people's behaviour. LGBTQ psychologists have been particularly concerned with the representation of LGBTQ people in the media. As Victoria (Clarke, 2001; Clarke and Kitzinger, 2004, 2005), Damien (Riggs, 2006c) and Sonja (Ellis and Kitzinger, 2002) have explored in their research, negative representations of LGBTQ people in the media contribute to widespread negative perceptions of LGBTQ people. Furthermore, both Damien (Riggs, 2007b) and Victoria (Clarke, 2002a, 2002b) have suggested that simply countering negative representations of LGBTQ people with (ostensibly) 'positive' representations may not be enough to prevent the former from occurring. Rather, there is a need to analyse the rhetoric of both negative *and* 'positive' or sympathetic media representations in order to understand in detail the often subtle and complex ways in which they work to portray LGBTQ people in a negative light (Peel and Harding, 2008). This process of analysis will help us to develop truly positive representations of LGBTQ people that are based on the reality of their lives.

Future directions

In addition to all of the gaps and absences we have highlighted throughout the book, we now make some broader suggestions about how the field should develop. We encourage readers to develop their own vision for the future of LGBTQ psychology.

- *Representing diversity.* There is a need to continue to develop sampling and analytic approaches that ensure the representation of diverse groups of LGBTQ people. It is also important that the research tools we use and the theoretical frameworks we employ reflect the actual worldviews of our participants, rather than reflecting a white, middle-class understanding of the world.
- *Moving away from a white, middle-class norm.* We need to ensure that 'diverse samples' include marginalised social groups *and* the 'usual suspects'. Too often 'diversity' is treated as referring only to people who are not white or middle-class, which means that, for example, a focus on 'race' in LGBTQ psychological research tends to translate into a focus on the experiences of

non-white people. This of course overlooks the fact that white people are also members of a racial group. As a result of 'race equalling non-white', we know very little about how white, middle-class LGBTQ people live out their lives and do identity development and coming out, relationships, family and parenting, and ageing *as* white, middle-class people. This does not mean that we should continue to focus research on the most privileged groups of LGBTQ people, but that we should recognise that everyone occupies a position in relation to race and class (and gender, age …) and we are all part of 'diversity'.

- *LGBTQ-positive mainstream psychology.* There is a need to consider what an LGBTQ-positive mainstream psychology would actually look like. How could we re-envisage psychology so that it would genuinely encompass a diverse range of experiences, rather than simply 'adding-in' LGBTQ people and leaving the heteronormative framework of mainstream psychology intact?
- *LGBTQ-specific research and comparative research.* We should continue to promote LGBTQ-specific research that celebrates the lives of LGBTQ people. At the same time, we should acknowledge the benefits of comparative research that avoids treating heterosexual people as the benchmark and seeks to identify actual and important differences between groups and the implications of these differences (e.g., the disparities between LGBTQ and heterosexual and non-trans people on key health indicators).
- *An international approach.* There is a need to develop a truly international approach to LGBTQ psychology that both recognises the cultural and national specificity of LGBTQ lives and allows for comparisons and collaborations between countries.

Main chapter points

This chapter:

- Outlined the cultural specificity of current research on LGBTQ people and the limitations of western concepts of gender and sexuality.
- Discussed the use of intersectional approaches within LGBTQ psychology and the relationship between privilege and disadvantage.
- Outlined some applications of LGBTQ research to a range of areas in psychology.
- Discussed some of the key directions for the future of LGBTQ psychology.

Questions for discussion and classroom exercises

1. Why do you think LGBTQ psychology is important? What are some of the key contributions that LGBTQ psychologists have made to understanding the lives of LGBTQ people and to psychology more broadly?

2. What questions do you think LGBTQ psychologists should ask in the future? If you were going to conduct a project in LGBTQ psychology, what would you investigate?

3. Discuss the pros and cons of the following two views of the future of LGBTQ psychology: (a) LGBTQ psychology should remain a separate, specialist area of psychology that focuses specifically on the needs and concerns of LGBTQ people; (b) LGBTQ psychology should be viewed as a central component of the discipline of psychology that has numerous implications for mainstream psychology and the various sub-fields and areas of research and practice that constitute it.

4. Consider how your own life is shaped through many different identity categories. What does it mean for you to experience the world through the intersections of all of these different aspects of your identity? If you were asked to rank the various aspects of your identity in order from most to least important, how would you rank them? Is this a difficult or easy thing to do? Does it limit your experience of the world?

5. Consider some of the non-western identity categories discussed in this chapter (nádleehí, fa'afafine) and in Chapter 2 (tom, dee). What are some of the problems in labelling non-western people who identify with such categories with western labels such as 'lesbian', 'gay' or 'trans'? Could (and should) the DSM diagnosis of 'Gender Identity Disorder' (GID) be applied to such people? What do non-western sexuality and gender categories reveal about the limitations of western categories?

6. If you were an educational psychologist reading this book how might the knowledge you have gained influence your practice? Consider the same question for a clinical psychologist/therapist, health psychologist, sport psychologist and occupational psychologist.

Further reading

Clarke, V., Burns, M. and Burgoyne, C. (2008) 'Who would take whose name?' Accounts of naming practices in same-sex relationships. *Journal of Community and Applied Social Psychology*, 18, 420–39.
Victoria Clarke and colleagues have explored how same-sex couples negotiate relational practices such as sharing (or not sharing) a last name. In this research they attempt to 'get beyond' a comparative paradigm (the study only includes same-sex couples), while also acknowledging that same-sex couples negotiate practices such as naming within a hetero-normative social context. In so doing they explore how heterosexual conventions (such as name-sharing) inevitably form a backdrop to same-sex couples' conversations about naming.

Ellis, S. J. (2009) Diversity and inclusivity at university: a survey of the experiences of lesbian, gay, bisexual and trans (LGBT) students in the UK. *Higher Education*, 57(6), 723.
Sonja Ellis explores the extent to which universities in the UK are perceived by LGBT students as 'gay friendly'. A sample of 291 students from forty-two universities completed an online survey which asked about their awareness of homophobic bullying on campus, the extent to which they felt able to be open about their sexuality/gender identity, and whether or not they felt that LGBT issues were adequately represented both in the curriculum and in the university's practices. The findings showed that homophobia is still a significant issue in universities and is primarily perpetrated by students against other students. The paper highlights the importance of being more proactive in addressing diversity and inclusivity, because the absence of a zero tolerance climate has enabled homophobia on campus to persist.

Peel, E. (2009) Intergroup relations in action: questions asked about lesbian, gay and bisexual issues in diversity training. *Journal of Community and Applied Social Psychology*, 19, 271–85.
Elizabeth Peel outlines the types of questions that heterosexuals ask about lesbian, gay and bisexual issues in diversity training about sexualities. She identifies six different themes in the questions (such as questions about the trainer's life, experiences and practices) and compares 'real' questions and answers to the decontextualised questions provided in training manuals. This paper highlights the importance of 'going where the action is'; Liz argues that 'intergroup relations' research should focus more on analyses of the 'real' social world in action, and rely less on reports of the social world.

Riggs, D. W. (2007c) Queer theory and its future in psychology: exploring issues of race privilege. *Social and Personality Psychology Compass*, 1, 39–52.
Damien Riggs outlines six main ways in which research on LGBTQ people in psychology needs to pay attention to issues of race and race privilege, including the need to: (1) acknowledge the intellectual traditions that the field builds on; (2) examine how particular accounts of 'the individual' are racialised; (3) examine how sexualities are always racialised; (4) recognise the contingency of social constructionist critiques of race; (5) acknowledge the cultural contingency of terms used within LGBTQ communities; and (6) recognise the limits of assuming that there will always be easy connections between diverse groups of people within LGBTQ communities.

Glossary

additive models of identity Models based on the assumption that it is possible and appropriate to examine a single aspect of someone's identity in isolation from the other aspects of their identity (e.g., it is possible to examine and understand a person's experience as a gay man in isolation from his status as a white, middle-class, middle-aged, able-bodied man). An alternative approach to identity is the intersectional approach, which understands all the different aspects of our identity as interconnected and impossible to separate and examine in isolation (see Chapters 4 and 11).

androgyny The phenomenon of not clearly fitting into either of the binary categories of 'male' or 'female', typically on the basis of physical appearance, dress or mannerisms.

assimilationist A negative evaluation of the desire of some LGBTQ people to belong to the mainstream of society, or a requirement from mainstream society for LGBTQ people to present their lives and experiences in ways that conform to dominant (heterosexual) norms and practices.

barebacking A term for unprotected anal intercourse (UAI) between non-heterosexual men. Barebacking is associated with a particular sub-culture where some men who have sex with men reject notions of HIV risk and safer sex practices for various reasons. UAI is a less value-laden term and connected more with one-off instances of unsafe sex.

BDSM An acronym for 'bondage, domination, sadism, masochism', also known as S&M or SM (sadomasochism). The terms 'sadism' (deriving pleasure from watching/inflicting pain and domination) and 'masochism' (deriving pleasure from pain and submission) were first coined by Richard von Krafft-Ebing in *Psychopathia sexualis* (1886). Krafft-Ebing took sadism from the last name of the Marquis de Sade (1740–1814), a writer of pornographic fiction, and masochism from the last name of Leopold von Sacher-Masoch (1836–95), the author of the book *Venus in Furs*. BDSM is a sub-cultural term used by people (of varying sexual identities including heterosexual) who engage in consensual sexual practices which include wearing leather, latex and uniforms, using sex toys and creating sexual 'scenes' usually involving sexually 'sadistic'/dominant and 'masochistic'/submissive partners. BDSM is pathologised in the DSM and some aspects of BDSM are illegal in many countries.

berdache See two-spirit.

biomedical model A model of health, illness and disease prevalent in western medicine since the nineteenth century that focuses on physical processes, which, in the context of health psychology, is often viewed as reductionist because the influence of psychological, social and cultural factors is excluded.

biopsychosocial model An approach to health, illness and disease that acknowledges that biological, psychological and social factors all play a role. This model is typically seen as an improvement on the more reductionist biomedical model, although from a critical health psychology perspective this model does not go far enough in engaging with the socio-cultural dimensions of health and illness.

biphobia A parallel term to homophobia that refers to psychological and social prejudice and discrimination against bisexual people.

birth (or biological, natal, genetic) mother/father The woman/man who conceived a child in a planned lesbian/gay family or in a lesbian/gay step-family. See also co-parent.

bisexual A person who experiences sexual and emotional attachments to both women and men.

calabai/calalai See two-spirit.

closeted An LGBTQ person who does not reveal their sexuality and/or gender identity.

colonisation The theft or appropriation of one group's land by another group on the basis of the presumed right of the colonising group to take the land. Typically this presumption of a right to ownership was informed by the view that First Nation or Indigenous people did not have a right to claim ownership over land on the basis that they did not engage with land in ways recognisable to colonisers.

coming out This means both coming to recognise and identify oneself as non-heterosexual or trans, and disclosing that information to others (often referred to as 'coming out of the closet'). Coming out as non-heterosexual or trans is only necessary because of the normativity of heterosexuality and of the social dominance of a binary sex/gender system, in which we are presumed to be either male *or* female, always and forever.

congenital inversion A term widely used by early sexologists that refers to the 'natural' or inborn inversion (or turning around) of the sexual instinct – so a congenitally inverted man desires men and a congenitally inverted woman desires women.

contextualism A theoretical approach informing some qualitative research, which assumes that meaning is related to the context in which it is produced. A number of different theoretical approaches can broadly be described as contextualist (including standpoint theory, phenomenology and critical realism), and contextualism is associated with qualitative methods of data analysis such as Grounded Theory and Interpretative Phenomenological Analysis.

conversation analysis See conversation analysts.

conversation analysts Those who engage in the qualitative study of talk-in-interaction. Conversation analysis (or CA) attempts to describe the orderliness, structure and sequential patterns of interaction in institutional talk (i.e., talk that occurs in a formal setting) and in everyday conversation (for an introduction to CA see Atkinson and Heritage, 1994; Psathas, 1995).

conversion therapy The active attempt to change a person's sexuality from non-heterosexual to heterosexual using a variety of techniques or 'treatments'.

co-parent In families where the children are genetically related to at least one of the parents, the non-birth parent(s) is often referred to as the 'co-parent(s)' (sometimes both parents are biologically related to the child, for example, when the brother of the co-parent donates sperm to the birth mother). The use of the terms 'birth mother' and 'co-mother' are complicated by the fact that in some instances both women in a lesbian couple may get pregnant (either sequentially or simultaneously), and lesbian couples may exchange ova to enable both women to claim biological status to the same infant. Some non-heterosexual families contain multiple co-parents: for example, a gay couple and a lesbian couple may co-parent together. See also social parent.

critical health psychology An approach to health research premised on principles associated with critical psychology: including using (predominantly) qualitative methods and critical/constructionist theories, aiming to promote positive social change for people marginalised on health grounds, and taking a more socio-cultural approach to health and illness than is typical in mainstream health psychology.

critical psychology An umbrella term for a range of different approaches to psychology that challenge the core assumptions of mainstream psychology (see Chapter 2).

critical realism A theoretical approach informing some work within critical psychology which assumes that the way reality is experienced and interpreted is shaped by culture, language and political interests.

cross-dressing The act of wearing clothes commonly associated with the 'other' gender within a particular society.

cross-gender identification Transsexual people often experience themselves as 'living in the wrong body' and so are said to have the gender identity of 'the other' sex.

deconstructing A strategy of analysis (also referred to as deconstructionism) concerned with exposing unquestioned assumptions and internal contradictions that is associated with the work of the French post-structuralist thinker Jacques Derrida (1930–2004) (e.g., Derrida, 1998).

dichotomous model of sexuality The division of sexuality into two, and only two, categories: heterosexuality and homosexuality. Also known as the binary model of sexuality or the heterosexual/homosexual binary. There are also dichotomous (or binary) models of sex (male/female) and of gender (masculine/feminine).

different-sex relationships Intimate relationships between two people of different sex/genders. An alternative to 'heterosexual relationships' (which excludes bisexuals in different-sex relationships) and 'opposite-sex relationships' (that problematically polarises men and women).

discourse A term with a wide range of meanings. Broadly speaking, it refers to patterned meaning within spoken or written language.

discourse analysis A form of qualitative analysis that centres on the detailed examination of patterns of meaning within texts, and the effects and implications of particular patterns of meaning.

discursive psychology A form of discourse analysis that focuses on psychological themes. Discursive psychology is also associated with a more 'fine-grained' approach to discourse analysis and more detailed analyses of textual data.

divorced lesbian mothers/gay fathers Lesbians and gay men who have had children in the context of a heterosexual relationship. Either the term 'lesbian/gay stepfamily' or the term 'lesbian/gay post-divorce family' is used to describe a family where a woman forms a relationship with another woman, or a man forms a relationship with another man, and one or both adults in the relationship has children. In the case of step-families, children could be from former heterosexual and/or same-sex relationships.

dominant group The group(s) within a society which claims a position of dominance and uses that position to ensure that its worldview is promoted above all others.

donor insemination A technically straightforward (but often emotionally complex and time consuming) way of attempting to conceive, where sperm is inserted into the vagina using a needle-less syringe. Donor insemination is performed by a nurse or doctor in a conception clinic; some women also self-inseminate. Donor insemination is not to be confused with *in vitro* fertilisation (IVF), a complex and expensive reproductive technology, used only when couples or women have had great difficulty conceiving.

double discrimination/jeopardy The idea that certain members of LGBTQ communities are marginalised both on the basis of their non-heterosexual or trans identities *and* on the basis of another factor (such as race, gender or age). This term expresses the multiple ways in which privilege and marginalisation intersect and the multiple identity positions we occupy. It is also used to refer to the ways in which bisexual and trans people are discriminated against both in mainstream society *and* in lesbian and gay communities.

drag kings/queens Men/women who dress in the clothing of the 'other' sex in order to parody gender norms and challenge gender binaries, and/or as a form of artistic expression.

embodiment At its simplest, embodiment refers to the experience of being in one's body, the experience of the materiality of one's body. Theoretically, the term is typically used to examine the meanings associated with a range of bodily forms: for example, the ways in which gender or racial norms are inscribed on bodies.

epidemiology The study of the prevalence of diseases in different populations (e.g., in LGBTQ communities), and why diseases occur. Epidemiological research is considered very important in the arena of public health and in the development of evidence-based practice in medicine and related fields.

fa'afafine See two-spirit.

families of choice The notion that LGBTQ people (among others) form families that are primarily organised not on the basis of biological relationships, but on the basis of supportive and caring relationships with other adults and children (to whom they may or may not be related through birth, marriage or legal adoption).

families of origin The families we are raised in/by.

female-to-male-transsexual (FTM) A natal female who transitions to his preferred male gender identity, through hormonal and/or surgical treatment; another, increasingly widely used term to refer to a FTM trans person is transman.

feminist psychology A recognised sub-field of psychology (also known as the psychology of women) that is informed by the political goals of the feminist movement and is concerned with topics relevant to women's lives and the operation of gender within society (see Chapter 2).

First Nation A group of people who have a prior claim to land now occupied by other groups of people who appropriated or stole the land. Despite the ongoing effects of dispossession, many First Nations people continue to claim sovereign rights over land, and to practise their connections and relationship to their land. First Nations land boundaries do not accord with those of existing global configurations, and First Nations people typically retain their own languages and group names while also engaging with western descriptions of the world.

gay Men who identify with this category experience their sole or primary sexual and emotional attachments to other men.

gay liberation A radical gay and lesbian political movement prominent in the 1970s concerned with homosexual oppression and sexual liberation for all. Gay liberationists often spoke of 'smashing the family' and other social institutions that had a role in the oppression of gay men and lesbians, and heterosexual women. Gay liberationists sought to rebuild society in line with ideals of peace, justice and economic equality.

gender identity clinic A psychiatric and surgical 'treatment' centre for transsexual people.

Gender Identity Disorder A diagnostic category in the DSM most commonly applied to transsexual people. Key criteria for the application of the category include a persistent and strong cross-gender identification and persistent discomfort about one's assigned sex.

gender inversion theory of homosexuality The notion that gay men are feminine people in male bodies and lesbians are masculine people in female bodies.

gender reassignment The surgical and hormonal process of transitioning from one sex to another.

genderist/non-genderist Parallel terms to heterosexist/non-heterosexist, which refer to discrimination on the basis of gender identity and specifically discrimination against trans people. A non-genderist approach rejects such discrimination and is affirmative of trans people's experiences and perspectives.

hate crimes Acts of violence or victimisation committed against a person or a group on the grounds of their actual or presumed membership of a particular social category. Crimes committed against people on the basis of their actual or presumed sexuality and/or gender identity are known as homophobic/transphobic hate crimes.

health inequalities Variation in the morbidity and mortality rates of different groups. Typically health inequalities are seen in terms of socio-economic status (i.e., poorer people suffer from greater ill health and die younger than richer people), but the term can also be applied to other 'demographic' characteristics such as sexuality and gender. Public health policy is often concerned with reducing health inequalities in the population.

hegemonic masculinity A form of masculinity which is dominant or which is accepted as the norm, and to which all men are expected to conform. Hegemonic masculinity incorporates the following assumptions: men should not display emotion, men should take a dominant role in interaction, and men should generally eschew all things 'feminine' (whether that be clothing, interests or activities).

heteronormativity A concept developed in queer theory that describes the social privileging of heterosexuality and the assumption that heterosexuality is the only natural and normal sexuality.

heteropatriarchy See patriarchy.

heterosex Sex between women and men, particularly penis-in-vagina intercourse. This term was developed to avoid the heterosexist equation of the generic term 'sex' with heterosexual sex.

heterosexism See heterosexist/non-heterosexist.

heterosexist/non-heterosexist To characterise someone, or something, as heterosexist is to indicate that they are, or it is, assuming heterosexuality to be inherently normal and superior to homosexuality and that everyone is or should be hetero-sexual (Fish, 2007). Heterosexism infuses social institutions and everyday inter-actions. A non-heterosexist approach avoids such assumptions.

heterosexual This is a term that is assumed to be widely understood and not to require any definition, but we disagree! We use the term to refer to people whose sole or primary sexual and emotional attachments are to people of 'the other' sex.

heterosexual/homosexual binary See dichotomous model of sexuality.

homophobia Negative attitudes towards lesbians and gay men that may manifest them-selves through anxiety, disgust, aversion, anger, discomfort or fear of lesbians and gay men, or of homosexuality more generally.

homosexuals and homosexuality It is helpful to distinguish between the term 'homo-sexual' (used to refer to a type of person) and 'homosexuality' (used to refer to a type of sexuality). Very few LGBQ people would use the term homosexual to describe themselves because it is thought to have rather negative, clinical con-notations. However, the term 'homosexuality' is widely used to refer to the phenomenon of same-sex attraction.

ideology An organised collection of ideas; a way of looking at things. Ideologies can be epistemological and refer to major paradigms within academic disciplines and areas of research (e.g., positivism, post-positivism); they can also be political and refer to a set of ideas or principles about how society should operate that inform the work of political movements and organisations.

Indigenous A term used to describe the group of people who first lived on a land. Indigenous people across a range of contexts are similar in regard to histories of dispossession and colonisation of their lands, but have different creation myths, spiritual practices and relationships to land.

individualised A concept is described as individualised (or individualising) because it explains social issues in terms of the behaviour of individual people. For example, we could argue that the concept of homophobia offers an individualised explan-ation of lesbian and gay social marginalisation because it focuses on individual attitudes rather than the organisation of society around a heterosexual norm.

institutionalised homophobia This term acknowledges that heterosexuality is both an individual sexuality and a social institution that regulates our behaviour and practices.

instruments of regulation This is a way of saying that certain constructs (e.g., the notion of a 'gay identity') work to limit and constrain our behaviour and practices in particular ways, and in the interests of particular groups and institutions.

internalised homophobia Negative feelings towards oneself as a lesbian or gay man resulting from having internalised the negative attitudes of others and of the wider society towards homosexuality.

intersectional An understanding of identity that recognises the multiple and concurrent ways in which identities intersect with one another. This approach does not view identities in an additive way (i.e., women + lesbian + black = more oppressed than just women + lesbian), but rather sees all aspects of an individual's expe-rience combining to produce a particular position in the world that may involve both privilege and disadvantage.

intersex A set of medical conditions where people are born with 'sex' chromosomes, external genitalia or an internal reproductive system that is not considered 'standard' for either male or female. Intersexed infants are typically attributed a male or female gender identity and may undergo treatment to align their body with social norms, although intersex activists have called for surgery not to be performed on non-consenting infants. Intersex people describe their sexual and gender identities in varied ways.

inversion A term for homosexuality and other forms of gender inversion (such as trans and intersex), widely used by early sexologists, which reflected the theory that homosexuality (and other forms of inversion) results from the inborn reversal of gender traits (e.g., female inverts were thought to be disposed to traditionally masculine pursuits and dress).

lesbian Women who identify with this category experience their sole or primary sexual and emotional attachments to other women; some women prefer to use the label 'gay woman'.

lesbian feminists Throughout the 1970s, lesbian feminism offered lesbians a vision of the 'lesbian nation', a women-centred utopia, 'a sort of haven in a heartless (male/heterosexual) world' (Stein, 1998/1992: 553), and a basis for political action. Lesbian feminists sought both to build a community apart from the mainstream (some chose to withdraw from all kinds of relationships with men) and to challenge mainstream norms and values. Both gay liberationists and lesbian feminists engaged in direct political action, organising marches, staging sit-ins and the like. They rejected the majority-appeasing methods of earlier gay and lesbian movements and worked instead for social transformation. **Radical lesbian feminists** developed a distinct form of lesbian feminism associated with radical feminist analyses of the operation of gender within society. Many lesbians continue to subscribe to lesbian feminist values.

lesbian and gay movement A term used to refer broadly to the political movement concerned with advancing the interests of lesbians and gay men. Within this broad movement there have been a wide range of different political eras, organisations and campaigns.

lesbian and gay studies An interdisciplinary field of study that has developed over the last few decades concerned with issues related to sexuality and gender identity (also known as 'queer studies'). Growing numbers of universities offer courses in lesbian and gay studies and there are numerous readers and edited collections that provide excellent introductions to the field (e.g., Abelove *et al.*, 1993, Richardson and Seidman, 2002).

liberal-humanistic A prevailing philosophy in late modern western cultures, which emphasises the uniqueness and rights of the individual. In relation to sexuality, this ideological framework stresses the essential humanness of LGBTQ people and the relatively trivial nature of their sexuality.

mainstream psychology The dominant approach to psychology, based on a set of assumptions related to positivist-empiricist and realist frameworks, including the notion that it is possible to amass objective facts about the world. Although we use the term 'mainstream' to describe an approach to LGBTQ psychology that is associated with the norms and values of mainstream psychology, given the marginal status of LGBTQ psychology with the discipline as whole it is debatable whether this approach to LGBTQ psychology can be truly regarded as mainstream.

male-to-female-transsexual (MTF) Natal males who transition to their preferred female gender identity, through hormonal and/or surgical treatment; another, increasingly widely used term to refer to a MTF trans person is **transwoman**.

Marxism A political philosophy and practice developed from the ideas of Karl Marx and Friedrich Engels. There are many different varieties of Marxism, but a central principle is that capitalism is based on the exploitation of workers by the owners of the means of production. Marxist theories tend to view the capitalist system as the root of all oppression.

mononormativity A term used by bisexual communities to refer to the normative status of only desiring sex and relationships with people of one sex/gender.

MSM The term MSM (men who have sex with men) was developed by HIV/AIDS researchers to enable the inclusion of men who have sex with men but do not identify with labels such as 'gay' or 'queer' in sexual health research and promotion. MSM deliberately emphasises sexual *behaviour* rather than sexual *identity*. The parallel term WSW (women who have sex with women) also appears in the context of sexual health research.

mundane heterosexism Heterosexism embedded in everyday language and practice, to the extent that it is unnoticed and therefore considered normal.

nádleehí See two-spirit.

natal sex A person's designated sex at birth.

naturalistic data Data that exist in the world (such as newspaper reports or doctor–patient interactions) rather than data collected specifically for the purposes of research.

non-genderist See genderist.

non-heterosexist See heterosexist.

non-heterosexual A relatively recent term used to refer collectively to LGBQ people. Although it is a negative term in the sense that it defines people as what they are not, some researchers regard it as useful because it is clear and inclusive.

non-reproductive sexuality See sodomy

non-trans A collective term for people who do not identify as trans, which provides a way of distinguishing between trans and non-trans people that avoids pathologising trans people or representing them as 'abnormal'.

normalisation A process of presenting something generally regarded as non-normative as normal and ordinary. The concept of normalisation was developed in the context of critiques of liberal-assimilationist politics, and the tendency to present lesbians and gay men as 'just the same as' heterosexual people (see Clarke, 2002b).

normative People often struggle with language when discussing LGBTQ identities, especially when they want to signal that these identities are not 'normal', in the sense that most people identify as heterosexual and as non-trans. We choose to avoid words like 'normal' because they imply a moral judgement; we prefer the term 'normative' to refer to what is constructed as the norm within dominant social values and 'non-normative' to refer to what is constructed as outside the norm.

oppression A term for social marginalisation associated with political movements such as Marxism, feminism and gay liberation. Within such movements oppression refers to using power to silence and subordinate a group of people.

passing Broadly speaking, passing refers to persons being viewed as members of a social group that they are not a part of (e.g., a gay man presenting himself as heterosexual). Typically, people attempt to pass so that they can gain the benefits associated with membership of a particular group, and/or to avoid the stigmatisation that is associated with membership of their own group. Passing can also be incidental, such as when someone is presumed to be a member of a group different from their own (e.g., when lesbian or gay parents are presumed to be heterosexual on the basis of the assumption that all parents are heterosexual).

pathologisation The literal meaning of pathology is disease, so 'the pathologising model of homosexuality' is another way of saying the disease or illness model of homosexuality. To pathologise homosexuality is to present it as having disease-like or 'abnormal' attributes.

patriarchal oppression Usually refers to the oppression of women in a male-dominated society.

patriarchy An important concept within feminism. The literal meaning of patriarchy is the organisation of society around family units where fathers have primary authority; feminists use the term more broadly to refer to a male-dominated society. The term heteropatriarchy was developed by lesbian feminists to refer to a male-dominated society in which heterosexuality is privileged.

penis-in-vagina intercourse A term developed by feminists and queer theorists to avoid the elision of 'sex' or 'penetrative sex' with this specific sex act (see Myerson et al., 2007). This term gives this particular sex act its full name when it normally has no marker because of its normative status as the generic sex act.

people with same-sex attractions This rather clumsy phrase is increasingly used in the literature because it signals a more inclusive understanding of same-sex sexuality and many people's reluctance to identify with particular sexuality categories such as 'lesbian' and 'gay', and even 'non-heterosexual' or 'queer'.

phenomenology A philosophy that is influential in qualitative research (see Langdridge, 2007a). There are many varieties of phenomenology, but broadly speaking it is the analysis of people's subjective experiences. Phenomenological approaches to qualitative research typically acknowledge that the process of interpreting people's experiences is inevitably shaped by the researcher's (subjective) experience of the world.

planned lesbian/gay families Families where the adults decided to have children after coming out as lesbian or gay.

political Social relations involving authority or power; to describe something as 'political' is to acknowledge that it relates to issues of power and ideology.

political lesbians Women who chose to be lesbian as a result of political commitments to feminism.

polyamorous See polyamory.

polyamory The practice of having more than one intimate relationship at the same time, with the knowledge and consent of everyone involved. Such relationships may be emotional, sexual or a combination of both.

post-modernism A worldview that challenges the concept of modernity, which promotes a linear and 'progressive' model of the world and the view that certain societies or groups are more 'evolved' than others. Post-modernism posits instead that there is no linear trajectory for societies, and that our experiences as individuals are fragmented and multiple rather than coherent and linear. However, it is also recognised that, as a result of the dominance of modernist ways of viewing the world, we experience ourselves as coherent and linear.

post-structuralism Post-structuralist theorists have been hugely influential across the social sciences and humanities. Post-structuralism developed in France in the 1960s and is strongly associated with the work of Michel Foucault (1978) and Jacques Derrida (1998). Like social constructionism, post-structuralism rejects the possibility of discovering objective facts about the world and the traditional (structural) view of language as a system of communication that describes the world as it is. Post-structuralists argue that language is contingent and is constitutive of world.

post-structuralist See post-structuralism.

post-structuralist/Foucauldian discourse analysis A form of discourse analysis (popular in psychology and in other academic disciplines) that is associated with the work of the French post-structuralist thinker Michel Foucault, and in particular with his analysis of the operation of power within society. This form of discourse analysis focuses on the ideological functions of discourse and the ways in which different discourses make certain subject positions available.

post-transition See pre-transition.

power Most basically, the ability to enforce a particular worldview above all others. Power is often thought of as a possession, something that dominant groups *have* and marginalised groups lack. Post-structuralist theorists such as Michel Foucault have challenged this view of power, arguing instead for a relational model of power, which posits that power is everywhere, and we cannot achieve freedom *from* power. For post-structuralist influenced queer theorists, the goal of oppositional politics is resisting (and working against) power rather than seeking liberation from power.

pre-/post-transition Terms used to refer to the periods (or states) prior to and after transsexual people 'transition' away from their natal sex to their chosen sex. The transition process usually consists of a number of different elements, such as adopting the dress and appearance of the chosen sex and undergoing hormonal and/or surgical treatment.

privilege The benefits that accrue to certain groups of people (e.g., white people, heterosexual people, middle-class people) on the basis of their membership in socially dominant groups. Privilege comes hand-in-hand with disadvantage, with the former typically coming at the expense of the latter.

psychology of women See feminist psychology.

public sex environments (PSEs) Public spaces where (mainly) MSM have sex; also known as 'cruising grounds', or, in the case of public toilets, 'cottages' (in the UK) or 'beats' (in Australia).

Q-methodology A research method developed by the psychologist William Stephenson (1902–89) that is used to study people's viewpoints. Unlike normal factor analysis ('R method'), Q looks for correlations between participants across a sample of variables. Q factor analysis reduces the many individual viewpoints of the participants down to a few 'factors' that represent shared ways of thinking (see Kitzinger, 1987).

qualitative psychology Psychological research that draws on qualitative research methods; that is, methods concerned with generating meaning and understanding and are typically based on the collection of textual data such as interviews and focus groups.

queer A complex term with different layers of meaning; used in the past as a derogatory term for homosexuals but reclaimed as a positive and confrontational self-description in the 1980s by activists and theorists seeking to challenge social norms around sexuality and gender identity. Queer is used both as a generic term to describe LGBT people and as a term associated with a particular body of critical theory (queer theory) that questions the usefulness of identity categories such as 'lesbian' and 'gay'. People who use the label queer to describe themselves often want to signal their allegiance to values associated with queer theory and queer activism. This is how we use this term.

queer heterosexuals Heterosexuals who identify with the tenets of queer theory and attempt to find ways to do heterosexuality differently, and to 'get beyond' heteronormative understandings of sex and relationships between women and men.

queer nuclear families Families that consist of two same-sex parents and a child or children. This term is used to draw attention to the ways in which the constitution of queer families is not necessarily radical, and often conforms to the structure of the quintessential (heterosexual) nuclear family.

queer theorists See queer theory.

queer theory A body of critical theory that has been hugely influential across the humanities and social sciences. It developed out of feminist critiques of essentialist models of gender and is strongly influenced by the work of the French post-structuralist thinker Michel Foucault (1978). A major focus of queer theory is the critique of heteronormative binary models of sex/gender and sexuality that privilege heterosexuality and non-trans genders over all other sexualities and genders. This critique highlights the contingency of heterosexuality on the refutation of non-heterosexuality and thus challenges the binary heterosexual/homosexual model of sexuality.

questioning The 'Q' in LGBTQ is often intended to have a double meaning, referring both to 'queer' and to 'questioning'; that is, to people who are questioning and exploring their sexuality (similar terms are 'bicurious' and 'heteroflexible').

racially marginalised The experience of social disadvantage, isolation or marginalisation on the basis of racial categories, where some groups of people located outside of the norm of whiteness are constructed as less valid or worthy of social inclusion.

radical lesbian feminist See lesbian feminists.

realism The worldview that there is a direct correspondence between objects and interpretation; that we 'know' an object is something because there are inherent facts about it that we can perceive and understand.

reflexive This refers to the notion that knowledge is actively constructed rather than 'discovered' and that the researcher has a role in constructing knowledge. Reflexive research is that which acknowledges the role of the researcher in the production of knowledge, and in which the researcher reflects on his or her positioning and the ways in which this may have shaped the collection and analysis of data.

regulatory role of psychology This concept refers to the way in which psychological knowledge supports the status quo. Critical psychologists have argued that psychological theories and research are not 'neutral'; rather, they often support dominant and oppressive ideologies such as 'a woman's place is in the home' and 'children need a mother and a father'.

resistance A way of opposing the use of power to oppress and dominate particular groups. The term resistance is used both to refer broadly to fighting back against power and to refer specifically, in the context of a Foucauldian analysis of the operation of power, to the ways in which we can work against power, when power is conceived of as relational and inescapable (rather than as a possession of dominant groups that marginalised groups can work to liberate themselves from).

rhetoric A form of argumentation; the use of particular constructions of talk to convince another of the validity or superiority of your position.

safer sex Taking precautionary measures during sex with a partner to avoid the transmission of STIs (sexually transmitted infections) and, in heterosex, the prevention of pregnancy through the use of a 'barrier method' (i.e., a condom, diaphragm or female condom). The term 'safer' (as opposed to 'safe') is used to acknowledge that no precaution is 100 per cent safe.

same-sex relationships Sexual/romantic relationships between two people of the same sex/gender. The term 'same-sex relationship' provides a way of indicating relationship status without direct reference to sexual identity, so it is (potentially) inclusive of bisexual and other non-heterosexual people in same-sex relationships.

Section 28 (of the Local Government Act 1988) This was introduced by the Conservative Thatcher Government in 1988, amid fears about children having access to books about gay parenting (in particular the book *Jenny lives with Eric and Martin*), and prohibited local authorities from 'intentionally promot[ing] homosexuality or publish[ing] material with the intention of promoting homosexuality', and schools from teaching 'the acceptability of homosexuality as a pretended family relationship'. Section 28 was overturned in Scotland in 2000, and three years later in the rest of the UK. It is widely regarded as one of the catalysts for a resurgence in lesbian and gay political activism (and the rise of groups and organisations like Stonewall and OutRage!) in the UK in the late 1980s.

separatist This term is applied to feminists who choose to withdraw from all sexual, emotional and physical contact with men. Separatism was particularly popular among radical lesbian feminists in the 1970s and was seen as a way for women to survive in a hostile male-dominated society and to form strong bonds with other women.

sex change surgery A range of surgical procedures that assist transsexual people in achieving a bodily appearance that is consistent with their chosen sex.

sex/gender This term acknowledges that it is not possible within mainstream thinking to separate theoretically the concepts of 'sex' and 'gender'; each is implicated in the construction of the other. For example, sex is often viewed as primary and gender is the cultural 'icing' on the biological 'cake' of sex. However, a close analysis of sex and gender reveals that the (sexed) body is heavily gendered: for example, the vagina is constructed as passive, a canal through which babies pass and which is *penetrated* by the active penis (see Clarke and Braun, 2009).

sexual fluidity The notion that sexuality is not fixed and therefore people's sexual identity and practices can change over time.

sexual identity A term derived from a modern western understanding of sexuality, influenced by the work of early sexologists, that views sexuality as a central component of self and integral to our identity. This model organises sexuality in terms of types of people (homosexuals, heterosexuals) rather than forms of behaviour. The term 'sexual identity' has also been used by psychologists as an umbrella term (in the context of child development) for sexual orientation, gender identity (our sense of ourselves as male or female) and gender role (the degree to which our behaviours and practices conform to those designated as appropriately masculine or appropriately feminine within the wider culture).

sexual orientation The notion, popular in many countries (both western and non-western), that a fixed, internal psychological or biological structure organises and directs our sexual behaviour. Although it is acknowledged that people may act in ways that contradict or conflict with their sexual orientation, 'true' expressions of sexuality are taken to be those that are consistent with people's (self-identified or externally labelled) sexual orientation.

social construction(ism) An understanding of the world in which objects are understood as not having inherent meaning, but rather develop meanings in relation to particular social, cultural and historical contexts (see Chapter 2).

social parent The non-birth parent or parents in a lesbian/gay family (see also co-parent).

socio-centric Broadly speaking, societies or communities that are orientated towards the needs of the society or community, rather than towards those of the individual; such societies are also known as collectivist.

sodomy/non-reproductive sexuality Before the work of sexologists radically changed how sex and sexuality were viewed in the west, sexuality was typically divided into reproductive sexuality = good (i.e., sex between a man and a woman that potentially results in conception) and non-reproductive sexuality (or sodomy) = bad (i.e., all non-reproductive sexual acts such as oral sex between women or between a woman and a man, and anal intercourse between men or between a woman and a man).

sperm donor A man who provides sperm either to a clinic or in a private arrangement for another person(s) to conceive a child. Men who donate sperm to a clinic are typically not legally recognised as parents, but laws regarding the legal status of private donors vary widely (in the UK, for example, private sperm donors technically have the same rights as unmarried fathers). While some sperm donors may be a part of the lives of children conceived as a result of their donation, many have little or no involvement.

Standards of Care Based on the work of the US-based doctor Harry Benjamin (1885–1986), the Standards of Care guide the psychiatric and medical 'treatment' of transsexualism and gender identity disorder in many western countries.

standpoint theory A theory informing qualitative work in psychology and other social science disciplines that is strongly associated with the work of feminists such as Dorothy Smith (1990), Sandra Harding (1991) and Patricia Hill Collins (1990). Standpoint theory acknowledges that all standpoints (the position from which people view the world) are partial; people's standpoints are influenced by their social group membership.

straight-acting queers LGBTQ people who do not exhibit any mannerisms, behaviour or dress that appear to fit an LGBTQ stereotype.

subclinical (health problem) A health problem or illness that remains below the surface of 'detection' by health professionals and/or for which an individual does not seek help and support from health professionals.

surrogacy Some gay men have used 'traditional surrogacy' (where the surrogate mother is genetically related to the baby) or 'gestational surrogacy' (where the baby carried in pregnancy by the surrogate is genetically related to another woman who has donated the egg) to have a biological child. Surrogacy is controversial, and feminists in particular have been critical of the use of women's bodies in this way. Surrogacy can also be very expensive if arrangements are made through an agency (US$100,000 is not unusual, Lev, 2006).

trans An umbrella term for people whose sex/gender diverges in some way from the sex/gender they were assigned at birth, including those who identify with the label transsexual. Transsexuals experience a discrepancy between their gender identity and the sex they were assigned at birth and often seek treatment to modify their body. The term transgender is often used to describe people who live outside of dominant gender norms without seeking surgical intervention; it is also used as an umbrella term to describe all those people whose gender identity does not mesh with their assigned sex. Some trans people identify as heterosexual, some as LGBQ, and others feel that there are no words to describe their sexuality and they refuse sexual categorisation.

transgender See trans.

transitioning The process of a trans person changing gender presentation from assigned sex to chosen sex. Typically people begin the process of transitioning by changing their mode of address and appearance to approximate their chosen gender identity. Latter stages of transitioning may include taking hormones and having surgery to change their physical anatomy to match their gender identity. Transitioning often also involves learning to change speech patterns and voice tone.

transmen See female-to-male transsexual.

transphobia A parallel term to homophobia that refers to psychological and social prejudice and discrimination against trans people.

transsexualism The phenomenon of experiencing a discrepancy between one's gender identity and natal sex.

transsexuals See trans.

transvestism Often presented as a pathological sexual fetish, transvestism refers to the phenomenon of people (usually men) experiencing pleasure from dressing in clothes typically associated with 'the other' sex/gender.

transwomen See male-to-female transsexual.

two-sex model A model of sex based on the assumption, that is deeply embedded in many cultures, that there are two, and only two, sexes.

two-spirit This is a term used to describe the experiences of Native American people who do not identify as heterosexual or as non-trans. Recent research indicates that the use of this catch-all phrase sidelines the specific terms used by individual Native American Nations (one example being the term nádleehí used by Navaho people; see Chapter 11). Other cultures have terms thought to be similar, such as fa'afafine in Samoan culture and calabai/calalai in Indonesian culture (see Chapters 4 and 11). It is important to note that terms such as 'two-spirit' are contested and reflect a western interpretation of non-western cultures.

usual suspects The group of people who constitute the typical sample in LGBTQ psychological research (i.e., white, middle-class lesbians and gay men).

West/western In a binary view of the world, where countries are (culturally, rather than necessarily geographically) positioned as either in the 'East' (e.g., Asia and Russia), or the 'West' (e.g., the USA, Europe, Australia, New Zealand), this term refers to a particular set of values that are presumed to be shared among nations located within the West. This is a relational term, with references to the West or the western world seen as the polar opposite of the East or the eastern world. While scholars continue to challenge and deconstruct this binary, the use of the term persists as a way to describe a particular worldview typically associated with individualism, consumerism and forms of domination such as colonisation.

whiteness This refers to a particular racialised way of being in, or seeing, the world in which the values and beliefs of white people are privileged. Whiteness is also understood as a form of 'cultural capital', where people can access the benefits of whiteness according to their approximation of the norms of whiteness.

women's studies A multidisciplinary field focused on women, gender and feminism, that incorporates most of the humanities and social sciences (also known as 'gender studies' or 'feminist studies'). Women's studies emerged and developed as a distinct field of study alongside second-wave feminism and the women's movement in the late 1960s and early 1970s, and many universities now offer degrees and courses in women's studies. See Robinson and Richardson (1997) for an introduction.

WSW See MSM.

Additional resources

We have listed a range of documentaries and feature films (that are widely accessible), as well as some web resources, that we have found useful in teaching and learning about LGBTQ (and intersex) issues.

Documentaries and feature films

History of LGBTQ psychology

Kinsey (Bill Condon Dir., 2004). The story of the life and work of Alfred Kinsey, the 'founding father' of modern sexology. The film provides an insight into Kinsey's research and methods, especially the less widely publicised aspects of his work.

History and politics of LGBTQ communities

Go fish (Rose Troche Dir., 1994). Probably one of the most well known lesbian films, centred on a burgeoning relationship between two lesbian women; the film shows a variety of lesbian lives and explores a number of issues that were 'live' in lesbian communities in the 1990s such as lesbian sex, lesbian stereotypes (within lesbian communities), butch/femme, lesbians having sex with men and coming out to family.

If these walls could talk 2 (Jane Anderson and Martha Coolidge Dirs., 2000). A collection of three short films, each depicting a different era in lesbian communities and politics, framed around the same house. The first film is set in the early 1960s and tells the story of an older lesbian (Edith) whose partner dies. Edith has to mourn her loss in a context of homophobia and a lack of same-sex partnership recognition. The second film is set in the early 1970s and explores the clashes between different approaches to lesbian lives and politics, centring on a controversial romance between a lesbian feminist (Linda) and a butch lesbian (Amy). The third film is set in 2000 and explores the experiences of an affluent, middle-class, white lesbian couple who want to have a baby and become parents.

Milk (Gus Van Sant Dir., 2008). A fictional account of the political life of Harvey Milk, a 'gay icon' and the first openly gay man to be elected to public office in the USA; Harvey Milk was assassinated by a colleague in 1978.

The film is interwoven with archive footage from the 1970s and provides a vivid insight into the experiences of gay and lesbian activists and communities in San Francisco at that time. There is also a documentary about Harvey Milk entitled *The times of Harvey Milk* (Rob Epstein Dir., 1984).

Paris is burning (Jennie Livingston Dir., 1990). A documentary following the lives of a group of impoverished African American and Latino drag queens and trans people and their involvement in underground dance and drag cultures. This film has been widely discussed in academic literature on queer theory and the 'performativity' of gender (see Sullivan, 2003).

Stonewall (Nigel Finch Dir., 1995). A fictional account of the events leading up to the Stonewall riots, one of the events considered to be a cornerstone of the modern lesbian and gay movement in the West. This history is also explored in two documentaries: *Before Stonewall: the making of a gay and lesbian community* (Greta Schiller, John Scagliotti and Robert Rosenberg Dirs., 1984) and *After Stonewall* (John Scagliotti Dir., 1999).

Trans and intersex experiences

Boys don't cry (Kimberly Peirce Dir., 1999). A fictionalised account of the life of a teenager, Brandon Teena, a young transman who had heterosexual relationships with young (natal) women. When his natal sex was discovered, he faced severe hostility (not least from the local police), which ultimately resulted in his rape and murder, and the murder of two of his friends. This film is based on the documentary *The Brandon Teena story* (Susan Muska and Gréta Olafsdóttir Dirs., 1998).

Hermaphrodites speak! (Cheryl Chase Dir., 1997). A group of intersex people discuss their experiences of growing up intersexed. Available from the Intersex Society of North America (website listed below).

Transgeneration (Jeremy Simmons Dir., 2005). This excellent eight-part series documents the lives of four young adults who identify as trans and their negotiation of university life. Topics covered include the surgical procedures they undergo and their differential access to these on the basis of socio-economic factors, the institutional issues they face transitioning whilst living on campus, their attempts at negotiating relationships with other young adults and with their birth families, and the supportive communities they build with other trans people.

Ma vie en rose (Alain Berliner Dir., 1997). The story of a young boy who considers himself a girl. The movie focuses on his parents' struggle to accept his identity, and the relationship he has with a boy who recognises him as a girl.

Normal (Jane Anderson Dir., 2003). This film centres on a Midwestern US father and husband, Roy, who, after twenty-five years of marriage, feels that living as a man has become intolerable and decides to have a sex change. The film explores his family's and his community's struggles to come to terms with this decision and Roy's transition to Ruth.

Homophobia

Big Eden (Thomas Bezucha Dir., 2000). A (flawed) attempt to imagine a community without homophobia. This film focuses on a burgeoning romance between two men in a small community in rural USA, and the community's involvement with their romance.

Brokeback Mountain (Ang Lee Dir., 2005). The story of a doomed love affair between two male ranch hands in the US Midwest in the 1960s–1980s. The film vividly explores the impact of homophobia (and 'internalised homophobia') on the men, and their relationship.

The gift (Louise Hogarth Dir., 2003). An insightful documentary about the experiences and motivations of men who engage in 'barebacking'. The documentary includes the voices of a wide range of gay men and examines their understandings of HIV/AIDS, as well as exploring how homophobia shapes gay men's experiences of HIV/AIDS.

The Matthew Shepard story (Roger Spottiswoode Dir., 2002) and *The Laramie Project* (Moises Kaufman Dir., 2002). Both of these feature films document the story of Matthew Shepard (and his family), a young gay man in the USA who was beaten and left to die by two other young men in 1998. Matthew Shepard's death became the subject of an anti-gay hate campaign by right-wing Christian organisations.

Trembling before G–D (Sandi Simcha Dubowski Dir., 2001). This film explores the experiences of Orthodox and Hasidic lesbian and gay Jewish people, in particular the difficulties they face in reconciling their sexual identities with their religious beliefs and practices.

Gay and lesbian youth and identity development

Beautiful thing (Hettie MacDonald Dir., 1996). This film is based on a play of the same name and tells the story of two white, working-class teenage boys living in a large council estate in London, who together explore their (homo)sexuality and form a relationship.

But I'm a cheerleader (Jamie Babbit Dir., 1999). Provides a humorous take on a serious issue – that of conversion therapy aimed at 'curing' young people of their non-heterosexual desires. This film is useful for exploring a wide range of issues in addition to conversion therapy, including the gender inversion theory of homosexuality and the origins of homosexuality (see Sullivan, 2003).

Get real (Simon Shore Dir., 1998). This film explores the difficulties of negotiating a playground love affair when it is between two (white, middle-class) young men. The film shows how homophobia can prevent non-heterosexual teenagers from exploring their feelings, and how the effects of the closet can be detrimental to early non-heterosexual relationships.

Queer as folk, series 1 and 2 (1999–2000). A provocative British television series documenting the lives of three gay men (two in their late twenties, one in his teens) living in and around Manchester's gay village. Useful for exploring a variety of issues including homophobic bullying in schools, coming out and developing an identity as a gay man, coming out to family members, lesbian and gay co-parenting, and sex and relationships between men. There is also a US version of this television series that ran from 2000 to 2005.

The incredibly true adventures of two girls in love (Maria Maggenti Dir., 1995). A love story between two teenage girls from very different social and economic backgrounds. Randy is white and working-class and lives with her lesbian aunts; she is an outsider at school, and is often taunted about her sexuality. Evie is black and middle-class, and popular at school, with a boyfriend.

Parenting and family

The L word, series 1–6 (2004–2009). A US television series following the lives and relationships of a group of (mostly) lesbian friends living in Los Angeles. Although criticised for portraying lesbians as long-haired, feminine and conventionally attractive, *The L word* has gained a huge following among lesbian communities and it useful for exploring a wide range of issues including lesbian parenting, coming out (at all stages of the life course), lesbian drag kings, relationships between lesbians and transmen, and lesbians in the military and the 'don't ask, don't tell' policy of the US military.

Man made: the story of two men and a baby (Emma Crimmings Dir., 2003). This Australian documentary tells the story of Tony and Lee, two white, middle-class gay men who start their family through surrogacy. The film follows their travels to the USA to negotiate and witness the birth of their child, and the beginning of their life as a family back home in Australia.

Modern times: pink parents (Lynn Alleway Dir., 1998). A documentary exploring the experiences of lesbian and gay parents. Lesbian couple Brenda and Buzz have a daughter through donor insemination and are trying for a second child. Chris, a gay man, is a prospective co-parent and currently donating sperm to a female friend. Hazel and Fliss have two children with a gay male friend who lives nearby. The documentary explores a number of different issues (often through a 'liberal heterosexual' lens) such as motivations for parenthood, homophobic bullying and male role models.

Our mom's a dyke (Juliette Olavarria Dir., 1996). A documentary about sisters coming to terms with their mother's new sexual identity. Made by the oldest sister, the film explores the sisters' journey from initial shock and embarrassment to acceptance and pride.

Rick and Steve: the happiest gay couple in all the world (Allan Brocka Dir., 2007). A humorous stop-motion animation series documenting the lives of Rick and Steve and their friends (including a lesbian couple Dana and Kirsten), who all live in the fictional 'gay ghetto' of West Lahunga Beach. Dana and Kirsten and Rick and Steve have a baby together. Useful for exploring a wide variety of issues, in addition to lesbian and gay parenting, including gay and lesbian stereotypes, same-sex relationships, families of choice, and living with HIV/AIDS.

Old age and ageing

Southern comfort (Kate Davis Dir., 2001). Tells the story of an older transman living in the southern USA and dying of ovarian cancer. The film focuses on his relationship with his female partner and the community in which he lives.

Love! Valour! Compassion! (Joe Mantello Dir., 1997). The story of a group of older gay men (and their younger boyfriends), which focuses on the long-term relationship of one couple and the experience of a gay man who is blind, as well as on issues of growing old and living in a context of HIV.

Websites

These websites include lots of useful information about and for members of LGBTQ communities.

Trans and intersex issues

Intersex Society of North America: www.isna.org/
Press for Change: www.pfc.org.uk/
The Gendys Network: www.gender.org.uk/gendys/index.htm
Transitioning FtM in Australia website: www.ftmaustralia.org/
United Kingdom Intersex Society: www.ukia.co.uk/

Bisexual issues

Bi Community News: www.bicommunitynews.co.uk/
Bi Org: http://bi.org/

LGBT community, politics and activism

Amnesty International: www.amnesty.org.uk/
Beyond masculinity: essays by queer men on gender and politics: www.beyond
   masculinity.com/articles/index.php
Gay and Lesbian Humanist Association: www.galha.org
International Lesbian and Gay Association (ILGA): www.ilga.org/
Metropolitan Community Churches: www.mccchurch.org/
Stonewall: www.stonewall.org.uk/

LGBTQ psychology and sexuality research

American Institute of Bisexuality: www.bisexual.org/home.html
The Kinsey Institute for Research in Sex, Gender, and Reproduction: www.
   kinseyinstitute.org/
Sexual Orientation, Science, Education and Policy (a website featuring the work
   of the renowned US LGBTQ psychologist Gregory Herek): http://psychology.
   ucdavis.edu/rainbow/index.html

LGB youth and coming out

Families and Friends of Lesbians and Gays (FFLAG): www.fflag.org.uk/
Parents, Families and Friends of Lesbians and Gays (PFLAG): http://www.pflag.org

Same-sex relationships, parenting and families

Gay Parent Mag: www.gayparentmag.com/
Loving More: www.lovemore.com/

Older LGBT people

Age Concern UK: http://www.ageconcern.org.uk
National LGBT Health Alliance (Australia): www.lgbthealth.org.au/ageing

Anti-LGB (Please note that all of these websites contain offensive and homophobic material)

Exodus International: www.exodus-international.org/
National Association for Research and Therapy of Homosexuality (NARTH):
   www.narth.com/
Westboro Baptist Church: www.godhatesfags.com/

References

Abelove, H. (1993) Freud, male homosexuality, and the Americans. In H. Abelove, M.A. Barale and D.M. Halperin (eds.), *The lesbian and gay studies reader* (pp. 381–93). New York: Routledge.

Abelove, H., Barale, M.A. and Halperin, D.M. (eds.) (1993) *The lesbian and gay studies reader*. New York: Routledge.

Abraham, I. (2009) 'Out to get us': queer Muslims and the clash of sexual civilisations in Australia. *Contemporary Islam*, 3(1), 79–97.

Adams, Jr., C.L. and Kimmel, D.C. (1997) Exploring the lives of older African American gay men. In B. Greene (ed.), *Ethnic and cultural diversity among lesbians and gay men* (pp. 132–51). Thousand Oaks, CA: Sage.

Adams, J., Braun, V. and McCreanor, T. (2004) Framing gay men's health: a critical review of policy documents. In D.W. Riggs and G.A. Walker (eds.), *Out in the Antipodes: Australian and New Zealand perspectives on gay and lesbian issues in psychology* (pp. 212–46). Perth: Brightfire Press.

Adams, J., McCreanor, T. and Braun, V. (2007) Alcohol and gay men: consumption, promotion and policy responses. In V. Clarke and E. Peel (eds.), *Out in psychology: lesbian, gay, bisexual, trans and queer perspectives* (pp. 369–90). Chichester: Wiley.

Adelman, M. (1986) *Long time passing: lives of older lesbians*. Boston, MA: Alyson.

Age Concern England (2005) *Planning for later life as a lesbian, gay man or bisexual person [Information sheet]*. London: Age Concern England. Available from: www.ageconcern.org.uk/AgeConcern/Documents/IS8_1205.pdf.

(2006) Opening doors – facts and figures. Available from: www.ageconcern.org.uk/AgeConcern/C12E7658DF594B09B18EB699ED319ED7.asp.

(2007) *Planning for later life: transgender people [Information sheet]*. London: Age Concern England. Available from: www.ace.org.uk/AgeConcern/Documents/IS30TransgenderJan2007.pdf.

Aguero, J.E., Bloch, L. and Byrne, D. (1984) The relationship among sexual beliefs, attitudes, experiences and homophobia. *Journal of Homosexuality*, 10, 95–107.

Amadio, D.M. and Chung, Y.B. (2004) Internalized homophobia and substance use among lesbian, gay, and bisexual persons. *Journal of Gay and Lesbian Social Services: Issues in Practice, Policy and Research*, 17(1), 83–101.

American Psychological Association (1998) A selected bibliography of lesbian, gay, and bisexual concerns in psychology: an affirmative perspective. Available from: www.apa.org/pi/lgbc/publications/pubsreports.html.

Amestoy, M.M. (2001) Research on sexual orientation labels' relationship to behaviors and desires. *Journal of Bisexuality*, 1(4), 91–113.

Anders, M. (2005) Miniature golf. *Journal of Bisexuality*, 5, 111–17.

Anderssen, N., Amlie, C. and Yitterøy, A. (2002) Outcomes for children with lesbian or gay parents. A review of studies from 1978 to 2000. *Scandinavian Journal of Psychology*, 43, 335–51.

Andrews, C. (2008) *Transitioning female-to-male in Australia: a guide for men, their families and service providers*. Morrisville, NC: Lulu Press.

Appleby, Y. (1994) Out on the margins. *Disability and Society*, 9(1), 19–32.

Archer, L. (2001) 'Muslim brothers, black lads, traditional Asians': British Muslim young men's constructions of race, religion and masculinity. *Feminism and Psychology*, 11(1), 79–105.

Asher, N.S. and Asher, K.C. (1999) Qualitative methods for an outsider looking: lesbian women and body image. In M. Kopala and L.A. Suzuki (eds.), *Using qualitative methods in psychology* (pp. 135–44). Thousand Oaks, CA: Sage.

Atkinson, J.M. and Heritage, J. (eds.) (1994) *Structures of social action: studies in conversation analysis*. Cambridge: Cambridge University Press.

Auger, J.A. (1990) Lesbians and aging: triple trouble or tremendous thrill. In S.D. Stone (ed.), *Lesbians in Canada* (pp. 25–34). Toronto: Between the Lines.

Ault, A. (1994) Hegemonic discourse in an oppositional community: lesbian feminists and bisexuality. *Critical Sociology*, 20(3), 107–22.

Axtell, S. (1999) Disability and chronic illness identity: interviews with lesbians and bisexual women and their partners. *International Journal of Sexuality and Gender Studies*, 4(1), 53–72.

Badgett, M.V.L. (1995) The wage effects of sexual orientation discrimination. *Industrial and Labor Relations Review*, 48(3), 726–39.

Bailey, J.V., Farquhar, C., Owen, C. and Mangtani, P. (2004) Sexually transmitted infections in women who have sex with women. *Sexually Transmitted Infections*, 80, 244–6.

Bailey, M.J. (1995) Biological perspectives on sexual orientation. In A.R. D'Augelli and C.J. Patterson (eds.), *Lesbian, gay, and bisexual identities over the lifespan: psychological perspectives* (pp. 102–35). New York: Oxford University Press.

Bailey, M.J., Bobrow, D., Wolfe, M. and Mikach, S. (1995) Sexual orientation of adult sons of gay fathers. *Developmental Psychology*, 31(1), 124–9.

Baldwin, J. (1955) *Notes of a native son*. Boston, MA: Beacon Press.

Balsam, K.F., Beauchaine, T.P., Mickey, R.M. and Rothblum, E.D. (2005) Mental health of lesbian, gay, bisexual, and heterosexual siblings: effects of gender, sexual orientation, and family. *Journal of Abnormal Psychology*, 114(3), 471–6.

Balsam, K.F., Huang, B., Fieland, K.C., Simoni, J.M. and Walters, K.L. (2004) Culture, trauma and wellness: a comparison of heterosexual and lesbian, gay, bisexual and two-spirit Native Americans. *Cultural Diversity and Ethnic Minority Psychology*, 10(3), 287–301.

Banks, C. (2003) The cost of homophobia: literature review on the human impact of homophobia in Canada. Gay and Lesbian Health Services Saskatoon, SK. Available at: www.lgbthealth.net/downloads/research/Human_Impact_of_Homophobia.pdf. Accessed 4 September 2008.

Barker, J.C. (2003) Lesbian aging: an agenda for social research. In G. Herdt and B. de Vries (eds.), *Gay and lesbian aging: research and future directions* (pp. 29–72). New York: Springer.

Barker, M. (2005) This is my partner, and this is my … partner's partner: constructing a polyamorous identity in a monogamous world. *International Journal of Constructivist Psychology*, 18, 75–88.

———(2007) Heteronormativity and the exclusion of bisexuality in psychology. In V. Clarke and E. Peel (eds.), *Out in psychology: lesbian, gay, bisexual, trans and queer perspectives* (pp. 95–117). Chichester: Wiley.

Barker, M., Bowes-Catton, H., Iantaffi, A., Cassidy, A. and Brewer, L. (2008) British bisexuality: a snapshot of bisexual identities in the UK. *Journal of Bisexuality*, 8(1/2), 141–62.

Barker, M., Hagger-Johnson, G., Hegarty, P., Hutchison, C. and Riggs, D.W. (2007) Responses from the BPS Lesbian and Gay Psychology Section to Crossley's 'Making sense of barebacking'. *British Journal of Social Psychology*, 46, 667–77.

Barnard, I. (2003) *Queer race: cultural interventions in the racial politics of queer theory*. New York: Peter Lang.

Barrett, H. and Tasker, F. (2001) Growing up with a gay parent: views of 101 gay fathers on their sons' and daughters' experiences. *Educational and Child Psychology*, 18(1), 62–77.

Barrett, R.R. (2003) Lesbian rituals and dianic tradition. *Journal of Lesbian Studies*, 7(2), 15–28.

Bauer, G.R. and Welles, S.L. (2001) Beyond assumption of negligible risk: sexually transmitted diseases and women who have sex with women. *American Journal of Public Health*, 91(8), 1282–6.

Baumeister, R.F. (2000) Gender differences in erotic plasticity: the female sex drive as socially flexible and responsive. *Psychological Bulletin*, 126(3), 347–74.

Beasley, C. (1999) *What is feminism? An introduction to feminist theory*. London: Sage.

Beehler, G.P. (2001) Confronting the culture of medicine: gay men's experiences with primary health care physicians. *Journal of the Gay and Lesbian Medical Association*, 5(4), 135–41.

Bell, A.P. and Weinberg, M.S. (1978) *Homosexualities: a study of diversity among men and women*. London: Mitchell Beazley.

Bell, A.P., Weinberg, M.S. and Hammersmith, S.K. (1981) *Sexual preference: its development in men and women*. Bloomington: Indiana University Press.

Benjamin, H. (1966) *The transsexual phenomenon*. New York: Julian Press.

Benkov, L. (1995) Lesbian and gay parents: from margin to center. *Journal of Feminist Family Therapy*, 7(1/2), 49–64.

Bennett, C. and Coyle, A. (2007) A minority within a minority: experiences of gay men with intellectual disabilities. In V. Clarke and E. Peel (eds.), *Out in psychology: lesbian, gay, bisexual, trans and queer perspectives* (pp. 125–45). Chichester: Wiley.

Bennett, K.C. and Thompson, N.L. (1991) *Accelerated ageing and male homosexuality: Australian evidence in a continuing debate*. New York: Harrington Park Press.

Bennett, S. (2003) Is there a primary mom? Parental perceptions of attachment bond hierarchies within lesbian adoptive families. *Child and Adolescent Social Work*, 20(3), 159–73.

Berger, R.M. (1980) Psychological adaptation of the older homosexual male. *Journal of Homosexuality*, 5(3), 161–75.

Bettinger, M. (2005) Polyamory and gay men: a family systems approach. *Journal of GLBT Family Studies*, 1(1), 97–116.

Bieber, I. (1965) Clinical aspects of male homosexuality. In J. Marmor (ed.), *Sexual inversion: the multiple roots of homosexuality*. New York: Basic Books.

Bigner, J.J. and Jacobsen, R. (1989a) The value of children to gay and heterosexual fathers. *Journal of Homosexuality*, 18, 167–72.

   (1989b) Parenting behaviors of homosexual and heterosexual fathers. *Journal of Homosexuality*, 18, 173–86.

Black, K.N. and Stevenson, M.R. (1984) The relationship of self-reported sex role characteristics and attitudes toward homosexuality. *Journal of Homosexuality*, 10, 83–93.

Blackwood, E. and Wieringa, S.E. (1999) (eds.), *Female desires: same-sex relations and transgender practices across cultures*. New York: Columbia University Press.

Blando, J.A. (2001) Twice hidden: older gay and lesbian couples, friends, and intimacy. *Generations*, 25(2), 87–9.

Blumstein, P. and Schwartz, P. (1983) *American couples: money, work, sex*. New York: William Morrow and Company.

Bockting, W., Robinson, B., Benner, A. and Scheltema, K. (2004) Patient satisfaction with transgender health services. *Journal of Sex and Marital Therapy*, 30(4), 277–94.

Bockting, W.O., Robinson B.E., Forberg, J. and Scheltema, K. (2005) Evaluation of a sexual health approach to reducing HIV/STD risk in the transgender community. *AIDS Care*, 17(3), 289–303.

Boehmer, U. (2002) Twenty years of public health research: inclusion of lesbian, gay, bisexual, and transgender populations. *American Journal of Public Health*, 92(7), 1125–30.

Bohan, J. (1996) *Psychology and sexual orientation: coming to terms*. New York: Routledge.

Bornstein, K. (1998) *My gender workbook: how to become a real man, a real woman, the real you, or something else entirely*. New York: Routledge.

Bos, H.M.W., van Balen, F. and van dem Boom, D.C. (2003) Planned lesbian families: their desire and motivation to have children. *Human Reproduction*, 18(10), 2216–24.

Boston Lesbian Psychologies Collective (eds.) (1987) *Lesbian psychologies: explorations and challenges*. Urbana: University of Illinois Press.

Bozett, F.W. (1981) Gay fathers: evolution of the gay-father identity. *American Journal of Orthopsychiatry*, 51(3), 552–9.

   (1988) Social control of identity by children of gay fathers. *Western Journal of Nursing Research*, 10(5), 550–65.

Brand, P.A., Rothblum, E.D. and Solomon, L.J. (1992) A comparison of lesbians, gay men, and heterosexuals on weight and restrained eating. *International Journal of Eating Disorders*, 11, 253–9.

Braun, V. (2000) Heterosexism in focus group research: collusion and challenge. *Feminism and Psychology*, 10(1), 133–40.

Braun, V. and Clarke, V. (2006) Using thematic analysis in psychology. *Qualitative Research in Psychology*, 3(2), 77–101.

Braun, V. and Kitzinger, C. (2001) 'Snatch,' 'hole,' or 'honey-pot'? Semantic categories and the problem on nonspecificity in female genital slang. *Journal of Sex Research*, 38(2), 146–58.

Brennan, T. and Hegarty, P. (2007) Who was Magnus Hirschfeld and why do we need to know? *History and Philosophy of Psychology*, 9(1), 12–28.

Brewaeys, A., Devroey, P., Helmerhorst, F.M., Van Hall, E.V. and Ponjaert, I. (1995) Lesbian mothers who conceived after donor insemination: a follow-up study. *Human Reproduction*, 10(10), 2731–5.

Brickell, C. (2001) Whose 'special treatment'? Heterosexism and the problems with liberalism. *Sexualities*, 4, 211–35.

Brown, C. (1998) *Social work and sexuality: working with lesbians and gay men*. London: Macmillan.

Brown, L.S. (1989) New voices, new visions: toward a lesbian/gay paradigm for psychology. *Psychology of Women Quarterly*, 13(4), 445–58.

(1992) While waiting for the revolution: the case for a lesbian feminist psychotherapy. *Feminism and Psychology*, 2(2), 239–53.

Brown, R.D., Clarke, B., Gortmaker, V. and Robinson-Keilig, R. (2004) Assessing the campus climate for gay, lesbian, bisexual, and transgender (GLBT) students using a multiple perspectives approach. *Journal of College Student Development*, 45(1), 8–26.

Browne, K. (2005) Snowball sampling: using social networks to research non-heterosexual women. *International Journal of Social Research Methodology*, 8(1), 47–60.

Bullock, D. (2004). Lesbian cruising: an examination of the concept and methods. *Journal of Homosexuality*, 47, 1–31.

Bullough, V.L. (2003) Magnus Hirschfeld, an often overlooked pioneer. *Sexuality and Culture*, 7(1), 62–77.

Burcombe, R.J., Makris, A., Pitam, M. and Finer, N. (2003) Breast cancer after bilateral subcutaneous mastectomy in a female-to-male trans-sexual. *The Breast*, 12, 290–3.

Burke, L.K. and Follingstad, D.R. (1999) Violence in lesbian and gay relationships: theory, prevalence, and correlational factors. *Clinical Psychology Review*, 19(5), 487–512.

Burman, E. (1994) *Deconstructing developmental psychology*. London: Routledge.

Burns, M., Burgoyne, C. and Clarke, V. (2008) Financial affairs? Money management in same-sex relationships. *Journal of Socio-Economics*, 37(2), 481–501.

Butler, J. (1990) *Gender trouble: feminism and the subversion of identity*. New York: Routledge.

(1993) *Bodies that matter: on the discursive limits of 'sex'*. New York: Routledge.

(1997) *The psychic life of power*. Standford, CA: Stanford University Press.

(2004) *Undoing gender*. New York: Routledge.

Butler, R.N. (1987) Ageism, in *The encyclopedia of ageing* (pp. 22–3). New York: Springer.

Cáceres, C.F. (2002) HIV among gay and other men who have sex with men in Latin America and the Caribbean: a hidden epidemic? *AIDS*, 16, s23–33.

Cahill, S., Battle, J. and Meyer, D. (2003) Partnering, parenting, and policy: family issues affecting Black lesbian, gay, bisexual, and transgender (LGBT) people. *Race and Society*, 6, 85–98.

Carragher, D.J. and Rivers, I. (2002) Trying to hide: a cross-national study of growing up for non-identified gay and bisexual male youth. *Clinical Child Psychology and Psychiatry*, 7(3), 457–74.

Carrington, C. (1999) *No place like home: relationships and family life among lesbians and gay men*. Chicago, IL: University of Chicago Press.

Cass, V.C. (1979) Homosexual identity formation: a theoretical model. *Journal of Homosexuality*, 4(3), 219–35.

(2005) Who is influencing whom? The relationship between identity, sexual orientation and indigenous psychologies. *Gay and Lesbian Issues and Psychology Review*, 1(2), 47–52.

Chaline, E. (2005) Researching sexual difference: a survey of gay S/M in the UK. *Lesbian and Gay Psychology Review*, 6, 240–52.

Chan, C.S. (1996) Don't ask, don't tell, don't know: sexual identity and expression among East Asian-American lesbians. In B. Zimmerman and T. A. H. McNaron (eds.), *The new lesbian studies: into the twenty-first century* (pp. 91–7). New York: The Feminist Press.

Chan, R.W., Brooks, R.C., Raboy, B. and Patterson, C.J. (1998) Division of labour among lesbian and heterosexual parents: associations with children's adjustment. *Journal of Family Psychology*, 12(3), 402–19.

Chandler, M., Panich, E., South, C., Margery, M., Maynard, N. and Newsome, M. (2005) The lion, the witch and the wardrobe: ageing GLBTI's (gay, lesbian, bisexual, transgender, and intersex people) and aged care: a literature review in the Australian context. *Geriaction*, 23, 15–21.

Chesney, M., Chambers, D.B., Taylor, J.M. and Johnson, L.M. (2003) Social support, distress, and well-being in older men living with HIV infection. *Journal of Acquired Immune Deficiency Syndromes*, 33, 185–93.

Clarke, V. (2000) 'Stereotype, attack and stigmatize those who disagree': employing scientific rhetoric in debates about lesbian and gay parenting. *Feminism and Psychology* 10(1), 142–9.

(2001) What about the children? Arguments against lesbian and gay parenting. *Women's Studies International Forum* 24(5), 555–70.

(2002a) Sameness and difference in research on lesbian parenting. *Journal of Community and Applied Social Psychology*, 12, 210–22.

(2002b) Resistance and normalisation in the construction of lesbian and gay families: a discursive analysis. In A. Coyle and C. Kitzinger (eds.), *Lesbian and gay psychology: new perspectives* (pp. 98–118). Oxford: BPS Blackwell.

(2005a) 'We're all very liberal in our views': students' talk about lesbian and gay parenting. *Lesbian and Gay Psychology Review*, 6(1), 2–15.

(2005b) Feminist perspectives on lesbian parenting: a review of the literature 1972–2002. *Psychology of Women Section Review*, 7(2), 11–23.

(2006) 'Gay men, gay men and more gay men': traditional, liberal and critical perspectives on male role models in lesbian families. *Lesbian and Gay Psychology Review*, 7(1), 19–35.

(2007) Man not included? A critical psychology analysis of lesbian families and male influences in child rearing. In F. Tasker and J.J. Bigner (eds.), *Gay and lesbian parenting: new directions* (pp. 309–49). New York: Haworth Press.

(2008) From outsiders to motherhood to reinventing the family: constructions of lesbian parenting in the psychological literature – 1886–2006. *Women's Studies International Forum*, 31, 118–28.

Clarke, V. and Braun, V. (2006) Avoiding heterosexism in teaching social psychology. Poster presented at the Society of Australasian Social Psychologists 35th Annual Conference, Australian National University, Canberra.

(2009) Gender. In D. Fox, I. Prilleltensky and S. Austin (eds.), *Critical psychology: an introduction*, 2nd edition (pp. 232–49). London: Sage.

(2009) Identifying and disrupting the heterosexist and genderist hidden curriculum in higher education: some lessons from psychology. In F. Columbus (ed.), *Sexuality education* (pp. 232–9). New York: Nova Science.

Clarke, V. and Broughton, J. (2005) Parents' pride: Victoria Clarke in conversation with Jenny Broughton. *Lesbian and Gay Psychology Review*, 6(1), 56–60.

Clarke, V., Burgoyne, C. and Burns, M. (2005) For love or money? Comparing lesbian and gay, and heterosexual relationships. *Psychologist* 18(6), 356–8.

(2006) Just a piece of paper? A qualitative exploration of same-sex couples' multiple conceptions of civil partnership and marriage. *Lesbian and Gay Psychology Review* 7(2), 141–61.

(2007) Romance, rights, recognition, responsibilities and radicalism: same-sex couples' views on civil partnership and marriage. In V. Clarke and E. Peel (eds.), *Out in psychology: lesbian, gay, bisexual, trans and queer perspectives* (pp. 173–93). Chichester: Wiley.

(2008) 'Who would take whose name?' Accounts of naming practices in same-sex relationships. *Journal of Community and Applied Social Psychology*, 18(5), 420–39.

Clarke, V. and Hopkins, J. (2002) Victoria Clarke in conversation with June Hopkins. *Lesbian and Gay Psychology Review*, 3(2), 44–7.

Clarke, V. and Kitzinger, C. (2004) Lesbian and gay parents on talk shows: resistance or collusion in heterosexism. *Qualitative Research in Psychology*, 1(3), 195–217.

(2005) 'We're not living on planet lesbian': constructions of male role models in debates about lesbian families. *Sexualities*, 8(2), 137–52.

Clarke, V., Kitzinger, C. and Potter, J. (2004) 'Kids are just cruel anyway': lesbian and gay parents talk about homophobic bullying. *British Journal of Social Psychology* 43(4), 531–50.

Clarke, V. and Peel, E. (eds.) (2004) Special feature on 'The social construction of lesbianism: a reappraisal'. *Feminism and Psychology* 14(4), 485–534.

(2005) LGBT psychology and feminist psychology: bridging the divide. *Psychology of Women Section Review* 7(2), 4–10.

(eds.) (2007a) *Out in psychology: lesbian, gay, bisexual, trans and queer perspectives.* Chichester: Wiley.

(2007b) From lesbian and gay psychology to LGBTQ psychologies: a journey into the unknown (or unknowable)? In V. Clarke and E. Peel (eds.), *Out in psychology: lesbian, gay, bisexual, trans and queer perspectives* (pp. 11–35). Chichester: Wiley.

(2007c) LGBT psychosocial theory and practice in the UK: a review of key contributions and current developments. In E. Peel, V. Clarke and J. Drescher (eds.), *British lesbian, gay, and bisexual psychologies: theory, research and practice* (pp. 7–25). New York: Haworth Press.

Clarke, V. and Rúdólfsdóttir, A.G. (2005) Love conquers all? An exploration of guidance books for family and friends of lesbians and gay men. *Psychology of Women Section Review* 7(2), 37–48.

Clarke, V. and Turner, K. (2007) Clothes maketh the queer? Dress, appearance and the construction of lesbian, gay and bisexual identities. *Feminism and Psychology*, 17(2), 267–76.

Clifford, C. and Orford, J. (2007) The experience of social power in the lives of trans people. In V. Clarke and E. Peel (eds.), *Out in psychology: lesbian, gay, bisexual, trans and queer perspectives* (pp. 195–216). Chichester: Wiley.

Clover, D. (2006) Overcoming barriers for older gay men in the use of health services: a qualitative study of growing older, sexuality and health. *Health Education Journal*, 65(1), 41–52.

Cochran, B.N., Stewart, A.J., Ginzler, J.A. and Cauce, A.M. (2002) Challenges faced by homeless sexual minorities: comparison of gay, lesbian, bisexual, and transgender homeless adolescents with their heterosexual counterparts. *American Journal of Public Health*, 92(5), 773–7.

Cochran, S.D. (2001) Emerging issues in research on lesbians' and gay men's mental health: does sexual orientation really matter? *American Psychologist*, 56(11), 931–47.

Cochran, S.D. and Mays, V.M. (1988) Disclosure of sexual preferences to physicians by black lesbian and bisexual women. *Western Journal of Medicine*, 149, 616–19.

(2000) Relation between psychiatric syndromes and behaviorally defined sexual orientation in a sample of the US population. *American Journal of Epidemiology*, 151(5), 516–23.

Cohen, C.J. (2005) Punks, bulldaggers, and welfare queens: the potential of queer politics? In E.P. Johnson and M.G. Henderson (eds.), *Black queer studies* (pp. 21–51). Durham, NC: Duke University Press.

Cohler, B.J. and Hammack, P.L. (2007) The psychological world of the gay teenager: social change, narrative, and 'normality'. *Journal of Youth and Adolescence*, 36(1), 47–59.

Coleman, E. (1982) Developmental stages of the coming out process. *Journal of Homosexuality*, 7(2/3), 31–43.

Collins, J.F. (2004) The intersection of race and bisexuality: a critical overview of the literature and past, present, and future of the 'borderlands'. *Journal of Bisexuality*, 4(1/2), 100–14.

Conger, J. (1975) Proceedings of the American Psychological Association Incorporated, for the year 1974: minutes of the annual meeting of the Council of Representatives. *American Psychologist*, 60, 620–51.

Cook-Daniels, L. (1997) Lesbian, gay male, bisexual and transgendered elders: elder abuse and neglect issues. *Journal of Elder Abuse and Neglect*, 9, 35–49.

(2000) I hope the blood never washes off your hands: transgender parenting crossing the lines. In J. Wells (ed.), *Home fronts: controversies in nontraditional parenting* (pp. 9–24). Los Angeles: Alyson Books.

Copper, B. (1987) The radical potential in lesbian mothering of daughters. In S. Pollack and J. Vaugn (eds.), *Politics of the heart: a lesbian parenting anthology* (pp. 233–40). Ithaca, NY: Firebrand Books.

Cosgrove, L. (2004) The aftermath of pregnancy loss: a feminist critique of the literature and implications for treatment. *Women and Therapy*, 27(3–4), 107–22.

Coyle, A. (2006) Discourse analysis. In G. M. Breakwell, C. Fife-Schaw, S. Hammond and J. A. Smith (eds.), *Research methods in psychology*, 3rd edition (pp. 366–87). London: Sage.

Coyle, A., Milton, M. and Annesley, P. (2001) The silencing of lesbian and gay voices in psycho-'therapeutic' texts, training and practice. In M. C. Steffens and U. Biechele (eds.), *Annual Review of Lesbian, Gay, and Bisexual Issues in European Psychology*, vol. I (pp. 95–124). Trier: ALGBP.

Coyle, A. and Wilkinson, S. (2002) Social psychological perspectives on lesbian and gay issues in Europe: the state of the art. *Journal of Community and Applied Social Psychology*, 12(3), 147–52.

Crawford, I. and Solliday, E. (1996) The attitudes of undergraduate college students toward gay parenting. *Journal of Homosexuality*, 30, 63–77.

Crawford, M. (1995) *Talking difference: on gender and language*. London: Sage.

(ed.) (2000) A reappraisal of gender: an ethnomethodological approach. *Feminism and Psychology*, 10(1), 7–72.

Crenshaw, K. M. (1991) Mapping the margins: intersectionality, identity politics, and violence against women of color. *Stanford Law Review*, 43(6), 1241–99.

Crimp, D. (1988) AIDS: cultural analysis/cultural activism. In D. Crimp (ed.), *AIDS: cultural analysis/cultural activism* (pp. 3–16). Cambridge, MA: MIT Press.

Croom, G. (2000) Lesbian, gay, and bisexual people of color: a challenge to representative sampling in empirical research. In B. Greene and G. Croom (eds.), *Education, research, and practice in lesbian, gay, bisexual, and transgender psychology* (pp. 263–81). Thousand Oaks, CA: Sage.

Crosbie-Burnett, M. and Helmbrecht, L. (1993) A descriptive empirical study of gay male stepfamilies. *Family Relations*, 42, 256–62.

Crossley, M. L. (2000) *Rethinking health psychology*. Milton Keynes: Open University Press.

Crowley, C., Harré, R. and Lunt, I. (2007) Safe spaces and sense of identity: views and experiences of lesbian, gay and bisexual young people. In E. Peel and V. Clarke (eds.), *British lesbian, gay and bisexual psychologies: theory, research and practice* (pp. 127–43). Binghamton, NY: Haworth Press.

D'Augelli, A. R. (1989) Lesbians' and gay men's experiences of discrimination and harassment in a university community. *American Journal of Community Psychology*, 17(3), 317–21.

(1992) Lesbian and gay male undergraduates' experiences of harassment and fear on campus. *Journal of Interpersonal Violence*, 7, 383–95.

(2003) Foreword: toward the future of lesbian, gay, bisexual, and transgender populations. In W. Meezan and J. I. Martin (eds.), *Research methods with gay, lesbian, bisexual, and transgender populations* (pp. xix–xxii). New York: Harrington Park Press.

D'Augelli, A. R. and Hart, M. M. (1987) Gay women, men, and families in rural settings: toward the development of helping communities. *American Journal of Community Psychology*, 15(1), 79–93.

Davies, D. (1996) Towards a model of gay affirmative therapy. In D. Davies and N. Charles (eds.), *Pink therapy: a guide for counsellors and therapists working with lesbian, gay and bisexual clients* (pp. 24–40). Buckingham: Open University Press.

Davis, C.M., Yarber, W.L., Bauserman, R., Schreer, G.E. and Davis, S.L. (eds.) (2004) *Handbook of sexuality-related measures*. Thousand Oaks, CA: Sage.

Demasi, S. (2003) 'I just want to be normal': women's initiation into heterosexual dating. In R. Heasley and B. Crane (eds.), *Sexual lives: a reader on the theories and realities of human sexualities* (pp. 108–19). Boston, MA: McGraw-Hill.

Denny, D. (2004) Changing models of transsexualism. In U. Leli and J. Drescher (eds.), *Transgender subjectivities: a clinician's guide* (pp. 25–40). New York: Haworth Press.

Derrida, J. (1998) *Of grammatology*, trans. G. Spivak. Baltimore, MD: Johns Hopkins University Press.

De Sutter, P. (2001) Gender reassignment and assisted reproduction: present and future reproduction options for transsexual people. *Human Reproduction*, 16(4), 612–14.

De Sutter, P., Kira, K., Verschoor, A. and Hotimsky, A. (2002) The desire to have children and the preservation of fertility in transsexual women: a survey. *International Journal of Transgenderism*, 6(3), www.symposion.com/ijt/index.htm.

Devor, H. (1993) Sexual orientation identities, attractions, and practices of female-to-male transsexuals. *Journal of Sex Research*, 30(6), 303–15.

de Vries, B. and Blando, J.A. (2003) The study of gay and lesbian aging: lessons for social gerontology. In G. Herdt and B. de Vries (eds.), *Gay and lesbian aging: research and future directions* (pp. 3–28). New York: Springer.

de Vries, A.L.C., Cohen-Kettenis, P.T. and Delemarre-van de Waal, H. (2007) Clinical management of gender dysphoria in adolescents. *International Journal of Transgenderism*, 9(3/4), 83–94.

di Ceglie, D. (1998) Children of transsexual parents: mental health issues and some principles of management. In D. de Ceglie and D. Freedman (eds.), *A stranger in my own body: atypical gender identity development and mental health* (pp. 266–74). London: Karnac.

DiLapi, E.M. (1989) Lesbian mothers and the motherhood hierarchy. *Journal of Homosexuality*, 18(1/2), 101–21.

D'Onofrio, S.A (2004) Polyamory. In J. Eadie (ed.), *Sexuality: the essential glossary* (pp. 164–5). London: Arnold.

Diamond, L.M. (2003) Was it a phase? Young women's relinquishment of lesbian/ bisexual identities over a 5-year period. *Journal of Personality and Social Psychology*, 84(2), 352–64.

    (2005) 'I'm straight, but I kissed a girl': the trouble with American media representations of female–female sexuality. *Feminism and Psychology*, 15(1), 104–10.

    (2006) *What we got wrong about sexuality and gender identity development: unexpected findings from a longitudinal study of young women*. Washington, DC: American Psychological Association.

    (2008) Female bisexuality from adolescence to adulthood: results from a 10-year longitudinal study. *Developmental Psychology*, 44(1), 5–14.

Dohrenwend, B.P. (2000) The roles of adversity and stress in psychopathology: some evidence and its implications for theory and research. *Journal of Health and Social Behavior*, 14(1), 1–19.

Doka, K. (1989) *Disenfranchised grief: recognising hidden sorrow*. New York: Lexington Books.

Dolan, K.A. and Davis, P.W. (2003) Nuances and shifts in lesbian women's constructions of STI and HIV vulnerability. *Social Science and Medicine*, 57(1), 25–38.

Douglas, C.A. (1990) *Love and politics: radical feminism and lesbian theories*. San Francisco, CA: ISM Press.

Dreger, A.D. (1998) *Hermaphrodites and the medical invention of sex*. Cambridge, MA: Harvard University Press.

Dryden, C. (1999) *Being married, doing gender: a critical analysis of gender relationships in marriage*. London: Routledge.

Dunne, G.A. (1997) *Lesbian lifestyles: women's work and the politics of sexuality*. London: Macmillan.

(1998) 'Pioneers behind our own front doors': towards greater balance in the organisation of work in partnerships. *Work, Employment and Society*, 12(2), 273–95.

(2001) The lady vanishes? Reflections on the experiences of married and divorced non-heterosexual fathers. *Sociological Research Online*, 6(3), www.socresonline.org.uk/6/3/dunne.html.

(2003) A passion for 'sameness'? Sexuality and gender accountability. In J. Weeks, J. Holland and M. Waites (eds.), *Sexualities and society: a reader* (pp. 57–68). Cambridge: Polity.

Edwards, D. and Potter, J. (1992) *Discursive psychology*. London: Sage.

Eliason, M.J. (1996) A survey of the campus climate for lesbian, gay, and bisexual university members. *Journal of Psychology and Human Sexuality*, 8(4), 39–58.

(2001) Bi-negativity: the stigma facing bisexual men. *Journal of Bisexuality*, 1(2/3), 137–54.

Eliason, M.J. and Schope, R. (2001) Does 'don't ask don't tell' apply to health care? Lesbian, gay and bisexual people's disclosure to health care providers. *Journal of the Gay and Lesbian Medical Association*, 5(4), 125–34.

Elliot, P. (2009) Engaging trans debates on gender variance: a feminist analysis. *Sexualities*, 12(1), 5–32.

Ellis, H. and Symonds, J.A. (2007) *Sexual inversion: a critical edition*, ed. I. Crozier. Basingstoke: Palgrave Macmillan.

Ellis, S.J. (2001) Doing being liberal: implicit prejudice in focus group talk about lesbian and gay human rights issues. *Lesbian and Gay Psychology Review*, 2(2), 43–9.

(2002a) Student support for lesbian and gay human rights: findings from a large-scale questionnaire study. In A. Coyle and C. Kitzinger (eds.), *Lesbian and gay psychology: new perspectives* (pp. 239–54). Oxford: BPS Blackwell.

(2002b) Moral reasoning and homosexuality: the acceptability of arguments about lesbian and gay issues. *Journal of Moral Education*, 31(4), 455–67.

(2004a) Ignorance is bliss? Undergraduate students and lesbian and gay culture. *Lesbian and Gay Psychology Review*, 5(2), 42–7.

(2004b) Young people and political action: who's taking responsibility for positive social change. *Journal of Youth Studies*, 7(1), 89–102.

(2004c) Rights-based reasoning in discussions about lesbian and gay issues: implications for moral educators. *Journal of Moral Education*, 33(1), 71–86.

(2007a) Community in the 21st century: issues arising from a study of British lesbians and gay men. In E. Peel, V. Clarke and J. Drescher (eds.), *British lesbian, gay and bisexual psychologies: theory, research and practice* (pp. 111–26). New York: Haworth Press.

(2007b) Homophobia, rights and community: contemporary issues in the lives of LGB people in the UK. In V. Clarke and E. Peel (eds.), *Out in psychology: lesbian, gay, bisexual, trans and queer perspectives* (pp. 311–30). Chichester: Wiley.

(2009) Diversity and inclusivity at university: a survey of the experiences of lesbian, gay, bisexual and trans (LGBT) students in the UK. *Higher Education*, 57(6), 723–39.

Ellis, S.J. and Kitzinger, C. (2002) Denying equality: an analysis of arguments against lowering the age of consent for sex between men. *Journal of Community and Applied Social Psychology*, 12, 167–80.

Ellis, S.J., Kitzinger, C. and Wilkinson, S. (2002) Attitudes towards lesbians and gay men and support for lesbian and gay human rights among psychology students. *Journal of Homosexuality*, 44(1), 121–38.

Epple, C. (1998) Coming to terms with Navajo nádleehí: a critique of berdache, 'gay', 'alternate gender', and 'two spirit'. *American Ethnologist*, 25(2), 267–90.

Epstein, S. (2003) Sexualising governance and medicalising identities: the emergence of a 'state-centered' LGBT health politics in the United States. *Sexualities*, 6(2), 131–71.

Equal Opportunities Commission (2006) *Facts about women and men in Great Britain*. London: EOC.

Ericksen, J.A. and Steffen, S.A. (1999) *Kiss and tell: surveying sex in the twentieth century*. Cambridge, MA: Harvard University Press.

Espin, O.M. (1995) 'Race', racism, and sexuality in the life narratives of immigrant women. *Feminism and Psychology*, 5(2), 223–38.

Evans, A.L., Scally, A.J., Wellard, S.J. and Wilson, J.D. (2007) Prevalence of bacterial vaginosis in lesbians and heterosexual women in a community setting. *Sexually Transmitted Infections*, 83, 470–5.

Evans, N.J. and Broido, E.M. (2002) The experiences of lesbian and bisexual women in college residence halls: implications for addressing homophobia and heterosexism. *Journal of Lesbian Studies*, 6(3/4), 29–42.

Factor, R.J. and Rothblum, E.D. (2008) A study of transgender adults and their non-transgender siblings on demographic characteristics, social support, and experiences of violence. *Journal of LGBT Health Research*, 3(3), 11–30.

Faderman, L. (1991) *Odd girls and twilight lovers: a history of lesbian life in twentieth century America*. New York: Columbia University Press.

Farquhar, C., Bailey, J. and Whittaker, D. (2001) *Are lesbians sexually healthy? A report of the 'Lesbian sexual behaviour and health survey'*. London South Bank University. Available at: www.lsbu.ac.uk/ahs/research/reports/clare/index.shtml, accessed 6 September 2008.

Feldman, J. (2002) New onset of type 2 diabetes mellitus with feminizing hormone therapy: case series. *International Journal of Transgenderism* 6(2). Available at: www.symposion.com/ijt/ijtvo06no02_01.htm, accessed 10 October 2008.

Feldman, J. and Bockting, W.O. (2003) Transgender health. *Minnesota Medicine*, 86(7), 25–32.

Fell, G., Mattiske, J. and Riggs, D.W. (2008). Challenging heteronormativity in psychological practice with lesbian, gay and bisexual clients: a workshop. *Gay and Lesbian Issues and Psychology Review*, 4(2), 127–40.

Fish, J. (1999) Sampling lesbians: how to get 1000 lesbians to complete a questionnaire. *Feminism and Psychology*, 9, 229–38.

(2006) *Heterosexism in health and social care.* Basingstoke: Palgrave Macmillan.

(2007) Far from mundane: theorising heterosexism for social work education. *Social Work Education*, 27(2), 182–93.

(2008) Navigating queer street: researching the intersections of lesbian, gay, bisexual and trans (LGBT) identities in health research. *Sociological Research Online*, 13(1), www.socresonline.org.uk/14/1/12.html.

Fish, J. and Anthony, D. (2005) UK national lesbians and health care survey. *Women and Health*, 41(3), 27–45.

Fish, J. and Wilkinson, S. (2000) Lesbians and cervical screening: preliminary results from a UK survey of lesbian health. *Psychology of Women Section Review*, 2, 45–68.

(2003) Understanding lesbians' healthcare behaviour: the case of breast self-examination. *Social Science and Medicine*, 56, 235–45.

Fitzgerald, S.B. (2004) Making the transition: understanding the longevity of lesbian relationships. In J.S. Weinstock and E.D. Rothblum (eds.), *Lesbian ex-lovers: the really long-term relationship* (pp. 177–92). New York: Harrington Park Press.

Flaks, D.K., Ficher, I., Masterpasqua, F. and Joseph, G. (1995) Lesbians choosing mother-hood: a comparative study of lesbian and heterosexual parents and their children. *Developmental Psychology*, 31(1), 105–14.

Flowers, P. (2001) Gay men and HIV/AIDS risk management. *Health*, 5(1), 50–75.

Flowers, P. and Buston, K. (2001) 'I was terrified of being different': exploring gay men's accounts of growing-up in a heterosexist society. *Journal of Adolescence*, 24(1), 51–65.

Flowers, P., Duncan, B. and Knussen, C. (2003) Reappraising HIV testing: an exploration of the psychosocial costs and benefits associated with learning one's HIV status in a purposive sample of Scottish gay men. *British Journal of Health Psychology*, 8, 179–94.

Flowers, P., Hart, G., Williamson, L., Frankis, J. and Der, G. (2002) Does bar-based, peer-led sexual health promotion have a community-level effect amongst gay men in Scotland? *International Journal of STD and AIDS*, 13, 102–8.

Flowers, P., Marriott, C. and Hart, G. (2000) The bar, the bogs and the bushes: the impact of locale on sexual cultures. *Culture, Health and Sexuality*, 2, 69–86.

Flowers, P., Sheeran, P., Beail, N. and Smith, J.A. (1997a) The role of psychosocial factors in HIV risk reduction among gay and bisexual men: a quantitative review. *Psychology and Health*, 12, 197–230.

Flowers, P., Smith, J.A., Sheeran, P. and Beail, N. (1997b) Health and romance: under-standing unprotected sex in relationships between gay men. *British Journal of Health Psychology*, 2, 73–86.

Folgerø, T. (2008) Queer nuclear families: reproducing and transgressing heteronorma-tivity. *Journal of Homosexuality*, 54(1/2), 124–49.

Foucault, M. (1978) *The history of sexuality*, vol. I., trans. R. Hurley. New York: Vintage Books.

Fox, D. and Prilleltensky, I. (eds.) (1997) *Critical psychology: an introduction.* London: Sage.

Fox, D., Prilleltensky, I. and Austin, S. (eds.) (2009) *Critical psychology: an introduction*, 2nd edition. London: Sage.

Fox, R.C. (1995) Bisexual identities. In A.R. D'Augelli and C.J. Patterson (eds.), *Lesbian, gay, and bisexual identities over the lifespan: psychological perspectives* (pp. 48–86). New York: Oxford University Press.

Fraley, S.S., Mona, L.R. and Theodore, P.S. (2007) The sexual lives of lesbian, gay, and bisexual people with disabilities: psychological perspectives. *Sexuality Research and Social Policy*, 4(1), 15–26.

Francher, J.S. and Henkin, J. (1973) The menopausal queen: adjustment to aging and the male homosexual. *American Journal of Orthopsychiatry*, 43, 670–4.

Frankis, J. and Flowers, P. (2005) Men who have sex with men (MSM) in public sex environments (PSEs): a systematic review of quantitative literature. *AIDS Care*, 17, 273–88.

Fraser, V. (2009). Online bodies and sexual subjectivities: in whose image? In B. Baird and D.W. Riggs (eds.), *The racial politics of bodies, nations and knowledges* (pp. 116–32). Cambridge: Cambridge Scholars Press.

Freedman, D., Tasker, F. and di Ceglie, D. (2002) Children and adolescents with transsexual parents referred to a specialist gender identity development service: a brief report of key developmental features. *Clinical Child Psychology and Psychiatry*, 7(3), 423–32.

Freud, S. (1953 [1905]) *Three essays on the theory of sexuality*. In *The standard edition of the complete psychological works of Sigmund Freud* (vol. LXXVIII, pp. 125–43). London: Hogarth Press.

Friend, R.A. (1991) Older lesbian and gay people: a theory of successful ageing. In J.A. Lee (ed.), *Gay midlife and maturity* (pp. 99–118). New York: Haworth Press.

Frith, H. (2000) Focusing on sex: using focus groups in sex research. *Sexualities*, 3(3), 275–97.

Fulcher, M., Sutfin, E.L. and Patterson, C.J. (2008) Individual differences in gender development: associations with parental sexual orientation, attitudes, and division of labor. *Sex Roles*, 58, 330–41.

Gabb, J. (2004) Critical differentials: querying the incongruities within research on lesbian families. *Sexualities*, 7(2), 167–82.

Gagné, P., Tewksbury, R. and McGaughey, D. (1997) Coming out and crossing over: identity formation and proclamation in a transgender community. *Gender and Society*, 11(4), 478–508.

Garfinkel, H. (1967). *Studies in ethnomethodology*. Cambridge: Polity Press.

Garnets, L., Hancock, K., Cochran, S., Goodchilds, J. and Peplau, L. (1991) Issues in psychotherapy with lesbians and gay men: a survey of psychologists. *American Psychologist*, 30, 964–72.

Garnets, L.D. and Kimmel, D.C. (eds.) (1993) *Psychological perspectives on lesbian and gay male experiences*. New York: Columbia University Press.

Gartrell, N., Rodas, C., Deck, A., Peyser, H. and Banks, A. (2006) The USA National Lesbian Family Study: interviews with mothers of 10-year-olds. *Feminism and Psychology*, 16(2), 175–92.

Gauthier, D.K. and Forsyth, C.J. (1999) Bareback sex, bug chasers, and the gift of death. *Deviant Behavior: An Interdisciplinary Journal*, 20, 85–100.

Gavey, N. (1996) Women's desire and sexual violence discourse. In S. Wilkinson (ed.), *Feminist social psychologies: international perspectives* (pp. 51–65). Buckingham: Open University Press.

Gay and Lesbian Medical Association (2001) *Healthy people 2010 companion document for lesbian, gay, bisexual, and transgender (LGBT) health*. San Francisco, CA: GLMA.

Gergen, K.J. (1973) Social psychology as history. *Journal of Personality and Social Psychology*, 26, 309–20.

Gianino, M. (2008) Adaptation and transformation: the transition to adoptive parenthood for gay male couples. *Journal of GLBT Family Studies*, 4(2), 205–43.

Gilman, S.E., Cochran, S.D., Mays, V.M., Hughes, M., Ostrow, D. and Kessler, R.C. (2001). Risk of psychiatric disorders among individuals reporting same-sex sexual partners in the National Comorbidity Survey. *American Journal of Public Health*, 91(6), 933–9.

Goldberg, A.E. (2007a) Talking about family: disclosure practices of adults raised by lesbian, gay, and bisexual parents. *Journal of Family Issues*, 28(1), 100–31.

(2007b) (How) does it make a difference? Perspectives of adults with lesbian, gay, and bisexual parents. *American Journal of Orthopsychiatry*, 77(4), 550–62.

Goldberg, A.E. and Allen, K.A. (2007) Imagining men: lesbian mothers' perceptions of male involvement during the transition to parenthood. *Journal of Marriage and Family*, 69, 352–65.

Golombok, S. (2000) *Parenting: what really counts?* London: Routledge.

(2007) Foreword: research on gay and lesbian parenting: a historical perspective across 30 years. In F. Tasker and J.J. Bigner (eds.), *Gay and lesbian parenting: new directions* (pp. xv–xxi). New York: Haworth Press.

Golombok, S., Perry, B., Burston, A., Murray, C., Mooney-Somers, J., Stevens, M. and Golding, J. (2003) Children with lesbian parents: a community study. *Developmental Psychology*, 39(1), 20–33.

Golombok, S., Spencer, A. and Rutter, M. (1983) Children in lesbian and single-parent households: psychosexual and psychiatric appraisal. *Child Psychology and Psychiatry*, 24, 551–72.

Golombok, S., Tasker, F. and Murray, C. (1997) Children raised in fatherless families from infancy: family relationships and the socioemotional development of children of lesbian and single heterosexual mothers. *Journal of Child Psychology and Psychiatry*, 38(7), 783–91.

Gordon, L.E. (2006) Bringing the U-haul: embracing and resisting sexual stereotypes in a lesbian community. *Sexualities*, 9, 171–92.

Gorman-Murray, A. (2008) Queering the family home: narratives from gay, lesbian and bisexual youth coming out in supportive family homes in Australia. *Gender, Place and Culture*, 15(1), 31–44.

Gottschalk, L. (2003) From gender inversion to choice and back: changing perceptions of the aetiology of lesbianism over three historical periods. *Women's Studies International Forum*, 26(3), 221–33.

Gough, B. (2002) 'I've always tolerated it but …': heterosexual masculinity and the discursive reproduction of homophobia. In A. Coyle and C. Kitzinger (eds.), *Lesbian and gay psychology: new perspectives* (pp. 219–38). Oxford: BPS Blackwell.

(2007) Coming out in the heterosexist world of sport: a qualitative analysis of web postings by heterosexual athletes. In E. Peel, V. Clarke and J. Drescher (eds.), *British lesbian, gay, and bisexual psychologies: theory, research and practice* (pp. 153–74). New York: Haworth Medical Press.

Gough, B. and McFadden, M. (2001) *Critical social psychology: an introduction.* Basingstoke: Palgrave.

Grack, C. and Richman, C.L. (1996) Reducing general and specific heterosexism through cooperative contact. *Journal of Psychology and Human Sexuality*, 8(4), 59–68.

Graham, S. (2004) While driving, drink water: bisexual and transgender intersections in South Sulawesi, Indonesia. *Journal of Bisexuality*, 3(3/4), 231–48.

Green, R. (1978) Sexual identity of 37 children raised by homosexual or transsexual parents. *American Journal of Psychiatry*, 135, 692–7.

(1987) *The 'sissy boy syndrome' and the development of homosexuality*. New Haven, CT: Yale University Press.

(1998) Transsexuals' children. *International Journal of Transgenderism*, 2(4), www.symposion.com/ijt/index.htm.

Greene, B. (1997) Ethnic minority lesbians and gay men: mental health and treatment issues. In B. Greene (ed.), *Ethnic and cultural diversity among lesbians and gay men* (pp. 216–39). London: Sage.

(2000) Beyond heterosexism and across the cultural divide: developing an inclusive lesbian, gay and bisexual psychology: a look to the future. In B. Greene and G.L. Croome (eds.), *Education, research and practice in lesbian, gay, bisexual and transgendered psychology: a resource manual* (pp. 1–45). Thousand Oaks, CA: Sage.

(2004) African American lesbians and other culturally diverse people in psychodynamic psychotherapies: useful paradigm or oxymoron? *Journal of Lesbian Studies*, 8(1/2), 57–77.

(2005) Psychology, diversity and social justice: beyond heterosexism and across the cultural divide. *Journal of Counseling Psychology Quarterly*, 18(4), 295–306.

Greene, B., Miville, M.L. and Ferguson, A.D. (2008) Lesbian and bisexual women of color, racism, heterosexism, homophobia and health: a recommended intervention and research agenda. In B. Wallace (ed.), *Toward equity in health: a new global approach to health disparities* (pp. 413–26). New York: Springer Publications.

Griffin, C. (2000) Absences that matter: constructions of sexuality in studies of young women's friendships. *Feminism and Psychology*, 10(2), 227–45.

Griffin, P. (1992) From hiding out to coming out: empowering lesbian and gay educators. In K.M. Harbeck (ed.), *Coming out of the classroom closet* (pp. 167–96). New York: Haworth Press.

Gross, M. (2006) Biparental and multiparental lesbian and gay families in France. *Lesbian and Gay Psychology Review*, 7(1), 36–47.

Grossman, A.H. and D'Augelli, A.R. (2006) Transgender youth: invisible and vulnerable. *Journal of Homosexuality*, 51(1), 111–28.

Grossman, A.H., D'Augelli, A.R., Salter, N.P. and Hubbard, S.M. (2006) Female-to-male and male-to-female transgender youth: comparing gender expression, gender atypicality, and parents' responses. *Journal of Gay, Lesbian, Bisexual and Transgender Counseling*, 1(1), 41–59.

Gurevich, M., Bower, J., Mathieson, C.M. and Dhayanandhan, B. (2007) 'What do they look like and are they among us?': bisexuality, (dis)closure and (un)viability. In V. Clarke and E. Peel (eds.), *Out in psychology: lesbian, gay, bisexual, trans and queer perspectives* (pp. 217–41). Chichester: Wiley.

Haag, A.M. and Chang, F.K. (1997) The impact of electronic networking on the lesbian and gay community. In J.D. Smith and R.J. Mancoske (eds.), *Rural gays and lesbians: building on the strengths of communities* (pp. 83–94). New York: Haworth Press.

Hale, J. (2006) Suggested rules for non-transsexuals writing about transsexuals, trans-sexuality, transsexualism, or trans. Available at: http://sandystone.com/hale.rules.html.

Hall, K.Q. (2003) Feminism, disability, and embodiment. *NWSA Journal*, 14(1), vii–xiii.

Halperin, C.T., Young, M.L., Waller, M., Martin, S. and Kupper. L. (2004) Prevalence of partner violence in same sex romantic and sexual relationships in a national sample of adolescents. *Journal of Adolescent Health*, 35(2), 124–31.

Halperin, D. (1990) *One hundred years of homosexuality and other essays on Greek love.* New York: Routledge.

  (2007) *What do gay men want? An essay on sex, risk and subjectivity.* Ann Arbor: University of Michigan Press.

Hamer, D.H., Hu, S., Magnuson, V.L., Hu, N. and Pattatucci, A.M.L. (1993) A linkage between DNA markers on the X chromosome and male sexual orientation. *Science*, 261, 321–7.

Han, A. (2006) 'I think you're the smartest race I've ever met': racialised economies of queer male desire. *ACRAWSA e-journal*, 2(2), www.ejournal.acrawsa.org.au, accessed 26 June 2008.

Hansen, G.L. (1982) Measuring prejudice against homosexuality (homosexism) among college students: a new scale. *Journal of Social Psychology*, 117, 233–6.

Harding, R. and Peel, E. (2006) 'We do'? International perspectives on equality, legality and same sex relationships. *Lesbian and Gay Psychology Review*, 7(2), 123–40.

  (2007a) Surveying sexualities: Internet research with non-heterosexuals. *Feminism and Psychology*, 17(2), 277–85.

  (2007b) Heterosexism at work: diversity training, discrimination law and the limits of liberal individualism. In V. Clarke and E. Peel (eds.), *Out in psychology: lesbian, gay, bisexual, trans and queer perspectives* (pp. 247–71). Chichester: Wiley.

Harding, S. (1991) *Whose science? Whose knowledge? Thinking from women's lives.* Ithaca, NY: Cornell University Press.

Harrison, J. and Riggs, D.W. (2006) Editorial: LGBTI ageing. *Gay and Lesbian Issues and Psychology Review*, 2(2), 42–3.

Hart, J. and Richardson, D. (eds.) (1981) *The theory and practice of homosexuality.* London: Routledge and Kegan Paul.

Hash, K.M. and Cramer, E.P. (2003) Empowering gay and lesbian caregivers and uncovering their unique experiences through the use of qualitative methods. In W. Meezan and J.I. Martin (eds.), *Research methods with gay, lesbian, bisexual, and transgender populations* (pp. 47–63). New York: Harrington Park Press.

Heaphy, B., Weeks, J. and Donovan, C. (1998) 'That's like my life': researching stories of non-heterosexual relationships. *Sexualities*, 1(4), 453–70.

Heaphy, B. and Yip, A.K.T. (2003) Uneven possibilities: understanding non-heterosexual ageing and the implications of social change. *Sociological Research Online*, 8(4), www.socresonline.org.uk/8/4/heaphy.html.

  (2006) Policy implications of ageing sexualities. *Social Policy and Society*, 5(4), 443–51.

Heaphy, B., Yip, A.K.T. and Thompson, D. (2003) *Lesbian, gay and bisexual lives over 50.* Nottingham: York House Publications.

  (2004) Ageing in a non-heterosexual context. *Ageing and Society*, 24, 881–902.

Hegarty, P. (1997) Materializing the hypothalamus: a performative account of the 'gay brain'. *Feminism and Psychology*, 7(3), 355–72.

(2002) 'It's not a choice, it's the way we're built': symbolic beliefs about sexual orientation in the US and Britain. *Journal of Community and Applied Social Psychology*, 12, 153–66.

(2003a) Pointing to a crisis? What finger-length ratios tell us about the construction of sexuality. *Radical Statistics*, 83, 16–30.

(2003b) Homosexual signs and heterosexual silences: Rorschach studies of male homosexuality from 1921 to 1967. *Journal of the History of Sexuality*, 12, 400–23.

(2007a) From genius inverts to gendered intelligence: Lewis Terman and the power of the norm. *History of Psychology*, 10, 132–55.

(2007b) What comes after discourse analysis for LGBTQ psychology? In V. Clarke and E. Peel (eds.), *Out in psychology: lesbian, gay, bisexual, trans and queer perspectives* (pp. 41–57). Chichester: Wiley.

Hegarty, P. and Buechel, C. (2006) Androcentric reporting of gender differences in APA articles, 1965–2004. *Review of General Psychology*, 10, 377–89.

Hegarty, P. and Golden, A.M. (2008) Attributions about the controllability of stigmatized traits: antecedents or justifications of prejudice? *Journal of Applied Social Psychology*, 38, 1023–44.

Hegarty, P. and Massey, S. (2006) Anti-homosexual prejudice … as opposed to what? Queer theory and the social psychology of anti-homosexual attitudes. *Journal of Homosexuality*, 52(1/2), 47–71.

Hegarty, P. and Pratto, F. (2001) The effects of category norms and stereotypes on explanations of intergroup differences. *Journal of Personality and Social Psychology*, 80, 723–35.

(2004) The differences that norms make: empiricism, social constructionism and the interpretation of group differences. *Sex Roles*, 50, 445–53.

Hennen, P. (2004) Fae spirits and gender trouble. *Journal of Contemporary Ethnography*, 33(5), 499–533.

Henrickson, M. (2007) Reaching out, hooking up: lavender netlife in a New Zealand study. *Sexuality Research and Social Policy*, 4(2), 38–49.

Herdt, G., Beeler, J. and Rawls, T.W. (1997) Life course diversity among older lesbians and gay men: a study in Chicago. *Journal of Gay, Lesbian, and Bisexual Identity*, 2(3/4), 231–46.

Herek, G.M. (1984) Attitudes toward lesbians and gay men: a factor-analytic study. *Journal of Homosexuality*, 10(1/2), 39–51.

(1990) The context of anti-gay violence: notes on cultural and psychological heterosexism. *Journal of Interpersonal Violence*, 5(3), 316–33.

(2004) Beyond 'homophobia': thinking about sexual prejudice and stigma in the twenty-first century. *Sexuality Research and Social Policy*, 1(2), 6–23.

(2009) Hate crimes and stigma-related experiences among sexual minority adults in the United States: prevalence estimates from a national probability sample. *Journal of Interpersonal Violence*, [DOI: 10.1177/0886260508316477].

Herek, G.M., Gillis, J.R. and Cogan, J.C. (1999) Psychological sequelae of hate-crime victimization among lesbian, gay, and bisexual adults. *Journal of Consulting and Clinical Psychology*, 67(6), 945–51.

Herek, G.M., Gillis, J.R., Cogan, J.C. and Glunt, E.K. (1997) Hate crime victimization among lesbian, gay, and bisexual adults: prevalence, psychological correlates, and methodological issues. *Journal of Interpersonal Violence*, 12(2), 195–215.

Herek, G.M., Kimmel, D.C., Amaro, H. and Melton, G.B. (1991) Avoiding heterosexual bias in psychological research. *American Psychologist*, 46(9), 957–63.

Hershberger, S.L. and D'Augelli, A.R. (1995) The impact of victimization on the mental health and suicidality of lesbian, gay, and bisexual youths. *Developmental Psychology*, 31, 65–74.

Hewitt, C. (1995) The socioeconomic position of gay men: a review of the evidence. *American Journal of Economics and Sociology*, 54(4), 461–79.

Hicks, S. (2005a) Lesbian and gay foster care and adoption: a brief UK history. *Adoption and Fostering*, 29, 42–55.

(2005b) Is gay parenting bad for kids? Responding to the 'very idea of difference' in research on lesbian and gay parents. *Sexualities*, 8(2), 153–68.

(2008) Gender role models … who needs 'em?! *Qualitative Social Work*, 7(1), 43–59.

Hicks, S. and McDermott, J. (1999) *Lesbian and gay fostering and adoption: extraordinary yet ordinary.* London: Jessica Kingsley.

Hill, D.B. and Willoughby, B.L.B. (2005) The development and validation of the genderism and transphobia scale. *Sex Roles*, 53(7/8), 531–44.

Hill, M. (1987) Child-rearing attitudes of black lesbian mothers. In Boston Lesbian Psychologies Collective (eds.), *Lesbian psychologies: explorations and challenges* (pp. 215–26). Chicago, IL: University of Illinois Press.

Hill Collins, P. (1990) *Black feminist thought: knowledge, consciousness and the politics of empowerment.* Boston, MA: Unwin Hyman.

Hiller, L., Visser, R., Kavanagh, A. and McNair, R. (2004) The drug use patterns of heterosexual and non-heterosexual women: data from the Women's Health Australia Study. In D.W. Riggs and G.A. Walker (eds.), *Out in the Antipodes: Australian and New Zealand perspectives on gay and lesbian issues in psychology* (pp. 192–211). Perth: Brightfire Press.

Hillier, L. (2002) 'It's a catch 22': same-sex-attracted young people on coming out to parents. In S.S. Feldman and D.A Rosenthal (eds.), *Talking sexuality: parent–adolescent communication* (pp. 75–91). San Francisco: Jossey Bass.

Hillier, L. and Harrison, L. (2007) Building realities less limited than their own: young people practising same-sex attraction on the internet. *Sexualities*, 10(1), 82–100.

Hillier, L., Turner, A. and Mitchell, A. (2005) Writing themselves in again: 6 years on. The 2nd national report on the sexuality, health and wellbeing of same sex attracted young people in Australia. Melbourne: Australian Research Centre in Sex, Health and Society (ARCSHS). Available at: www.latrobe.edu.au/arcshs.

Hillman, J. and Martin, R.A. (2002) Lessons about gay and lesbian lives: a spaceship exercise. *Teaching of Psychology*, 29(4), 308–11.

Hinchliff, S., Gott, M. and Galena, E. (2005) 'I daresay I might find it embarrassing': general practitioners' perspectives on discussing sexual health issues with lesbian and gay patients. *Health and Social Care in the Community*, 13(4), 345–53.

Hines, S. (2006) Intimate transitions: transgender practices of partnering and parenting. *Sociology*, 40(2), 353–71.

(2007) *Transforming gender: transgender practices of identity, intimacy and care.* University of Bristol: The Policy Press.

Hirschfeld, M. (1910) *Die transvestitien*. Berlin: Pulvermacher.

Hite, S. (1976) *The Hite report: a nationwide study of female sexuality*. New York: Macmillan.

Hodges, I. and Pearson, C. (2008) Silent minority: exploring British gay men's experience of the nature and content of psychology as a discipline. *Hellenic Journal of Psychology*, 5(1), 33–57.

Hollister, J. (2004) Beyond the interaction membrane: Laud Humphreys' tearoom tradeoff. *International Journal of Sociology and Social Policy*, 24(3–5), 73–94.

Hollway, W. (1989) *Subjectivity and method in psychology: gender, meaning and science*. London: Sage.

Holman, C.W. and Goldberg, J.M. (2007) Ethical, legal and psychosocial issues in the care of transgender adolescents. *International Journal of Transgenderism*, 9(3–4), 95–110.

Hooker, E. (1957) The adjustment of the male overt homosexual. *Journal of Projective Techniques*, 21, 18–31.

Hopkins, J.H. (1969) The lesbian personality. *British Journal of Psychiatry*, 115, 1433–6.

Hospers, H.J. and Kok, G. (1995) Determinants of safe and risk-taking sexual behaviour among gay men: a review. *AIDS Education and Prevention*, 7(1), 74–96.

Hostetler, A.J. and Cohler, B.J. (1997) Partnership, singlehood, and the lesbian and gay life course: a research agenda. *Journal of Gay, Lesbian, and Bisexual Identity*, 2(3/4), 199–230.

Hudson, W.W. and Ricketts, W.A. (1980) A strategy for the measurement of homophobia. *Journal of Homosexuality*, 5(4), 357–72.

Hughes, C. and Evans, A. (2003) Health needs of women who have sex with women. *British Medical Journal*, 327, 939–40.

Hughes, T.L. and Eliason, M.J. (2002) Substance use and abuse in lesbian, gay, bisexual and transgender populations. *Journal of Primary Prevention*, 22(3), 263–98.

Humphrey, J.C. (2000) Cracks in the feminist mirror? Research and reflections on lesbian and gay men working together. *Feminist Review*, 66, 95–130.

Humphreys, L. (1970) *Tearoom trade: impersonal sex in public places*. Chicago: Aldine.

Hunt, R. and Jensen, J. (2006) *The experiences of young gay people in Britain's schools*. London: Stonewall. Available at: www.stonewall.org.uk.

Hyde, Z., Comfort, J., Brown, G., McManus, A. and Howart, P. (2007) The health and well-being of lesbian and bisexual women in Western Australia, WA Centre for health promotion research, Curtain University of Technology, Perth, Western Australia. Available at: http://wachpr.curtin.edu.au/downloads/reports/51949LBWHWBSFinalReport.pdf, accessed 15 November 2007.

Iasenza, S. (2002) Beyond 'lesbian bed death': the passion and play in lesbian relationships. *Journal of Lesbian Studies*, 6(1), 111–20.

Ibáñez, T. and Íñiguez, L. (eds.) (1997) *Critical social psychology*. London: Sage.

Igartua, K.J., Gill, K. and Montoro, R. (2003) Internalized homophobia: a factor in depression, anxiety, and suicide in the gay and lesbian population. *Canadian Journal of Community Mental Health*, 22(2), 15–30.

International Lesbian and Gay Association (1998) Equality for lesbians and gay men. Available at: www.steff.suite.dk/report.pdf.

Israel, G.E. (2005) Translove: transgender persons and their families. *Journal of GLBT Family Studies*, 1(1), 53–67.

Jackson, P.A. (2000) An explosion of Thai identities: global queering and re-imagining queer theory. *Culture, Health and Sexuality*, 2(4), 405–24.

Jackson, S. (2006) Gender, sexuality and heterosexuality: the complexity (and limits) of heteronormativity. *Feminist Theory*, 7(1), 105–21.

Jalas, K. (2004) Butch lesbians and the struggle with recognition. *Lesbian and Gay Psychology Review*, 5(1), 15–21.

Jeffreys, S. (1985) *The spinster and her enemies: feminism and sexuality, 1880–1930*. London: Routledge.

(2003) *Unpacking queer politics: a lesbian feminist perspective*. Cambridge: Polity Press.

(2008) They know it when they see it: the UK Gender Recognition Act 2004. *British Journal of Politics and International Relations*, 10, 328–45.

Jivraj, S. and de Jong, A. (2004) *Muslim moral instruction on homosexuality*. London: Safra Project. Available at: www.safraproject.org/publications.htm, accessed 23 July 2007.

Johnson, K. (2007) Transsexualism: diagnostic dilemmas, transgender politics and the future of transgender care. In V. Clarke and E. Peel (eds.), *Out in psychology: lesbian, gay, bisexual, trans and queer perspectives* (pp. 445–64). Chichester: Wiley.

Jowett, A. and Peel, E. (2009) Chronic illness in non-heterosexual contexts: an online survey of experiences. *Feminism and Psychology*, 19(4), 454–74.

Juang, R. (2006) Transgendering the politics of recognition. In S. Stryker and S. Whittle (eds.), *The transgender studies reader* (pp. 706–19). New York: Routledge.

Kallman, F.J. (1952) Comparative twin study on the genetic aspects of male homosexuality. *Journal of Nervous and Mental Disease*, 115, 283–98.

Kandaswamy, P. (2008) State austerity and the racial politics of same-sex marriage in the United States. *Sexualities*, 11(6), 706–25.

Kando, T. (1976) Males, females, and transsexuals: a comparative study of sexual conservatism. *Journal of Homosexuality*, 1(1), 45–64.

Kerr, S.K. and Emerson, A.M. (2003) A review of lesbian depression and anxiety. In R.M. Mathy and S.K. Kerr (eds.), *Lesbian and bisexual women's mental health* (pp. 143–62). Binghamton, NY: Haworth Press.

Kessler, S.J. (1998) *Lessons from the intersexed*. New Brunswick, NJ: Rutgers University Press.

Kessler, S.J. and McKenna, W. (1978) *Gender: an ethnomethodological approach*. Chicago, IL: University of Chicago Press.

Kimmel, D.C. (1977a). Psychotherapy and the older gay man. *Psychotherapy: Theory, Research and Practice*, 14, 386–93.

(1977b) Patterns of aging among gay men. *Christopher Street*, November, 28–31.

(1978) Adult development and ageing: a gay perspective. *Journal of Social Issues*, 34(3), 113–30.

(1979) Life history interviews of aging gay men. *International Journal of Aging and Human Development*, 10(3), 239–48.

Kimmel, D.C., Rose, T. and David, S. (eds.) (2006) *Lesbian, gay, bisexual, and transgender aging: research and clinical perspectives*. New York: Columbia University Press.

King, B.R. and Black, K.N. (1999) Extent of relational stigmatization of lesbians and their children by heterosexual college students. *Journal of Homosexuality*, 37(2), 65–81.

King, M., McKeown, E., Warner, J., Ramsay, A., Johnson, K., Cort, C. *et al.* (2003) Mental health and quality of life of gay men and lesbians in England and Wales. *British Journal of Psychiatry*, 183, 552–8.

Kinsey, A.C., Pomeroy, W.B. and Martin, C.E. (1948) *Sexual behavior in the human male*. Philadelphia, PA: W. B. Saunders.

Kinsey, A.C., Pomeroy, W.B., Martin, C.E. and Gebhard, P.H. (1953) *Sexual behavior in the human female*. Philadelphia, PA: W. B. Saunders.

Kippax, S. and Smith, G. (2001) Anal intercourse and power in sex between men. *Sexualities*, 4, 413–34.

Kite, M.E. (1992). Individual differences in males' reactions to gay males and lesbians. *Journal of Applied Social Psychology*, 22(15), 1222–39.

Kitzinger, C. (1987) *The social construction of lesbianism*. London: Sage.

(1989) *Liberal humanism as an ideology of social control: the regulation of lesbian identities*. In K. Gergen and J. Shotter (eds.), *Texts of identity* (pp. 82–98). London: Sage.

(1991) Lesbians and gay men in the workplace: psychosocial issues. In M. Davidson and J. Earnshaw (eds.), *Vulnerable workers: psychosocial and legal issues* (pp. 224–40). London: Wiley.

(1995) Social constructionism: implications for lesbian and gay psychology. In A.R. D'Augelli and C.J. Patterson (eds.), *Lesbian, gay, and bisexual identities over the lifespan: psychological perspectives* (pp. 136–61). New York: Oxford University Press.

(1996a) The token lesbian chapter. In S. Wilkinson (ed.), *Feminist psychologies: international perspectives* (pp. 119–44). Buckingham: Open University Press.

(1996b) Speaking of oppression: psychology, politics, and the language of power. In E.D. Rothblum and L.A. Bond (eds.), *Preventing heterosexism and homophobia* (pp. 3–19). Thousand Oaks, CA: Sage.

(1996c) Towards a politics of lesbian friendships. In J.S. Weinstock and E.D. Rothblum (eds.), *Lesbian friendships: for ourselves and each other* (pp. 295–9). New York: New York University Press.

(1997) Lesbian and gay psychology: a critical analysis. In D. Fox and I. Prilleltensky (eds.), *Critical psychology: an introduction* (pp. 202–16). London: Sage.

(2000a) Women with Androgen Insensitivity Syndrome (AIS). In J. Ussher (ed.), *Women's health: an international reader* (pp. 387–94). Leicester: British Psychological Society.

(2000b) Doing feminist conversation analysis. *Feminism and Psychology*, 10(2), 163–93.

(2005a) Heteronormativity in action: reproducing the heterosexual nuclear family in after-hours medical calls. *Social Problems*, 52(4), 477–98.

(2005b) Speaking as a heterosexual: (how) does sexuality matter for talk-in-interaction. *Research on Language and Social Interaction* 38(3), 221–65.

Kitzinger, C. and Coyle, A. (1995) Lesbian and gay couples: speaking of difference. *Psychologist*, 8, 64–9.

(2002) Introducing lesbian and gay psychology. In A. Coyle and C. Kitzinger (eds.), *Lesbian and gay psychology: new perspectives* (pp. 1–29). Oxford: BPS Blackwell.

Kitzinger, C. and Peel, E. (2005) The de-gaying and re-gaying of AIDS: contested homophobias in lesbian and gay awareness training. *Discourse and Society*, 16(2), 173–97.

Kitzinger, C. and Perkins, R. (1993) *Changing our minds: lesbian feminism and psychology*. London: Onlywomen Press.

Kitzinger, C. and Wilkinson, S. (1995) Transitions from heterosexuality to lesbianism: the discursive production of lesbian identities. *Developmental Psychology*, 31(1), 95–104.

(2004) The rebranding of marriage: why we got married instead of registering a civil partnership. *Feminism and Psychology*, 14 (1), 127–50.

(2006) Genders, sexualities and equal marriage rights. *Lesbian and Gay Psychology Review*, 7(2), 174–9.

Kitzinger, C., Wilkinson, S., Coyle, A. and Milton, M. (1998) Towards lesbian and gay psychology. *Psychologist*, 11(11), 529–33.

Klein, F. (1978) *The bisexual option: a concept of one hundred percent intimacy*. New York: Arbor House.

Klein, K., Sepekoff, B. and Wolf, T.J. (1985) Sexual orientation: a multi-variable dynamic process. *Journal of Homosexuality*, 11(1/2), 35–49.

Klesse, C. (2006a) Polyamory and its 'others': contesting the terms of non-monogamy. *Sexualities*, 9(5), 565–83.

(2006b) Heteronormativity, non-monogamy and the marriage debate in the bisexual movement. *Lesbian and Gay Psychology Review*, 7(2), 162–73.

(2007) *The spectre of promiscuity: gay male and bisexual non-monogamies and polyamories*. Aldershot: Ashgate.

Knapp Whittier, D. (1997) Social conflict among 'gay' men in a small(er) Southern town. In J.G. Smith and R.J. Mancoske (eds.), *Rural gays and lesbians: building on the strengths of communities* (pp. 53–71). New York: Haworth Press.

Koh, A.S. and Ross, L.K. (2006) Mental health issues: a comparison of lesbian, bisexual, and heterosexual women. *Journal of Homosexuality*, 51(1), 33–57.

Kong, T.S.K., Mahoney, D. and Plummer, K. (2002) Queering the interview. In J.F. Gubrium and J.A. Holstein (eds.), *Handbook of interview research: context and method* (pp. 239–58). Thousand Oaks, CA: Sage.

Krafft-Ebing, R.V. (1997 [1886]) *Psychopathia sexualis: the case histories*. London: Creation Books.

Krane, V. and Kauer, K.J. (2007) Out on the ball fields: lesbians in sport. In V. Clarke and E. Peel (eds.), *Out in psychology: lesbian, gay, bisexual, trans and queer perspectives* (pp. 273–90). Chichester: Wiley.

Krestan, J. and Bepko, C.S. (1980) The problem of fusion in the lesbian relationship. *Family Process*, 19, 277–89.

Kuang, M., Mathy, R.M., Carol, H.M. and Nojima, K. (2003) The effects of sexual orientation, gender identity and gender role on the mental health of women in Taiwan's T-po lesbian community. *Journal of Psychology and Human Sexuality*, 15(4), 163–84.

Kurdek, L.A. (1991a) Correlates of relationship satisfaction in cohabiting gay and lesbian couples. *Journal of Personal and Social Psychology*, 61, 910–22.

(1991b). The dissolution of gay and lesbian couples. *Journal of Personal and Social Psychology*, 8, 265–78.

(2004) Are gay and lesbian cohabiting couples really different from heterosexual married couples? *Journal of Marriage and Family*, 66, 880–900.

(2005) What do we know about gay and lesbian couples? *Current Directions in Psychological Science*, 14, 251–4.

(2007) The allocation of household labor by partners in gay and lesbian couples. *Journal of Family Issues*, 28(1), 132–48.

Lacan, J. (1968) *The language of the self: the function of language in psychoanalysis.* Baltimore, MD: Johns Hopkins University Press.

Lacquer, T. (1990) *Making sex: body and gender from the Greeks to Freud.* Cambridge, MA: Harvard University Press.

Lampon, D. (1995) Lesbians and safer sex practices. *Feminism and Psychology*, 5(2), 170–6.

Land, V. and Kitzinger, C. (2005) Speaking as a lesbian: correcting the heterosexist presumption. *Research on Language and Social Interaction*, 38(4), 371–416.

(2007) Closet talk: the contemporary relevance of the closet in lesbian and gay interaction. In V. Clarke and E. Peel (eds.), *Out in psychology: lesbian, gay, bisexual, trans and queer perspectives* (pp. 147–71). Chichester: Wiley.

Landen, M. and Innala S. (2000). Attitudes toward transsexualism in a Swedish national survey. *Archives of Sexual Behavior*, 29 (4), 375–88.

Langdridge, D. (2007a) *Phenomenological psychology: theory, research and method.* Harlow: Pearson Education.

(2007b) Gay affirmative therapy: a theoretical framework and defence. In E. Peel, V. Clarke and J. Drescher (eds.), *British lesbian, gay and bisexual psychologies: theory, research and practice* (pp. 27–43). New York: Haworth Press.

Langdridge, D. and Barker, M. (2007) (eds.) *Safe, sane and consensual: contemporary perspectives on sadomasochism.* London: Palgrave Macmillan.

LaSala, M.C. (2003) When interviewing 'family': maximizing the insider advantage in the qualitative study of lesbians and gay men. In W. Meezan and J.I. Martin (eds.), *Research methods with gay, lesbian, bisexual, and transgender populations* (pp. 15–30). New York: Harrington Park Press.

Lasser, J. and Tharinger, D. (2003) Visibility management in school and beyond: a qualitative study of gay, lesbian, bisexual youth. *Journal of Adolescence*, 26(2), 233–44.

Layne, L.L. (2003) *Motherhood lost: a feminist account of pregnancy loss in America.* New York: Routledge.

Lee, A. (2008) Finding the way to the end of the rainbow: a researcher's insight investigating British old gay men's lives. *Sociological Research Online*, 13(1), www.socresonline.org.uk/13/1/6.html.

Lee, R. (2000) Health care problems of lesbian, gay, bisexual, and transgender patients. *Western Journal of Medicine*, 172, 403–8.

Leming, M.R. and Dickenson, G.E. (2002) *Understanding dying, death and bereavement*, 5th edition. Fort Worth, TX: Harcourt.

Leung, P., Erich, S. and Kanenberg, H. (2005) A comparison of family functioning in gay/lesbian, heterosexual and special needs adoptions. *Children and Youth Services Review*, 27(9), 1031–44.

Lev, A. (2004) *Transgender emergence: therapeutic guidelines for working with gender-variant people and their families.* Binghamton, NY: Haworth Clinical Practice Press.

(2006) Gay dads: choosing surrogacy. *Lesbian and Gay Psychology Review*, 7(1), 73–7.

LeVay, S. (1991) A difference in hypothalamic structure between heterosexual and homosexual men. *Science*, 253, 1034–7.

Levitt, E. and Klassen, A.D. (1974) Public attitudes toward homosexuality: part of the 1970 national survey by the Institute for Sex Research. *Journal of Homosexuality*, 1(1), 29–43.

Liao, L.M. (2007) Towards a clinical-psychological approach to address the heterosexual concerns of intersex women. In V. Clarke and E. Peel (eds.), *Out in psychology: lesbian, gay, bisexual, trans and queer perspectives* (pp. 391–408). Chichester: Wiley.

Lindsay, J., Perlesz, A., Brown, R., McNair, R., de Vaus, D. and Pitts, M. (2006) Stigma or respect: lesbian-parented families negotiating school settings. *Sociology*, 40(6), 1059–77.

Lipton, B. (2004) Gay men living with non-HIV chronic illnesses. *Journal of Gay and Lesbian Social Services*, 17(2), 1–23.

Litovich, M.L. and Langhout, R.D. (2004) Framing heterosexism in lesbian families: a preliminary examination of resilient coping. *Journal of Community and Applied Social Psychology*, 14, 411–35.

Lombardi, E. (2001) Enhancing transgender health care. *American Journal of Public Health*, 91(6), 869–72.

Lombardi, E. and Davis, S.M. (2006) Transgender health issues. In D.F. Morrow and L. Messinger (eds.), *Sexual orientation and gender expression in social work practice: working with gay, lesbian, bisexual and transgender people* (pp. 343–63). New York: Columbia University Press.

Lombardi, E.L., Wilchins, R.A., Priesing, D. and Malouf, D. (2001) Gender violence: transgender experiences with violence and discrimination. *Journal of Homosexuality*, 42(1), 89–101.

Lorde, A. (1987) Man child: a black lesbian-feminist's response. In S. Pollack and J. Vaughn (eds.), *Politics of the heart: a lesbian parenting anthology* (pp. 220–6). Ithaca, NY: Firebrand Books.

Lovell, J. and Riggs, D.W. (2009) Constructions of difference in children's storybooks and their implications in bullying behaviour. In B. Baird and D.W. Riggs (eds.), *The racial politics of bodies, nations and knowledges*. Cambridge: Cambridge Scholars Press.

Lubbe, C. (2008) The experiences of children growing up in lesbian-headed families in South Africa. *Journal of GLBT Family Studies*, 4(3), 325–59.

Lucksted, A. (2004) Lesbian, gay, bisexual, and transgender people receiving services in the public mental health system: raising issues. *Journal of Gay and Lesbian Psychotherapy*, 8(3–4), 25–42.

Lumby, M.E. (1976) Homophobia: the quest for a valid scale. *Journal of Homosexuality*, 2(1), 39–47.

Lurie, S. (2005) Identifying training needs of health care providers related to treatment and care of transgendered patients: a qualitative needs assessment conducted in New England. *International Journal of Transgenderism*, 8(2/3), 93–112.

Lyons, C.J. (2006) Stigma or sympathy? Attributions of fault to hate crime victims and offenders. *Social Psychology Quarterly*, 69(1), 39–59.

Maasen, T. (1998) Counselling gay men with multiple loss and survival problems: the bereavement group as a transitional object. *AIDS Care*, 10 (suppl. 1), S57–S63.

McBride, D. A. (2005) *Why I hate Abercrombie and Fitch: essays on race and sexuality.* New York: New York University Press.

MacBride-Stewart, S. (2004) Dental dams: a parody of straight expectations in the promotion of 'safer' lesbian sex. In D. W. Riggs and G. A. Walker (eds.), *Out in the Antipodes: Australian and New Zealand perpectives on gay and lesbian issues in psychology* (pp. 393–416). Perth: Brightfire Press.

MacCallum, F. and Golombok, S. (2004) Children raised in fatherless families from infancy: a follow-up study of children of lesbian and single heterosexual mothers at early adolescence. *Journal of Child Psychology and Psychiatry*, 45(8), 1407–19.

McCann, P., Augoustinos, M. and LeCouteur, A. (2004) 'Race' and the human genome project: constructions of scientific legitimacy. *Discourse and Society*, 15(6), 409–32.

McCauley, E. and Ehrhardt, A. A. (1978) Role expectations and definitions: a comparison of female transsexuals and lesbians. *Journal of Homosexuality*, 3(2), 137–47.

McClennen, J. C. (2003) Researching gay and lesbian domestic violence: the journey of a non-LGBT researcher. In W. Meezan and J. I. Martin (eds.), *Research methods with gay, lesbian, bisexual, and transgender populations* (pp. 31–45). New York: Harrington Park Press.

McDermott, E. (2004) Telling lesbian stories: interviewing and the class dynamics of 'talk'. *Women's Studies International Forum*, 27, 177–87.

(2006) Surviving in dangerous places: lesbian identity performances in the workplace, social class and psychological health. *Feminism and Psychology*, 16(2), 193–211.

MacDonald, Jr., A. P. and Games, R. G. (1974) Some characteristics of those who hold positive and negative attitudes toward homosexuals. *Journal of Homosexuality*, 1(1), 9–27.

McIntosh, P. (1998) White privilege: unpacking the invisible knapsack. In M. McGoldrick (ed.), *Re-visioning family therapy: race, culture, and gender in clinical practice* (pp. 147–52). New York: Guilford Press.

Mackenzie, G. O. (1999) 50 billion galaxies of gender: transgendering the millennium. In K. More and S. Whittle (eds.), *Reclaiming genders: transsexual grammars at the fin de siècle* (pp. 193–218). London: Continuum.

McLaren, S., Jude, B. and McLachlan, A. J. (2008) Sense of belonging to the general and gay communities as predictors of depression amongst Australian gay men. *International Journal of Men's Health*, 7, 90–9.

McLean, K. (2004) Negotiating (non)monogamy: bisexuality and intimate relationships. *Journal of Bisexuality*, 4(1/2), 84–97.

(2008). Silences and stereotypes: the impact of (mis)constructions of bisexuality on Australian bisexual men and women. *Gay and Lesbian Issues and Psychology Review*, 4(3), 158–65.

McLelland, M. (2003) Western intersections, Eastern approximations: living more 'like oneself': transgender identities and sexualities in Japan. *Journal of Bisexuality*, 3(3/4), 203–30.

McNamee, S. and Gergen, K. (eds.) (1992) *Therapy as social construction*. London: Sage.

McRobbie, A. (2004) Postfeminism and popular culture. *Feminist Media Studies*, 4(3), 255–64.

Madill, A. and Gough, B. (2008) Qualitative research and its place in psychological science. *Psychological Methods*, 13(3), 254–71.

Maguen, S., Floyd, F.J., Bakeman, R. and Armistead, L. (2002) Developmental milestones and disclosure of sexual orientation among gay, lesbian, and bisexual youths. *Journal of Applied Developmental Psychology*, 23(2), 219–33.

Maison, D. (1995) Do we say what we think? On the implications for research of an anti-discrimination norm. *Polish Psychological Bulletin*, 26, 175–87.

Malaney, G.D., Williams, E.A. and Geller, W.W. (1997) Assessing campus climate for gays, lesbians, and bisexuals at two institutions. *Journal of College Student Development*, 38(4), 365–75.

Malley, M. and Tasker, F. (2007) 'The difference that makes a difference': what matters to lesbians and gay men in psychotherapy. In E. Peel, V. Clarke and J. Drescher (eds.), *British lesbian, gay and bisexual psychologies: theory, research and practice* (pp. 93–109). New York: Haworth Press.

Mallon, G.P. (2006) *Lesbian and gay foster and adoptive parents*. Washington, DC: Child Welfare League of America.

Maney, D.W. and Cain, R.E. (1997) Preservice elementary teachers' attitudes toward gay and lesbian parenting. *Journal of School Health*, 67(6), 236–41.

Marrazzo, J.M., Coffey, P. and Bingham, A. (2005) Sexual practices, risk perception and knowledge of sexually transmitted disease risk among lesbian and bisexual women. *Perspectives on Sexual and Reproductive Health*, 37(1), 6–12.

Marshall, H. and Wollett, A. (2000) Fit to reproduce? The regulatory role of pregnancy texts. *Feminism and Psychology*, 10(3), 351–66.

Martin, J.I. and Meezan, W. (2003) Applying ethical standards to research and evaluations involving lesbian, gay, bisexual, and transgender populations. In W. Meezan and J.I. Martin (eds.), *Research methods with gay, lesbian, bisexual, and transgender populations* (pp. 181–201). New York: Harrington Park Press.

Martin, J.T., Puts, D.A. and Breedlove, S.M. (2008) Fluctuating asymmetry in the hands of homosexuals and heterosexuals: relationships to digit ratios and other sexually dimorphic anatomical traits. *Archives of Sexual Behavior*, 37(1), 119–32.

Mason-Schrock, D. (1996) Transsexuals' narrative construction of the 'true self'. *Social Psychology Quarterly*, 59(3), 176–92.

Mathy, R.M., Lehmann, B.A. and Kerr, D.L. (2003) Bisexual and transgender identities in a non-clinical sample of North Americans: suicidal intent, behavioural difficulties and mental health treatment. *Journal of Bisexuality*, 3(3/4), 93–109.

Matthews, C.R., Lorah, P. and Fenton, J. (2005) Toward a grounded theory of lesbians' recovery from addiction. *Journal of Lesbian Studies*, 9(3), 57–68.

Mays, V.M., Cochran, S.D., Bellinger, G. and Smith, R.G. (1992) The language of black gay men's sexual behavior: implications for AIDS risk reduction. *Journal of Sex Research*, 29(3), 425–34.

Meezan, W. and Martin, J.I. (2003) Exploring current themes in research on gay, lesbian, bisexual and transgender populations. In W. Meezan and J.I. Martin (eds.), *Research methods with gay, lesbian, bisexual, and transgender populations* (pp. 1–14). New York: Harrington Park Press.

Meyer, I.H. (2001) Why lesbian, gay, bisexual, and transgender public health? *American Journal of Public Health*, 91, 856–9.

Meyer, I.H. and Colton, M.E. (1999) Sampling gay men: random digit dialing versus sources in the gay community. *Journal of Homosexuality*, 37(4), 99–110.

Meyerowitz, J. (2002) *How sex changed: a history of transsexuality in the United States.* Cambridge, MA: Harvard University Press.

Miller, B. (1979) Gay fathers and their children. *Family Coordinator*, 28, 544–52.

(1987) Counselling gay husbands and fathers. In F.W. Bozett (ed.), *Gay and lesbian parents* (pp. 175–87). New York: Praeger.

Miller, D. and Higgins, D.J. (2006) The role of sexual orientation disclosure and harassment in predicting job satisfaction and organizational commitment. *Lesbian and Gay Psychology Review*, 7(2), 216–30.

Millham, J., San Miguel, C.L. and Kellogg, R. (1976) A factor-analytic conceptualization of attitudes toward male and female homosexuals. *Journal of Homosexuality*, 2(1), 3–10.

Milton, M. (2006) 'What you want, when you want it': relating in the age of Gaydar. *Lesbian and Gay Psychology Review*, 7(3), 306–9.

Milton, M. and Coyle, A. (2003). Sexual identity: affirmative practice with lesbian and gay clients. In R. Woolfe, W. Dryden and S. Strawbridge (eds.), *Handbook of Counselling Psychology*, 2nd edition (pp. 481–99). London: Sage.

Minton, H.L. (1997) Queer theory: historical roots and implications for psychology. *Theory and Psychology*, 7(3), 337–53.

(2002) *Departing from deviance: a history of homosexual rights and emancipatory science in America.* Chicago, IL: University of Chicago Press.

Mishna, F., Newman, P.A., Daley, A. and Soloman, S. (2008) Bullying of lesbian and gay youth: a qualitative investigation. *British Journal of Social Work*, DOI: 10.1093/bjsw/bcm148

Mitchell, J. (1974) *Psychoanalysis and feminism: Freud, Reich, Laing and Women.* New York: Vintage Books.

Monro, S. (2006) Growing up transgender: stories of an excluded population. In C. Leccardi and E. Ruspini (eds.), *A new youth? Young people, generations and family life* (pp. 298–320). Aldershot: Ashgate.

Montcalm, D.M. and Myer, L.L. (2000) Lesbian immunity from HIV/AIDS: fact or fiction? *Journal of Lesbian Studies*, 4(2), 131–47.

Moon, L. (2007) *Feeling queer or queer feelings? Radical approaches to counselling sex, sexualities and genders.* London: Routledge.

Moore, M.R. (2006) Lipstick or timberlands? Meanings of gender presentation in black lesbian communities. *Signs: Journal of Women in Culture and Society*, 32(1), 113–39.

Morgan, D. (1999) Risk and family practices: accounting for change and fluidity in family life. In E.B. Silva and C. Smart (eds.), *The new family?* (pp. 13–30) London: Sage.

Morin, S.F. (1977) Heterosexual bias in psychological research on lesbianism and male homosexuality. *American Psychologist*, 32, 629–37.

Morse, C.N., McLaren, S. and McLachlan, A.J. (2007) The attitudes of Australian heterosexuals toward same-sex parents. In F. Tasker and J.J. Bigner (eds.), *Gay and lesbian parenting: new directions* (pp. 425–55). New York: Haworth Press.

Mulick, P.S. and Wright, L.W. (2002) Examining the existence of biphobia in the hetero-sexual and homosexual populations. *Journal of Bisexuality*, 2(4), 45–64.

Munt, S.R. (1998) Introduction. In S.R. Munt (ed.), *Butch/femme: inside lesbian gender* (pp. 1–11). London: Cassell Academic.

Murray, M. (2004a) Criticizing health psychology. In M. Murray (ed.), *Critical health psychology* (pp. 1–11). London: Palgrave.

Murray, M. (ed.) (2004b) *Critical health psychology*. Basingstoke: Palgrave Macmillan.

Myerson, M., Crawley, S.L., Anstey, E.H., Kessler, J. and Okopny, C. (2007) Who's zoomin' who? A feminist, queer content analysis of 'interdisciplinary' human sexuality textbooks. *Hypatia*, 22(1), 92–113.

Nagoshi, J.L., Adams, K.A., Terrill, H.K., Hill, E.D., Brzuzy, S. and Nagoshi, C.T. (2008). Gender differences in correlates of homophobia and transphobia. *Sex Roles*, 59: 521–31.

Nairn, K. and Smith, A.B. (2003) Taking students seriously: their rights to be safe in school. *Gender and Education*, 15(2), 133–49.

Nanda, S. (2000) *Gender diversity: crosscultural variations*. Long Grove, IL: Waveland Press.

Nardi, P.M. (1992) Sex, friendship, and gender roles among gay men. In P.M. Nardi (ed.), *Men's friendships* (pp. 173–85). Newbury Park, CA: Sage.

Nardi, P.M. and Sherrod, D. (1994). Friendship in the lives of gay men and lesbians. *Journal of Social and Personal Relationships*, 11(2), 185–99.

Nelson, J.A. (1994). Comment on special issue on adolescence. *American Psychologist*, 48, 523–4.

Nemoto, T., Operario, D., Keatley, J. and Villegas, D. (2004) Social context of HIV risk behaviours among male-to-female transgenders of color. *AIDS Care*, 16(6), 724–35.

Nichols, M. (1987) Lesbian sexuality: issues and developing theory. In Boston Lesbian Psychologies Collective (eds.), *Lesbian psychologies* (pp. 97–125). Chicago, IL: University of Illinois Press.

   (2004) Lesbian sexuality/female sexuality: rethinking 'lesbian bed death'. *Sexual and Relationship Therapy*, 19(4): 363–71.

Nicolosi, J. (1991) *Reparative therapy of male homosexuality*. New York: Rowman and Littlefield.

Norman, A. (1985) *Triple jeopardy: growing old in a second homeland*. London: Centre for Policy on Ageing.

Norris, W.P. (1991) Liberal attitudes and homophobic acts: the paradoxes of homosexual experience in a liberal institution. *Journal of Homosexuality*, 22(3/4), 81–120.

O'Boyle, C.G. and Thomas, M.D. (1996) Friendships between lesbian and heterosex-ual women. In J.S. Weinstock and E.D. Rothblum (eds.), *Lesbian friendships: for ourselves and each other* (pp. 240–8). New York: New York University Press.

Ochs, R. (1996) Biphobia: it goes more than two ways. In B.A. Firestein (ed.), *Bisexuality: the psychology and politics of an invisible minority* (pp. 217–39). Thousand Oaks, CA: Sage.

Oerton, S. (1998) Reclaiming the 'housewife'? Lesbians and household work. In G. Dunne (ed.), *Living 'difference': lesbian perspectives on work and family life* (pp. 69–83). New York: Harrington Park Press.

Oosterhuis, H. (2000) *Krafft-Ebing, psychiatry, and the making of sexual identity.* Chicago, IL: University of Chicago Press.

O'Toole, C.J. (1996) Disabled lesbians: challenging monocultural constructs. *Sexuality and Disability*, 14(3), 221–36.

Paechter, C. (2000) Growing up with a lesbian mother: a theoretically-based analysis of personal experience. *Sexualities*, 3(4), 395–408.

Page, E.H. (2004) Mental health services experiences of bisexual women and bisexual men: an empirical study. *Journal of Bisexuality*, 4(1–2), 137–60.

Pallotta-Chiarolli, M. (2006) Polyparents having children, raising children, schooling children. *Lesbian and Gay Psychology Review*, 7(1), 48–53.

Parker, I. (1990) Discourse: definitions and contradictions. *Philosophical Psychology*, 3(2), 189–204.

(1992) *Discourse dynamics: a critical analysis for social and individual psychology.* London: Routledge.

Patterson, C.J. (1992) Children of lesbian and gay parents. *Child Development*, 63, 1025–42.

(1995) Families of the lesbian baby boom: parents' division of labor and children's adjustment. *Developmental Psychology*, 31(1), 115–25.

(2008). *Child development.* New York: McGraw Hill.

Patterson, C.J., Sutfin, E.L. and Fulcher, M. (2004) Division of labor among lesbian and heterosexual parenting couples: correlates of specialized versus shared patterns. *Journal of Adult Development*, 11(3), 179–89.

Peel E. (1999) Violence against lesbians and gay men: decision making in reporting and not reporting crime. *Feminism and Psychology*, 9(2), 161–7.

(2001a) Mundane heterosexism: understanding incidents of the everyday. *Women's Studies International Forum*, 24(5), 541–54.

(2001b) Neglect and tokenism: representations of violence against lesbians in textbooks. *Psychology of Women Section Review*, 3(1), 14–19.

(2001c) 'I am what I am?': using stereotypes in anti-heterosexism training. *Lesbian and Gay Psychology Review*, 2(2), 50–6.

(2002) Lesbian and gay awareness training: challenging homophobia, liberalism and managing stereotypes. In A. Coyle and C. Kitzinger (eds.), *Lesbian and gay psychology: new perspectives* (pp. 255–74). Oxford: BPS Blackwell.

(2005) Effeminate 'fudge nudgers' and tomboyish 'lettuce lickers': language and the construction of sexualities in diversity training. *Psychology of Women Section Review*, 7(2), 22–34.

(2009) Intergroup relations in action: questions asked about lesbian, gay and bisexual issues in diversity training. *Journal of Community and Applied Social Psychology*, 19, 271–85.

Peel, E. and Cain, R. (2008) Silent miscarriage and deafening heteronormativity: an experiential and critical feminist account. Experiencing Reproductive Loss: Working Together to Change Practice, 2 October, Open University, UK.

Peel, E. and Clarke, V. (eds.) (2005) Critiquing psychology: a reappraisal of *The social construction of lesbianism*. *Lesbian and Gay Psychology Review*, 6(2).

(2007) Low-key lesbians and grandiose gays: the gendered dynamics of civil partnership, ritual and recognition. British Psychological Society Psychology of Women Section Conference, 18–20 July, Cumberland Lodge, Windsor, UK.

Peel, E. and Coyle, A. (eds.) (2004) Special feature: heterosexual people working in lesbian and gay psychology. *Lesbian and Gay Psychology Review*, 5(2), 54–70.

Peel, E. and Harding, R. (2004) Divorcing romance, rights, and radicalism: beyond pro and anti in the lesbian and gay marriage debate. *Feminism and Psychology*, 14(4), 584–95.

(2008) Recognising and celebrating same sex relationships: beyond the normative debate. *Sexualities*, 11(6), 659–66.

Peel, E. and Thomson, M. (eds.) (2009) Lesbian, gay, bisexual, trans and queer health psychology: charting the terrain. *Feminism and Psychology*, 19(4).

Peplau, L.A. (2001) Rethinking women's sexual orientation: an interdisciplinary, relationship-focused approach. *Personal Relationships*, 8(1), 1–19.

Peplau, L.A. and Fingerhut, A.W. (2007) The close relationships of lesbians and gay men. *Annual Review of Psychology*, 58, 405–24.

Peplau, L.A. and Garnets, L.D. (2000) A new paradigm for understanding women's sexuality and sexual orientation. *Journal of Social Issues*, 56(2), 329–50.

Perkins, R. (1991) Therapy for lesbians: the case against. *Feminism and Psychology*, 1(3), 325–38.

Perlesz, A., Brown, R., Lindsay, J., McNair, R., de Vaus, D. and Pitts, M. (2006) Family in transition: parents, children and grandparents in lesbian families give meaning to 'doing family'. *Journal of Family Therapy*, 28, 175–99.

Perlesz, A. and McNair, R. (2004) Lesbian parenting: insiders' voices. *Australian and New Zealand Journal of Family Therapy*, 25(2), 129–40.

Petersen, A. and Lupton, D. (1996) *The new public health: health and self in the age of risk*. London: Sage.

Peterson, J.L., Bakeman, R., Stokes, J. and Community intervention trial for youth study team (2001) Racial/ethnic patterns of HIV sexual risk behaviours among young men who have sex with men. *Journal of the Gay and Lesbian Medical Association*, 5(4), 155–62.

Peterson, J.L., Coates, T.J., Catania, J.A., Middleton, L., Hilliard, B. and Hearst, N. (1992) High-risk sexual behaviour and condom use among gay and bisexual African-American men. *American Journal of Public Health*, 82, 1490–4.

Peterson, K.J. (1996) (ed.) *Health care for lesbians and gay men: confronting homophobia and heterosexism*. Binghamton, NY: Harrington Park Press.

Pillard, R.C. and Weinrich, J.D. (1986) Evidence of familial nature of male homosexuality. *Archives of General Psychiatry*, 43, 808–12.

Pitman, G.E. (2002) Outsider/insider: the politics of shifting identities in the research process. *Feminism and Psychology*, 12, 282–8.

Pitts, M., Couch, M., Mulcare, H., Croy, S. and Mitchell, A. (2009) Health and wellbeing of trans people in Australia and New Zealand. *Feminism and Psychology*, 19(4), 475–95.

Pitts, M., Smith, A., Mitchell, A. and Patel, S. (2006) *Private lives: a report on the health and wellbeing of GLBTI Australians*. Melbourne: Australian Research Centre in Sex, Health and Society.

Plumb, M. (1997) Blueprint for the future: the lesbian health advocacy movement. In J. White and M. Martinez (eds.), *The lesbian health book: caring for ourselves* (pp. 362–78). Seattle: Seal Press.

Pollack, S. (1987) Lesbian mothers: a lesbian-feminist perspective on research. In S. Pollack and J. Vaughn (eds.), *Politics of the heart: a lesbian parenting anthology* (pp. 316–24). Ithaca, NY: Firebrand Books.

Porche, M. and Purvin, D. (2008) Never in our lifetime: legal marriage for same-sex couples in long-term relationships. *Family Relations*, 57, 144–59.

Potter, J. and Wetherell, M. (1987) *Discourse and social psychology: beyond attitudes and behaviour*. London: Sage.

Potter, J., Wetherell, M., Gill, R. and Edwards, D. (1990) Discourse: noun, verb or social practice? *Philosophical Psychology*, 3(2), 205–17.

Price, E. (2005) All but invisible: older gay men and lesbians. *Nursing Older People*, 17(4), 16–18.

Price, J. (1998) *Navigating differences: friendships between gay and straight men*. New York: Harrington Park Press.

Price, J.H. (1982) High school students' attitudes toward homosexuality. *Journal of School Health*, 52, 469–74.

Prilleltensky, I. and Fox, D. (1997) Introducing critical psychology: values, assumptions, and the status quo. In D. Fox and I. Prilleltensky (eds.), *Critical psychology: an introduction* (pp. 3–20). London: Sage.

Psathas, G. (1995) *Conversation analysis*. Thousand Oaks, CA: Sage.

Pugh, S. (2002) The forgotten: a community without a generation – older lesbians and gay men. In D. Richardon and S. Seidman (eds.), *Handbook of lesbian and gay studies* (pp. 161–81). London: Sage.

Rachlin, K., Green, J. and Lombardi, E. (2008) Utilization of health care among female-to-male transgender individuals in the United States. *International Journal of Transgenderism*, 54(3), 243–58.

Rahman, Q. (1999) The psychology of human sexual orientation: what is it and why bother? *Lesbian and Gay Psychology Section Newsletter*, 2, 6–10.

Rahman, Q., Andersson, D. and Govier, E. (2005) A specific sexual orientation-related difference in navigation strategy. *Behavioral Neuroscience*, 119(1), 311–16.

Raja, S. and Stokes, J.P. (1998) Assessing attitudes towards lesbians and gay men: the modern homophobia scale. *Journal of Gay, Lesbian and Bisexual Identity*, 3, 113–34.

Raymond, J. (1979) *The transsexual empire: the making of the she-male*. New York: Columbia University Press.

Razzano, L.A., Matthews, A. and Hughes, T.L. (2002) Utilization of mental health services: a comparison of lesbian and heterosexual women. *Journal of Gay and Lesbian Social Services*, 14(1), 51–66.

Reason, P. and Bradbury, H. (eds.) (2001) *Handbook of action research: participative inquiry and practice*. Thousand Oaks, CA: Sage.

Reid, J.D. (1995) Development in later life: older lesbian and gay lives. In A.R. D'Augelli and C.J. Patterson (eds.), *Lesbian, gay, and bisexual identities over the lifespan: psychological perspectives* (pp. 215–40). New York: Oxford University Press.

Reid, K. (2008) Dancing our own steps: a queer families' project. *International Journal of Narrative Therapy and Community Work*, 2, 61–8.

Renzetti, C.M. and Miley, C.H. (eds.) (1996) *Violence in gay and lesbian domestic partnerships*. Binghamton, NY: Haworth Press.

Rich, A. (1980) Compulsory heterosexuality and lesbian existence. *Signs: Journal of Women in Culture and Society*, 5, 631–60.

Richards, G. (1997). *'Race', racism and psychology: towards a reflexive history.* New York: Routledge.

Richardson, D. and Seidman, S. (eds.) (2002) *Handbook of lesbian and gay studies.* London: Sage.

Rickards, T. and Wuest, J. (2006) The process of losing and regaining credibility when coming-out at midlife. *Health Care for Women International*, 27, 530–47.

Rieger, G., Chivers, M. L. and Bailey, J. M. (2005) Sexual arousal patterns of bisexual men. *Psychological Science*, 16(8), 579–84.

Riggs, D. W. (2004a) The politics of scientific knowledge: constructions of sexuality and ethics in the conversion therapy literature. *Lesbian and Gay Psychology Review*, 5(1), 6–14.

(2004b) Resisting heterosexism in foster carer training: valuing queer approaches to adult learning and relationality. *Canadian Journal of Queer Studies*, 1(1). Available from: http://jqstudies.oise.utoronto.ca/journal/viewarticle.php?id=3&layout=html.

(2005) Locating control: psychology and the cultural production of 'healthy subject positions'. *Culture, Health and Sexuality*, 7, 87–100.

(2006a) 'Serosameness' or 'serodifference'? Resisting polarised discourses of identity and relationality in the context of HIV. *Sexualities*, 9, 431–44.

(2006b) *Priscilla, (white) queen of the desert: queer rights/race privilege.* New York: Peter Lang.

(2006c) Developmentalism and the rhetoric of 'best interests of the child': challenging heteronormative constructions of families and parenting. *Journal of GLBT Family Studies*, 2(1), 87–112.

(2007a) Recognising race in LGBTQ psychology: privilege, power and complicity. In V. Clarke and E. Peel (eds.), *Out in psychology: lesbian, gay, bisexual, trans and queer perspectives* (pp. 59–76). Chichester: Wiley.

(2007b) *Becoming parent: lesbians, gay men and family.* Tenerife: Post Pressed.

(2007c) Queer theory and its future in psychology: exploring issues of race privilege. *Social and Personality Psychology Compass*, 1, 39–52.

(ed.) (2007d) *Taking up the challenge: critical race and whiteness studies in a post-colonising nation.* Adelaide: Crawford House.

(2008) Using multinomial logistic regression analysis to develop a model of Australian gay and heterosexual sperm donors' motivations and beliefs. *International Journal of Emerging Technologies and Society*, 6(2), 106–23.

(2009a) Institutional stressors and individual strengths: policy and practice directions for working with Australian lesbian and gay foster carers. *Practice: Social Work in Action*, 21(2), 77–90.

(2009b). The ground upon which we stand: reading sexuality through race. *Lesbian and Gay Psychology Review*, 10(1), 42–6.

(2009c) The health and well-being implications of emotion work undertaken by gay sperm donors, *Feminism and Psychology*, 19(4), 517–33.

Riggs, D. W., and Augoustinos, M. (2007) Learning difference: representations of diversity of storybooks for children of lesbian and gay parents. *Journal of GLBT Family Studies*, 3(3/4), 133–56.

Riggs, D.W. and Choi, P.Y.L. (2006) Heterosexism, racism and psychology: challenging or colluding with privilege? *Psychologist*, 19, 288–91.

Riggs, D.W., McLaren, S. and Mayes, A. (2009) Attitudes toward parenting in a lesbian and gay community convenience sample. *Journal of Gay and Lesbian Mental Health*, 13(1), 1–11.

Ringer, R.J. (2001) Constituting nonmonogamies. In M. Bernstein and R. Reimann (eds.), *Queer families, queer politics: challenging culture and the state* (pp. 137–51). New York: Columbia University Press.

Ritchie, A. and Barker, M. (2005) Explorations in feminist participant-led research: conducting focus group discussions with polyamorous women. *Psychology of Women Section Review*, 7(2), 47–59.

(2006) 'There aren't words for what we do or how we feel so we have to make them up': constructing polyamorous languages in a culture of compulsory monogamy. *Sexualities*, 9(5), 584–601.

Rivers, I. (2000) Social exclusion, absenteeism and sexual minority youth. *Support for Learning*, 15(1), 13–18.

(2001) The bullying of sexual minorities at school: its nature and long-term correlates. *Educational and Child Psychology*, 18(1), 33–46.

(2002) Developmental issues for lesbian and gay youth. In A. Coyle and C. Kitzinger (eds.), *Lesbian and gay psychology: new Perspectives* (pp. 30–44). Oxford: BPS Blackwell.

Roback, H.B., Strassberg, D.S., McKee, E. and Cunningham, J. (1978) Self-concept and psychological adjustment differences between self-identified male transsexuals and male homosexuals. *Journal of Homosexuality*, 3(1), 15–20.

Roberts, D. (2002) *Shattered bonds: the color of child welfare*. New York: Basic Books.

Roberts, S.J., Grindel, C.G., Patsdaughter, C.A., Reardon, K. and Tarmina, M.S. (2004) Mental health problems and use of services of lesbians: results of the Boston lesbian health project II. *Journal of Gay and Lesbian Social Services: Issues in Practice, Policy and Research*, 17(4), 1–16.

Robinson, B.E. and Skeen, P. (1982) Sex-role orientation of gay fathers versus gay nonfathers. *Perception and Motor Skills*, 55, 1055–9.

Robinson, V. and Richardson, D. (eds.) (1997) *Introducing women's studies*, 2nd edition. Basingstoke: Palgrave Macmillan.

Rochlin, M. (2003) Heterosexuality questionnaire. In R. Heasley and B. Crane (eds.), *Sexual lives: a reader on the theories and realities of human sexualities* (pp. 403–4). Boston: McGraw-Hill.

Rodriguez, E.M. and Ouellette, S.C. (2000) Gay and lesbian Christians: homosexual and religious identity integration in the members and participants of a gay-positive church. *Journal for the Scientific Study of Religion*, 39(3), 333–47.

Rofes, E. (2007) Thriving: gay men's health in the 21st century. Available from: www.ericrofes.com/pdf/THRIVING, accessed 19 June, 2008.

Rolfe, A. (2008) 'We don't': the meanings of civil partnerships for people choosing not to have one. British Psychological Society Psychology of Women Section Conference, 16–18 July, Cumberland Lodge, Windsor, UK.

Röndahl, G., Innala, S. and Carlsson, M. (2004) Nursing staff and nursing students' emotions towards homosexual patients and their wish to refrain from nursing, if the option existed. *Scandinavian Journal of Caring Sciences*, 18, 19–26.

Ross, L., Epstein, R., Goldfinger, C., Steele, L., Anderson, S. and Strike, C. (2008) Lesbian and queer mothers navigating the adoption system: the impacts of mental health. *Health Sociology Review*, 17, 260–72.

Ross, M.W. (2005) Typing, doing and being: sexuality and the Internet. *Journal of Sex Research*, 42, 342–52.

Rostad, F. and Long, B.C. (2007) Striving for holistic success: how lesbians come out on top. In V. Clarke and E. Peel (eds.), *Out in psychology: lesbian, gay, bisexual, trans and queer perspectives* (pp. 311–30). Chichester: Wiley.

Rothblum, E.D. (1992) We may be your worst nightmare, but we are also your future. *Feminism and Psychology*, 2(2), 271–4.

(2002) Gay and lesbian body images. In T.F. Cash and T. Pruzinsky (eds.), *Body images: a handbook of theory, research, and clinical practice* (pp. 257–65). New York: Guilford Press.

(2004) 'Out'standing in her field: looking back at Celia Kitzinger's *The social construction of lesbianism*. *Feminism and Psychology*, 14(4), 503–6.

(2007) From science fiction to computer-generated technology: sampling lesbian, gay, and bisexual individuals. In I.H. Meyer and M.E. Northridge (eds.), *The health of sexual minorities: public health perspectives on lesbian, gay, bisexual, and transgender populations* (pp. 442–54). New York: Springer.

Rothblum, E.D., Balsam, K.F., Todosijevic, J. and Solomon, S.E. (2006) Same-sex couples in civil unions compared with same-sex couples not in civil unions and heterosexual siblings: an overview. *Lesbian and Gay Psychology Review*, 7(2), 180–8.

Rothblum, E.D. and Factor, R.J. (2001) Lesbians and their sisters as a control group: demographic and mental health factors. *Psychological Science*, 12(1), 63–9.

Rounds, K.A. (1988) AIDS in rural areas: challenges to providing care. *Social Work*, 33(3), 257–61.

Rust, P.C. (1993) Neutralizing the political threat of the marginal woman: lesbians' beliefs about bisexual women. *Journal of Sex Research*, 30(3), 214–28.

(1995) *Bisexuality and the challenge to lesbian politics: sex, loyalty and revolution*. New York: New York University Press.

(2000) *Bisexuality in the United States*. New York: Columbia University Press.

Ryan, C. and Rivers, I. (2003) Lesbian, gay, bisexual and transgender youth: victimization and its correlates in the USA and UK. *Culture, Health and Sexuality*, 5(2), 103–19.

Ryan, H., Wortley, P.M., Easton, A., Pederson, L. and Greenwood, G. (2001) Smoking among lesbians, gays, and bisexuals: a review of the literature. *American Journal of Preventive Medicine*, 21(2), 142–9.

Ryan, S. (2007) Parent–child interaction styles between gay and lesbian parents and their adopted children. In F. Tasker and J.J. Bigner (eds.), *Gay and lesbian parenting: new directions* (pp. 105–32). New York: Haworth Press.

Saffron, L. (1998) Raising children in an age of diversity: advantages of having a lesbian mother. *Journal of Lesbian Studies*, 2(4), 35–47.

Sakamoto, I., Chin, M., Chapra, A. and Ricciardi, J. (2009) A 'normative' homeless woman? Marginalisation, emotional injury and social support of transwomen experiencing homelessness. *Gay and Lesbian Issues and Psychology Review*, 5(1), 2–19.

Sandfield, A. and Percy, C. (2003) Accounting for single status: heterosexism and ageism in heterosexual women's talk about marriage. *Feminism and Psychology*, 13(4), 475–88.

Sandfort, T.G.M. (2003) Studying sexual orientation change: a methodological review of the Spitzer study, 'Can some gay men and lesbians change their sexual orientation?' *Journal of Gay and Lesbian Psychotherapy*, 7(3), 15–29.

Santillo, V.M. and Lowe, F.C. (2005) Prostate cancer and the gay male. *Journal of Gay and Lesbian Psychotherapy*, 9, 9–27.

Saphira, M. and Glover, M. (2000) New Zealand national lesbian health survey. *Journal of the Gay and Lesbian Medical Association*, 4(2), 49–56.

Savin-Williams, R.C. (1994) Verbal and physical abuse as stressors in the lives of lesbian, gay male and bisexual youths: associations with school problems, running away, substance abuse, prostitution and suicide. *Journal of Consulting and Clinical Psychology*, 62, 261–9.

(2001) A critique of research on sexual-minority youths. *Journal of Adolescence*, 24(1), 5–13.

(2005) *The new gay teenager*. Cambridge, MA: Harvard University Press.

Savin-Williams, R.C. and Ream, G.L. (2003) Sex variations in the disclosure to parents of same-sex attractions. *Journal of Family Psychology*, 17(3), 429–38.

Schleifer, D. (2006) Make me feel mighty real: gay female-to-male transgenderists negotiating sex, gender, and sexuality. *Sexualities*, 9, 57–75.

Schroeder, M. and Shidlo, A. (2001) Ethical issues in sexual orientation conversion therapies: an empirical study of consumers. *Journal of Gay and Lesbian Psychotherapy*, 5(3/4), 131–66.

Sedgwick, E.K. (1990) *Epistemology of the closet*. Berkeley, CA: University of California Press.

Seil, D. (2004) The diagnosis and treatment of transgendered patients. In U. Leli and J. Drescher (eds.), *Transgender subjectivities: a clinician's guide* (pp. 99–116). New York: Haworth Press.

Shakespeare, T. (1999) Coming out and coming home. *Journal of Gay, Lesbian, and Bisexual Identity*, 4(1), 39–51.

Sharpe, S. (2002) 'It's just really hard to come to terms with': young people's views on homosexuality. *Sex Education*, 2(3), 263–77.

Sherkat, D.E. (2002) Sexuality and religious commitment in the United States: an empirical examination. *Journal for the Scientific Study of Religion*, 41(2), 313–23.

Shernoff, M. (1998) *Gay widowers: life after the death of a partner*. New York: Harrington Park Press.

Shidlo, A. and Schroeder, M. (2002) Changing sexual orientation: a consumers' report. *Professional Psychology: Research and Practice*, 33(3), 249–59.

Shipman, B. and Smart, C. (2007) 'It's made a huge difference': recognition, rights and the personal significance of civil partnership. *Sociological Research Online*, 19(1) www.socresonline.org.uk/12/1/shipman.html.

Short, L. (2007) Lesbian mothers living well in the context of heterosexism and discrimination: resources, strategies and legislative change. *Feminism and Psychology*, 17(1), 57–74.

Short, L., Riggs, D.W., Perlesz, A., Brown, R. and Kane, G. (2007) *Lesbian, gay, bisexual and transgender (LGBT) parented families: a literature review prepared for the Australian Psychological Society.* Melbourne: Australian Psychological Society. Available from: www.psychology.org.au/Assets/Files/LGBT-Families-Lit-Review.pdf.

Siegelman, M. (1972) Adjustment of homosexual and heterosexual women. *British Journal of Psychiatry*, 120, 447–81.

Siever, M.D. (1994) Sexual orientation and gender as factors in socioculturally acquired vulnerability to body satisfaction and eating disorders. *Journal of Consulting and Clinical Psychology*, 62, 252–60.

Simoni, J.M. (1996) Confronting heterosexism in the teaching of psychology. *Teaching of Psychology*, 23(4), 220–6.

Simonsen, G., Blazina, C. and Watkins, C.E. (2000) Gender role conflict and psychological well-being among gay men. *Journal of Counseling Psychology*, 47(1), 85–9.

Skinner, W.F. and Otis, M.D. (1996) Drug and alcohol use among lesbian and gay people in a southern U.S. sample: epidemiological, comparative, and methodological findings from the Trilogy Project. *Journal of Homosexuality*, 30(3), 59–92.

Smith, B. (2007) Gay, lesbian, bisexual and transgendered (GLBT) experiences with earth-spirited faith. *Journal of Homosexuality*, 52(3/4), 235–48.

Smith, D.E. (1990) *Texts, facts, and femininity: exploring the relations of ruling.* London: Routledge.

Smith, J.A. and Osborn, M. (2003) Interpretative phenomenological analysis. In J.A. Smith (ed.), *Qualitative psychology: a practical guide to methods* (pp. 51–80). London: Sage.

Smith, K.T. (1971) Homophobia: a tentative personality profile. *Psychological Reports*, 29, 1091–4.

Solomon, S.E., Rothblum, E.D. and Balsam, K.F. (2005) Money, housework, sex, and conflict: same-sex couples in civil unions, those not in civil unions, and heterosexual married siblings. *Sex Roles*, 52(9/10), 561–75.

Sophie, J. (1987) Internalised homophobia and lesbian identity. *Journal of Homosexuality*, 14(1), 53–65.

Sotelo, M.J. (2000) Political tolerance among adolescents towards homosexuals in Spain. *Journal of Homosexuality*, 39(1), 95–105.

Speer, S.A. (2001) Reconsidering the concept of hegemonic masculinity: discursive psychology, conversation analysis, and participants' orientations. *Feminism and Psychology* 11(1), 107–35.

(2002) Sexist talk: gender categories, participants' orientations and irony. *The Journal of Sociolinguistics* 6(3), 347–77.

(2005) The interactional organization of the gender attribution process. *Sociology* 39(1), 67–87.

(2009) On the role of reported, third party compliments in passing as a 'real' woman. In S.A. Speer and E.H. Stokoe (eds.), *Conversation and gender.* Cambridge: Cambridge University Press.

Speer, S.A. and Green, R. (2007) On passing: the interactional organization of appearance attributions in the psychiatric assessment of transsexual patients. In V. Clarke and E. Peel (eds.), *Out in psychology: lesbian, gay, bisexual, trans and queer perspectives* (pp. 335–68). Chichester: Wiley.

(2008) Transsexual identities: constructions of gender in an NHS Gender Identity Clinic. Online document available from: www.open.ac.uk/socialsciences/identities/findings/Speer.pdf.

Speer, S.A. and Parsons, C. (2006) Gatekeeping gender: some features of the use of hypothetical questions in the psychiatric assessment of transsexual patients. *Discourse and Society* 17(6), 785–812.

Speer, S.A. and Potter, J. (2000) The management of heterosexist talk: conversational resources and prejudiced claims. *Discourse and Society*, 11(4), 543–72.

(2002) From performatives to practices: Judith Butler, discursive psychology, and the management of heterosexist talk. In P. McIlvenny (ed.), *Talking gender and sexuality* (pp. 151–80). Amsterdam: John Benjamins.

Spitzer, R.L. (2003) Can some gay men and lesbians change their sexual orientation? 200 participants reporting a change from homosexual to heterosexual orientation. *Archives of Sexual Behavior*, 32(5), 403–17.

Springer, C.A. and Lease, S.H. (2000) The impact of multiple AIDS-related bereavement in the gay male population. *Journal of Counseling and Development*, 78, 297–304.

Springer, K. (2002) Third wave black feminism? *Signs: Journal of Women in Culture and Society*, 27(4), 1059–82.

Stacey, J. (1996) *In the name of the family: rethinking family values in the postmodern age.* Boston, MA: Beacon Press.

(2006) Gay parenthood and the decline of paternity as we knew it. *Sexualities*, 9(1), 27–55.

Stacey, J. and Biblarz, T.J. (2001) (How) does the sexual orientation of parents matter? *American Sociological Review*, 66, 159–83.

Stam, H.J. (2000) Theorising health and illness: functionalism, subjectivity and reflexivity. *Journal of Health Psychology*, 5(3), 273–83.

Stein, A. (1998/1992) 'Sisters and queers': the decentering of lesbian feminism. In P.M. Nardi and B.E. Schneider (eds.), *Social perspectives in lesbian and gay studies* (pp. 553–63). New York: Routledge.

Stevens, P.E. (1992) Lesbian health care research: a review of the literature from 1970 to 1990. *Health Care for Women International*, 13(2), 91–120.

Stoller, R. (1968) *Sex and gender: on the development of masculinity and femininity.* New York: Science House.

Stone, S. (1991) The 'empire' strikes back: a posttranssexual manifesto. In K. Straub and J. Epstein (eds.), *Body guards: the cultural politics of gender ambiguity* (pp. 280–304). New York: Routledge.

Stonewall Cymru (2003) *Counted out: findings from the 2002–3 Stonewall Cymru survey of lesbian, gay and bisexual people in Wales.* London: Stonewall.

Sullivan, N. (2003) *A critical introduction to queer theory.* Edinburgh: Edinburgh University Press.

Suter, E.A., Daas, K.L. and Bergen, K.M. (2008) Negotiating lesbian family identity via symbols and rituals. *Journal of Family Issues*, 29(1), 26–47.

Szymanski, D.M. and Chung, Y.B. (2001) The lesbian internalized homophobia scale: a rational/theoretical approach. *Journal of Homosexuality*, 41(2), 37–52.

Szymanski, D.M., Chung, Y.B. and Balsam, K.F. (2001) Psychosocial correlates of internalized homophobia in lesbians. *Measurement and Evaluation in Counseling and Development*, 34(1), 27–38.

Tafoya, T. (1997) Native gay and lesbian issues: the two-spirited. In B. Greene (ed.), *Ethnic and cultural diversity among lesbians and gay men* (pp. 1–9). Thousand Oaks, CA: Sage.

Tasker, F. (2002) Lesbian and gay parenting. In A. Coyle and C. Kitzinger (eds.), *Lesbian and gay psychology: new perspectives* (pp. 81–97). Oxford: BPS Blackwell.

(2005) Lesbian mothers, gay fathers, and their children: a review. *Developmental and Behavioral Pediatrics*, 26(3), 224–40.

Tasker, F. and Golombok, S. (1997) *Growing up in a lesbian family: effects on child development*. New York: Guilford Press.

(1998) The role of co-mothers in planned lesbian-led families. *Journal of Lesbian Studies*, 2(4), 49–68.

Tasker, F. and Patterson, C. J. (2007) Research on gay and lesbian parenting: retrospect and prospect. In F. Tasker and J. J. Bigner (eds.), *Gay and lesbian parenting: new directions* (pp. 9–34). New York: Haworth Press.

Taulke-Johnson, R. (2008) Moving beyond homophobia, harassment and intolerance: gay male university students' alternative narratives. *Discourse: Studies in the Cultural Politics of Education*, 29(1), 121–33.

Taulke-Johnson, R. A. and Rivers, I. (1999) Providing a safe environment for lesbian, gay and bisexual students living in university accommodation. *Youth and Policy*, 64, 74–89.

Tavris, C. (1993) *Mismeasure of women: why women are not the better sex, the inferior sex, or the opposite sex*. New York: Touchstone.

Taylor, Y. (2008) 'That's not really my scene': working-class lesbians in (and out of) place. *Sexualities*, 11(5), 523–46.

Tee, N. and Hegarty, P. (2006) Predicting opposition to the civil rights of trans persons in the United Kingdom. *Journal of Community and Applied Social Psychology*, 16, 70–80.

Terry, J. (1990) Lesbians under the medical gaze: scientists search for remarkable differences. *Journal of Sex Research*, 27(3), 317–39.

(1999) *An American obsession: science, medicine and homosexuality in modern society*. Chicago, IL: University of Chicago Press.

Thomas, A. B., Ross, M. W. and Harris, K. K. (2007) Coming out online: interpretations of young men's stories. *Sexuality Research and Social Policy*, 4(2), 5–17.

Thomas, C. (ed.) (2000) *Straight with a twist: queer theory and the subject of heterosexuality*. Champaign: University of Illinois Press.

Thomas, G. (2007) *The sexual demon of colonial power: pan-African embodiment and erotic schemes of empire*. Bloomington: Indiana University Press.

Thompson, B. W. (2000) *Mothering without a compass: white mother's love, black son's courage*. Minneapolis: University of Minnesota Press.

Thompson, E. and Morgan, E. (2008) 'Mostly straight' young women: variations in sexual behaviour and identity development. *Developmental Psychology*, 44(1), 15–21.

Thompson, G. H. and Fishburn, W. R. (1977) Attitudes toward homosexuality among graduate counseling students. *Counselor Education and Supervision* (December), 121–30.

Thompson, Jr., N. L., McCandless, B. R. and Strickland, B. R. (1971) Personal adjustment of male and female homosexuals and heterosexuals. *Journal of Abnormal Psychology*, 78(2), 237–40.

Tikkanen, R. and Ross, M.W. (2000) Looking for sexual compatibility: experiences among Swedish men in visiting internet gay chat rooms. *Cyberpsychology and Behaviour*, 3, 605–16.

Tillmann-Healy, L.M. (2001) *Between gay and straight: understanding friendship across sexual orientation*. Walnut Creek, CA: Altamira Press.

Touroni, E. and Coyle, A. (2002) Decision-making in planned lesbian parenting: an interpretative phenomenological analysis. *Journal of Community and Applied Social Psychology*, 12, 194–209.

Townsend, M. (1998) Mental health issues and same-sex marriage. In R.P. Cabaj and D.W. Purcell (eds.), *On the road to same-sex marriage: a supportive guide to psychological, political and legal issues*. San Francisco: Jossey-Bass.

Troiden, R.R. (1979) Becoming homosexual: a model of gay identity acquisition. *Psychiatry: Journal for the Study of Interpersonal Processes*, 42(4), 362–73.

Turner, A., Chen, T.C., Barber, T.W., Malabanan, A.O., Holick, M.F. and Tangpricha, V. (2004) Testosterone increases bone mineral density in female-to-male transsexuals: A case series of 15 subjects. *Clinical Endocrinology*, 61, 560–6.

Turrell, S.C. (2000) A descriptive analysis of same sex relationship violence for a diverse sample. *Journal of Family Violence*, 15(3), 281–93.

Unger, R.K. (1996) Using the master's tools: epistemology and empiricism. In S. Wilkinson (ed.), *Feminist social psychologies: international perspectives* (pp. 165–81). Buckingham: Open University Press.

Unger, R. and Crawford, M. (2003) *Women and gender: a feminist psychology*, 4th edition. New York: McGraw-Hill.

van Eden-Moorefield, B., Proulx, C.M. and Pasley, K. (2008) A comparison of internet and face-to-face (FTF) qualitative methods in studying the relationships of gay men. *Journal of GLBT Family Studies*, 4(2), 181–205.

Vanfraussen, K., Ponjaert-Kristoffersen, I. and Brewaeys, A. (2002) What does it mean for youngsters to grow up in a lesbian family created by means of donor insemination? *Journal of Reproductive and Infant Psychology*, 20(4), 237–52.

van Hoye, G. and Lievens, F. (2003). The effects of sexual orientation on hirability ratings: an experimental study. *Journal of Business and Psychology*, 18(1), 15–30.

Wahler, J. and Gabbay, S.G. (1997) Gay male aging: a review of the literature. *Journal of Gay and Lesbian Social Services*, 6(3), 1–20.

Wainright, J.L., Russell, S.T. and Patterson, C.J. (2004) Psychosocial adjustment, school outcomes, and romantic relationships of adolescents with same-sex parents. *Child Development*, 75(6), 1886–98.

Walter, C.A. (2003) *The loss of a life partner: narratives of the bereaved*. New York: Columbia University Press.

Walters, S.D. (1996) From here to queer: radical feminism, postmodernism, and the lesbian menace (or, why can't a woman be more like a fag?). *Signs: Journal of Women in Culture and Society*, 21(4), 830–69.

Wang, J., Häusermann, M., Vounatsou, P., Aggleton, P. and Weiss, M.G. (2007) Health status, behavior, and care utilization in the Geneva Gay Men's Health Survey. *Preventative Medicine*, 44(1), 70–5.

Warner, D.N. (2004) Towards a queer research methodology. *Qualitative Research in Psychology*, 1, 321–37.

Warner, J., McKeown, E., Griffin, M., Johnson, K., Ramsay, A., Cort, C. and King, M. (2004) Rates and predictors of mental illness in gay men, lesbians and bisexual men and women. *British Journal of Psychiatry*, 185, 479–85.

Warner, Michael (1991) Introduction: fear of a queer planet. *Social Text*, 9 (4 [29]), 3–17.

Warwick, I., Aggleton, P. and Douglas, N. (2001) Playing it safe: addressing the emotional and physical health of lesbian and gay pupils in the U.K. *Journal of Adolescence*, 24(1), 129–40.

Weeks, J., Heaphy, B. and Donovan, C. (2001) *Same sex intimacies: families of choice and other life experiments*. London: Routledge.

Weinberg, G. (1972) *Society and the healthy homosexual*. New York: St Martin's.

Weinberg, M.S. (1969) The ageing male homosexual. *Medical Aspects of Sexuality*, 3(12), 66–72.

Weinberg, M.S., Williams, C.J. and Pryor, D.W. (1994) *Dual attraction: understanding bisexuality*. New York: Oxford University Press.

Weinrich, J.D. and Klein, F. (2002) Bi-gay, bi-straight, and bi-bi: three bisexual subgroups identified using cluster analysis of the Klein Sexual Orientation Grid. *Journal of Bisexuality*, 2(4), 109–40.

Weinstock, J.S. (1998) Lesbian, gay, bisexual, and transgender friendships in adulthood. In C.J. Patterson and A.R. D'Augelli (eds.), *Lesbian, gay, and bisexual identities in families: psychological perspectives* (pp. 122–53). New York: Oxford University Press.

(2004) Lesbian FLEX-ibility: friend and/or family connections among lesbian ex-lovers. In J.S. Weinstock and E.D. Rothblum (eds.), *Lesbian ex-lovers: the really long-term relationship* (pp. 193–238). New York: Harrington Park Press.

Weinstock, J.S. and Rothblum, E.D. (1996) (eds.) *Lesbian friendships: for ourselves and each other*. New York: New York University Press.

Weiss, J.T. (2004) GL vs. BT: the archaeology of biphobia and transphobia within the US gay and lesbian community. *Journal of Bisexuality*, 3(1), 25–55.

Wells, J. (1997) Introduction. In J. Wells (ed.), *Lesbians raising sons: an anthology* (pp. ix–xv). Los Angeles, CA: Alyson Books.

Westerman, T.G. (2004) Engagement of Indigenous clients in mental health services: what role do cultural differences play? *Australian e-journal for the Advancement of Mental Health*, 3(3). Available from: www.gtp.com.au/ips/inewsfiles/P21.pdf, accessed 11 November 2008.

Weston, K. (1991) *Families we choose: lesbians, gays, kinship*. New York: Columbia University Press.

Wetherell, M. and Potter, J. (1992) *Mapping the language of racism: discourse and the legitimation of exploitation*. London: Harvester Wheatsheaf.

Wheeler, D.P. (2003) Methodological issues in conducting community-based health and social services research among urban black and African American LGBT populations. In W. Meezan and J.I. Martin (eds.), *Research methods with gay, lesbian, bisexual, and transgender populations* (pp. 65–78). New York: Harrington Park Press.

Whipple, V. (2006) *Lesbian widows: invisible grief*. New York: Haworth Press.

White, T. and Ettner, R. (2007) Adaptation and adjustment in children of transsexual parents. *European Child and Adolescent Psychiatry*, 16(4), 215–21.

Whittle, S., Turner, L. and Al-Alami, M. (2007) *Engendered penalties: transgender and transsexual people's experiences of inequality and discrimination*. London: Press for Change.

Wilkinson, S. (1997a) Feminist psychology. In D. Fox and I. Prilleltensky (eds.), *Critical psychology: an introduction* (pp. 247–64). London: Sage.

(1997b) Prioritizing the political: feminist psychology. In T. Ibáñez and L. Íñiguez (eds.), *Critical social psychology* (pp. 178–94). London: Sage.

(1998a) Focus groups in health research: exploring the meanings of health and illness. *Journal of Health Psychology*, 3(3), 329–48.

(1998b) Focus groups in feminist research: power, interaction, and the co-construction of meaning. *Women's Studies International Forum*, 21(1), 111–25.

(2002) Lesbian health. In A. Coyle and C. Kitzinger (eds.), *Lesbian and gay psychology: new perspectives* (pp. 117–34). Oxford: BPS Blackwell.

Wilkinson, S. and Kitzinger, C. (eds.) (1993) *Heterosexuality: a feminism and psychology reader*. London: Sage.

(1996a) The queer backlash. In D. Bell and R. Klein (eds.), *Radically speaking: feminism reclaimed* (pp. 375–82). Melbourne: Spinifex Press.

(eds.) (1996b) *Representing the other: a feminism and psychology reader*. London: Sage.

Willging, C. E., Salvador, M. and Kano, M. (2006) Unequal treatment: mental health care for sexual and gender minority groups in a rural state. *Psychiatric Services*, 57(6), 867–70.

Williamson, I. and Spence, K. (2001) Towards an understanding of risk factors for eating disturbance amongst gay men. *Health Education*, 5, 217–27.

Willig, C. (2001) *Introducing qualitative research in psychology: adventures in theory and method*. Buckingham: Open University Press.

Willoughby, B. L. B., Doty, N. D. and Malik, N. M. (2008) Parental reactions to their child's sexual orientation disclosure: a family stress perspective. *Parenting: Science and Practice*, 8, 70–91.

Wilton, T. (1997) *Good for you: handbook of lesbian health and wellbeing*. London: Cassell.

(2000) *Sexualities in health and social care: a textbook*. Buckingham: Open University Press.

Winter, S., Webster, B. and Cheung, P. K. E. (2008) Measuring Hong Kong undergraduate students' attitudes towards transpeople. *Sex Roles*, 59: 670–83.

Witten, T. M. (2002) Geriatric care and management issues for the transgendered and intersexed populations. *Geriatric Care and Management Journal*, 12(3), 20–4.

(2003) Transgender aging: an emerging population and an emerging need. *Sexologies*, 12, 14–19. Available from: www.transcience.org/abstracts/Abstract-English-sexology.pdf.

Witten, T. M and Whittle, S. (2004) Transpanthers: the greying of transgender and the law. *Deakin Law Review*, 23, 1–17.

Wojnar, D. (2007) Miscarriage experiences of lesbian couples. *Journal of Midwifery and Women's Health*, 52(5), 479–85.

Wojnar, D. and Swanson, K. M. (2006) Why shouldn't lesbian women who miscarry receive special consideration? A viewpoint. *Journal of GLBT Family Studies*, 2(1), 1–12.

Worth, H. (2001) Bad-assed honeys with a difference: South Auckland fa'afafine talk about identity. *Intersections: Gender, History and Culture in the Asian Context*, 6. Available from: http://intersections.anu.edu.au, accessed 14 October 2008.

Wren, B. (2002) 'I can accept my child is transsexual but if I ever see him in a dress I'll hit him': dilemmas in parenting a transgendered adolescent. *Clinical Child Psychology and Psychiatry*, 7, 377–97.

Yip, A. K. T. (2004) Negotiating space with family and kin in identity construction: the narrative of British non-heterosexual Muslims. *Sociological Review*, 52(3), 336–50.

Zhou, J. N., Hofman, M. A., Gooren, L. J. G. and Swaab, D. F. (1995) A sex difference in the human brain and its relation to transsexuality. *Nature*, 378, 68–70.

Index